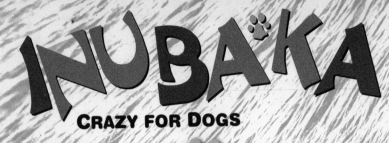

INUBAKA

CRAZY FOR DOGS

10

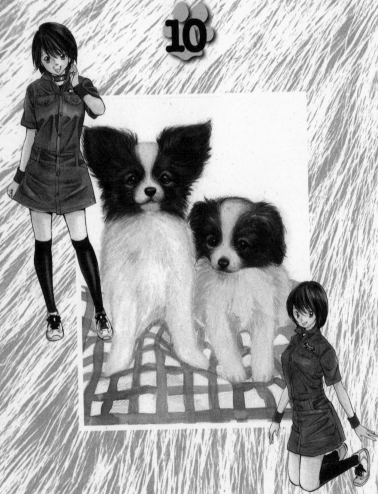

YUKIYA SAKURAGI

Contents

Story thus far

Teppei is the manager of the recently opened pet shop Woofles. He intended to breed his black Labrador Noa with a champion dog, but instead Noa was "taken advantage of" by an unknown and unfixed male dog!

The unknown dog's owner was Suguri Miyauchi and her dog was a mutt named Lupin. Suguri is now working at Woofles to make up for her dog's actions.

Suguri's enthusiasm is more than a little unique. She has eaten dog food (and said it was tasty), caught dog poop with her bare hands, and caused dogs to have "happy pee" in her presence. Teppei is starting to realize that Suguri is indeed a very special girl.

Woofles hires a professional cameraman for an in-store doggie photo-shoot! Out of all the adorably dressed-up dogs, dog otaku Akiba and his tuxedo-dressed pup Zidane were the most enthusiastic of them all. But when Zidane sneezed, his suit tore in half! Humiliated by Chizuru's nasty fat jokes, Akiba finally loses it! He decides to put Zidane on a diet.

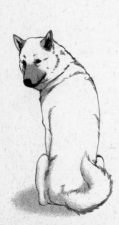
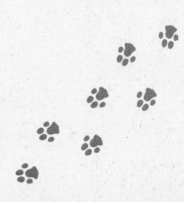

CHARACTERS

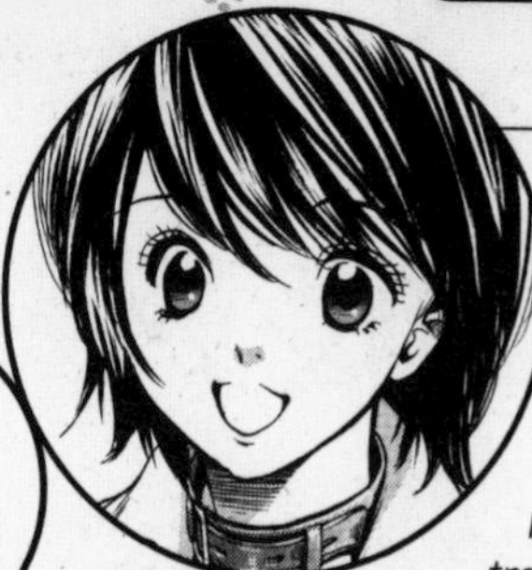

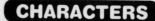

Suguri Miyauchi

She seems to possess an almost supernatural connection with dogs. When she approaches them they often urinate with great excitement! She is crazy for dogs and can catch their droppings with her bare hands. She is currently a trainee at the Woofles Pet Shop.

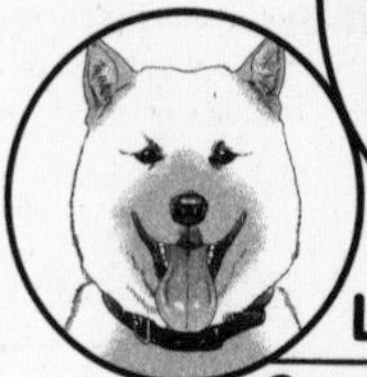

Lupin

♂ *Mutt (mongrel)*

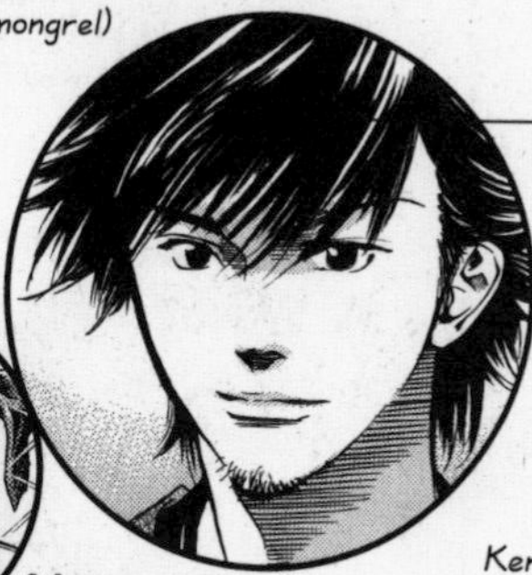

Teppei Iida

He is the manager of the recently opened pet shop Woofles. He is aware of Suguri's special ability and has hired her to work in his shop. He also lets Suguri and Kentaro crash with him.

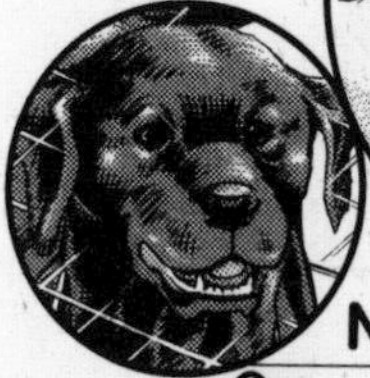

Noa

♀ *Labrador retriever*

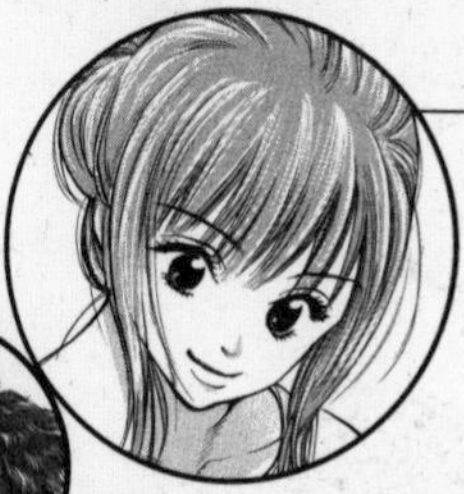

Momoko Takeuchi

Woofles Pet Shop (second location) pet groomer. At first she was a girl with many problems and she rarely smiled. But after meeting Suguri, she's changed, and the two are now best friends.

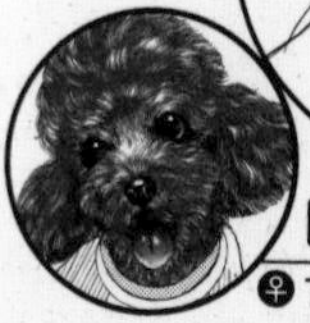

Mel

♀ *Toy poodle*

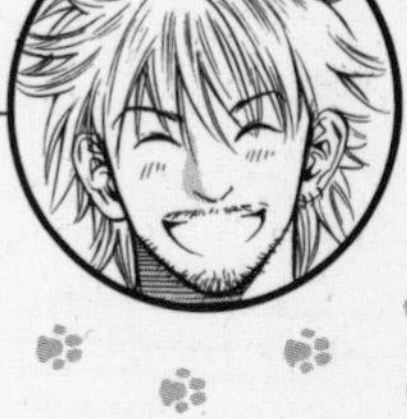

Kentaro Osada

A wannabe musician and buddy of Teppei's from high school. Teppei saved Kentaro when he was a down-and-out beggar. He has a crush on the piano instructor Kanako, but not her dog...

Melon
♂ *Chihuahua*

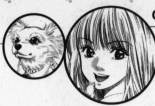

Chizuru Sawamura

She adopted a Chihuahua, Melon, after her long-time pet golden retriever Ricky alerted her that Melon was ill. She works at a hostess bar to repay Melon's medical fees.

Kanako Mori

She teaches piano on the second floor of the same building as Woofles. Her love for her dog, Czerny, is so great that it surprises even Suguri!

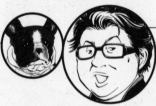

Czerny
♀ *Pomeranian*

Zidane
♂ *French bulldog*

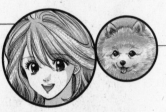

Hiroshi Akiba

Pop-idol otaku turned dog otaku. His dream is to publish a photo collection of his dog, Zidane. He is a government employee.

Mari Yamashita

She is a model whose nickname is Yamarin. She decided to keep an unsold papillon, Lucky, which was her costar in a bread commercial.

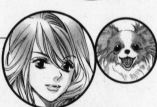

Lucky
♂ *Papillon*

Chanta
♀ *Shiba*

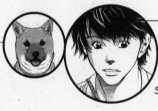

Kim

A Korean friend of Kentaro. He had a phobia of dogs, but he has been working hard to get over it in order to get close to Suguri, whom he has a crush on. He bought a Shiba dog named Chanta! He goes to sleep with her!

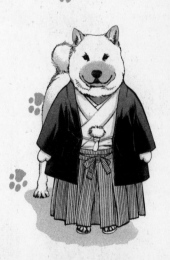

INUBAKA

CHAPTER 98: ZIDANE'S DIET PLAN PART 1

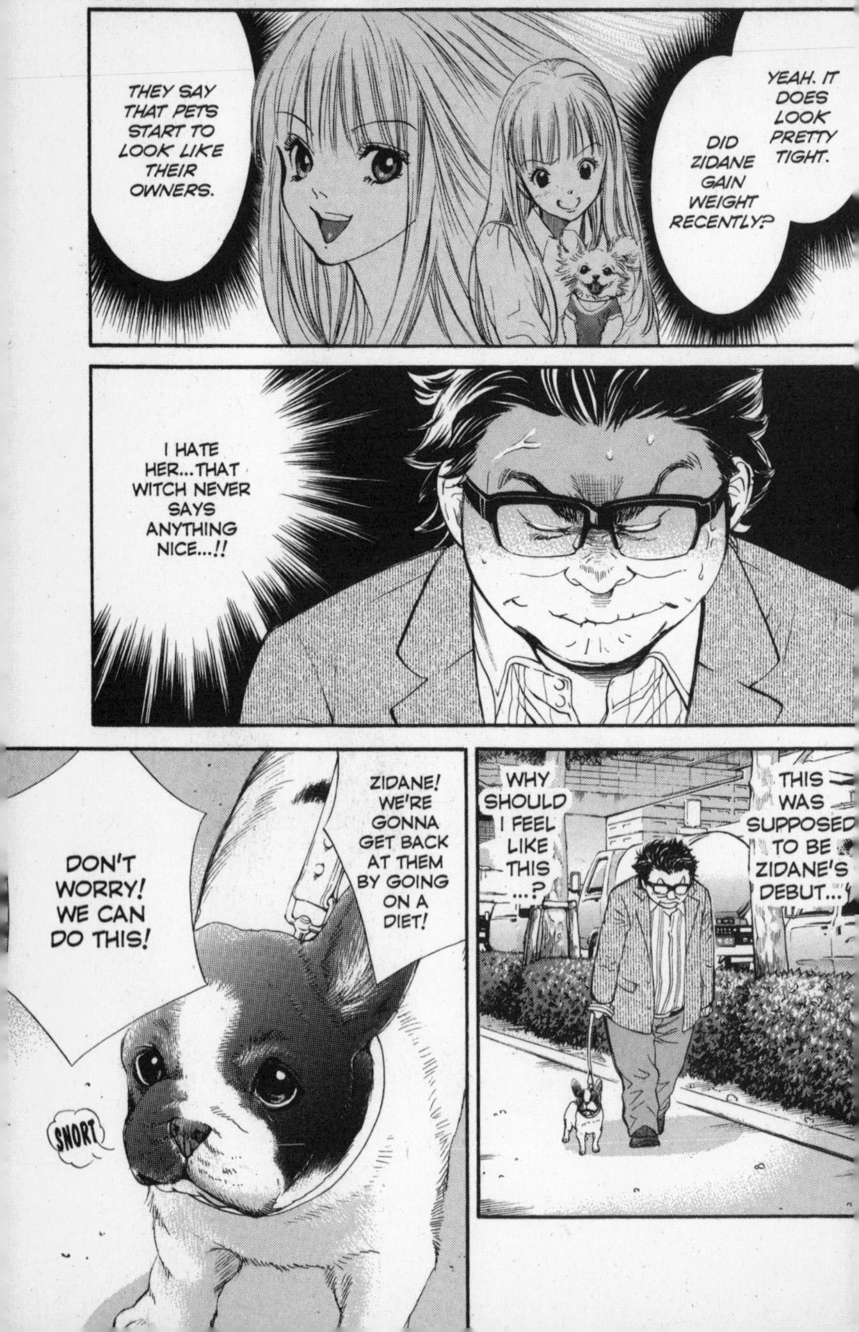

YEAH. IT DOES LOOK PRETTY TIGHT.
DID ZIDANE GAIN WEIGHT RECENTLY?
THEY SAY THAT PETS START TO LOOK LIKE THEIR OWNERS.
I HATE HER...THAT WITCH NEVER SAYS ANYTHING NICE...!!
THIS WAS SUPPOSED TO BE ZIDANE'S DEBUT...
WHY SHOULD I FEEL LIKE THIS ...?
ZIDANE! WE'RE GONNA GET BACK AT THEM BY GOING ON A DIET!
DON'T WORRY! WE CAN DO THIS!
SNORT

CHAPTER 98: ZIDANE'S DIET PLAN PART 1

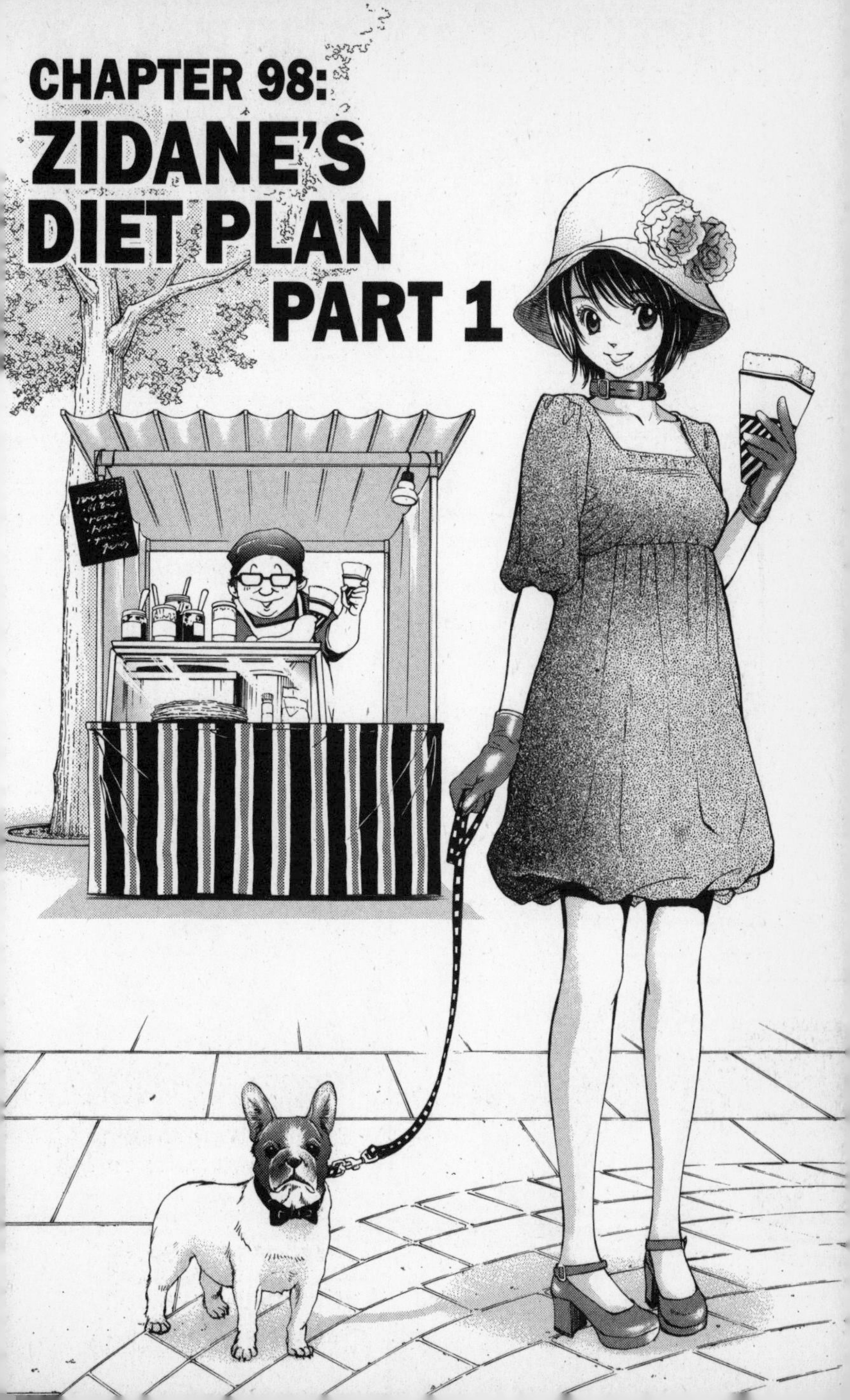

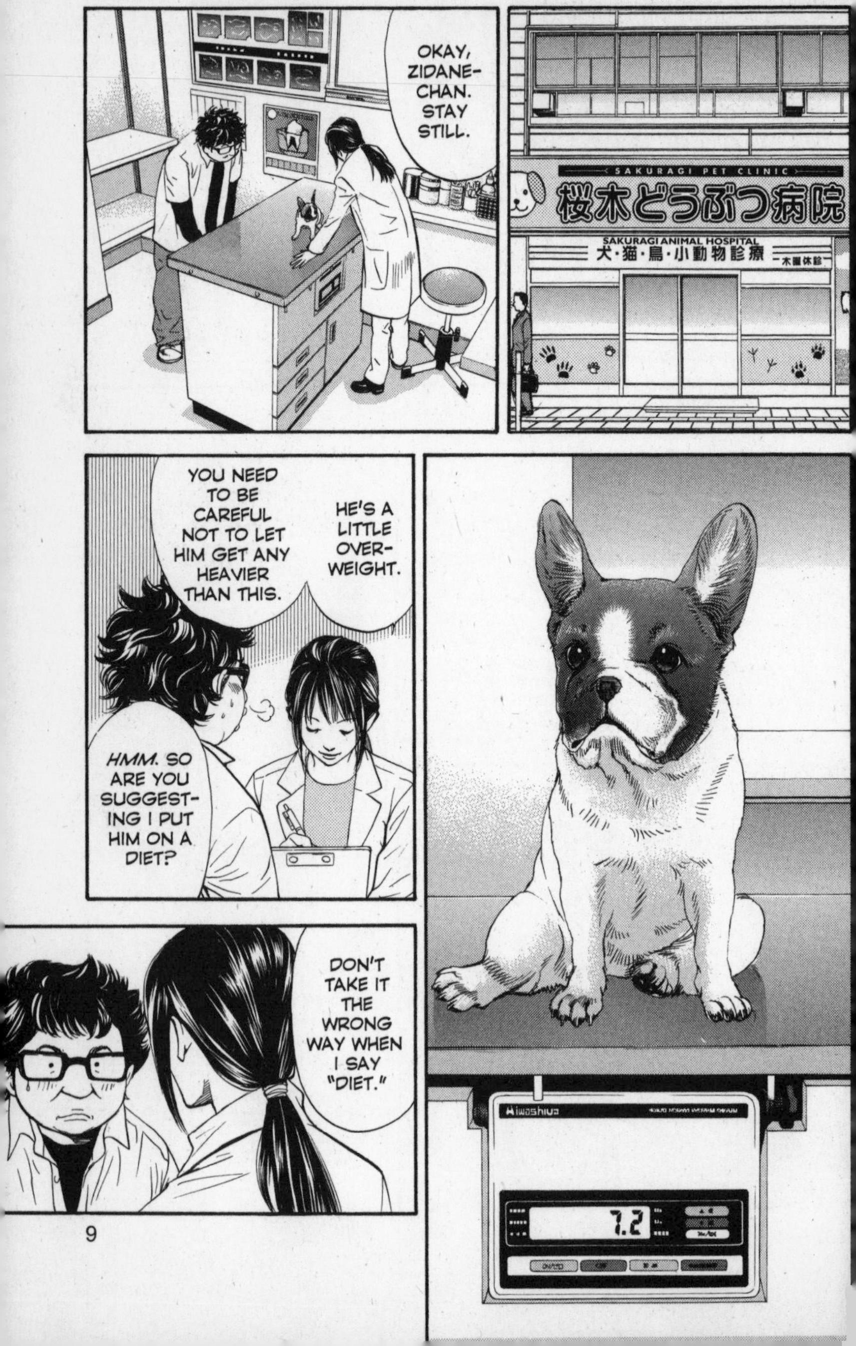
SAKURAGI PET CLINIC
桜木どうぶつ病院
SAKURAGI ANIMAL HOSPITAL
犬・猫・鳥・小動物診療
木曜休診
OKAY, ZIDANE-CHAN. STAY STILL.
7.2
HE'S A LITTLE OVER-WEIGHT.
YOU NEED TO BE CAREFUL NOT TO LET HIM GET ANY HEAVIER THAN THIS.
HMM. SO ARE YOU SUGGEST-ING I PUT HIM ON A DIET?
DON'T TAKE IT THE WRONG WAY WHEN I SAY "DIET."

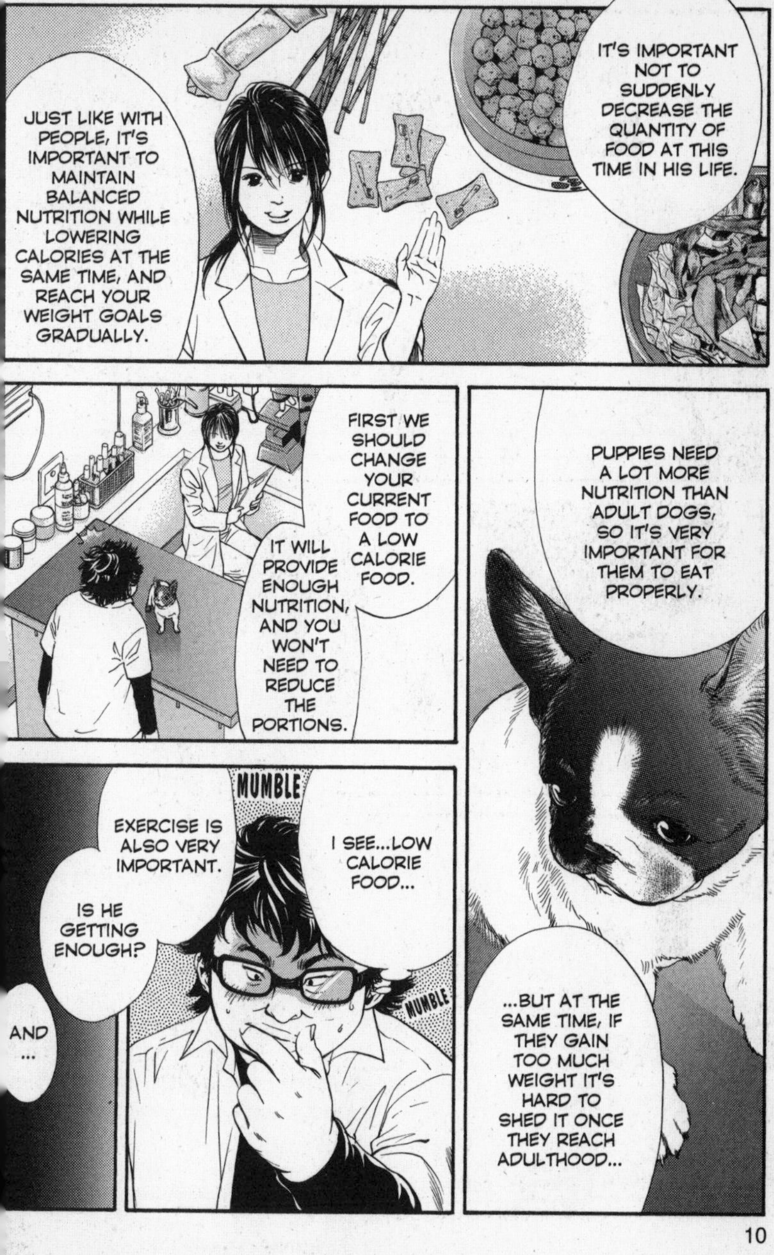
IT'S IMPORTANT NOT TO SUDDENLY DECREASE THE QUANTITY OF FOOD AT THIS TIME IN HIS LIFE.
JUST LIKE WITH PEOPLE, IT'S IMPORTANT TO MAINTAIN BALANCED NUTRITION WHILE LOWERING CALORIES AT THE SAME TIME, AND REACH YOUR WEIGHT GOALS GRADUALLY.
PUPPIES NEED A LOT MORE NUTRITION THAN ADULT DOGS, SO IT'S VERY IMPORTANT FOR THEM TO EAT PROPERLY.
...BUT AT THE SAME TIME, IF THEY GAIN TOO MUCH WEIGHT IT'S HARD TO SHED IT ONCE THEY REACH ADULTHOOD...
FIRST WE SHOULD CHANGE YOUR CURRENT FOOD TO A LOW CALORIE FOOD.
IT WILL PROVIDE ENOUGH NUTRITION, AND YOU WON'T NEED TO REDUCE THE PORTIONS.
MUMBLE
I SEE...LOW CALORIE FOOD...
MUMBLE
EXERCISE IS ALSO VERY IMPORTANT.
IS HE GETTING ENOUGH?
AND ...

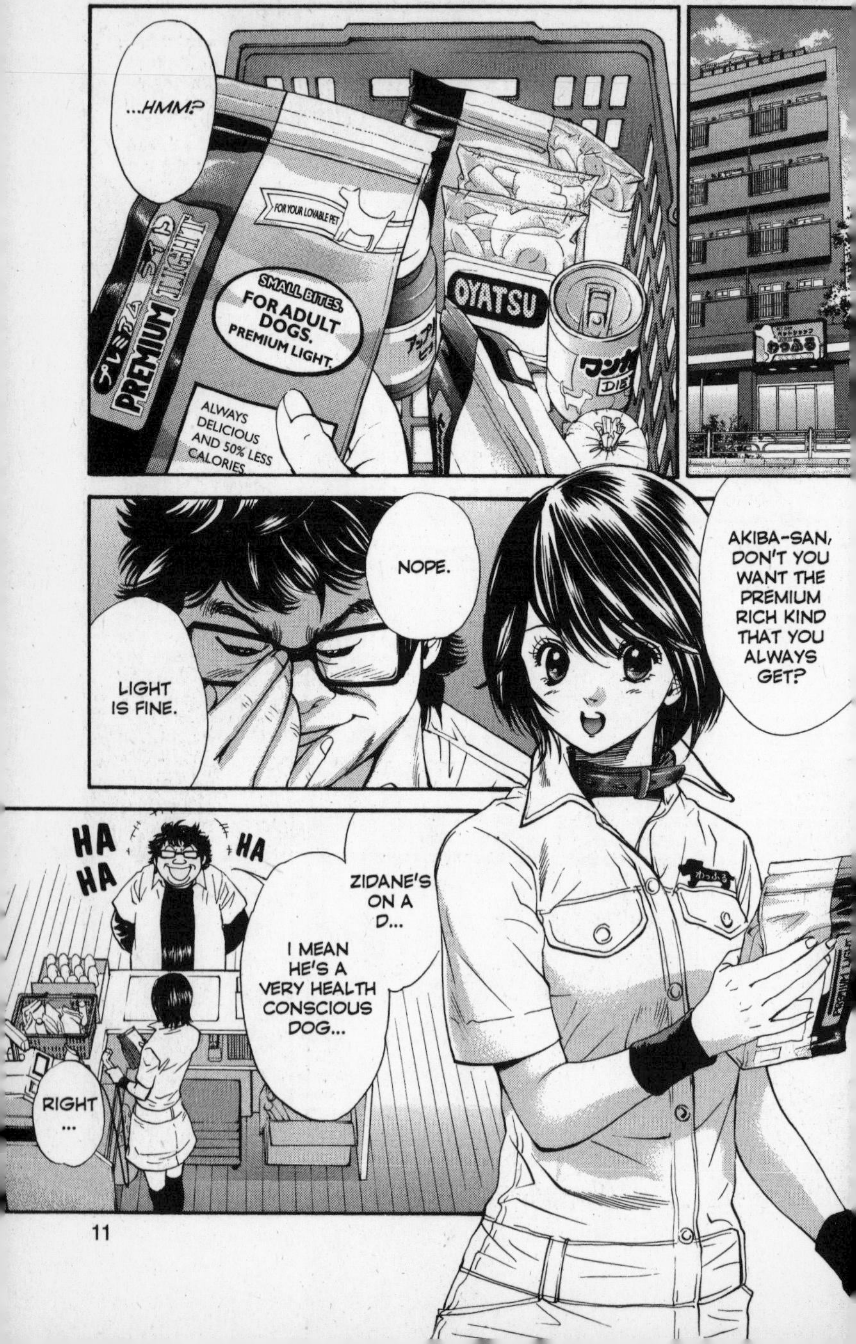
...HMM?
PREMIUM LIGHT
FOR YOUR LOVABLE PET
SMALL BITES. FOR ADULT DOGS. PREMIUM LIGHT.
ALWAYS DELICIOUS AND 50% LESS CALORIES.
OYATSU
AKIBA-SAN, DON'T YOU WANT THE PREMIUM RICH KIND THAT YOU ALWAYS GET?
NOPE.
LIGHT IS FINE.
ZIDANE'S ON A D...
I MEAN HE'S A VERY HEALTH CONSCIOUS DOG...
HA HA
HA HA
RIGHT ...

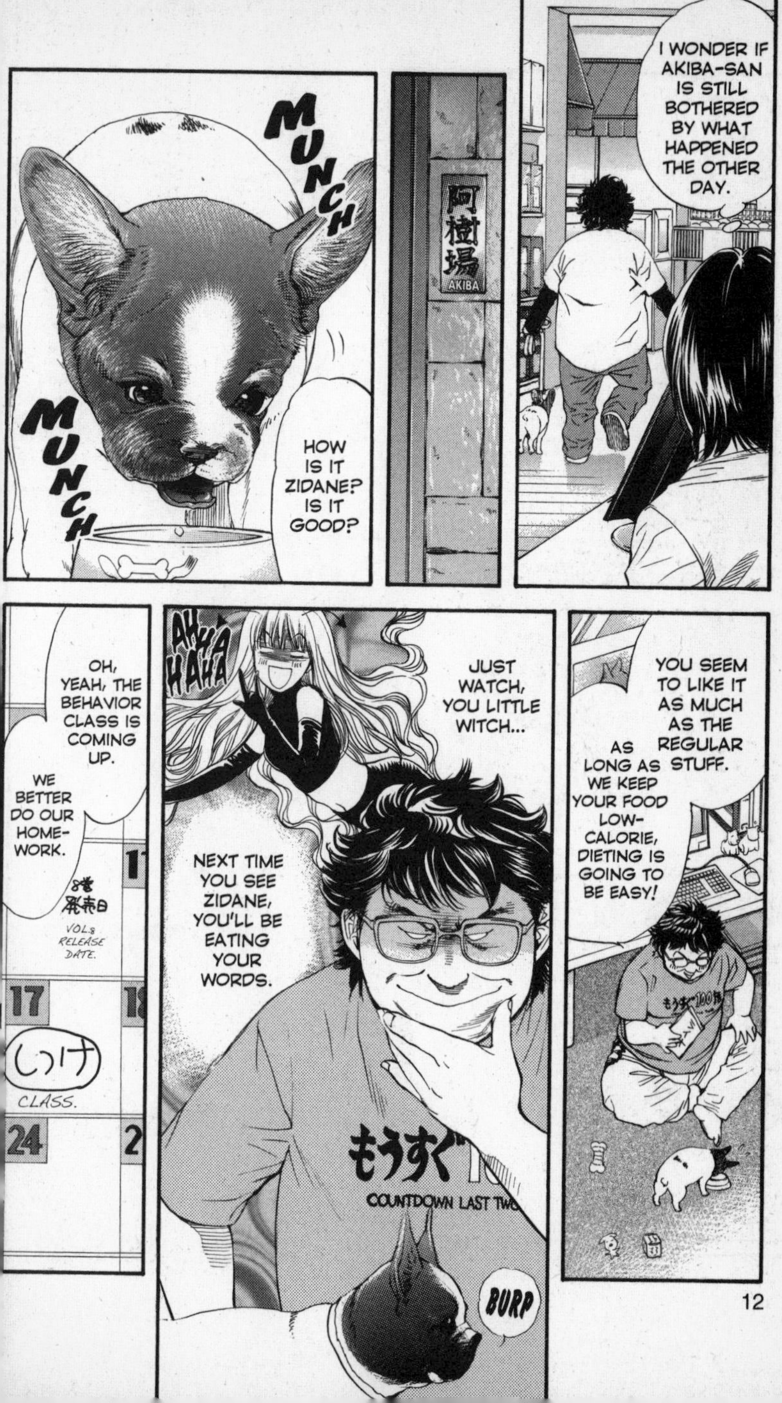
I WONDER IF AKIBA-SAN IS STILL BOTHERED BY WHAT HAPPENED THE OTHER DAY.
阿樹場
AKIBA
MUNCH
MUNCH
HOW IS IT ZIDANE? IS IT GOOD?
YOU SEEM TO LIKE IT AS MUCH AS THE REGULAR STUFF.
AS LONG AS WE KEEP YOUR FOOD LOW-CALORIE, DIETING IS GOING TO BE EASY!
JUST WATCH, YOU LITTLE WITCH...
AHAHAHA
NEXT TIME YOU SEE ZIDANE, YOU'LL BE EATING YOUR WORDS.
COUNTDOWN LAST TWO
BURP
OH, YEAH, THE BEHAVIOR CLASS IS COMING UP.
WE BETTER DO OUR HOMEWORK.
8巻発売日
VOL.8 RELEASE DATE.
17
18
しつけ
CLASS.
24

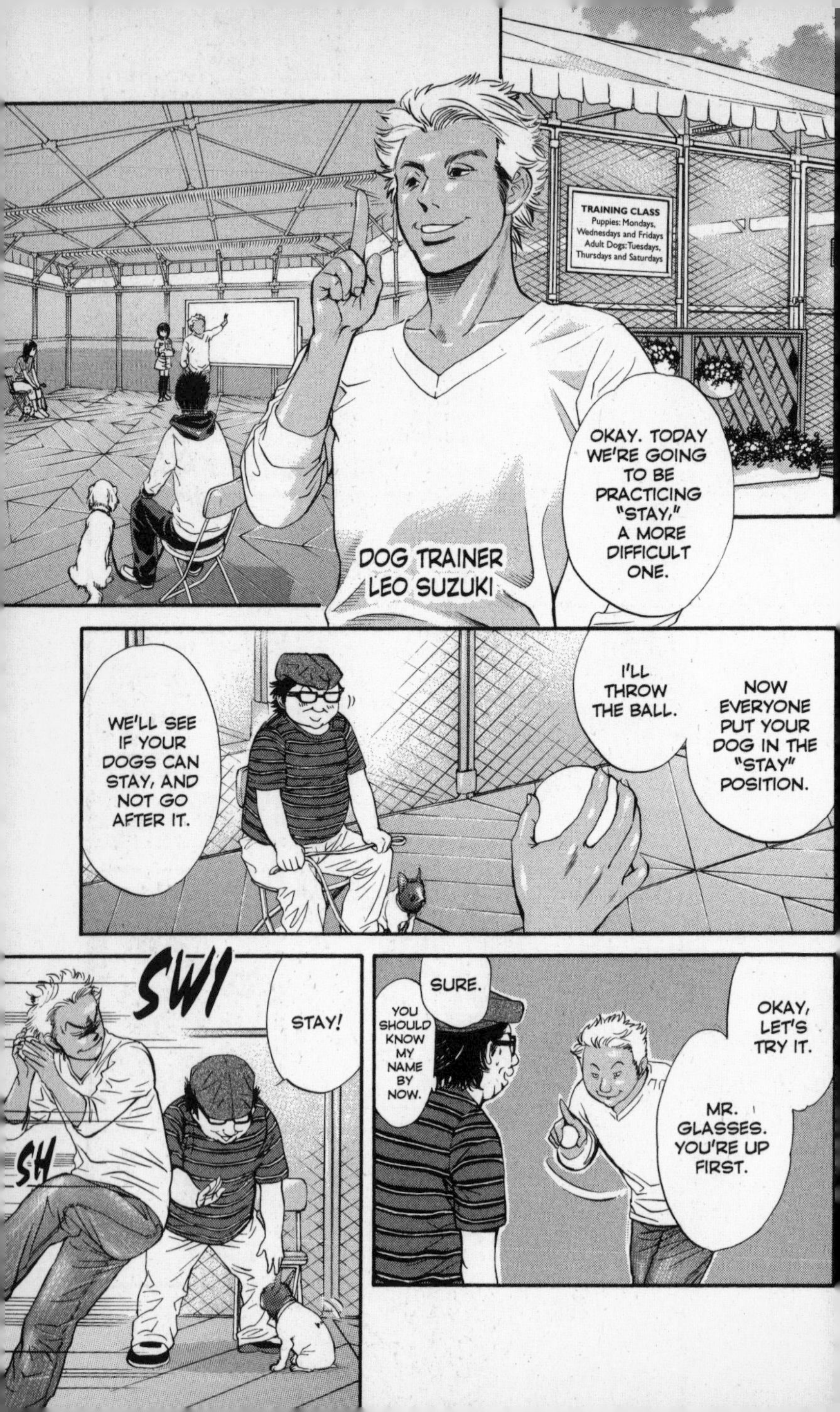
TRAINING CLASS
Puppies: Mondays, Wednesdays and Fridays
Adult Dogs: Tuesdays, Thursdays and Saturdays
OKAY. TODAY WE'RE GOING TO BE PRACTICING "STAY," A MORE DIFFICULT ONE.
DOG TRAINER LEO SUZUKI
NOW EVERYONE PUT YOUR DOG IN THE "STAY" POSITION.
I'LL THROW THE BALL.
WE'LL SEE IF YOUR DOGS CAN STAY, AND NOT GO AFTER IT.
OKAY, LET'S TRY IT.
MR. GLASSES. YOU'RE UP FIRST.
SURE.
YOU SHOULD KNOW MY NAME BY NOW.
STAY!
SWI
SH

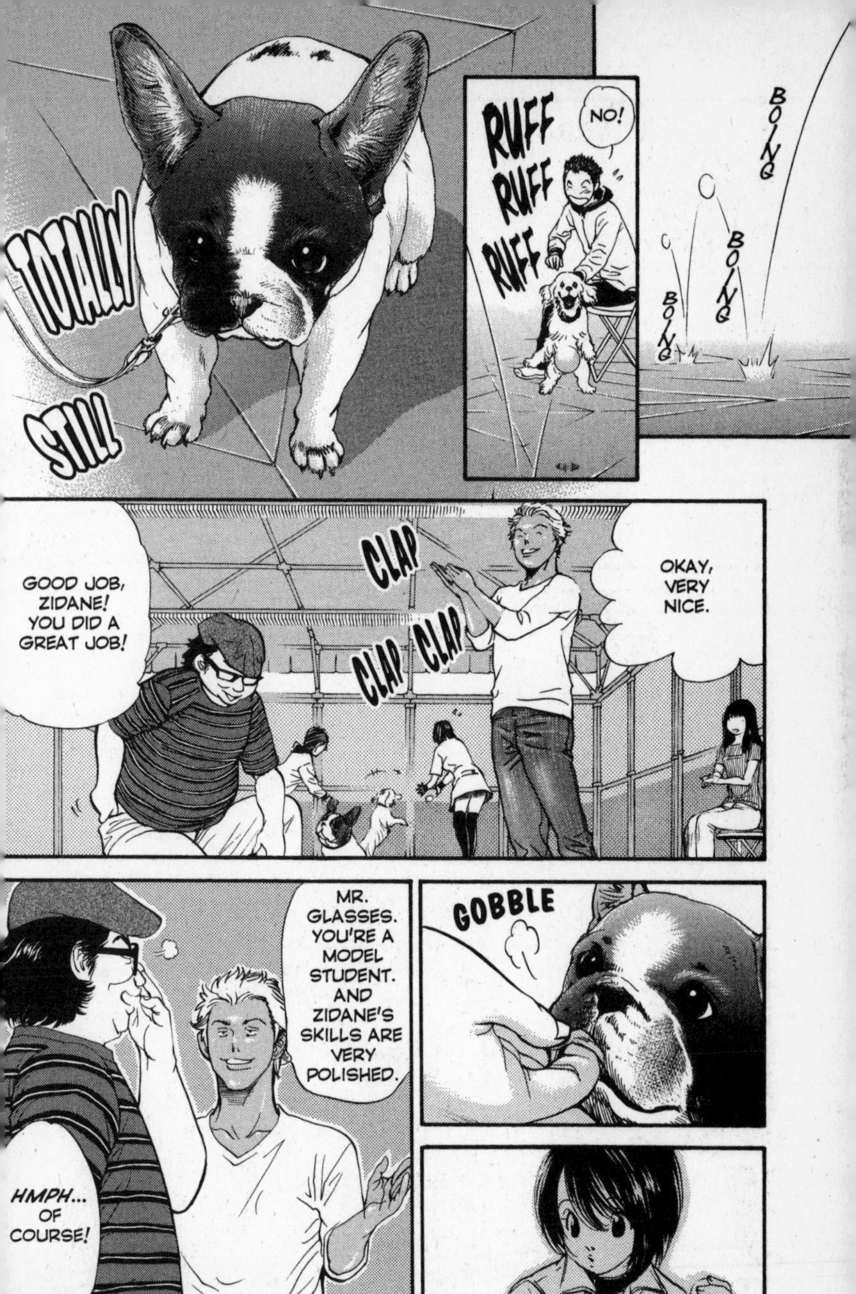
BOING
BOING
BOING
NO!
RUFF
RUFF
RUFF
TOTALLY
STILL
OKAY, VERY NICE.
CLAP
CLAP CLAP
GOOD JOB, ZIDANE! YOU DID A GREAT JOB!
GOBBLE
MR. GLASSES. YOU'RE A MODEL STUDENT. AND ZIDANE'S SKILLS ARE VERY POLISHED.
HMPH... OF COURSE!

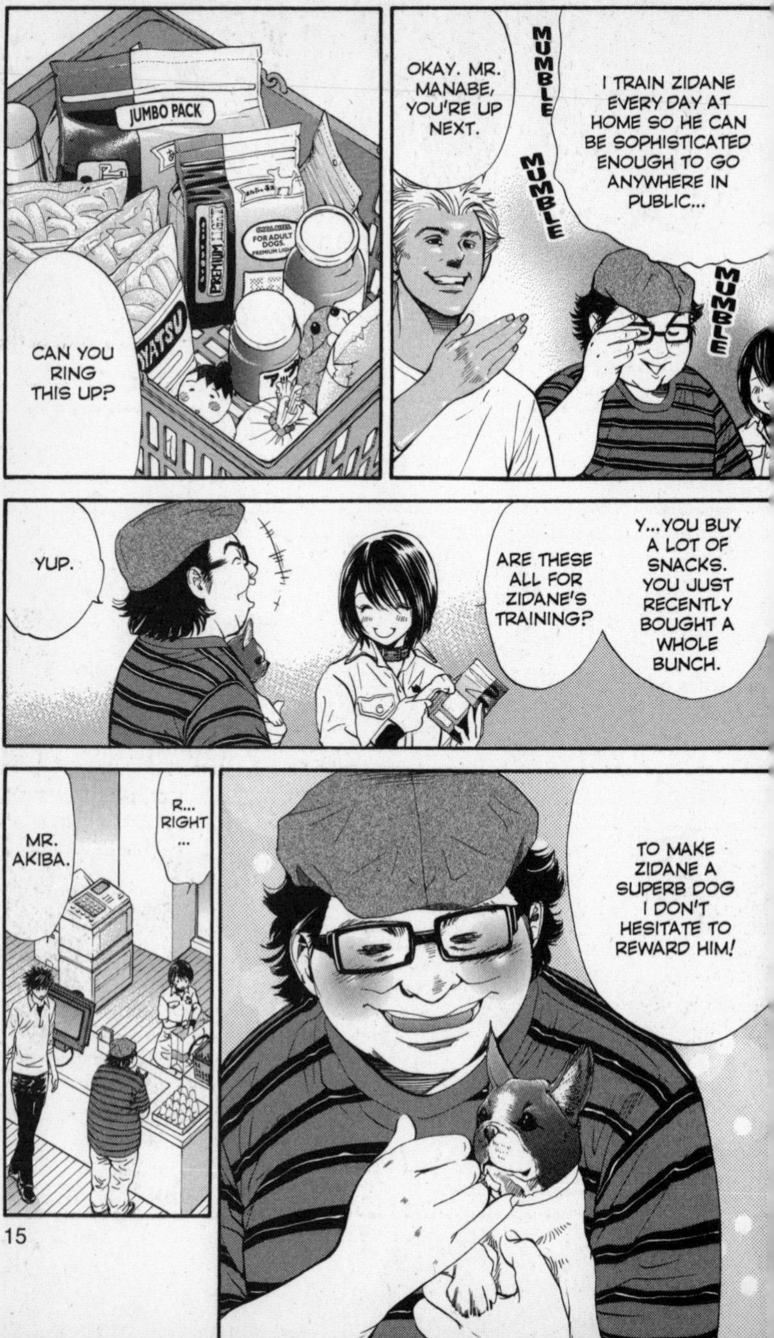
I TRAIN ZIDANE EVERY DAY AT HOME SO HE CAN BE SOPHISTICATED ENOUGH TO GO ANYWHERE IN PUBLIC...
MUMBLE
MUMBLE
MUMBLE
OKAY. MR. MANABE, YOU'RE UP NEXT.
JUMBO PACK
FOR ADULT DOGS
CAN YOU RING THIS UP?
Y...YOU BUY A LOT OF SNACKS. YOU JUST RECENTLY BOUGHT A WHOLE BUNCH.
ARE THESE ALL FOR ZIDANE'S TRAINING?
YUP.
TO MAKE ZIDANE A SUPERB DOG I DON'T HESITATE TO REWARD HIM!
R... RIGHT ...
MR. AKIBA.

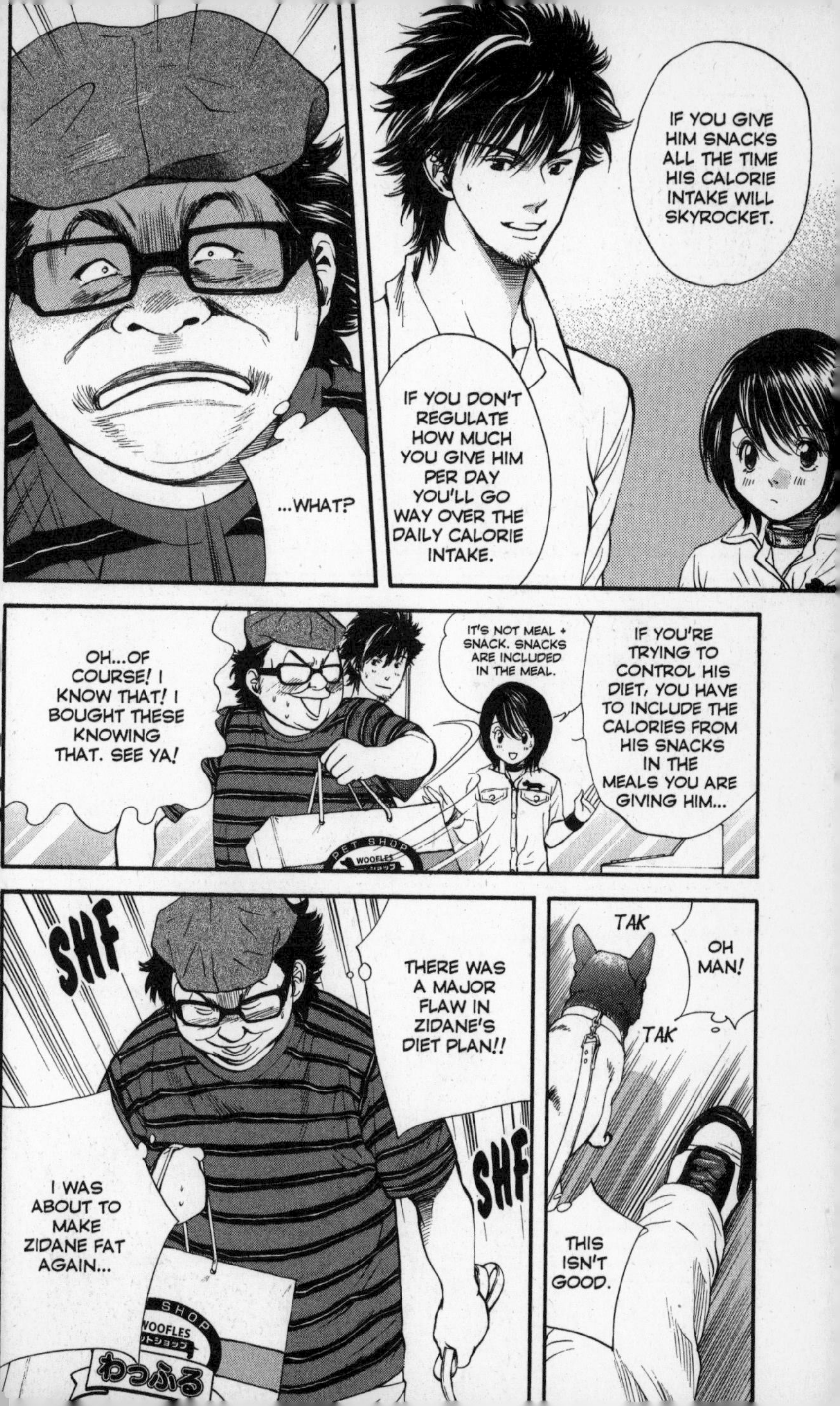
IF YOU GIVE HIM SNACKS ALL THE TIME HIS CALORIE INTAKE WILL SKYROCKET.
IF YOU DON'T REGULATE HOW MUCH YOU GIVE HIM PER DAY YOU'LL GO WAY OVER THE DAILY CALORIE INTAKE.
...WHAT?
IF YOU'RE TRYING TO CONTROL HIS DIET, YOU HAVE TO INCLUDE THE CALORIES FROM HIS SNACKS IN THE MEALS YOU ARE GIVING HIM...
IT'S NOT MEAL + SNACK. SNACKS ARE INCLUDED IN THE MEAL.
OH...OF COURSE! I KNOW THAT! I BOUGHT THESE KNOWING THAT. SEE YA!
PET SHOP
WOOFLES
TAK
OH MAN!
TAK
THIS ISN'T GOOD.
SHF
THERE WAS A MAJOR FLAW IN ZIDANE'S DIET PLAN!!
SHF
I WAS ABOUT TO MAKE ZIDANE FAT AGAIN...
SHOP
WOOFLES
わっふる

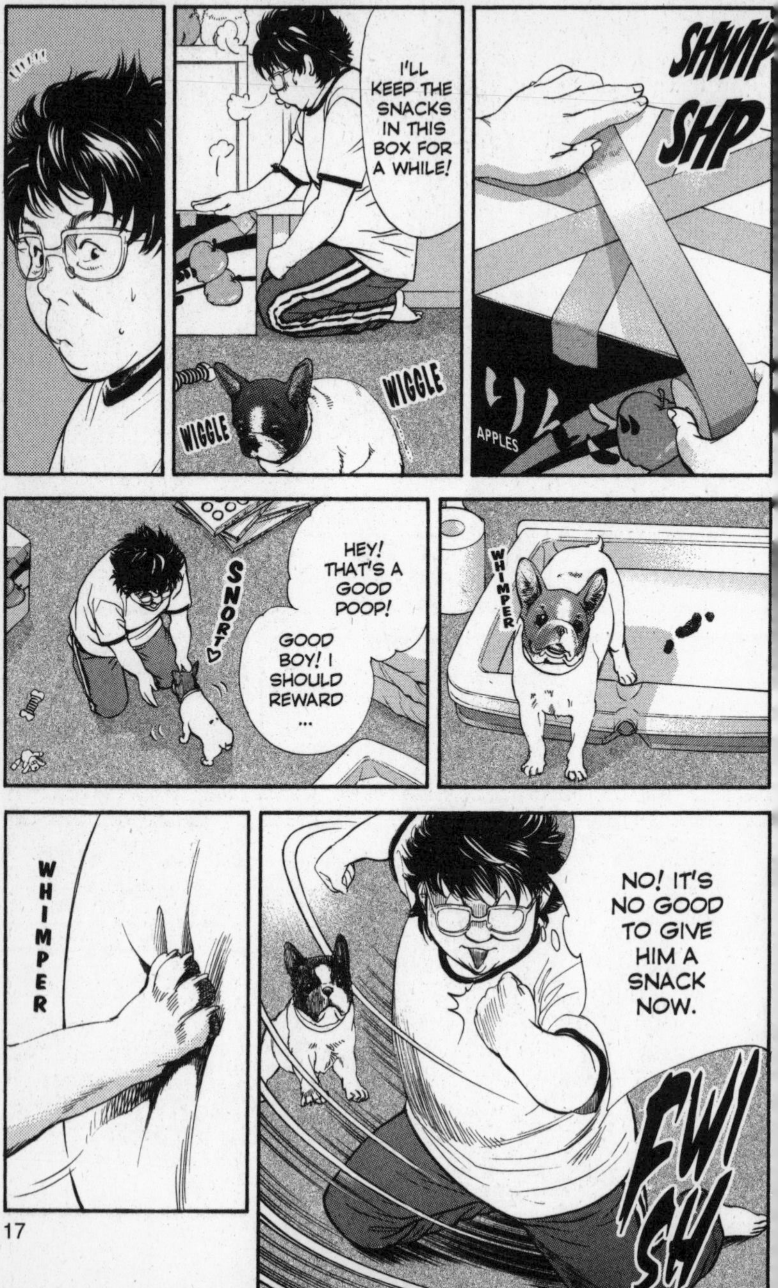
SHWIP
SHP
APPLES
I'LL KEEP THE SNACKS IN THIS BOX FOR A WHILE!
WIGGLE
WIGGLE
WHIMPER
HEY! THAT'S A GOOD POOP!
GOOD BOY! I SHOULD REWARD ...
SNORT♡
NO! IT'S NO GOOD TO GIVE HIM A SNACK NOW.
FWISH
WHIMPER

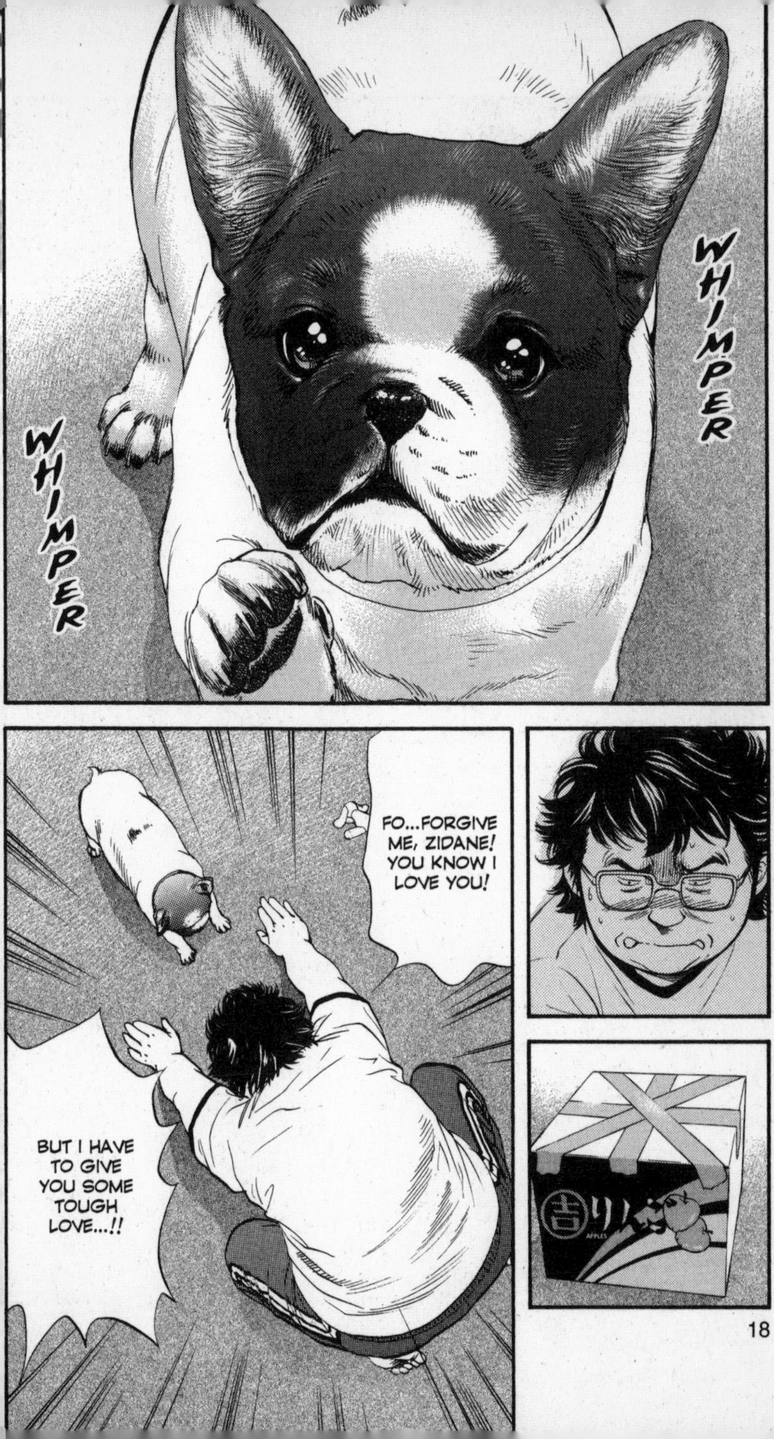

WHIMPER
WHIMPER
FO...FORGIVE ME, ZIDANE! YOU KNOW I LOVE YOU!
BUT I HAVE TO GIVE YOU SOME TOUGH LOVE...!!

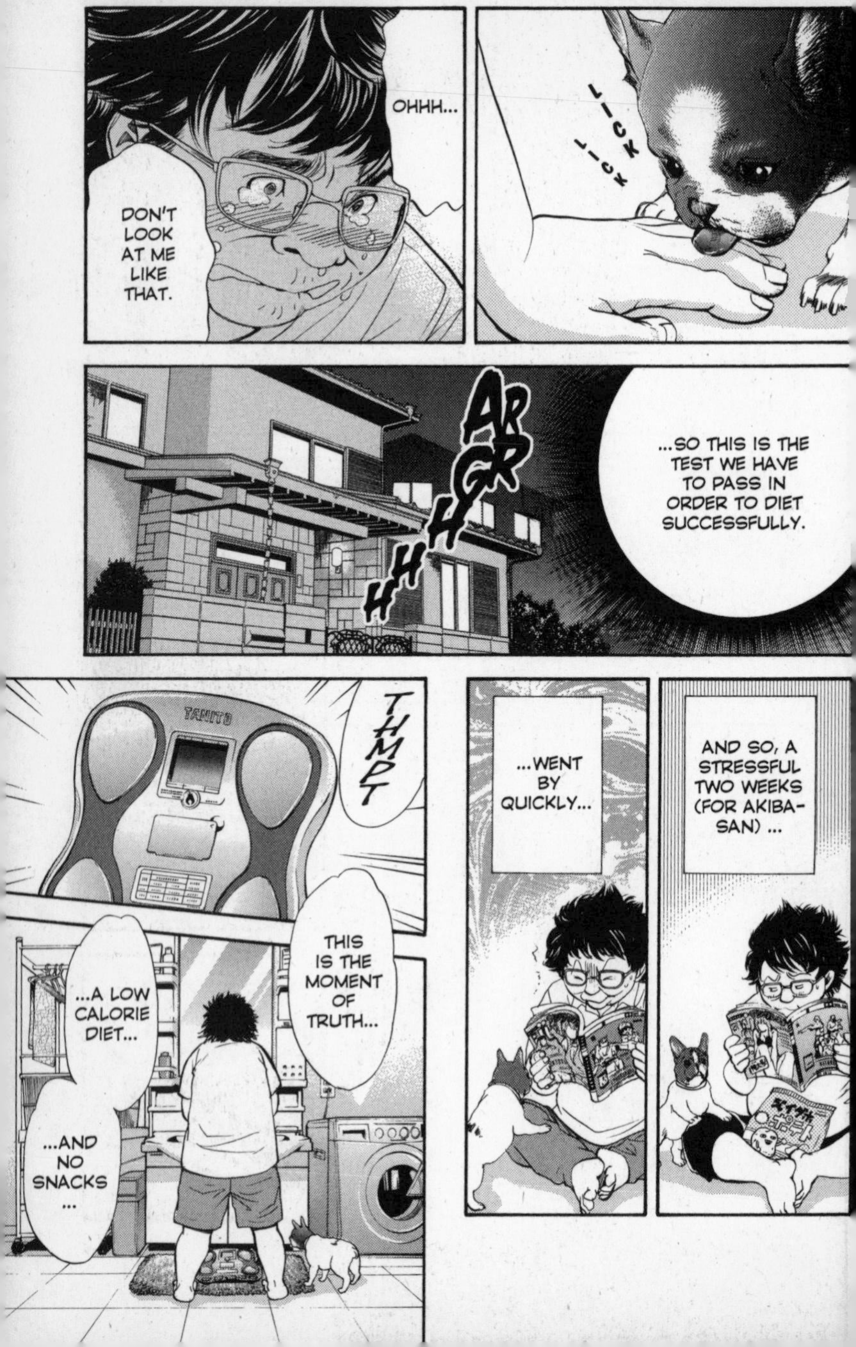
LICK
LICK
OHHH...
DON'T LOOK AT ME LIKE THAT.
...SO THIS IS THE TEST WE HAVE TO PASS IN ORDER TO DIET SUCCESSFULLY.
ARGRHHHH
AND SO, A STRESSFUL TWO WEEKS (FOR AKIBA-SAN) ...
...WENT BY QUICKLY...
TANITO
THMPT
THIS IS THE MOMENT OF TRUTH...
...A LOW CALORIE DIET...
...AND NO SNACKS ...

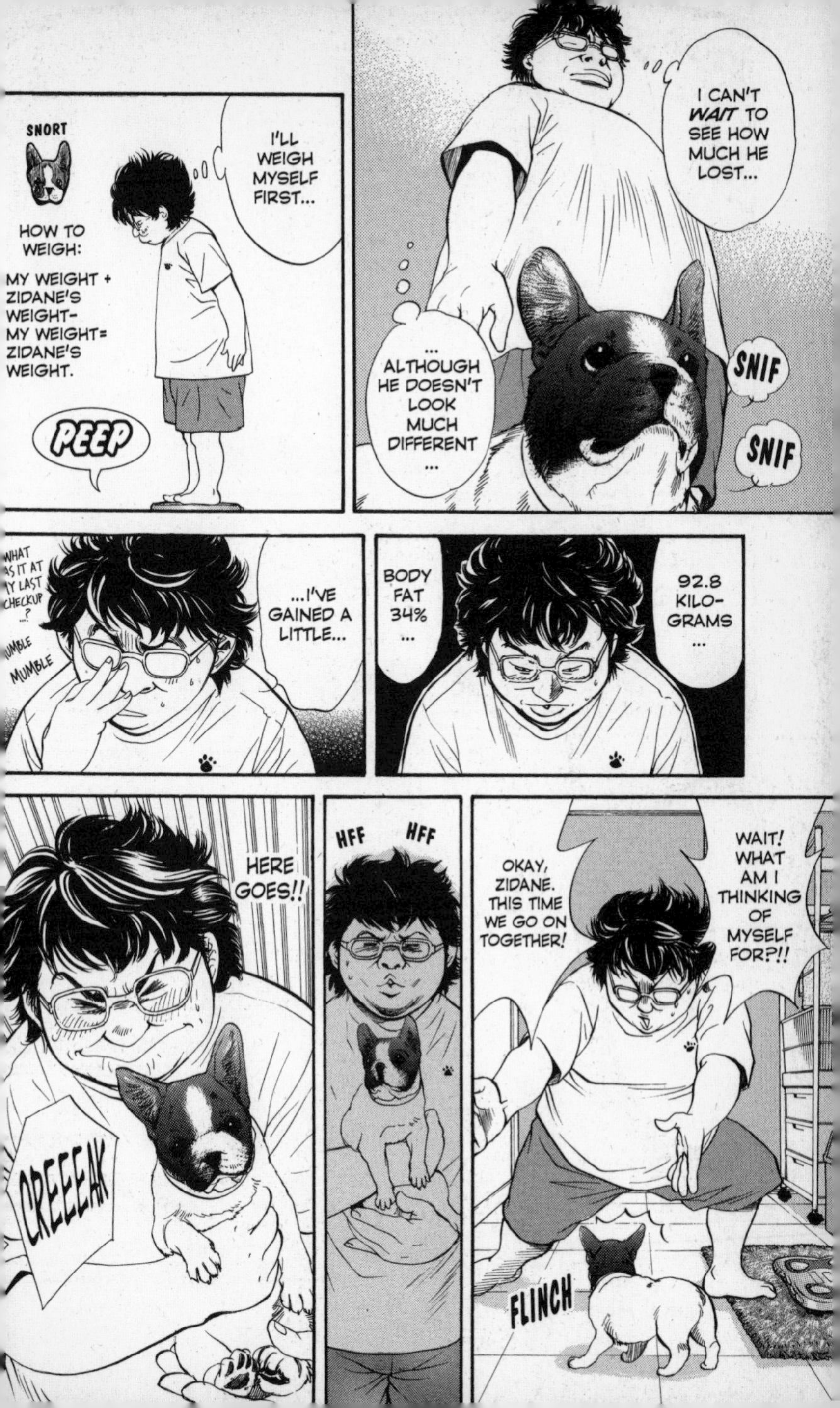
I CAN'T *WAIT* TO SEE HOW MUCH HE LOST...
... ALTHOUGH HE DOESN'T LOOK MUCH DIFFERENT ...
SNIF
SNIF
I'LL WEIGH MYSELF FIRST...
SNORT
HOW TO WEIGH:
MY WEIGHT + ZIDANE'S WEIGHT- MY WEIGHT= ZIDANE'S WEIGHT.
PEEP
92.8 KILO- GRAMS ...
BODY FAT 34% ...
...I'VE GAINED A LITTLE...
CHECKUP ...?
MUMBLE
WAIT! WHAT AM I THINKING OF MYSELF FOR?!!
OKAY, ZIDANE. THIS TIME WE GO ON TOGETHER!
FLINCH
HFF HFF
HERE GOES!!
CREEEAK

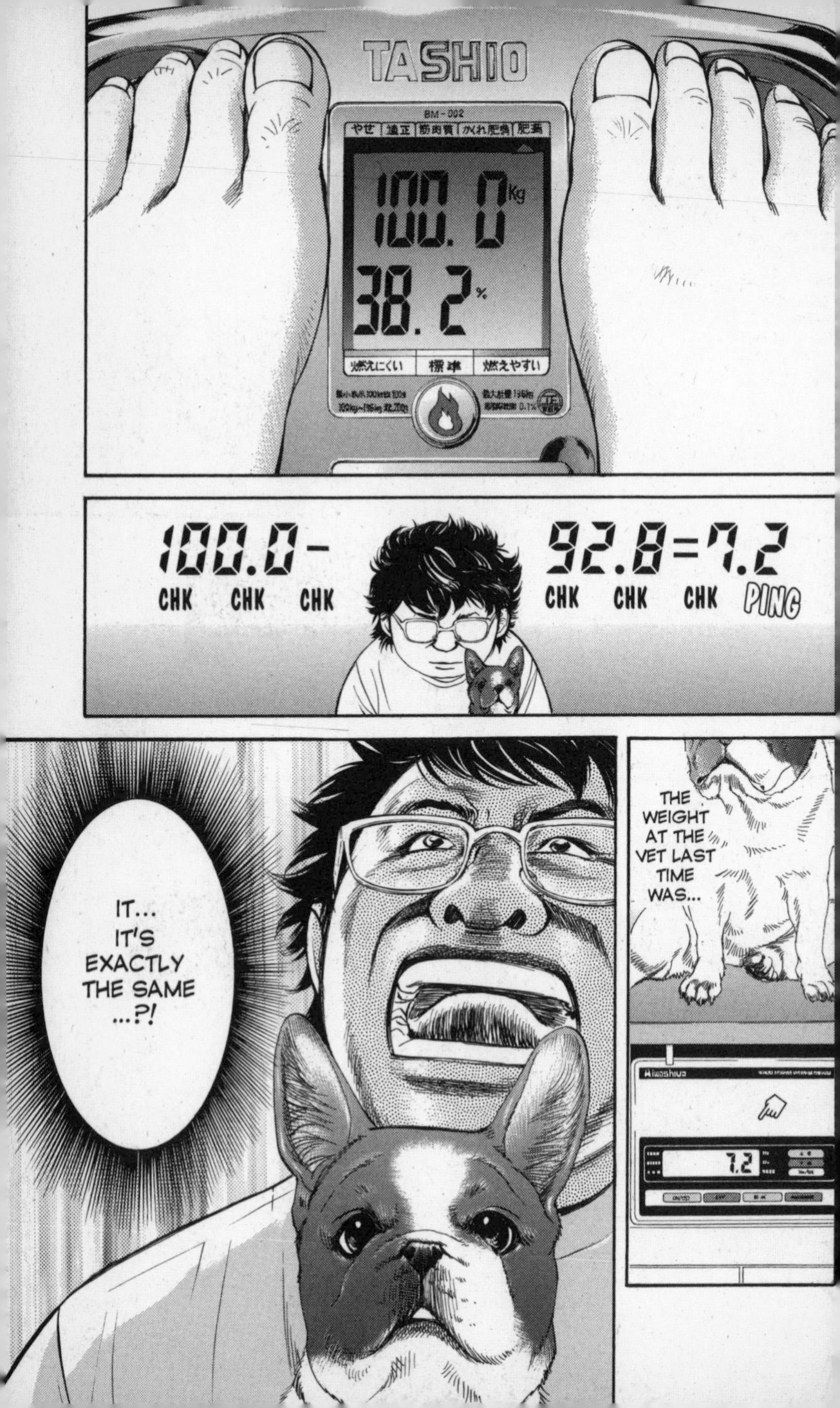
TASHIO
BM-002
やせ 適正 筋肉質 かくれ肥満 肥満
100.0 Kg
100.0
38.2 %
燃えにくい 標準 燃えやすい
100.0-
CHK CHK CHK
92.8=7.2
CHK CHK CHK
PING
THE WEIGHT AT THE VET LAST TIME WAS...
7.2
IT... IT'S EXACTLY THE SAME ...?!

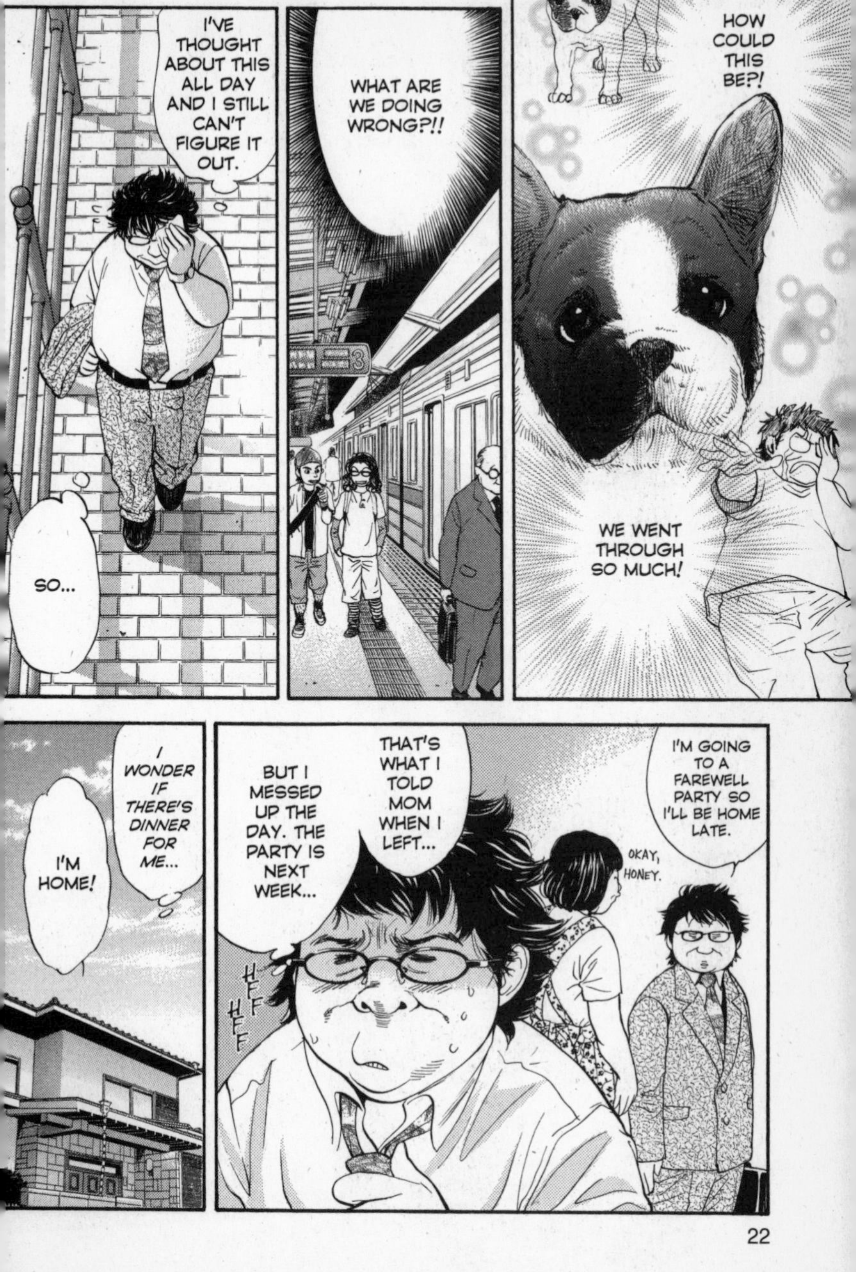
HOW COULD THIS BE?!
WE WENT THROUGH SO MUCH!
WHAT ARE WE DOING WRONG?!!
I'VE THOUGHT ABOUT THIS ALL DAY AND I STILL CAN'T FIGURE IT OUT.
SO...
I'M GOING TO A FAREWELL PARTY SO I'LL BE HOME LATE.
OKAY, HONEY.
THAT'S WHAT I TOLD MOM WHEN I LEFT...
BUT I MESSED UP THE DAY. THE PARTY IS NEXT WEEK...
HEF HEF
I WONDER IF THERE'S DINNER FOR ME...
I'M HOME!

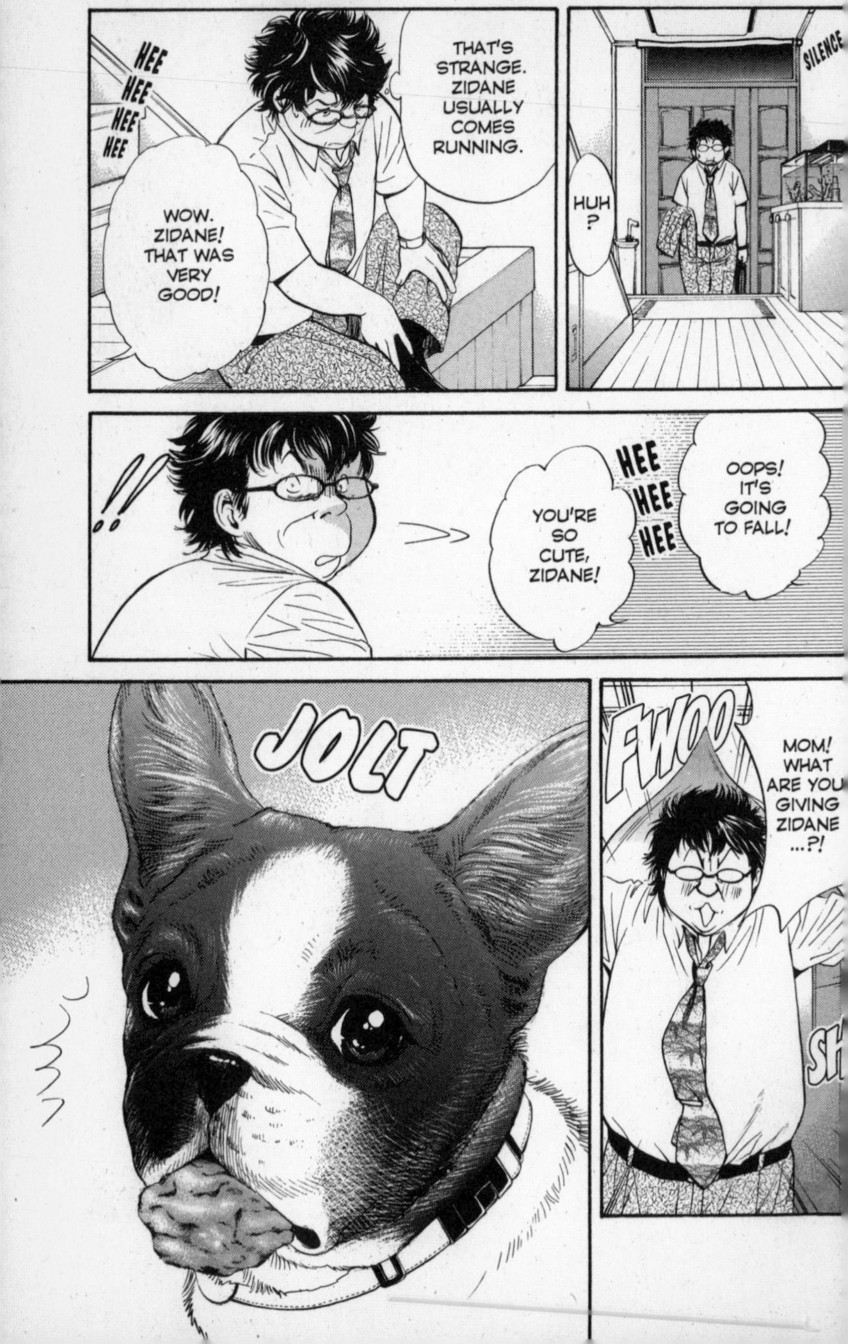
SILENCE
HUH?
THAT'S STRANGE. ZIDANE USUALLY COMES RUNNING.
HEE HEE HEE HEE
WOW. ZIDANE! THAT WAS VERY GOOD!
OOPS! IT'S GOING TO FALL!
HEE HEE HEE
YOU'RE SO CUTE, ZIDANE!
!!
FWOO
MOM! WHAT ARE YOU GIVING ZIDANE ...?!
JOLT

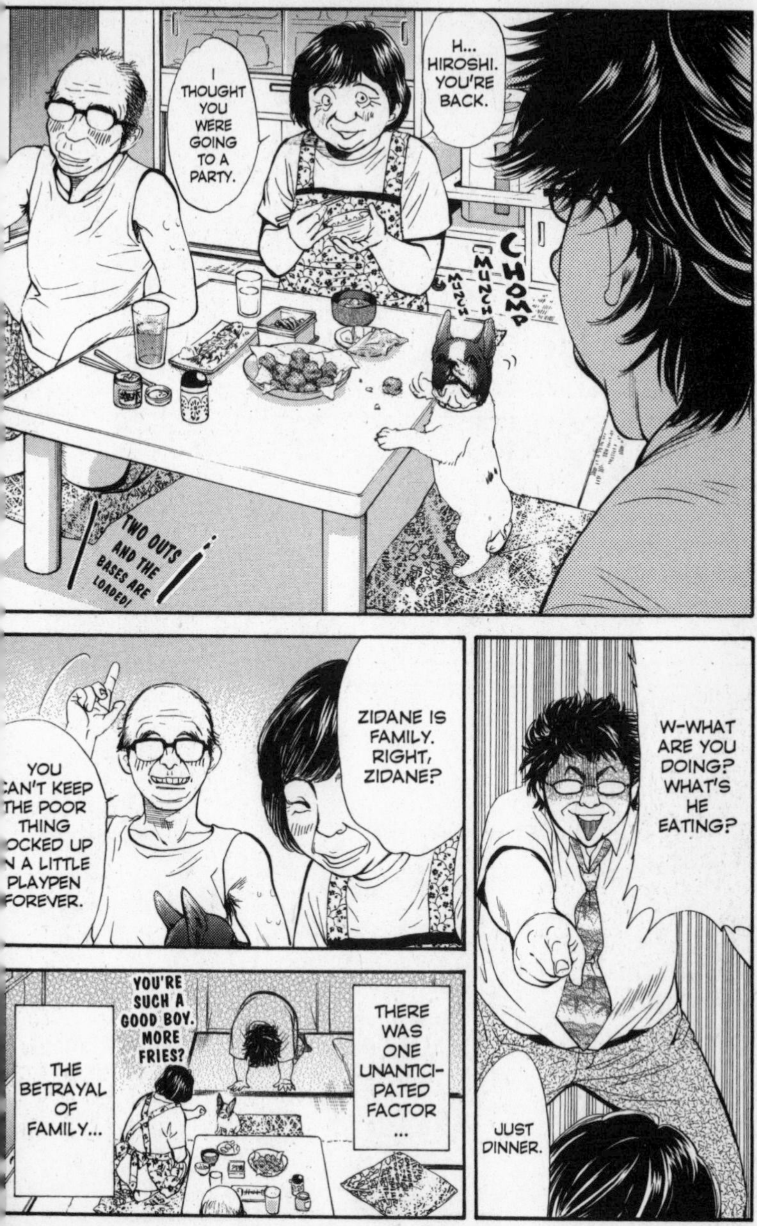
H... HIROSHI. YOU'RE BACK.
I THOUGHT YOU WERE GOING TO A PARTY.
CHOMP
MUNCH
MUNCH
TWO OUTS AND THE BASES ARE LOADED!
W-WHAT ARE YOU DOING? WHAT'S HE EATING?
JUST DINNER.
ZIDANE IS FAMILY. RIGHT, ZIDANE?
YOU AN'T KEEP THE POOR THING OCKED UP N A LITTLE PLAYPEN FOREVER.
THERE WAS ONE UNANTICI-PATED FACTOR ...
YOU'RE SUCH A GOOD BOY. MORE FRIES?
THE BETRAYAL OF FAMILY...

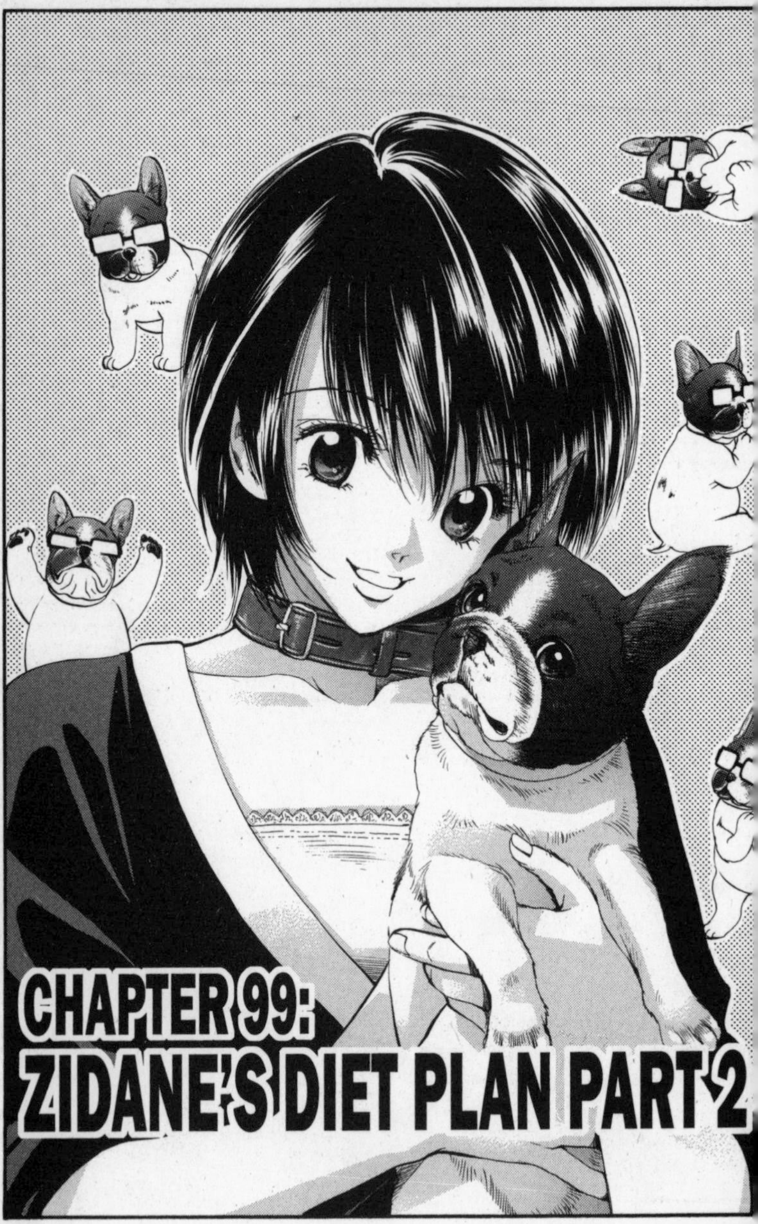
CHAPTER 99:
ZIDANE'S DIET PLAN PART 2

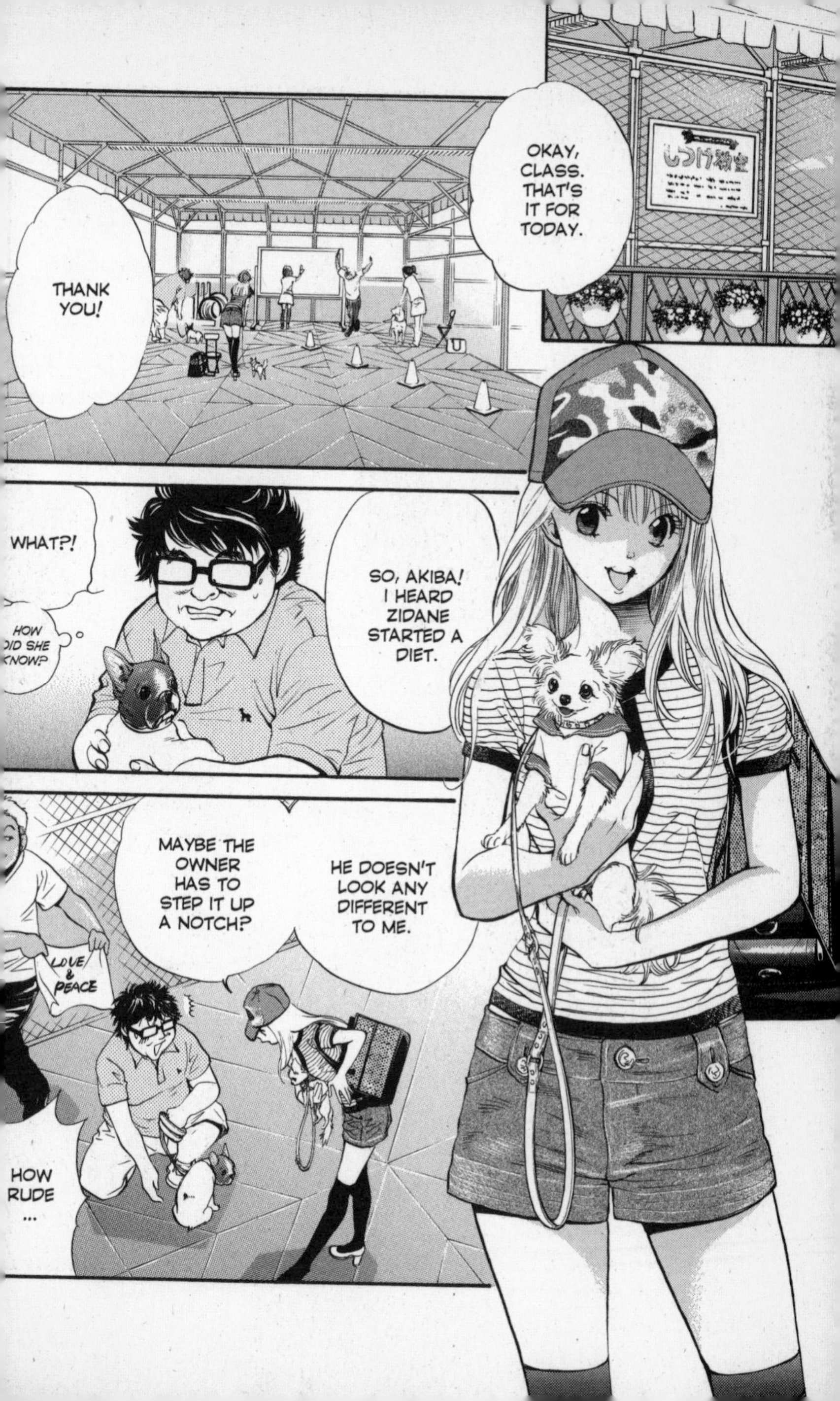
OKAY, CLASS. THAT'S IT FOR TODAY.
THANK YOU!
SO, AKIBA! I HEARD ZIDANE STARTED A DIET.
WHAT?!
HOW DID SHE KNOW?
HE DOESN'T LOOK ANY DIFFERENT TO ME.
MAYBE THE OWNER HAS TO STEP IT UP A NOTCH?
LOVE & PEACE
HOW RUDE ...

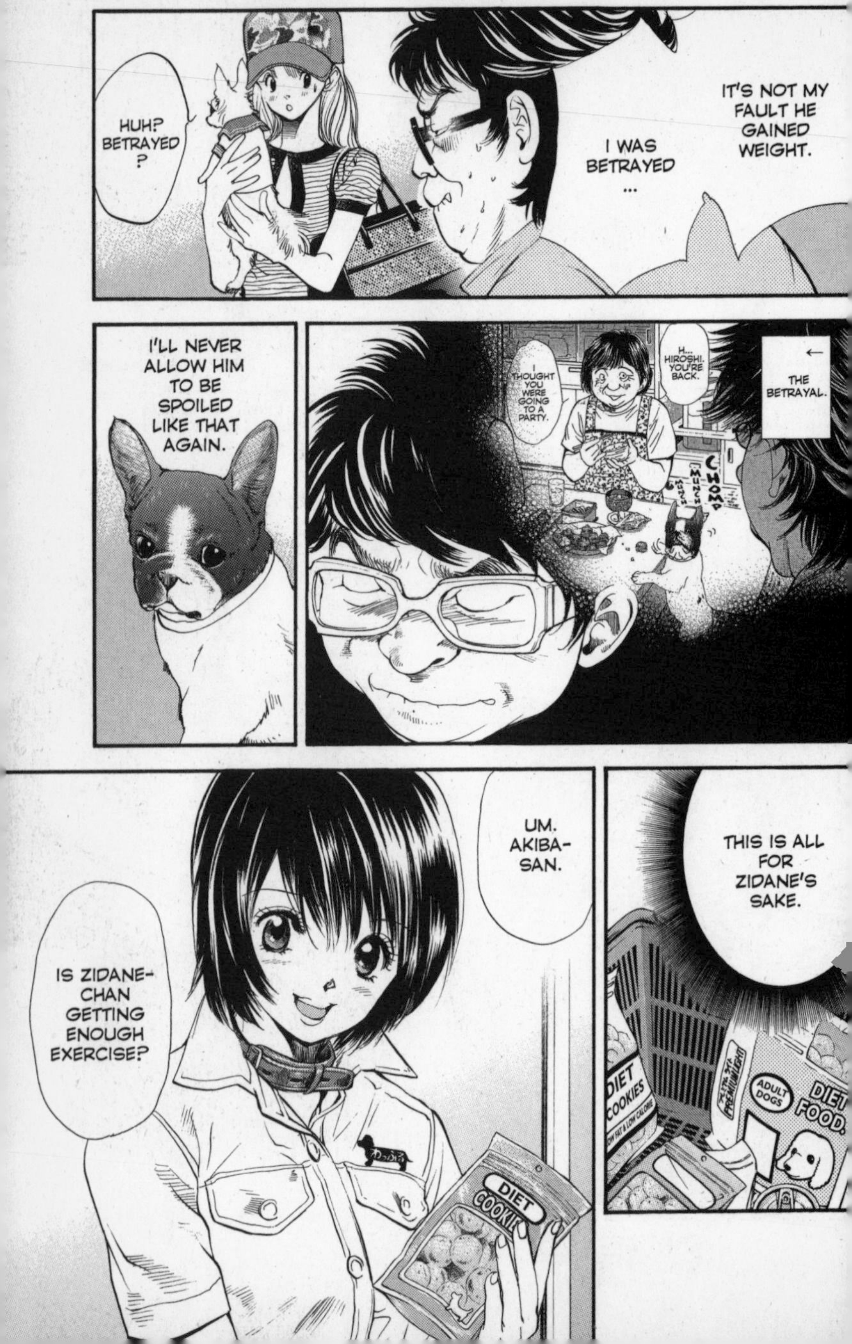

IT'S NOT MY FAULT HE GAINED WEIGHT.
I WAS BETRAYED ...
HUH? BETRAYED ?
← THE BETRAYAL.
H... HIROSHI. YOU'RE BACK.
I THOUGHT YOU WERE GOING TO A PARTY.
CHOMP
MUNCH MUNCH
I'LL NEVER ALLOW HIM TO BE SPOILED LIKE THAT AGAIN.
THIS IS ALL FOR ZIDANE'S SAKE.
DIET COOKIES
PREMIUM LIGHT
ADULT DOGS
DIET FOOD.
UM. AKIBA-SAN.
IS ZIDANE-CHAN GETTING ENOUGH EXERCISE?
DIET

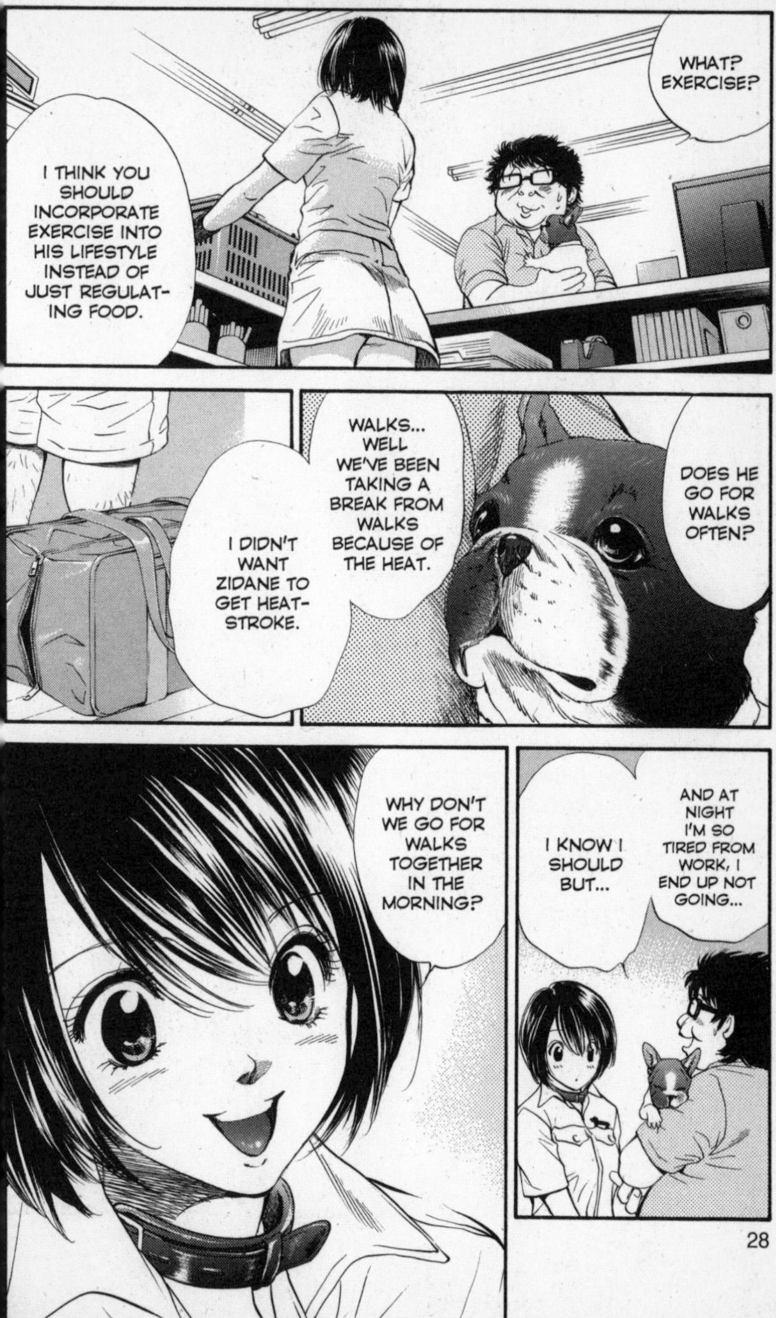
WHAT? EXERCISE?
I THINK YOU SHOULD INCORPORATE EXERCISE INTO HIS LIFESTYLE INSTEAD OF JUST REGULATING FOOD.
DOES HE GO FOR WALKS OFTEN?
WALKS... WELL WE'VE BEEN TAKING A BREAK FROM WALKS BECAUSE OF THE HEAT.
I DIDN'T WANT ZIDANE TO GET HEAT-STROKE.
AND AT NIGHT I'M SO TIRED FROM WORK, I END UP NOT GOING...
I KNOW I SHOULD BUT...
WHY DON'T WE GO FOR WALKS TOGETHER IN THE MORNING?

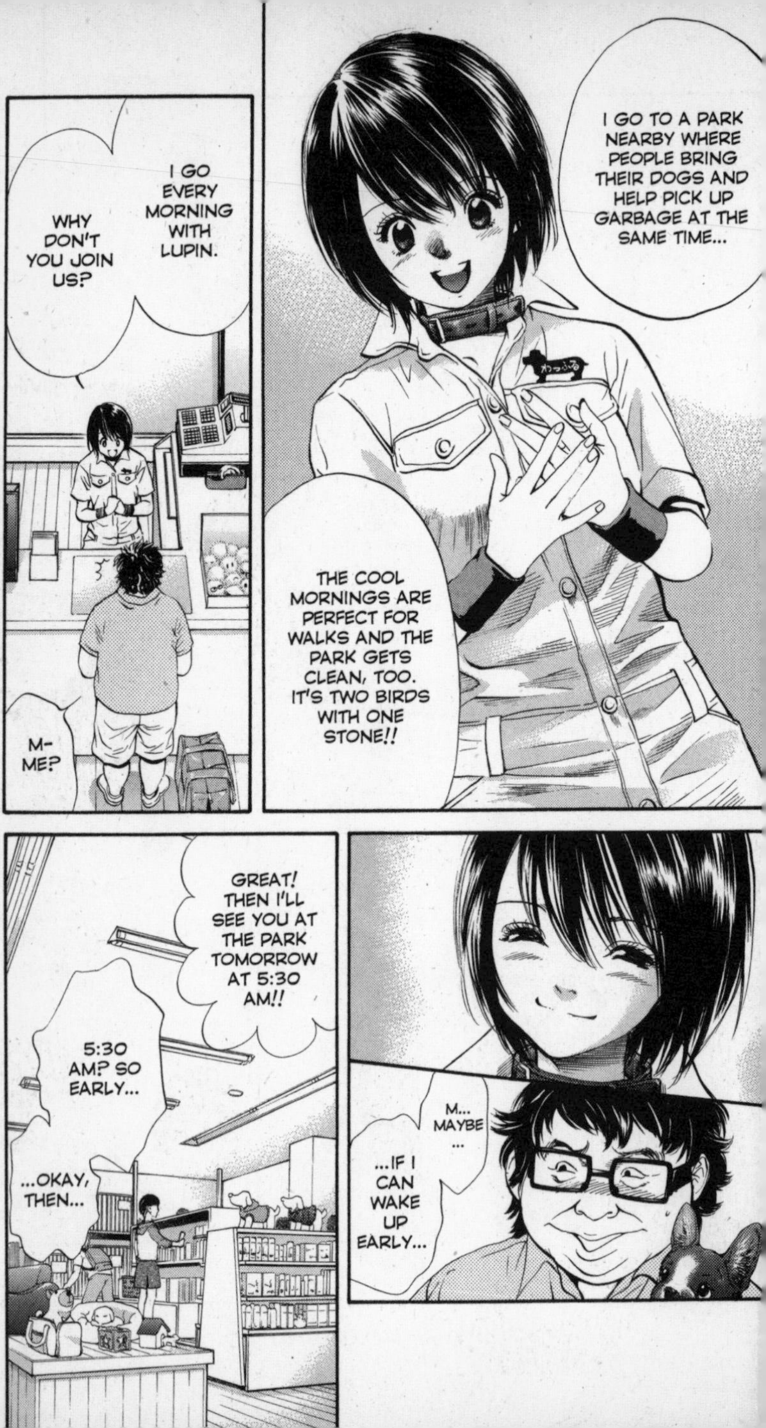
I GO TO A PARK NEARBY WHERE PEOPLE BRING THEIR DOGS AND HELP PICK UP GARBAGE AT THE SAME TIME...
THE COOL MORNINGS ARE PERFECT FOR WALKS AND THE PARK GETS CLEAN, TOO. IT'S TWO BIRDS WITH ONE STONE!!
I GO EVERY MORNING WITH LUPIN.
WHY DON'T YOU JOIN US?
M-ME?
M... MAYBE ...
...IF I CAN WAKE UP EARLY...
GREAT! THEN I'LL SEE YOU AT THE PARK TOMORROW AT 5:30 AM!!
5:30 AM? SO EARLY...
...OKAY, THEN...

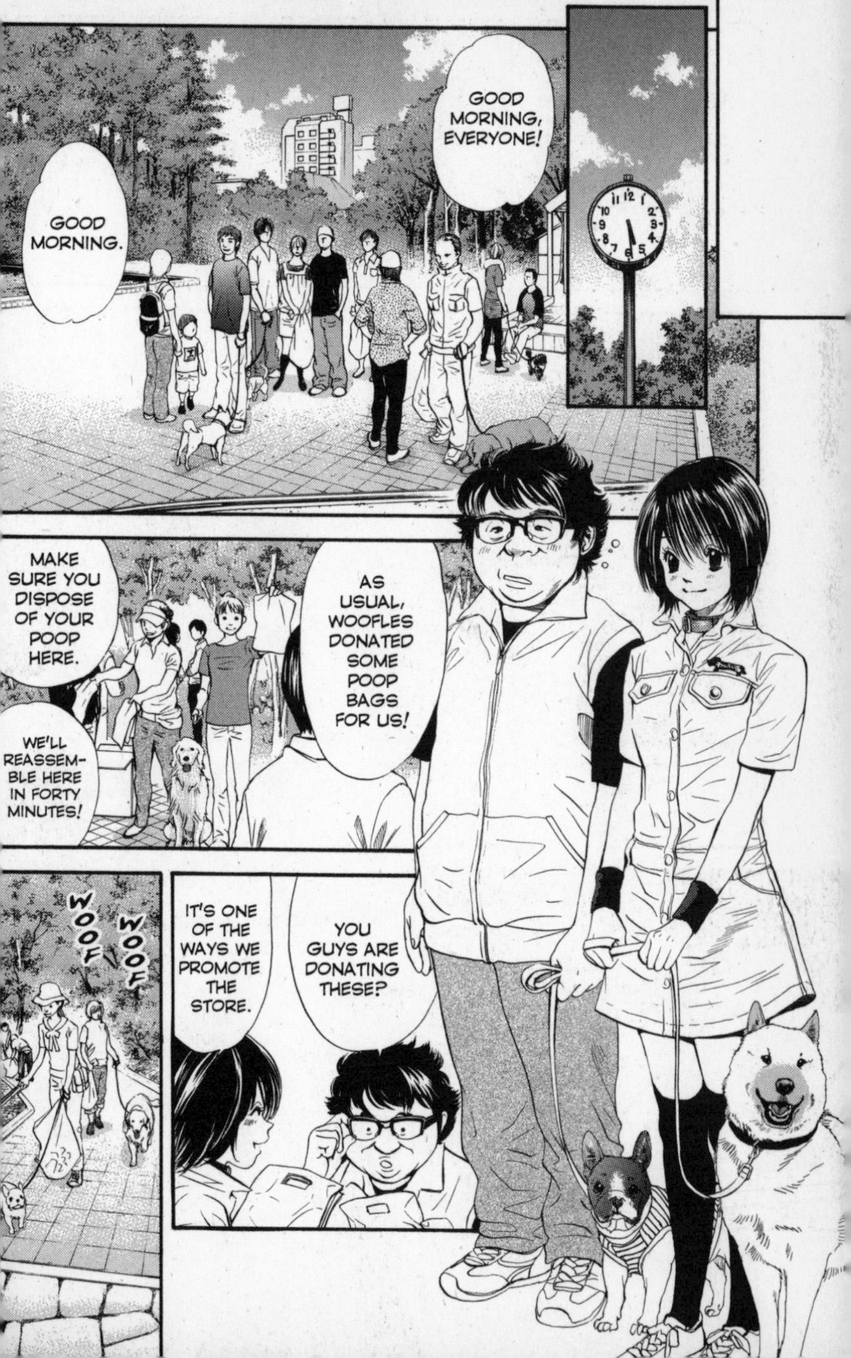
GOOD MORNING, EVERYONE!
GOOD MORNING.
AS USUAL, WOOFLES DONATED SOME POOP BAGS FOR US!
MAKE SURE YOU DISPOSE OF YOUR POOP HERE.
WE'LL REASSEM-BLE HERE IN FORTY MINUTES!
YOU GUYS ARE DONATING THESE?
IT'S ONE OF THE WAYS WE PROMOTE THE STORE.
WOOF
WOOF

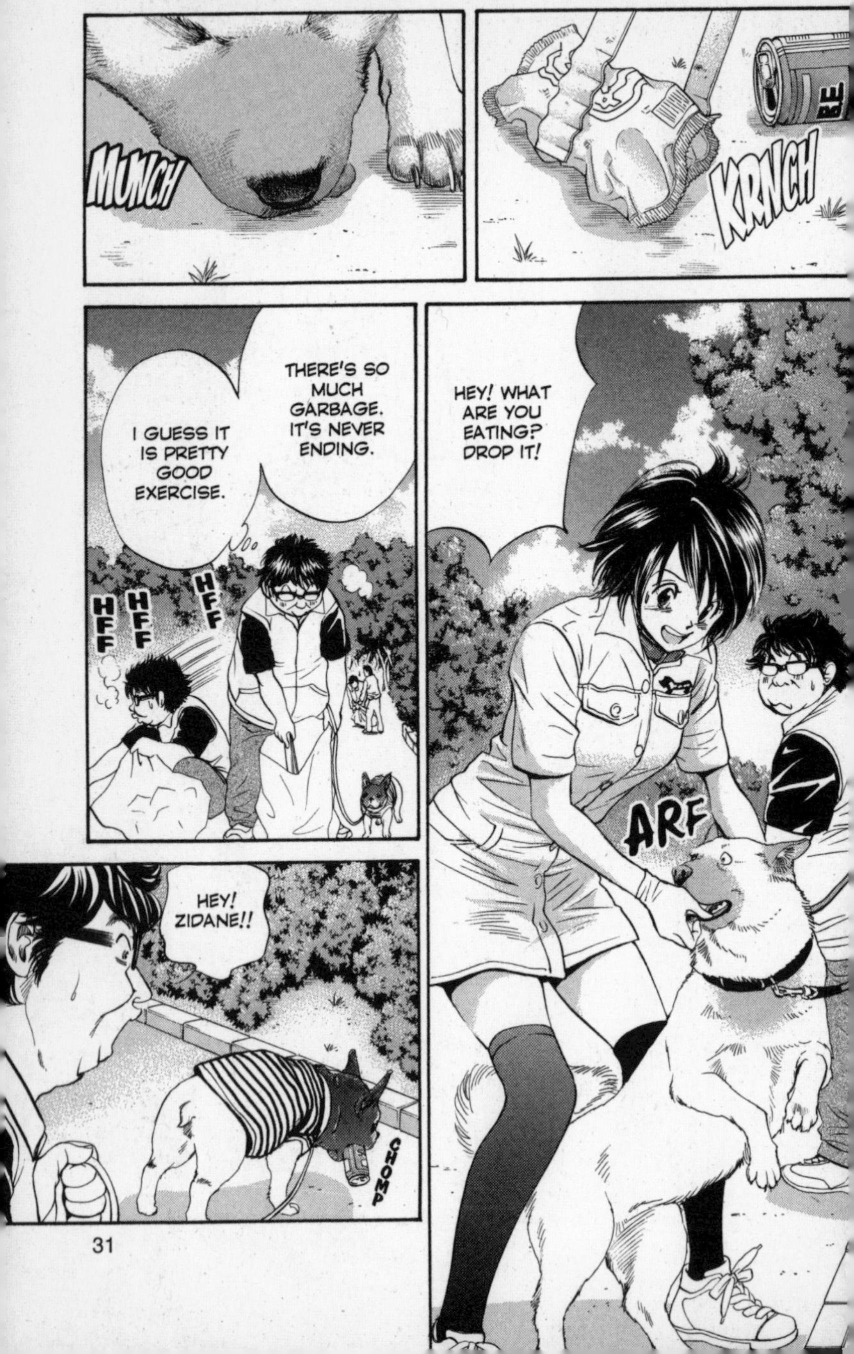
KRNCH
MUNCH
HEY! WHAT ARE YOU EATING? DROP IT!
ARF
THERE'S SO MUCH GARBAGE. IT'S NEVER ENDING.
I GUESS IT IS PRETTY GOOD EXERCISE.
HFF
HFF
HFF
HEY! ZIDANE!!
CHOMP

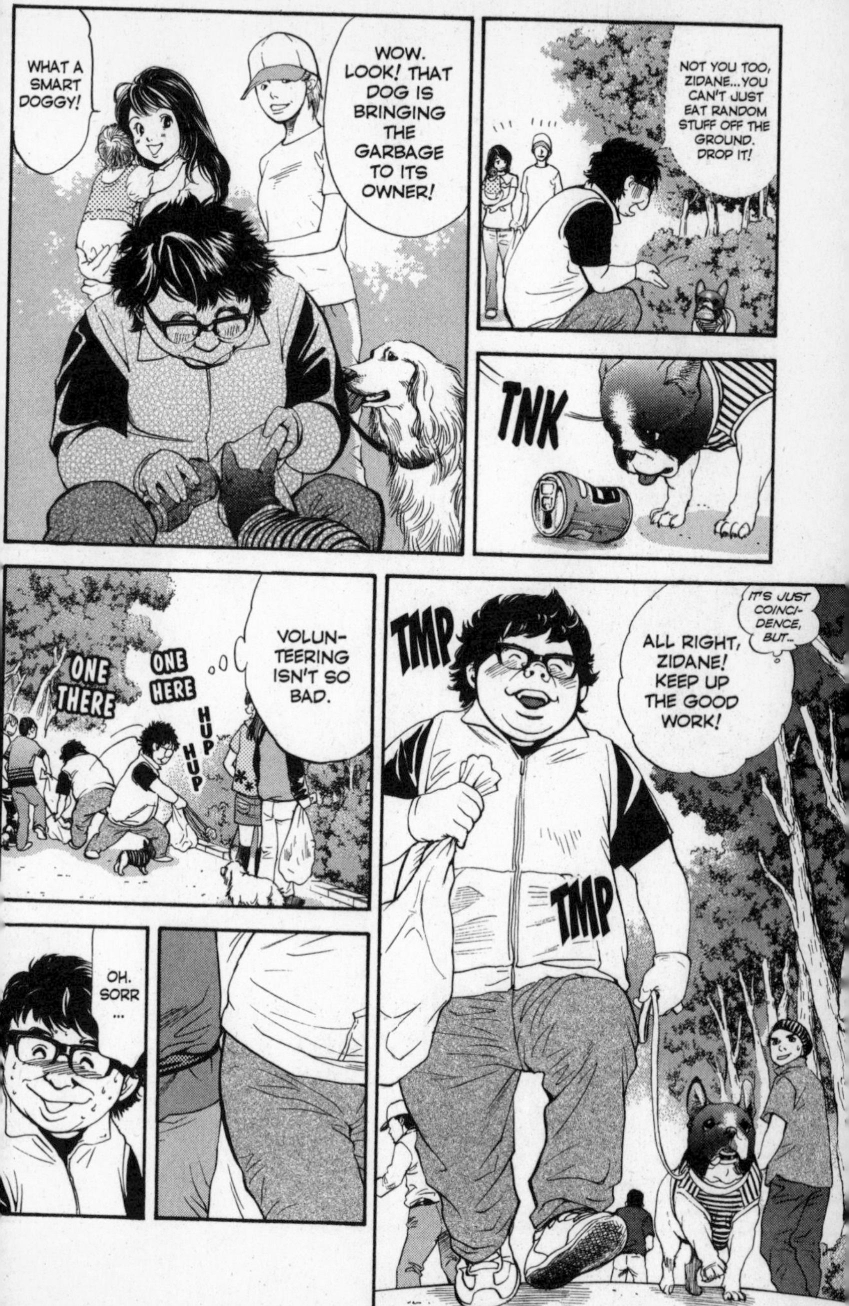
NOT YOU TOO, ZIDANE...YOU CAN'T JUST EAT RANDOM STUFF OFF THE GROUND. DROP IT!
TNK
WOW. LOOK! THAT DOG IS BRINGING THE GARBAGE TO ITS OWNER!
WHAT A SMART DOGGY!
IT'S JUST COINCIDENCE, BUT...
ALL RIGHT, ZIDANE! KEEP UP THE GOOD WORK!
TMP
TMP
VOLUNTEERING ISN'T SO BAD.
HUP
HUP
ONE HERE
ONE THERE
OH. SORR...

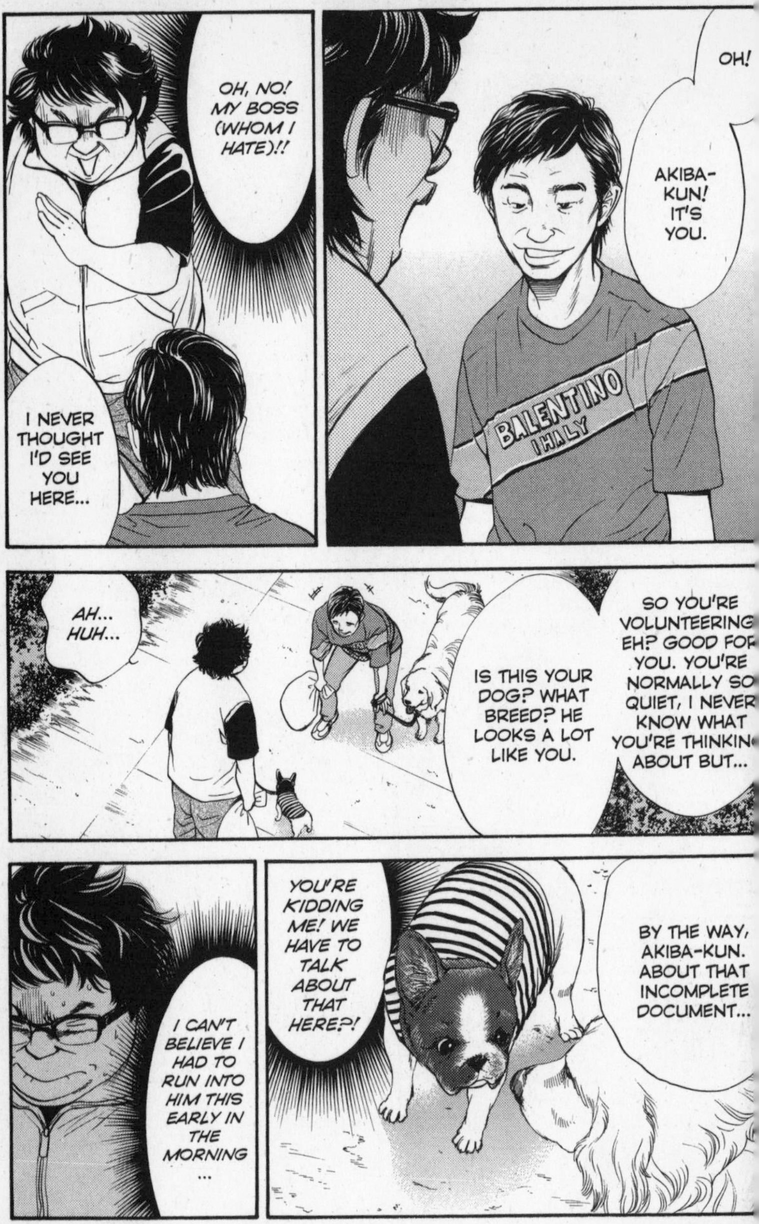
OH!
AKIBA-KUN! IT'S YOU.
OH, NO! MY BOSS (WHOM I HATE)!!
I NEVER THOUGHT I'D SEE YOU HERE...
SO YOU'RE VOLUNTEERING EH? GOOD FOR YOU. YOU'RE NORMALLY SO QUIET, I NEVER KNOW WHAT YOU'RE THINKIN ABOUT BUT...
IS THIS YOUR DOG? WHAT BREED? HE LOOKS A LOT LIKE YOU.
AH... HUH...
BY THE WAY, AKIBA-KUN. ABOUT THAT INCOMPLETE DOCUMENT...
YOU'RE KIDDING ME! WE HAVE TO TALK ABOUT THAT HERE?!
I CAN'T BELIEVE I HAD TO RUN INTO HIM THIS EARLY IN THE MORNING ...
BALENTINO IHALY

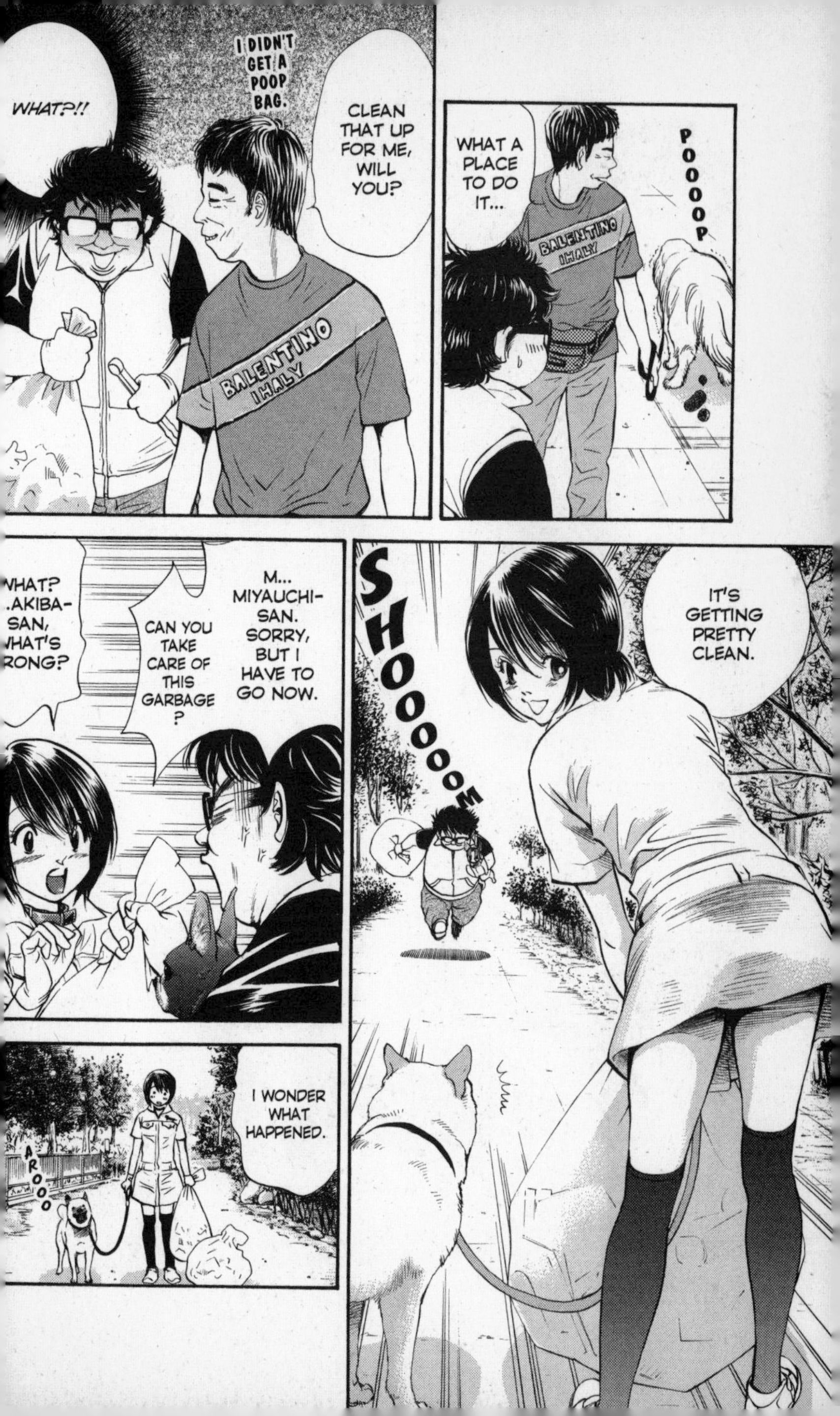
POOOOP
WHAT A PLACE TO DO IT...
CLEAN THAT UP FOR ME, WILL YOU?
I DIDN'T GET A POOP BAG.
WHAT?!!
IT'S GETTING PRETTY CLEAN.
SHOOOOOOM
M... MIYAUCHI-SAN. SORRY, BUT I HAVE TO GO NOW.
CAN YOU TAKE CARE OF THIS GARBAGE?
WHAT? .AKIBA-SAN, WHAT'S RONG?
I WONDER WHAT HAPPENED.
AROOOO

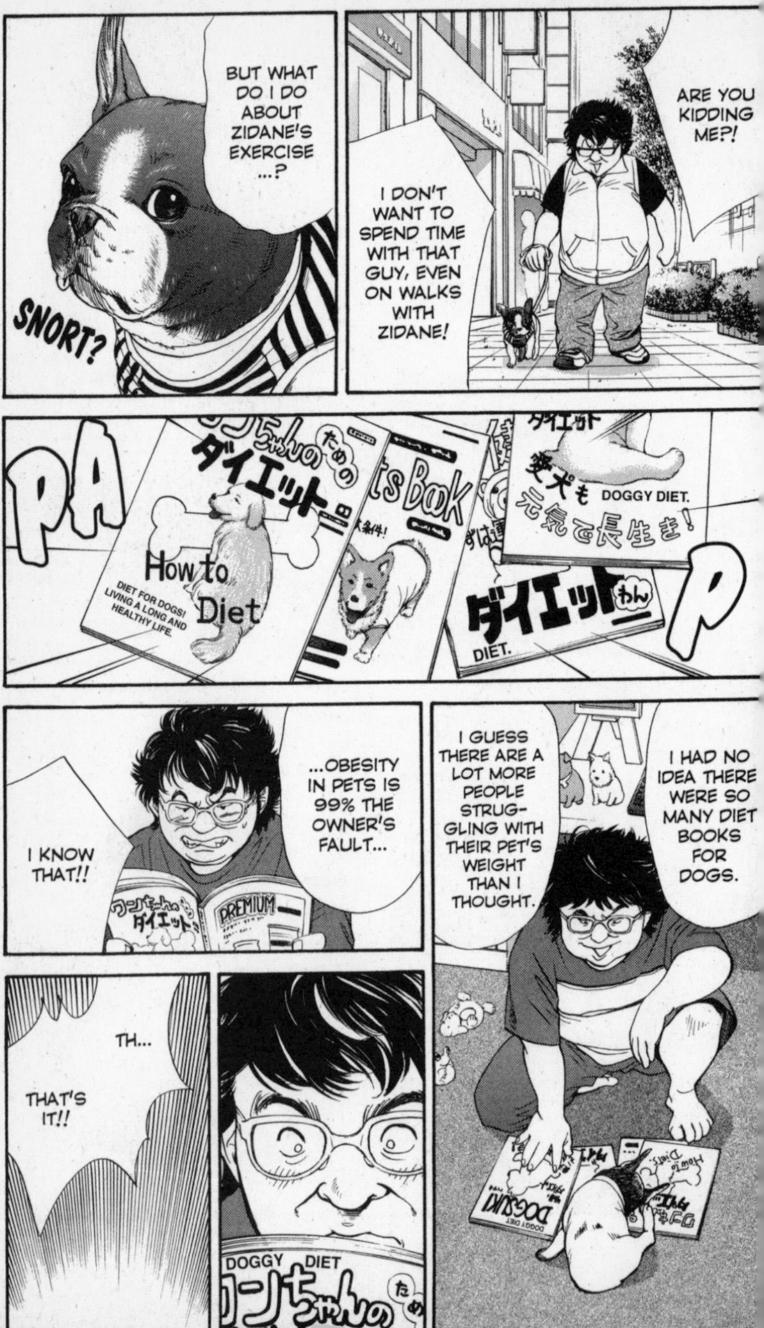
ARE YOU KIDDING ME?!
I DON'T WANT TO SPEND TIME WITH THAT GUY, EVEN ON WALKS WITH ZIDANE!
BUT WHAT DO I DO ABOUT ZIDANE'S EXERCISE ...?
SNORT?
P
愛犬も元気で長生き!
DOGGY DIET.
ダイエットわん
DIET.
How to Diet
DIET FOR DOGS! LIVING A LONG AND HEALTHY LIFE.
PA
I HAD NO IDEA THERE WERE SO MANY DIET BOOKS FOR DOGS.
I GUESS THERE ARE A LOT MORE PEOPLE STRUG-GLING WITH THEIR PET'S WEIGHT THAN I THOUGHT.
...OBESITY IN PETS IS 99% THE OWNER'S FAULT...
I KNOW THAT!!
PREMIUM
DOGGY DIET
TH...
THAT'S IT!!

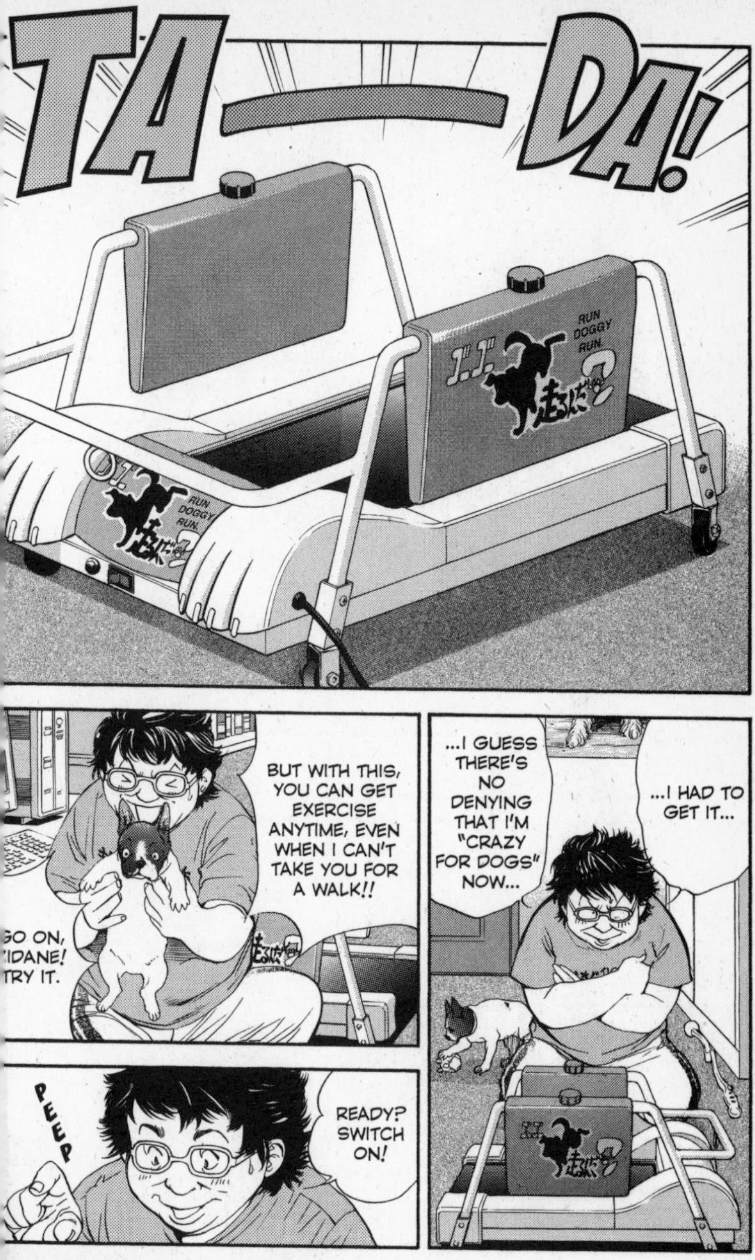
TA—DA!
RUN DOGGY RUN.
RUN DOGGY RUN.
...I HAD TO GET IT...
...I GUESS THERE'S NO DENYING THAT I'M "CRAZY FOR DOGS" NOW...
BUT WITH THIS, YOU CAN GET EXERCISE ANYTIME, EVEN WHEN I CAN'T TAKE YOU FOR A WALK!!
GO ON, ZIDANE! TRY IT.
READY? SWITCH ON!
PEEP

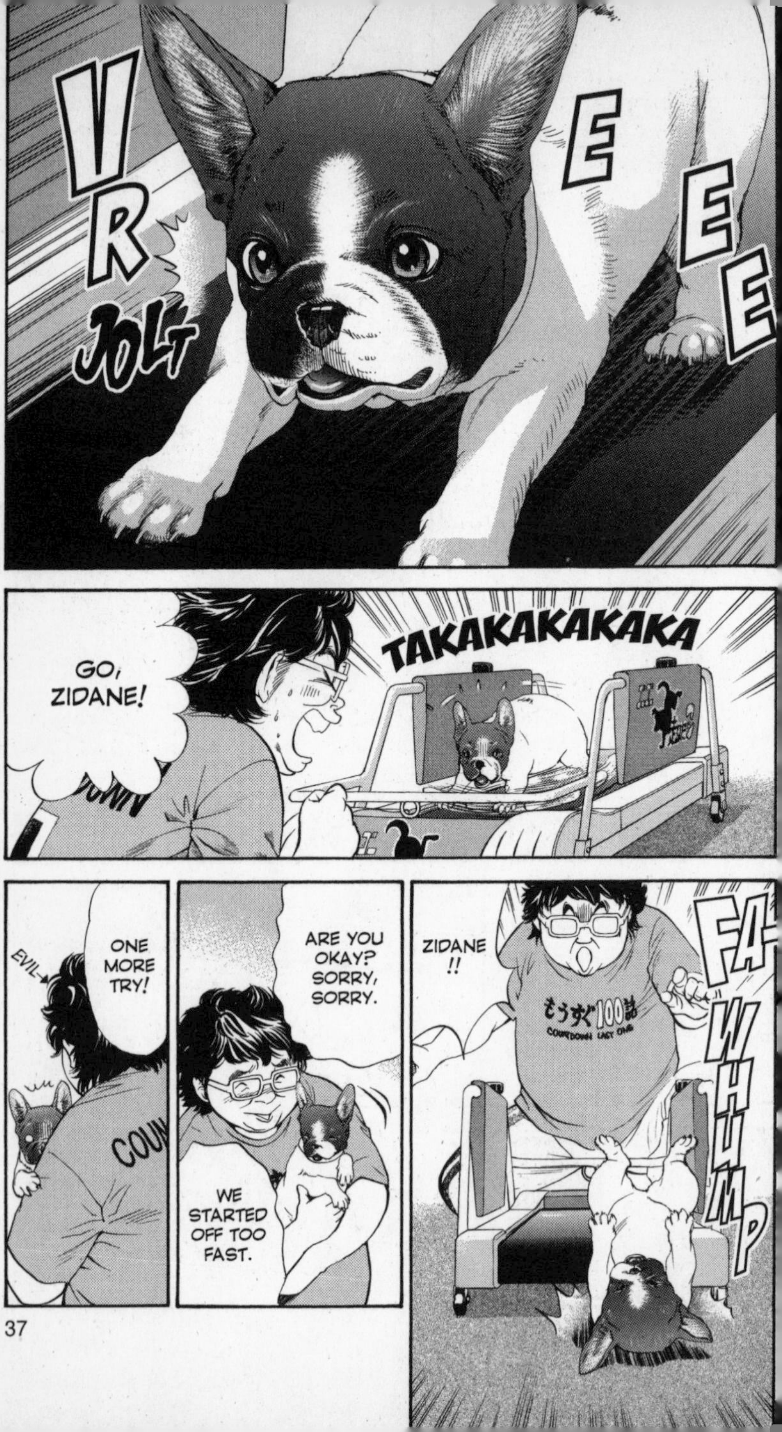
VR
EEE
JOLT
TAKAKAKAKAKA
GO, ZIDANE!
ZIDANE !!
FA-WHUMP
もうすぐ100話
ARE YOU OKAY? SORRY, SORRY.
WE STARTED OFF TOO FAST.
EVIL
ONE MORE TRY!

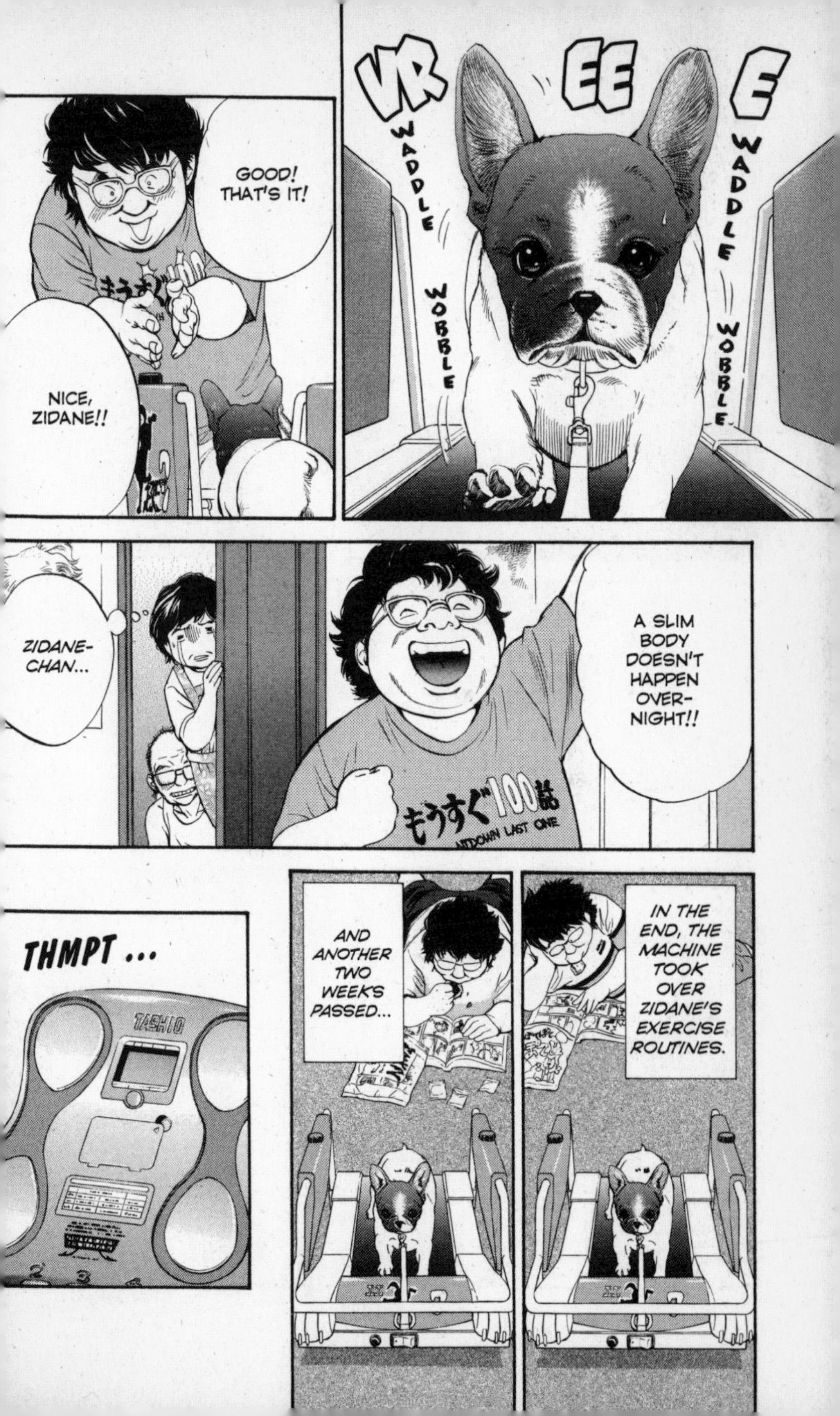
VR EE E
WADDLE
WOBBLE
WADDLE
WOBBLE
GOOD! THAT'S IT!
NICE, ZIDANE!!
A SLIM BODY DOESN'T HAPPEN OVER-NIGHT!!
もうすぐ100話
ZIDANE-CHAN...
IN THE END, THE MACHINE TOOK OVER ZIDANE'S EXERCISE ROUTINES.
AND ANOTHER TWO WEEKS PASSED...
THMPT ...
TASHIO

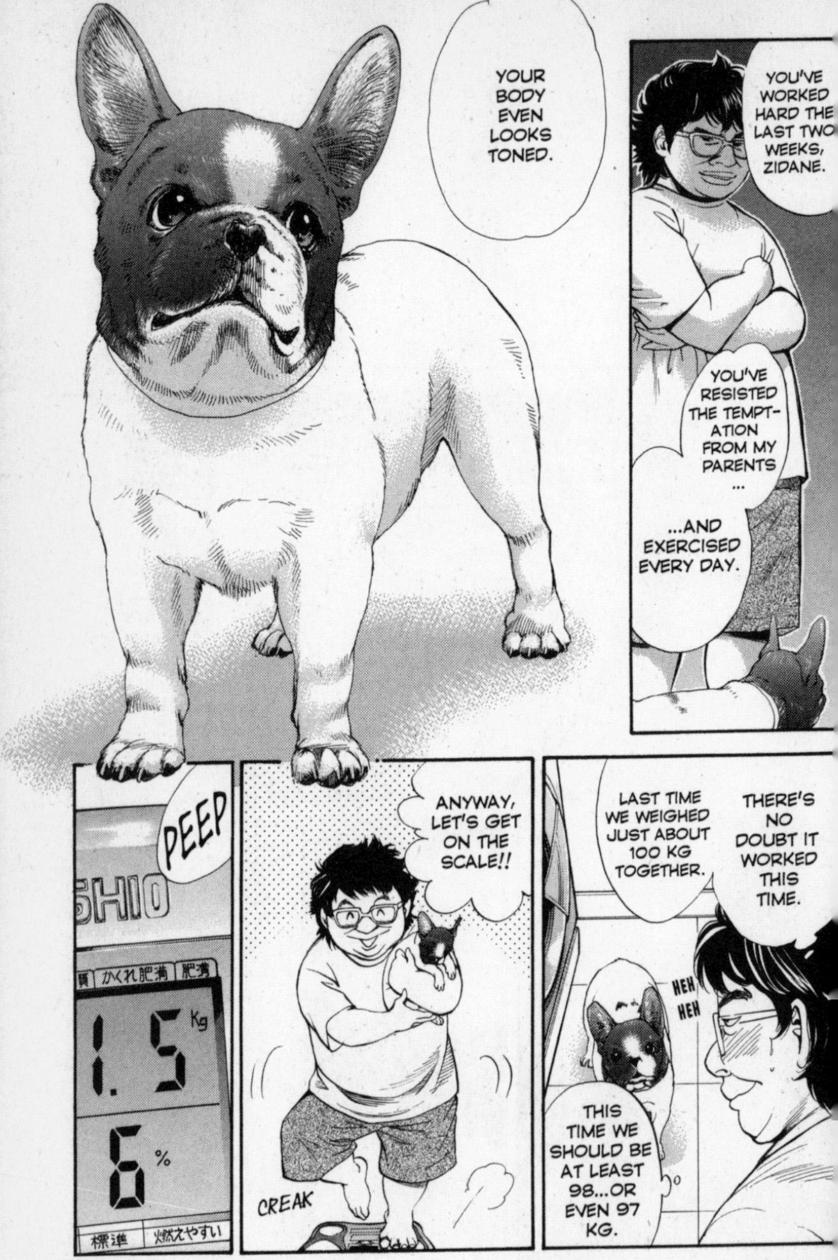
YOU'VE WORKED HARD THE LAST TWO WEEKS, ZIDANE.
YOU'VE RESISTED THE TEMPT-ATION FROM MY PARENTS ...
...AND EXERCISED EVERY DAY.
YOUR BODY EVEN LOOKS TONED.
THERE'S NO DOUBT IT WORKED THIS TIME.
LAST TIME WE WEIGHED JUST ABOUT 100 KG TOGETHER.
HEH HEH
THIS TIME WE SHOULD BE AT LEAST 98...OR EVEN 97 KG.
ANYWAY, LET'S GET ON THE SCALE!!
CREAK
PEEP
SHIO
かくれ肥満
肥満
1.5 Kg
6 %
標準
燃えやすい

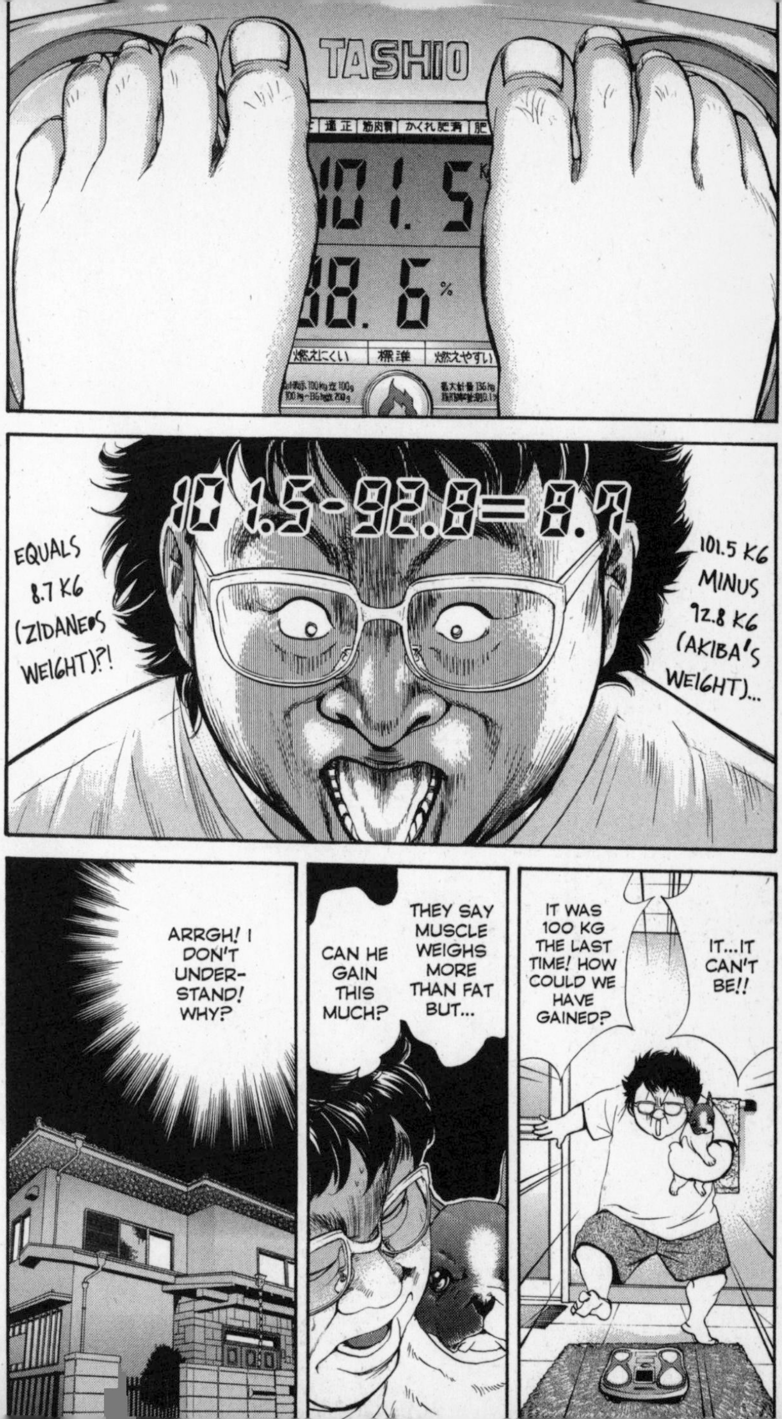
TASHIO
燃えにくい
標準
燃えやすい
101.5-92.8=8.7
101.5 KG MINUS 92.8 KG (AKIBA'S WEIGHT)...
EQUALS 8.7 KG (ZIDANE'S WEIGHT)?!
IT...IT CAN'T BE!!
IT WAS 100 KG THE LAST TIME! HOW COULD WE HAVE GAINED?
THEY SAY MUSCLE WEIGHS MORE THAN FAT BUT...
CAN HE GAIN THIS MUCH?
ARRGH! I DON'T UNDER-STAND! WHY?

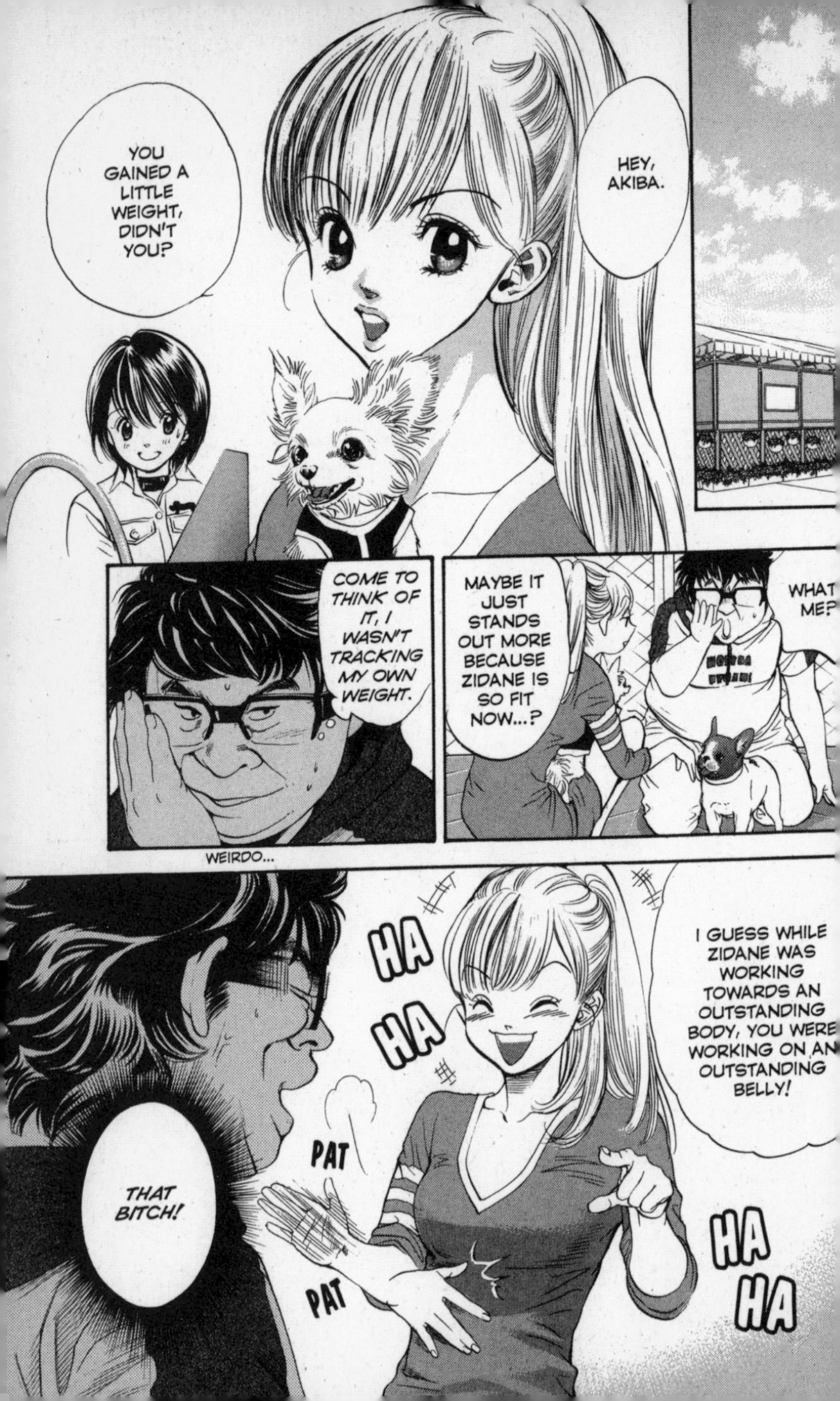

HEY, AKIBA.
YOU GAINED A LITTLE WEIGHT, DIDN'T YOU?
WHAT ME?
MAYBE IT JUST STANDS OUT MORE BECAUSE ZIDANE IS SO FIT NOW...?
COME TO THINK OF IT, I WASN'T TRACKING MY OWN WEIGHT.
WEIRDO...
I GUESS WHILE ZIDANE WAS WORKING TOWARDS AN OUTSTANDING BODY, YOU WERE WORKING ON AN OUTSTANDING BELLY!
HA HA
HA HA
HA
HA
PAT
PAT
THAT BITCH!

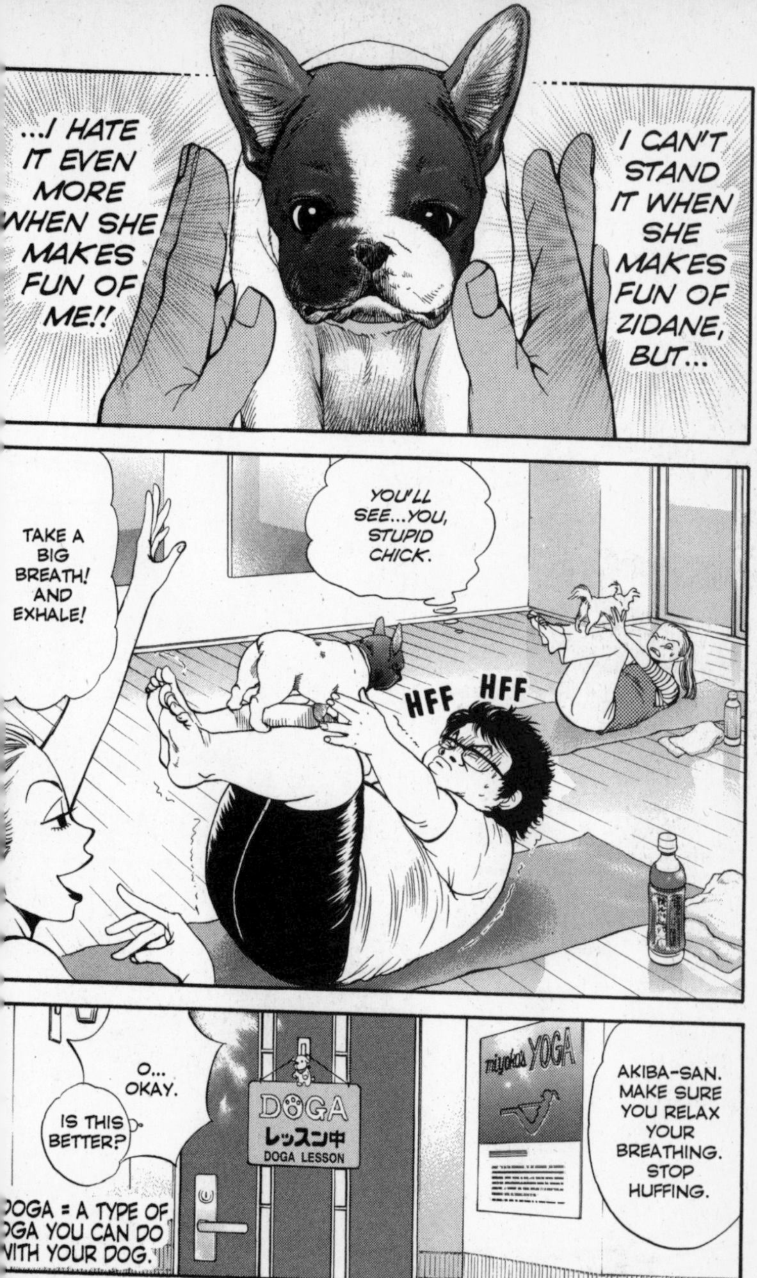
I CAN'T STAND IT WHEN SHE MAKES FUN OF ZIDANE, BUT...
...I HATE IT EVEN MORE WHEN SHE MAKES FUN OF ME!!
YOU'LL SEE...YOU, STUPID CHICK.
HFF HFF
TAKE A BIG BREATH! AND EXHALE!
AKIBA-SAN. MAKE SURE YOU RELAX YOUR BREATHING. STOP HUFFING.
miyoko's YOGA
DOGA
レッスン中
DOGA LESSON
O... OKAY.
IS THIS BETTER?
OGA = A TYPE OF
OGA YOU CAN DO
WITH YOUR DOG.

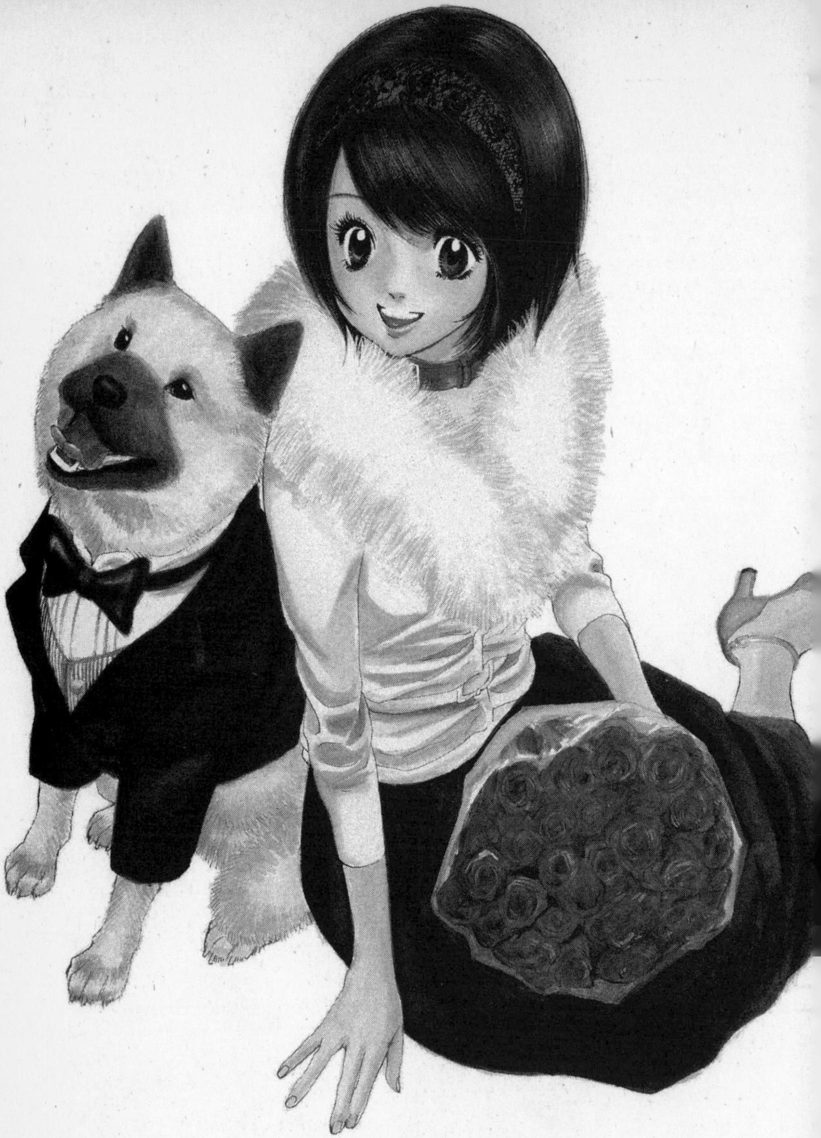

CHAPTER 100:

LEGEND OF LITTLE LUPIN

INUBAKA 10TH VOLUME GREETINGS.

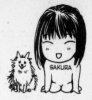

SAKURA

HOW TIME FLIES. WE'VE ALREADY REACHED OUR 10TH VOLUME.
MY LOVELY DOG BLANC, WHO WAS ONLY 7 MONTHS OLD WHEN THE FIRST VOLUME CAME OUT, IS 3 YEARS OLD THIS YEAR. AND THESE DAYS, I'M SURPRISED BY HOW TIME JUST SEEMS TO FLY EVEN FASTER COMPARED TO THE EARLY PART OF THE SERIES. WITH THE SUPPORT OF MY WONDERFUL STAFF MEMBERS, AND THE ENCOURAGEMENT I RECEIVE THROUGH ALL THE LETTERS AND DOGGY PICTURES FROM OUR READERS, WE'VE COME THIS FAR AND I'D LIKE TO THANK ALL OF YOU FOR YOUR CONTINUOUS SUPPORT! I PROMISE TO CONTINUE TO DO MY VERY BEST, WHILE I'M STILL HEALTHY...I THINK I'M HEALTHY. THAT REMINDS ME, I HAVE TO GO FOR A CHECK UP...BEING OVER 30 AND ALL...

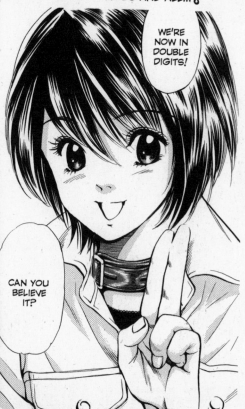

WE'RE NOW IN DOUBLE DIGITS!

CAN YOU BELIEVE IT?

I STILL LOVE DOGS, BUT LATELY I'VE BEEN FINDING CATS ADORABLE.

AN AMERICAN SHORT HAIR THAT I THINK IS MY NEIGHBOR'S CAT LETS ME PET HER, AND THAT MAKES ME SO HAPPY. (CATS TEND TO RUN AWAY A LOT...) SHE DOES KIND OF HAVE SCARY EYES, BUT SHE COMES RIGHT UP TO ME ON HER OWN AND IS JUST SOOO CUTE.

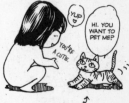

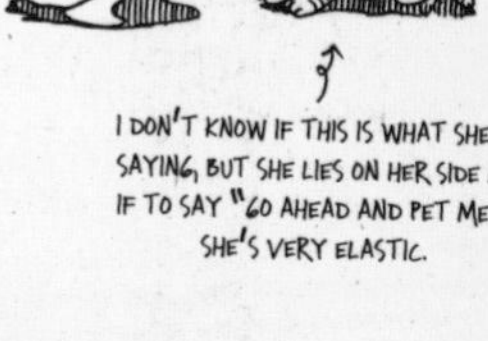

YUP

YOU'RE A CUTIE.

HI. YOU WANT TO PET ME?

I DON'T KNOW IF THIS IS WHAT SHE IS SAYING, BUT SHE LIES ON HER SIDE AS IF TO SAY "GO AHEAD AND PET ME." SHE'S VERY ELASTIC.

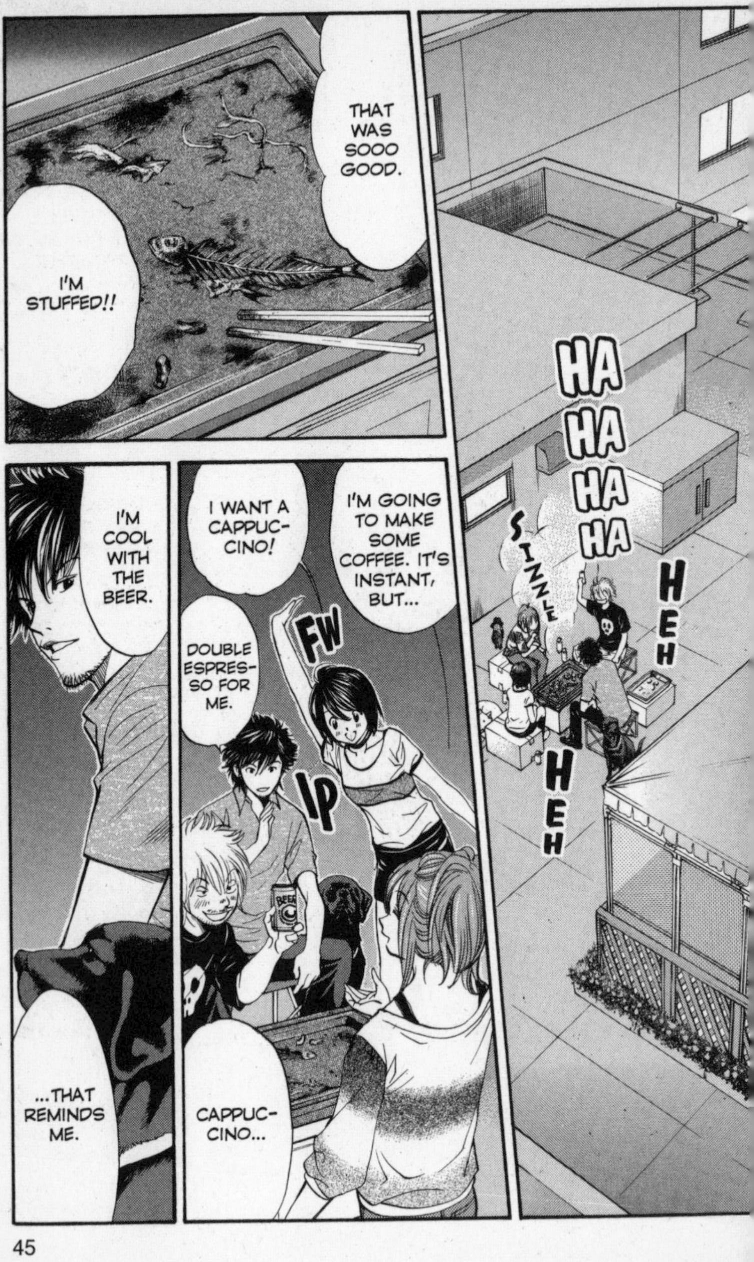

HA HA HA HA
HEH HEH
SIZZLE
HEH HEH
THAT WAS SOOO GOOD.
I'M STUFFED!!
I'M GOING TO MAKE SOME COFFEE. IT'S INSTANT, BUT...
I WANT A CAPPUC-CINO!
FWIP
DOUBLE ESPRES-SO FOR ME.
CAPPUC-CINO...
I'M COOL WITH THE BEER.
...THAT REMINDS ME.

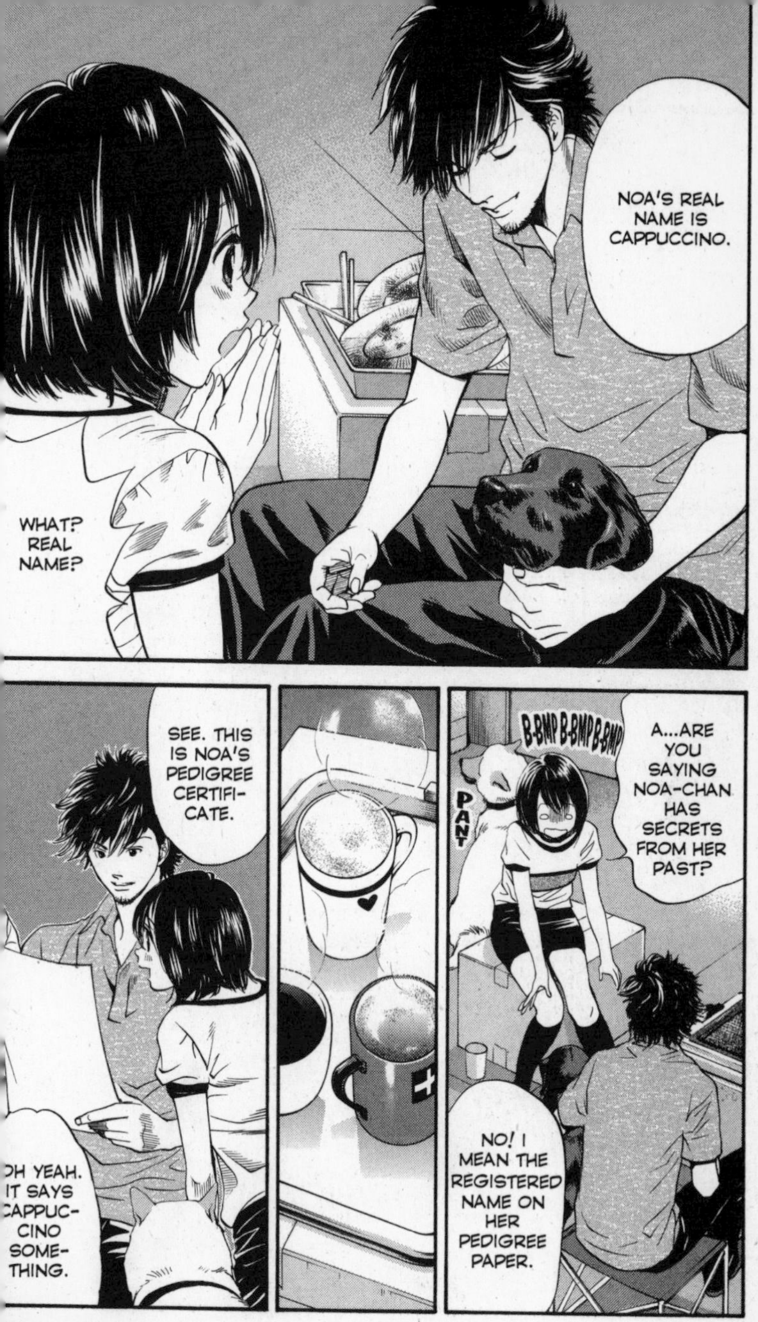
NOA'S REAL NAME IS CAPPUCCINO.
WHAT? REAL NAME?
B-BMP B-BMP B-BMP
A...ARE YOU SAYING NOA-CHAN HAS SECRETS FROM HER PAST?
PANT
NO! I MEAN THE REGISTERED NAME ON HER PEDIGREE PAPER.
SEE. THIS IS NOA'S PEDIGREE CERTIFI-CATE.
OH YEAH. IT SAYS CAPPUC-CINO SOME-THING.

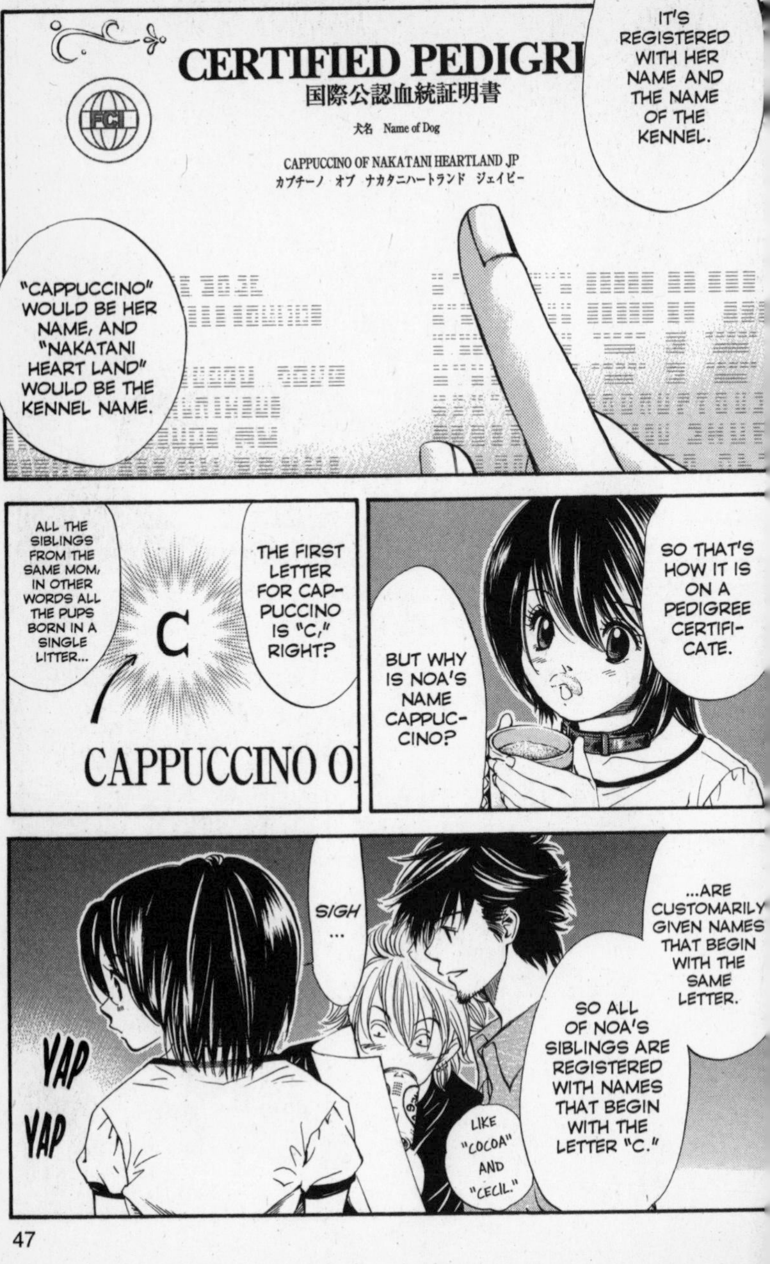
IT'S REGISTERED WITH HER NAME AND THE NAME OF THE KENNEL.
CERTIFIED PEDIGRI
国際公認血統証明書
FCI
犬名 Name of Dog
CAPPUCCINO OF NAKATANI HEARTLAND JP
カプチーノ オブ ナカタニハートランド ジェイピー
"CAPPUCCINO" WOULD BE HER NAME, AND "NAKATANI HEART LAND" WOULD BE THE KENNEL NAME.
SO THAT'S HOW IT IS ON A PEDIGREE CERTIFICATE.
BUT WHY IS NOA'S NAME CAPPUCCINO?
THE FIRST LETTER FOR CAPPUCCINO IS "C," RIGHT?
C
CAPPUCCINO O
ALL THE SIBLINGS FROM THE SAME MOM, IN OTHER WORDS ALL THE PUPS BORN IN A SINGLE LITTER...
...ARE CUSTOMARILY GIVEN NAMES THAT BEGIN WITH THE SAME LETTER.
SIGH...
SO ALL OF NOA'S SIBLINGS ARE REGISTERED WITH NAMES THAT BEGIN WITH THE LETTER "C."
LIKE "COCOA" AND "CECIL."
YAP
YAP

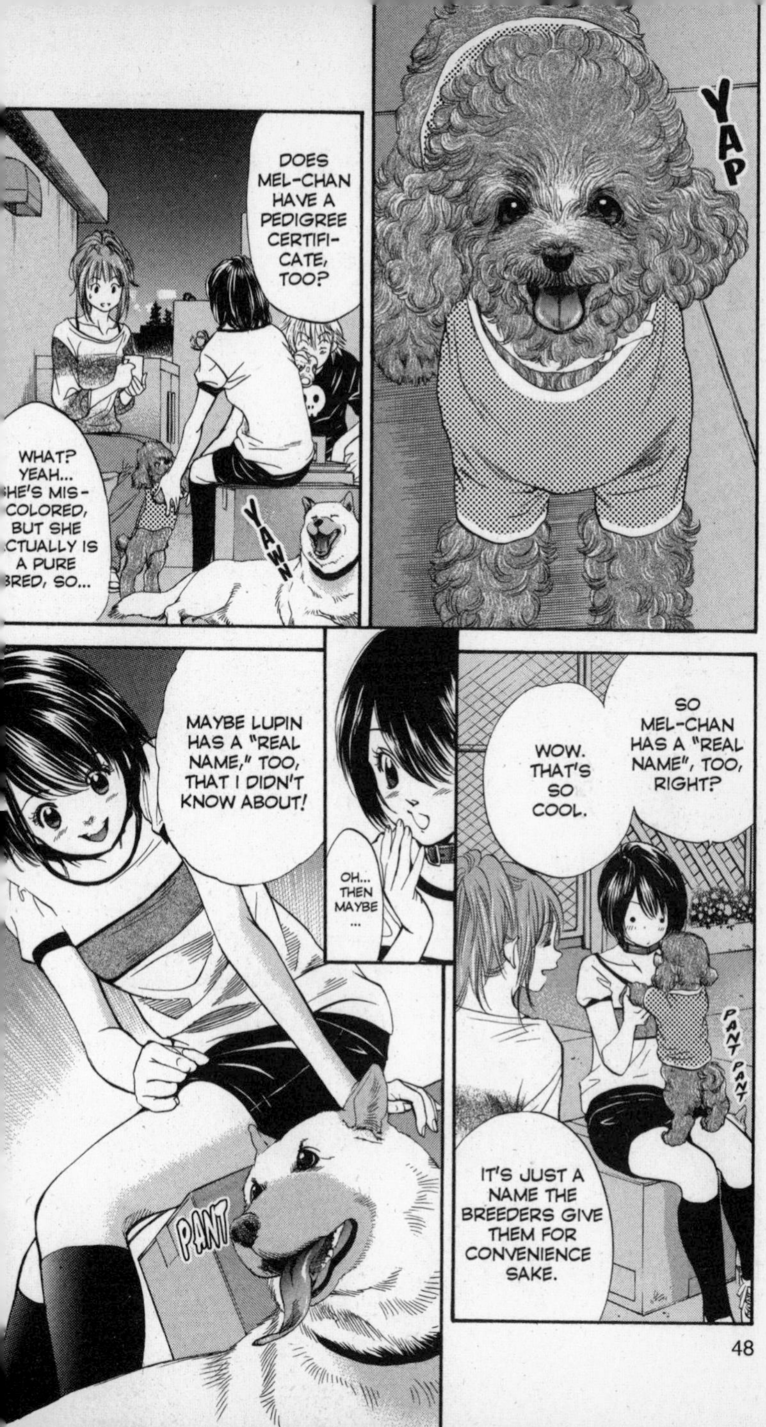
YAP
DOES MEL-CHAN HAVE A PEDIGREE CERTIFI-CATE, TOO?
WHAT? YEAH... HE'S MIS-COLORED, BUT SHE CTUALLY IS A PURE BRED, SO...
YAWN
SO MEL-CHAN HAS A "REAL NAME", TOO, RIGHT?
WOW. THAT'S SO COOL.
IT'S JUST A NAME THE BREEDERS GIVE THEM FOR CONVENIENCE SAKE.
PANT PANT
OH... THEN MAYBE ...
MAYBE LUPIN HAS A "REAL NAME," TOO, THAT I DIDN'T KNOW ABOUT!
PANT

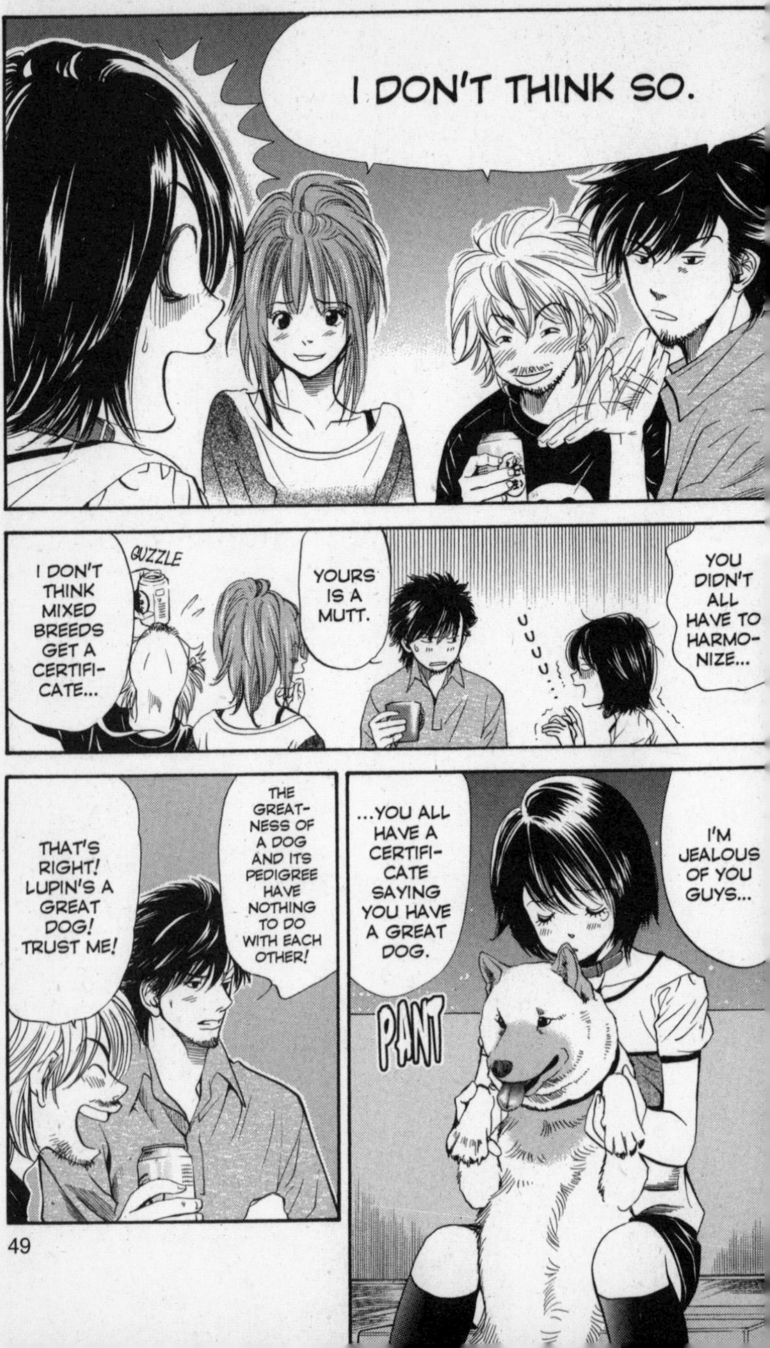
I DON'T THINK SO.
YOU DIDN'T ALL HAVE TO HARMONIZE...
UUUU...
YOURS IS A MUTT.
GUZZLE
I DON'T THINK MIXED BREEDS GET A CERTIFICATE...
I'M JEALOUS OF YOU GUYS...
...YOU ALL HAVE A CERTIFICATE SAYING YOU HAVE A GREAT DOG.
PANT
THE GREATNESS OF A DOG AND ITS PEDIGREE HAVE NOTHING TO DO WITH EACH OTHER!
THAT'S RIGHT! LUPIN'S A GREAT DOG! TRUST ME!

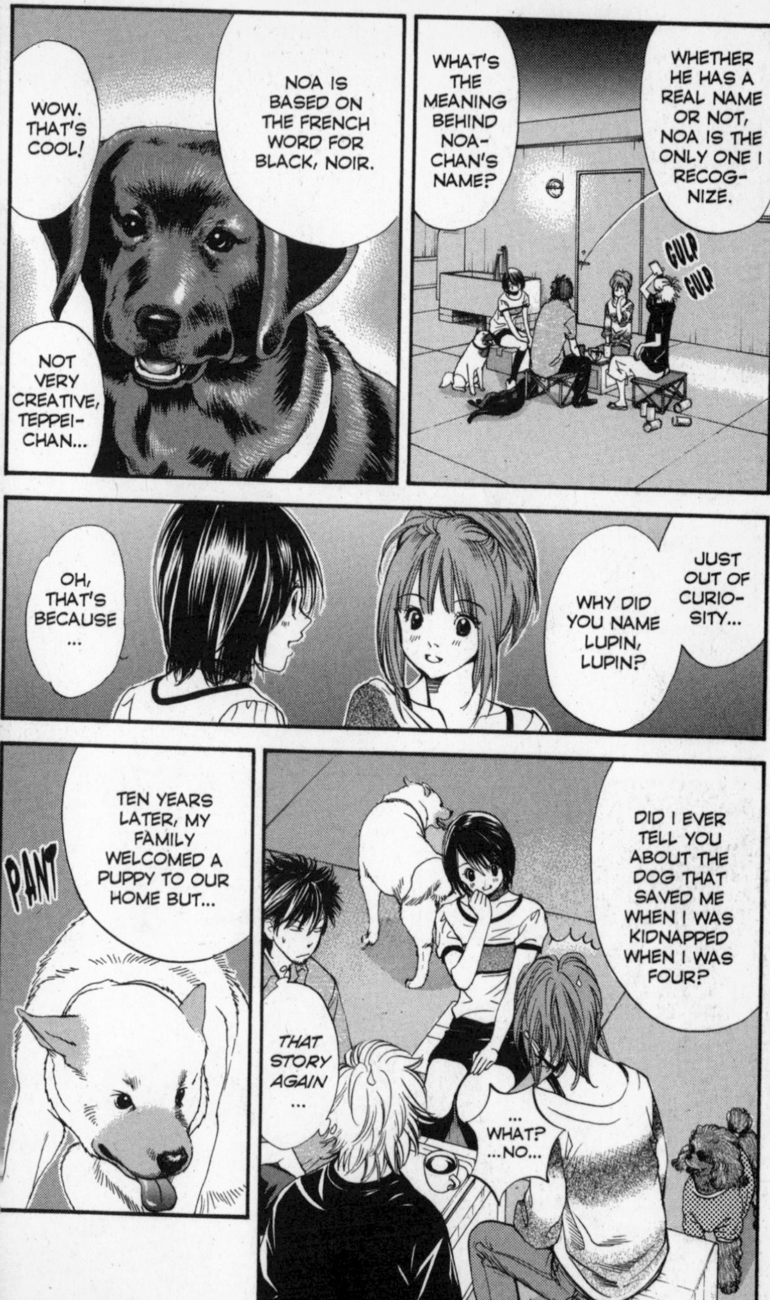
WHETHER HE HAS A REAL NAME OR NOT, NOA IS THE ONLY ONE I RECOGNIZE.
GULP GULP
WHAT'S THE MEANING BEHIND NOA-CHAN'S NAME?
NOA IS BASED ON THE FRENCH WORD FOR BLACK, NOIR.
WOW. THAT'S COOL!
NOT VERY CREATIVE, TEPPEI-CHAN...
JUST OUT OF CURIOSITY...
WHY DID YOU NAME LUPIN, LUPIN?
OH, THAT'S BECAUSE ...
DID I EVER TELL YOU ABOUT THE DOG THAT SAVED ME WHEN I WAS KIDNAPPED WHEN I WAS FOUR?
... WHAT? ...NO...
THAT STORY AGAIN ...
TEN YEARS LATER, MY FAMILY WELCOMED A PUPPY TO OUR HOME BUT...
PANT

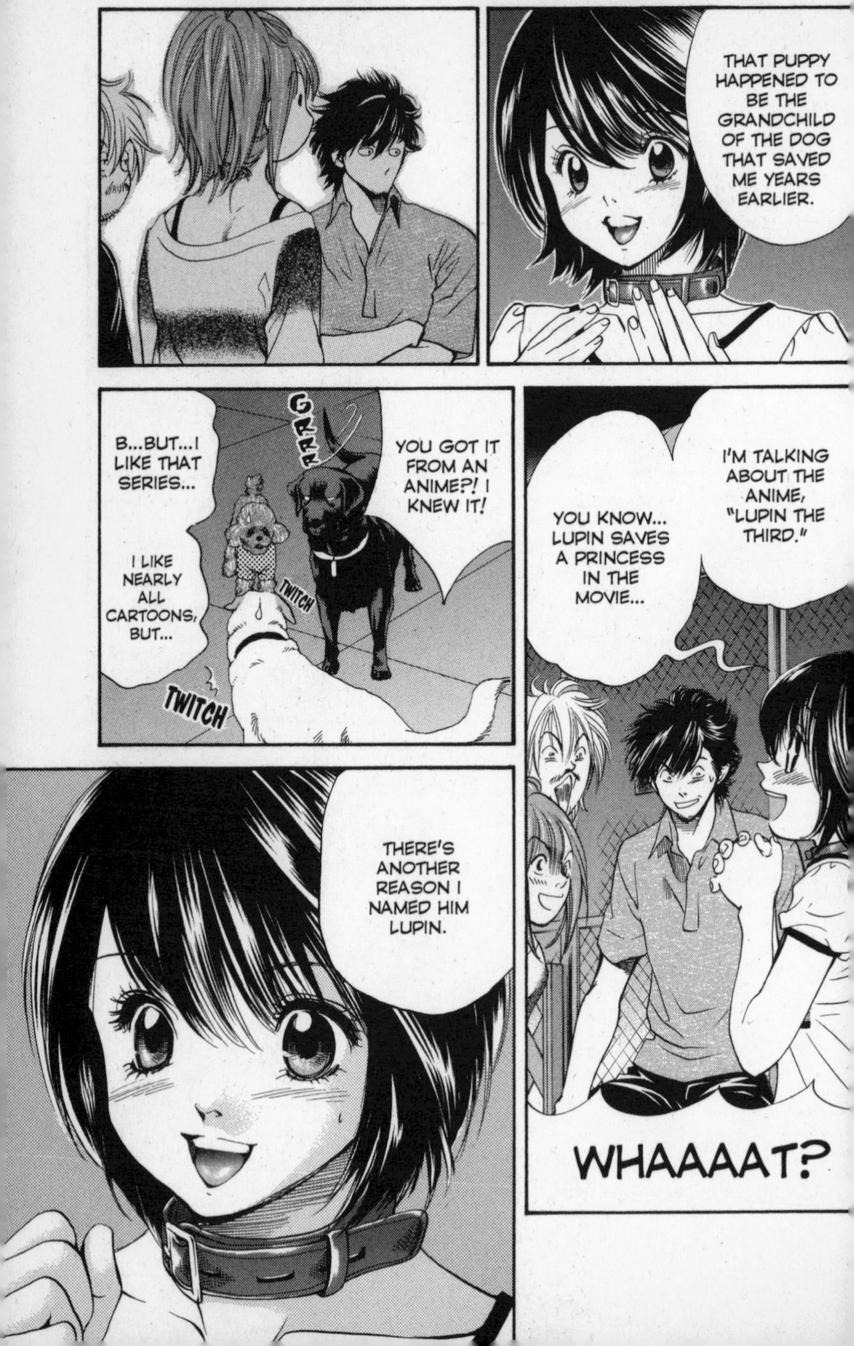
THAT PUPPY HAPPENED TO BE THE GRANDCHILD OF THE DOG THAT SAVED ME YEARS EARLIER.
I'M TALKING ABOUT THE ANIME, "LUPIN THE THIRD."
YOU KNOW... LUPIN SAVES A PRINCESS IN THE MOVIE...
WHAAAAT?
YOU GOT IT FROM AN ANIME?! I KNEW IT!
GRRR
B...BUT...I LIKE THAT SERIES...
I LIKE NEARLY ALL CARTOONS, BUT...
TWITCH
TWITCH
THERE'S ANOTHER REASON I NAMED HIM LUPIN.

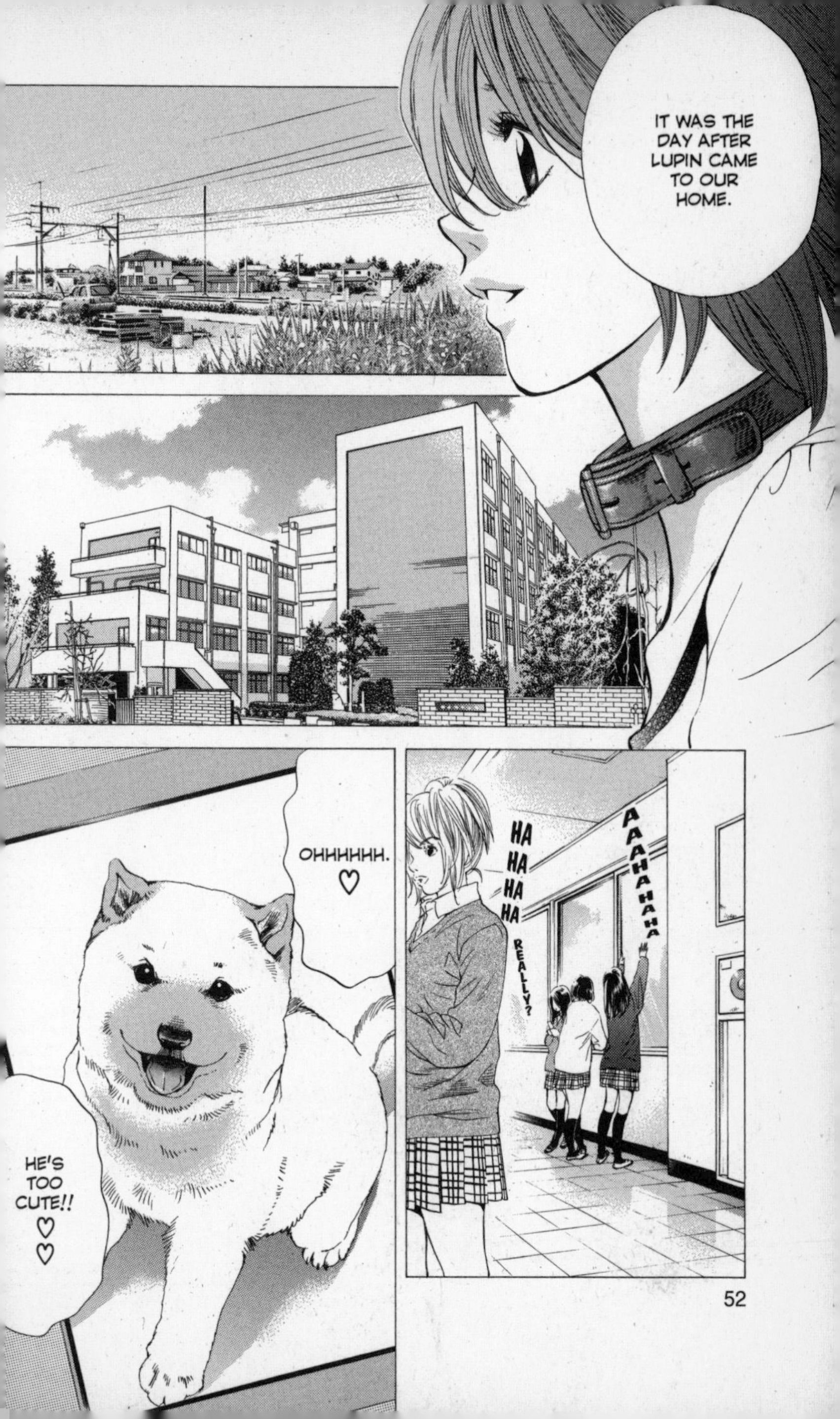
IT WAS THE DAY AFTER LUPIN CAME TO OUR HOME.
AAAHAHAHA
HA HA HA HA
REALLY?
OHHHHHH. ♡
HE'S TOO CUTE!! ♡ ♡

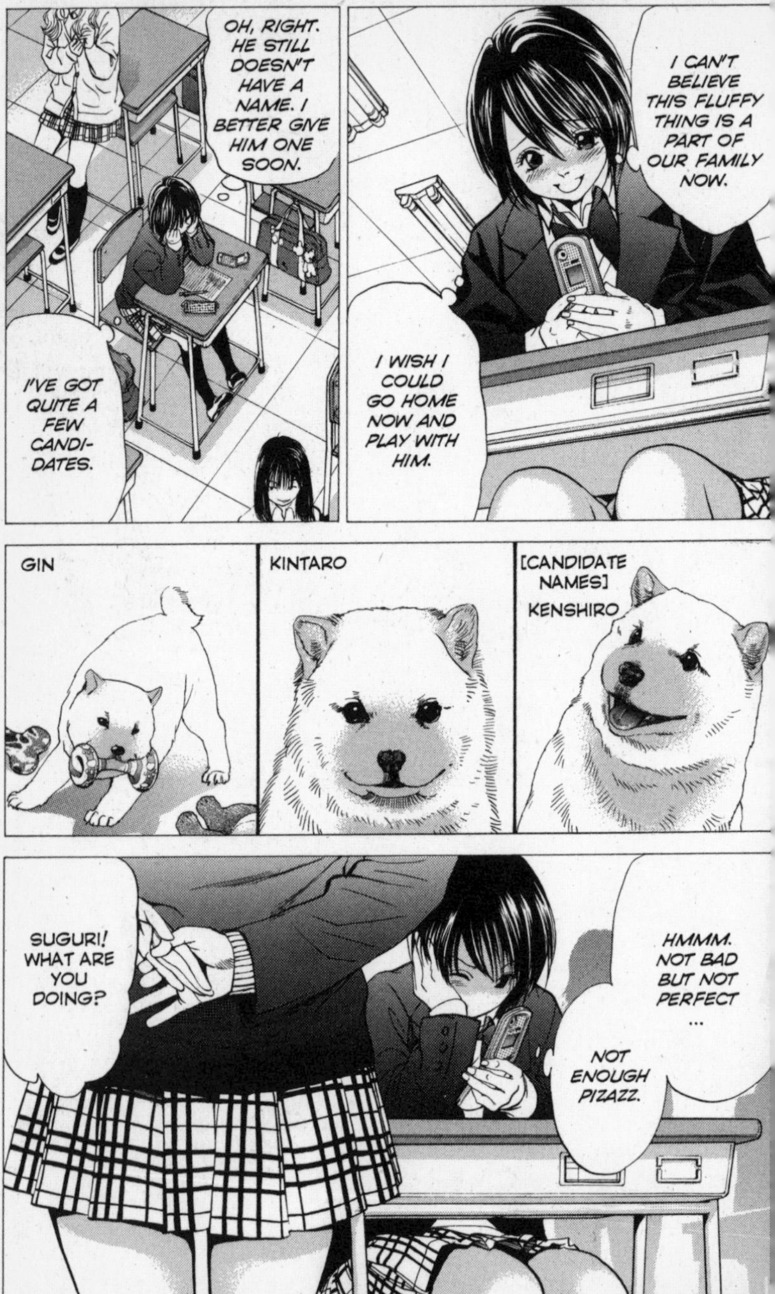
I CAN'T BELIEVE THIS FLUFFY THING IS A PART OF OUR FAMILY NOW.
I WISH I COULD GO HOME NOW AND PLAY WITH HIM.
OH, RIGHT. HE STILL DOESN'T HAVE A NAME. I BETTER GIVE HIM ONE SOON.
I'VE GOT QUITE A FEW CANDI-DATES.
[CANDIDATE NAMES]
KENSHIRO
KINTARO
GIN
HMMM. NOT BAD BUT NOT PERFECT ...
NOT ENOUGH PIZAZZ.
SUGURI! WHAT ARE YOU DOING?

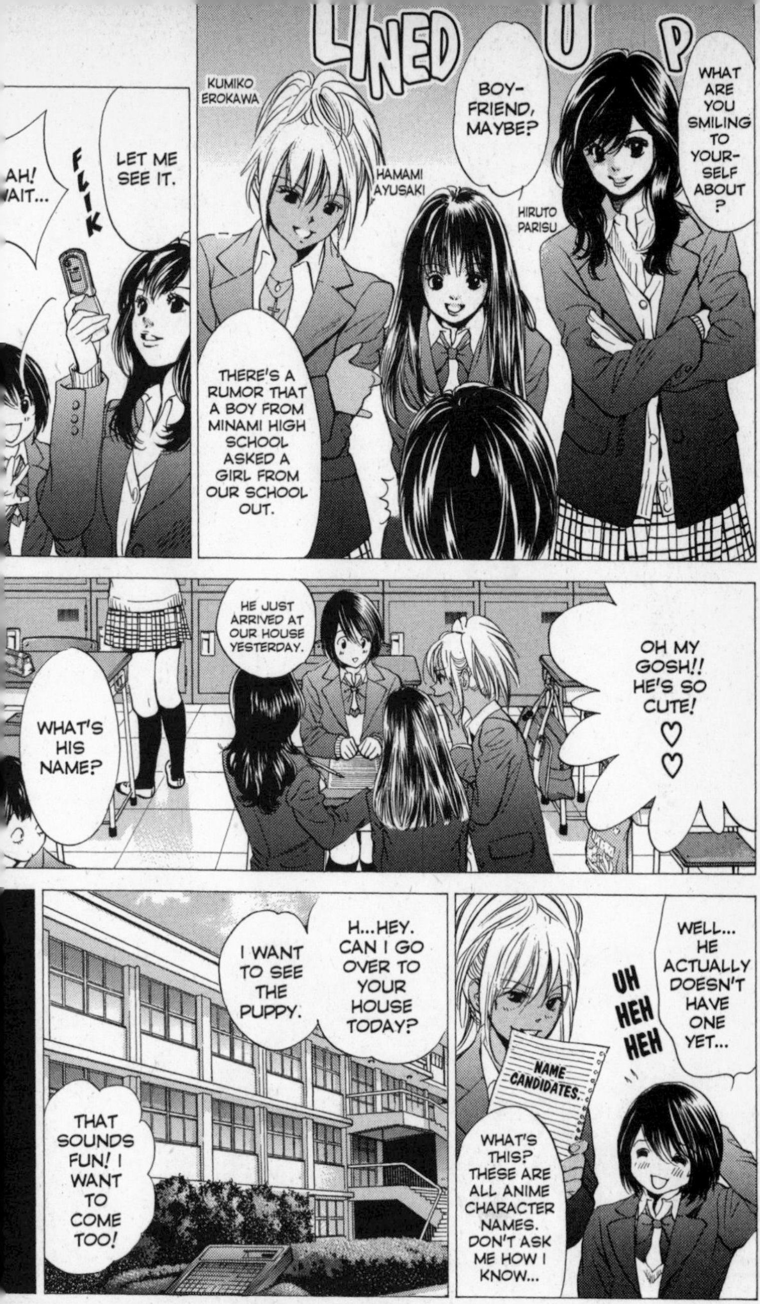
LINED UP
WHAT ARE YOU SMILING TO YOURSELF ABOUT?
BOY-FRIEND, MAYBE?
KUMIKO EROKAWA
HAMAMI AYUSAKI
HIRUTO PARISU
THERE'S A RUMOR THAT A BOY FROM MINAMI HIGH SCHOOL ASKED A GIRL FROM OUR SCHOOL OUT.
LET ME SEE IT.
FLIK
AH!
OH MY GOSH!! HE'S SO CUTE! ♡ ♡
HE JUST ARRIVED AT OUR HOUSE YESTERDAY.
WHAT'S HIS NAME?
WELL... HE ACTUALLY DOESN'T HAVE ONE YET...
UH HEH HEH
NAME CANDIDATES..
WHAT'S THIS? THESE ARE ALL ANIME CHARACTER NAMES. DON'T ASK ME HOW I KNOW...
H...HEY. CAN I GO OVER TO YOUR HOUSE TODAY?
I WANT TO SEE THE PUPPY.
THAT SOUNDS FUN! I WANT TO COME TOO!

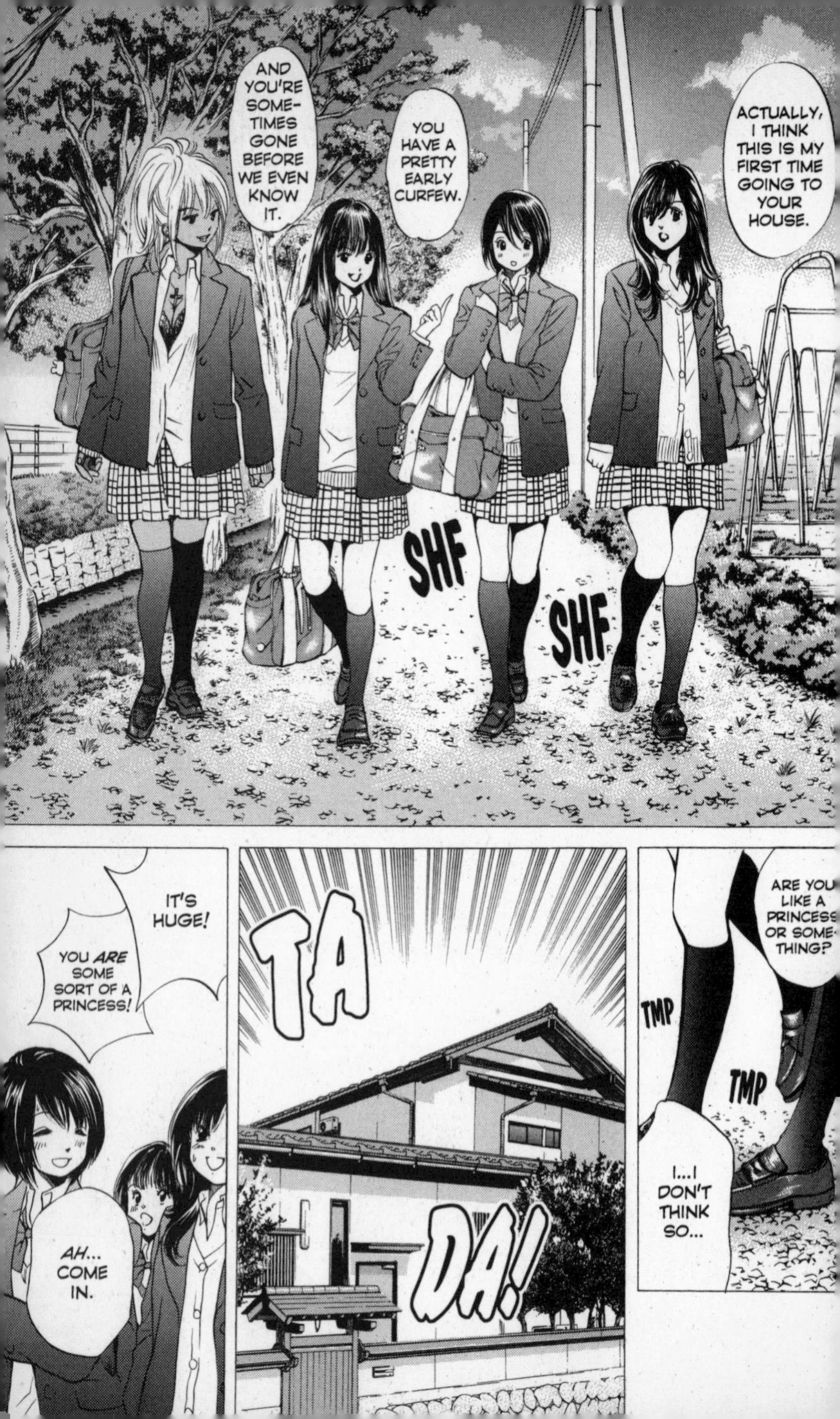
ACTUALLY, I THINK THIS IS MY FIRST TIME GOING TO YOUR HOUSE.
YOU HAVE A PRETTY EARLY CURFEW.
AND YOU'RE SOME-TIMES GONE BEFORE WE EVEN KNOW IT.
SHF
SHF
ARE YOU LIKE A PRINCESS OR SOME-THING?
TMP
TMP
I...I DON'T THINK SO...
TA
DA!
IT'S HUGE!
YOU *ARE* SOME SORT OF A PRINCESS!
AH... COME IN.

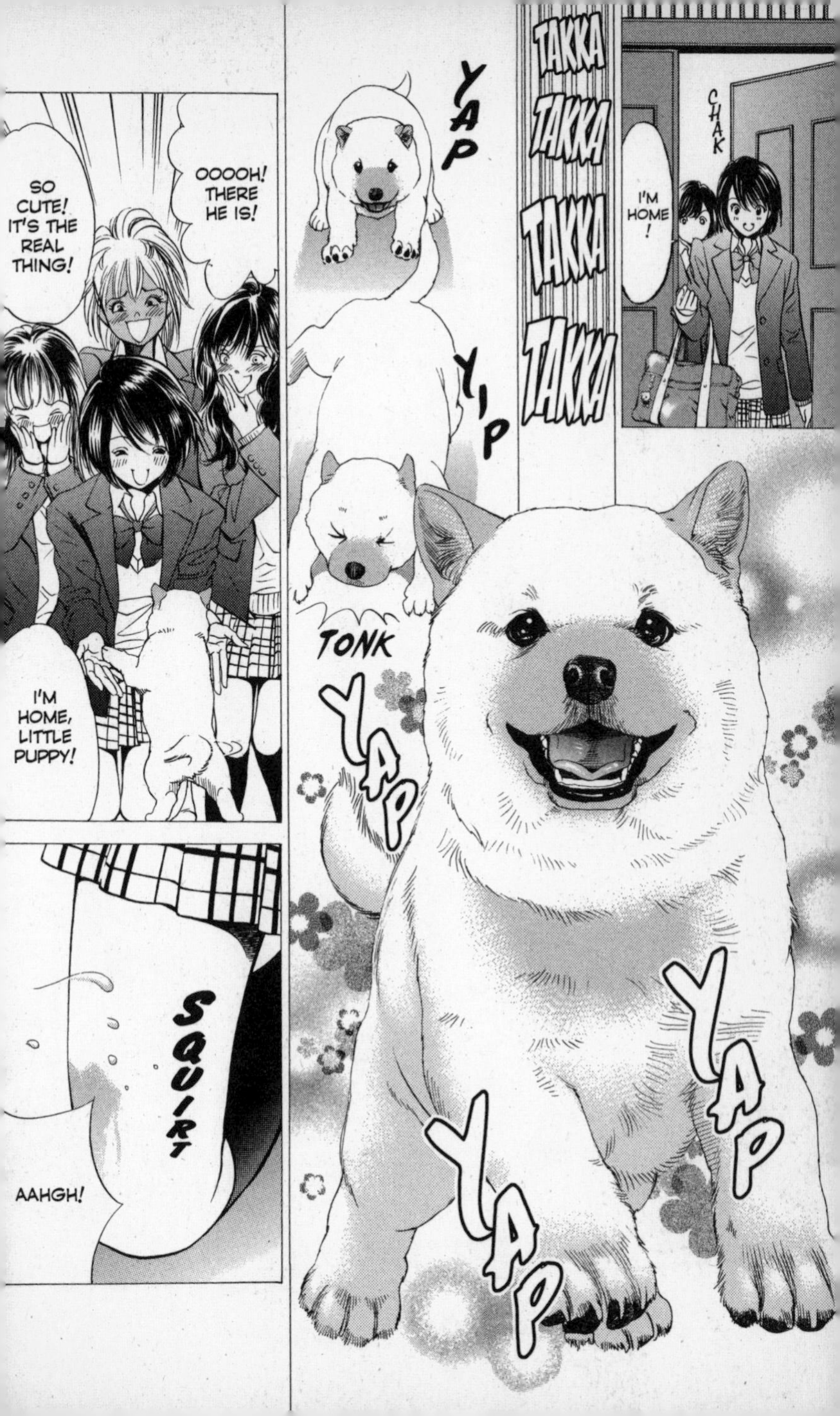
CHAK
I'M HOME!
TAKKA TAKKA TAKKA TAKKA
YAP
YIP
TONK
YAP
YAP
YAP
OOOOH! THERE HE IS!
SO CUTE! IT'S THE REAL THING!
I'M HOME, LITTLE PUPPY!
SQUIRT
AAHGH!

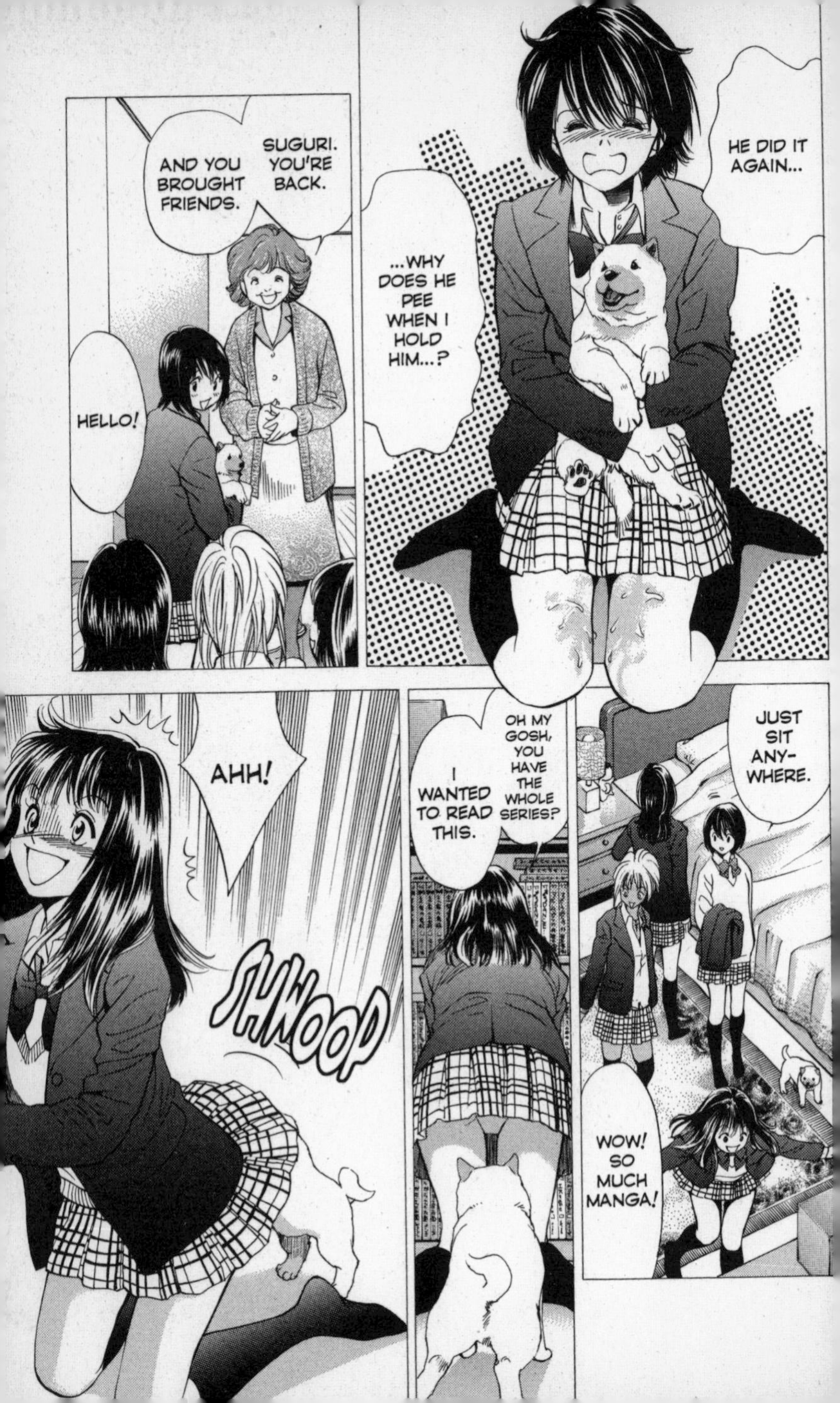
HE DID IT AGAIN...
...WHY DOES HE PEE WHEN I HOLD HIM...?
SUGURI. YOU'RE BACK.
AND YOU BROUGHT FRIENDS.
HELLO!
JUST SIT ANY-WHERE.
WOW! SO MUCH MANGA!
OH MY GOSH, YOU HAVE THE WHOLE SERIES?
I WANTED TO READ THIS.
AHH!
SHWOOP

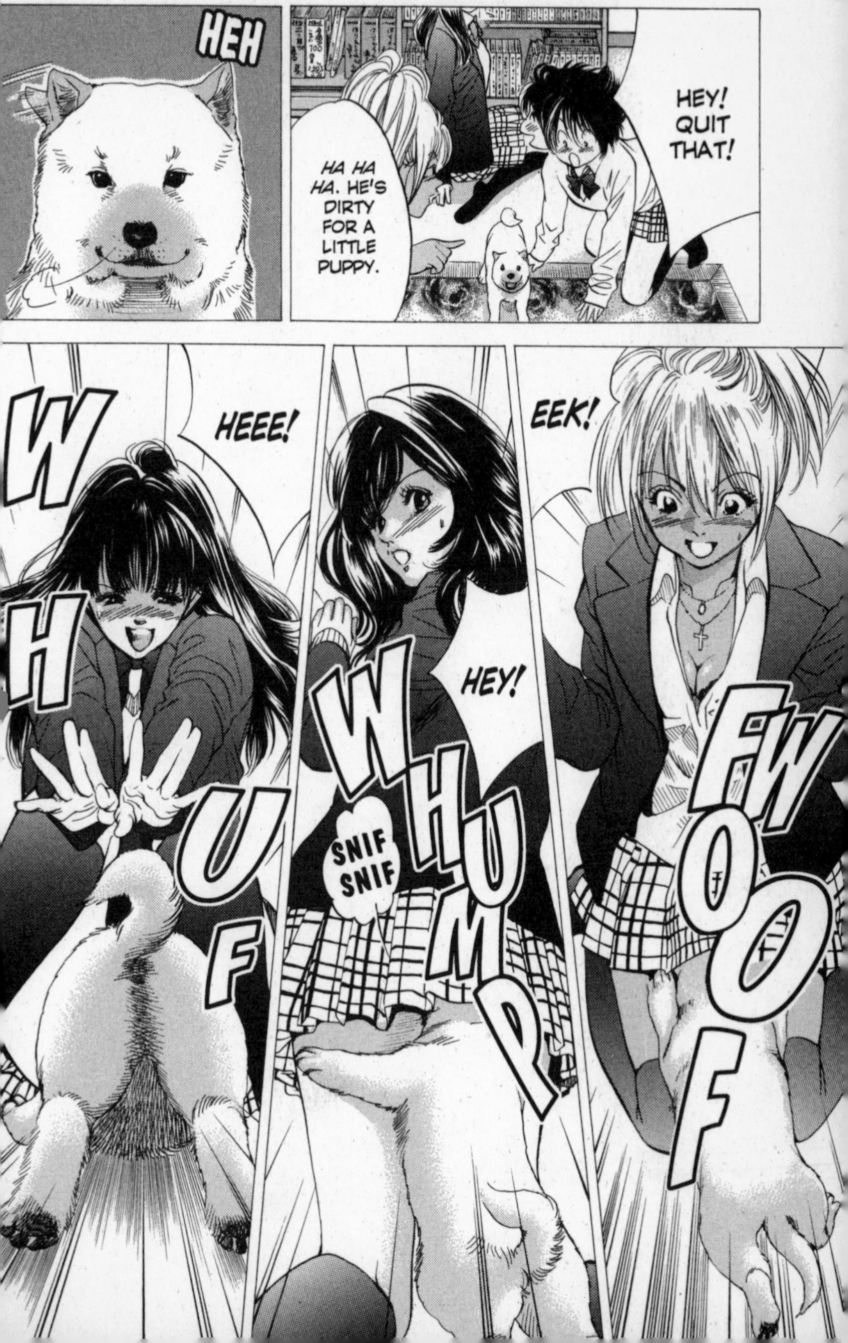
HEY! QUIT THAT!
HA HA HA. HE'S DIRTY FOR A LITTLE PUPPY.
HEH
EEK!
FWOOF
HEY!
WHUMP
SNIF SNIF
HEEE!
WHUF

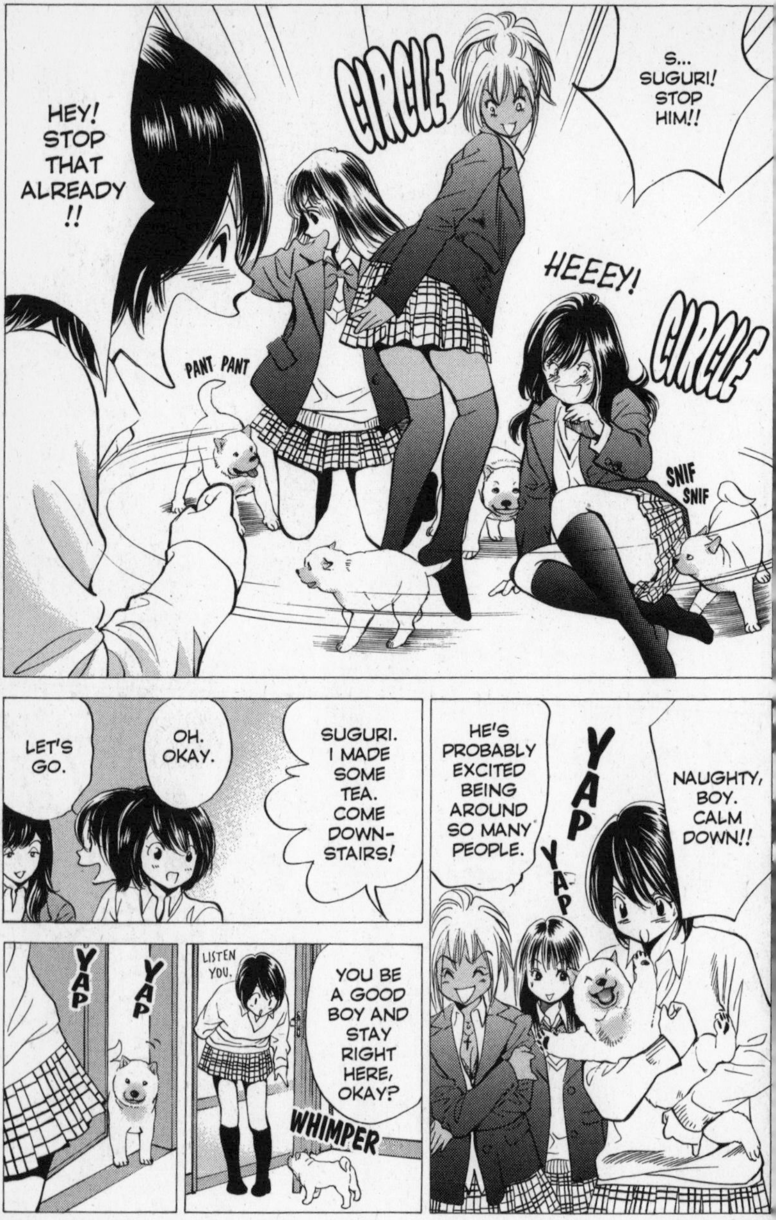
S... SUGURI! STOP HIM!!
CIRCLE
HEY! STOP THAT ALREADY!!
HEEEY!
CIRCLE
PANT PANT
SNIF SNIF
NAUGHTY, BOY. CALM DOWN!!
YAP
HE'S PROBABLY EXCITED BEING AROUND SO MANY PEOPLE.
YAP YAP
SUGURI. I MADE SOME TEA. COME DOWN-STAIRS!
OH. OKAY.
LET'S GO.
YOU BE A GOOD BOY AND STAY RIGHT HERE, OKAY?
LISTEN YOU.
WHIMPER
YAP
YAP

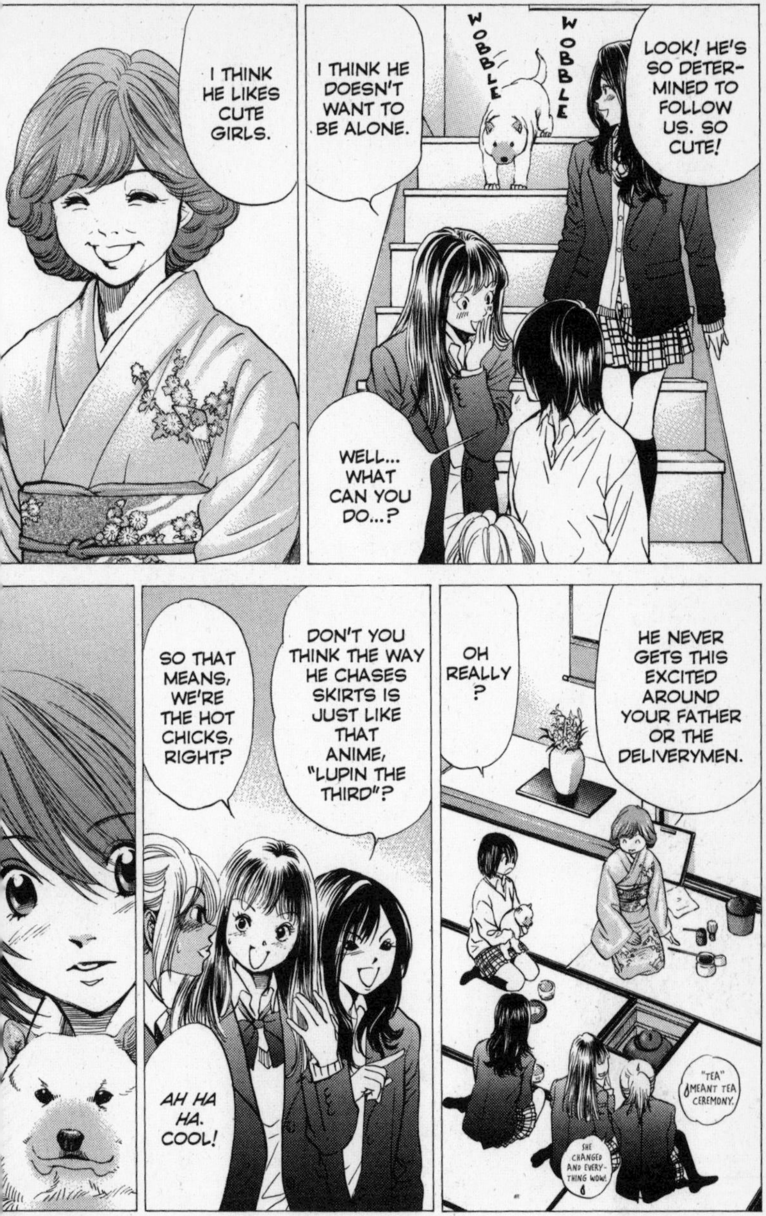
LOOK! HE'S SO DETERMINED TO FOLLOW US. SO CUTE!
WOBBLE
WOBBLE
I THINK HE DOESN'T WANT TO BE ALONE.
WELL... WHAT CAN YOU DO...?
I THINK HE LIKES CUTE GIRLS.
HE NEVER GETS THIS EXCITED AROUND YOUR FATHER OR THE DELIVERYMEN.
OH REALLY?
"TEA" MEANT TEA CEREMONY.
SHE CHANGED AND EVERYTHING WOW!
DON'T YOU THINK THE WAY HE CHASES SKIRTS IS JUST LIKE THAT ANIME, "LUPIN THE THIRD"?
SO THAT MEANS, WE'RE THE HOT CHICKS, RIGHT?
AH HA HA. COOL!

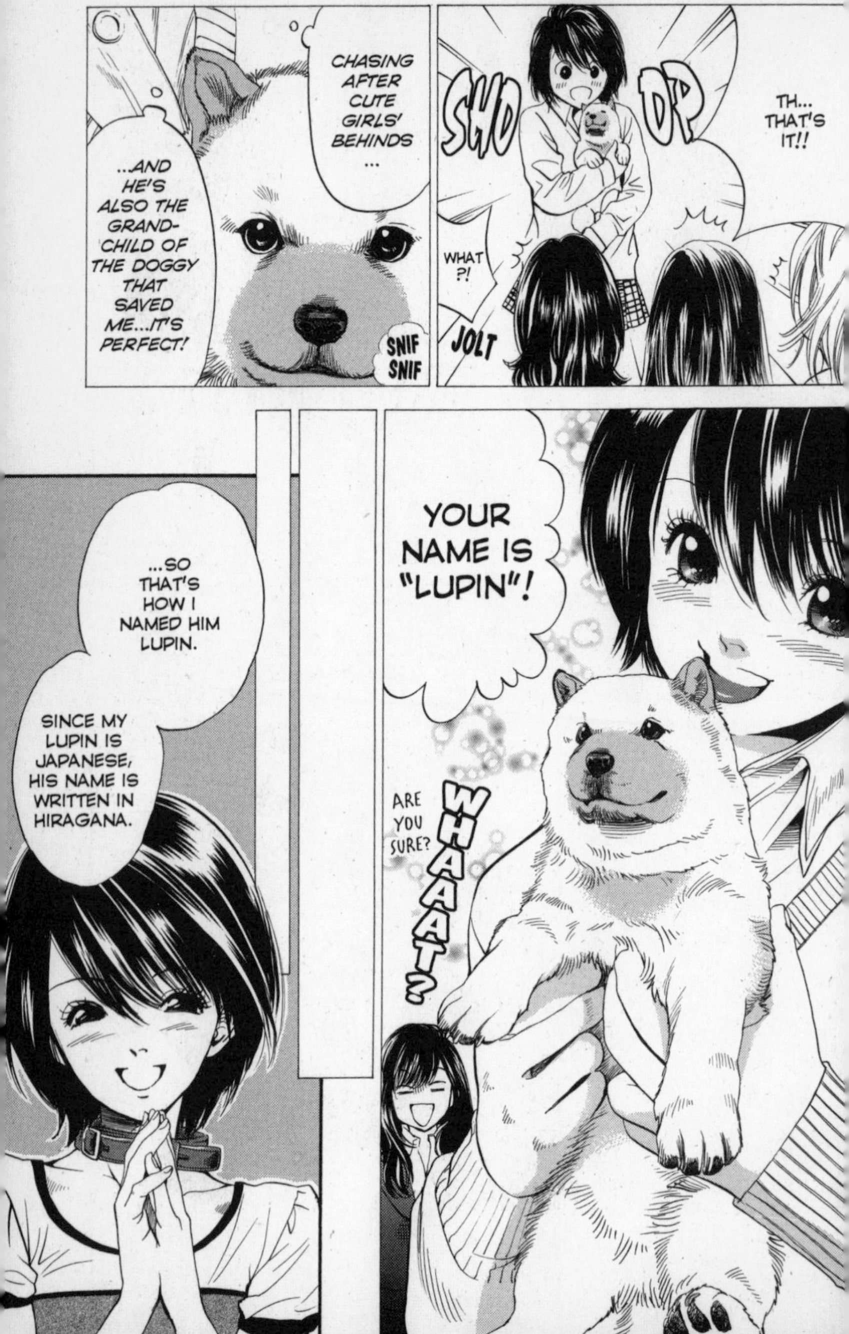
TH... THAT'S IT!!
SHOOP
WHAT?!
JOLT
CHASING AFTER CUTE GIRLS' BEHINDS...
...AND HE'S ALSO THE GRANDCHILD OF THE DOGGY THAT SAVED ME...IT'S PERFECT!
SNIF SNIF
YOUR NAME IS "LUPIN"!
WHAAAAT?
ARE YOU SURE?
...SO THAT'S HOW I NAMED HIM LUPIN.
SINCE MY LUPIN IS JAPANESE, HIS NAME IS WRITTEN IN HIRAGANA.

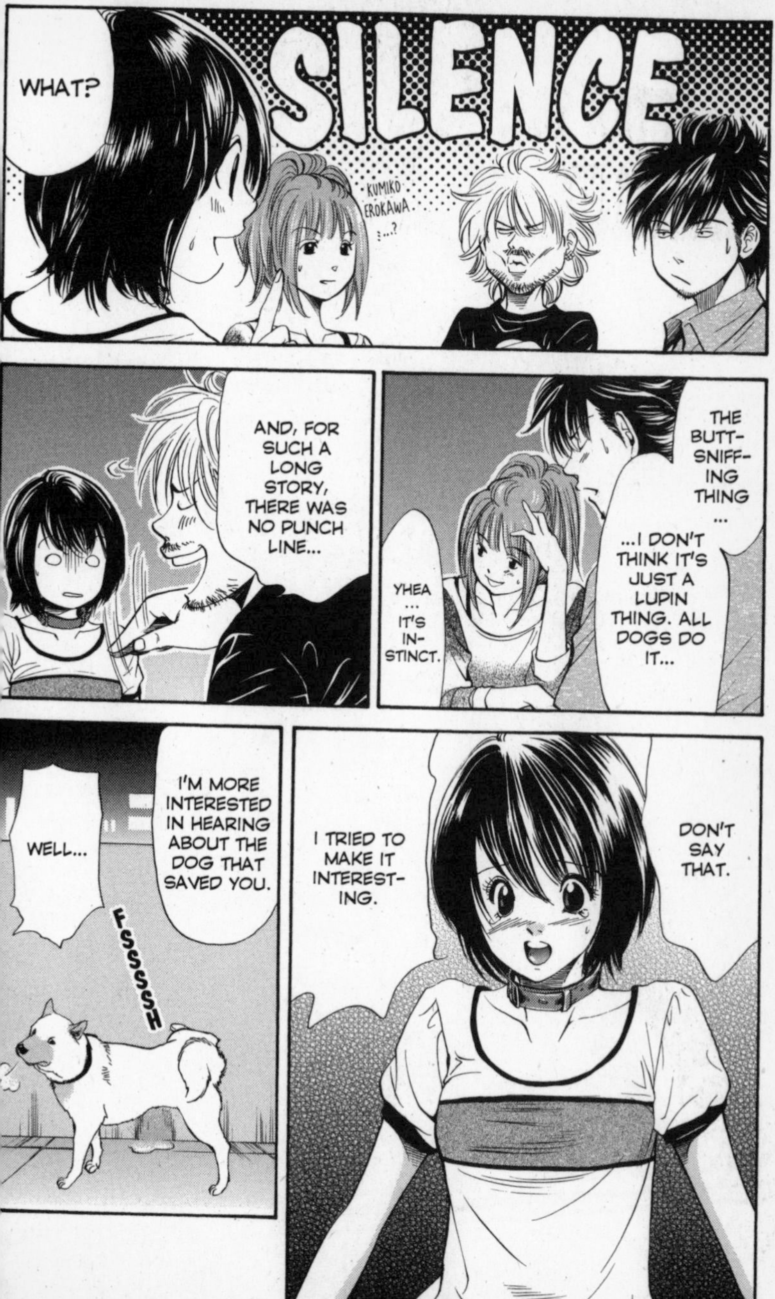
SILENCE
WHAT?
KUMIKO EROKAWA ...?
THE BUTT-SNIFFING THING ...
...I DON'T THINK IT'S JUST A LUPIN THING. ALL DOGS DO IT...
YHEA ... IT'S INSTINCT.
AND, FOR SUCH A LONG STORY, THERE WAS NO PUNCH LINE...
DON'T SAY THAT.
I TRIED TO MAKE IT INTERESTING.
I'M MORE INTERESTED IN HEARING ABOUT THE DOG THAT SAVED YOU.
WELL...
FSSSSH

CHAPTER 101: TARGET

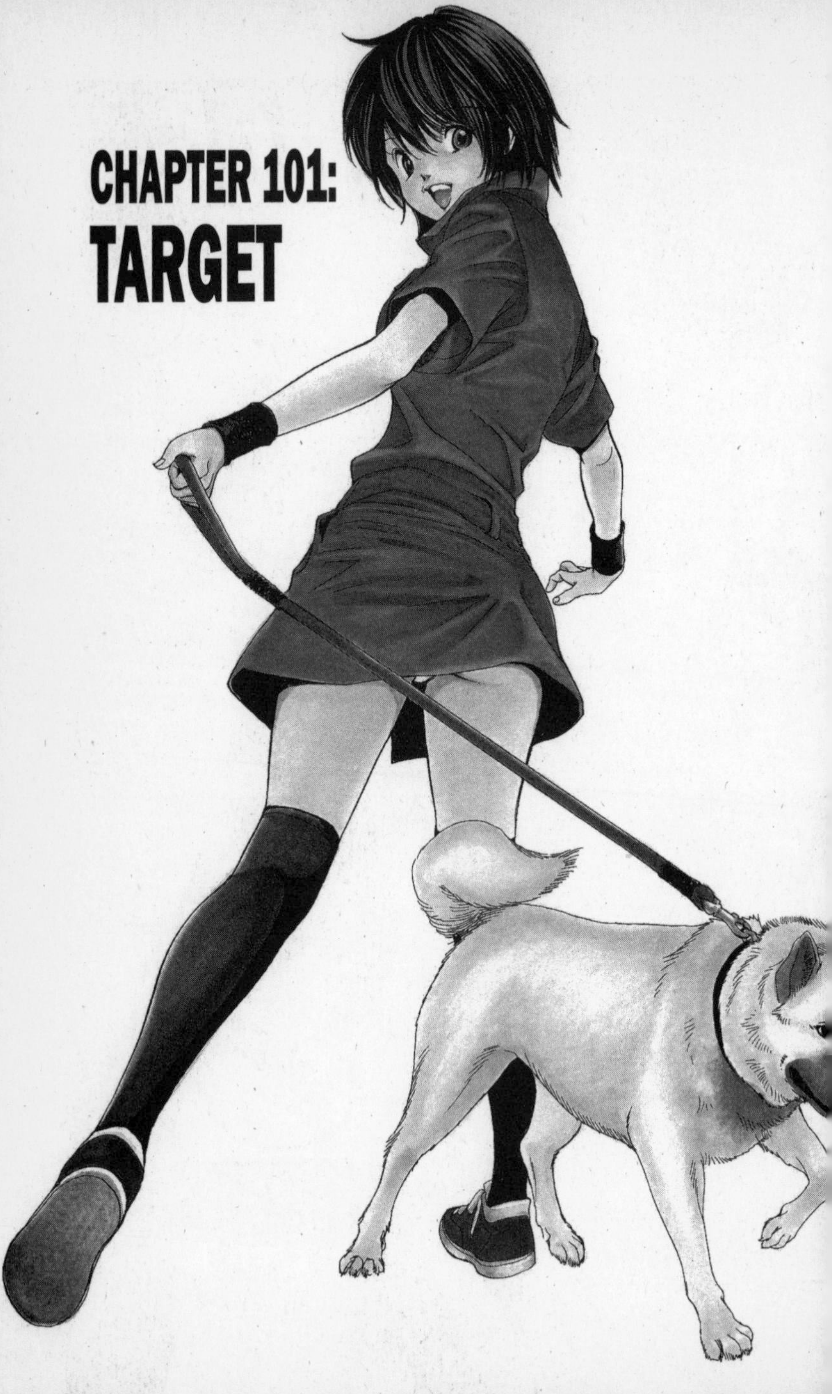

SUGURI'S UNIFORM COLLECTION

WE'VE COLLECTED ALL OF SUGURI'S UNIFORMS THAT APPEARED FROM CHAPTERS 2 TO 108. WHICH ONE DO YOU LIKE?

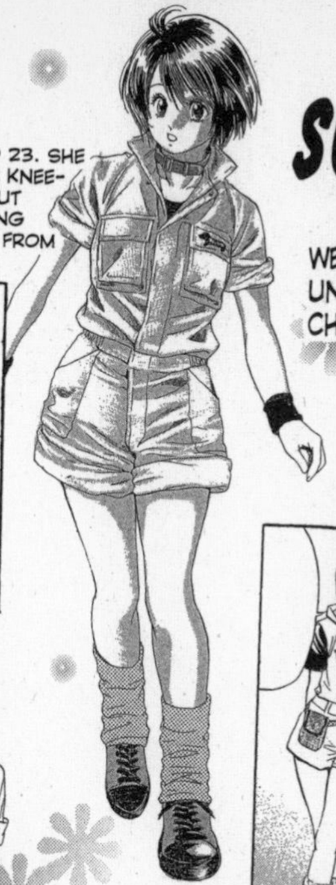

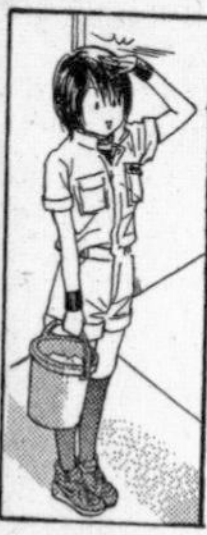

⊙TYPE 1

ROM CH. 2 TO 23. SHE SED TO WEAR KNEE-IGH SOCKS BUT TARTS WEARING EG WARMERS FROM H. 20.

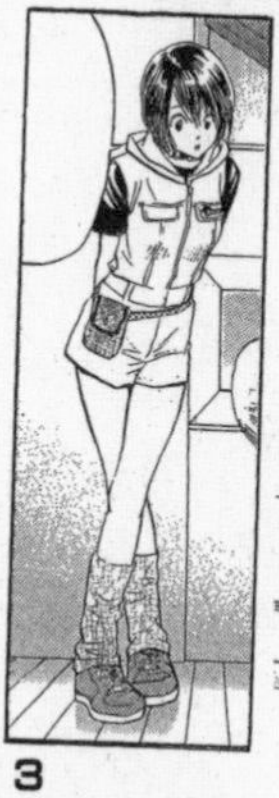

⊙TYPE 2

THROUGH CH. 24 TO 43. THE WAIST POUCH DISAPPEARS SOMEWHERE IN THE BETWEEN.

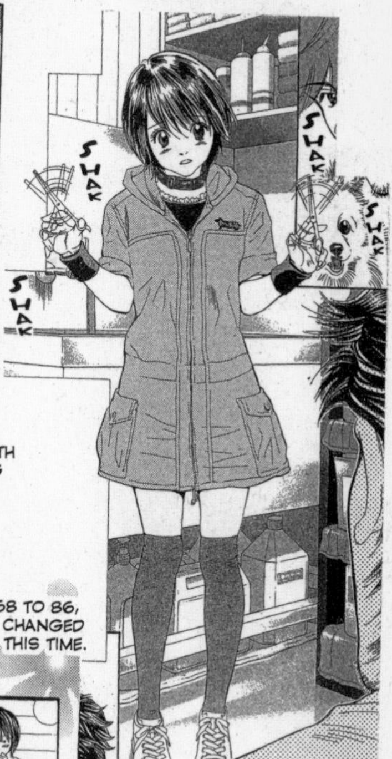

SHAK
SHAK
SHAK
SHAK

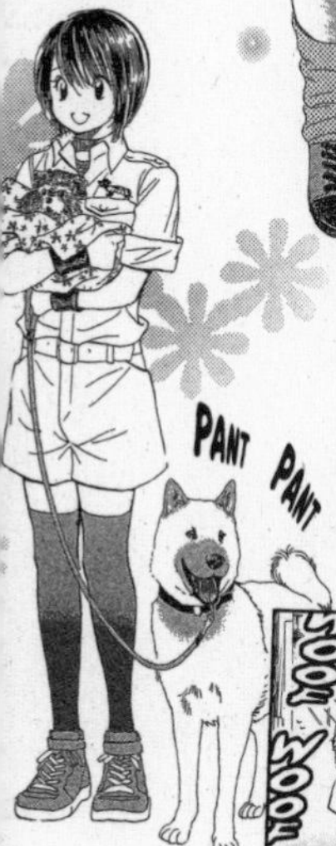

PANT PANT

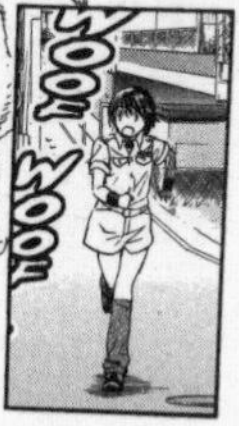

WOOF
WOOF

⊙TYPE 3

THROUGH CH 44 TO 67. BOTH KNEE-HIGH SOCKS AND LEG WARMERS COULD BE SEEN.

⊙TYPE 4

THROUGH CH. 68 TO 86, AND CH. 101. IT CHANGED TO A MINISKIRT THIS TIME.

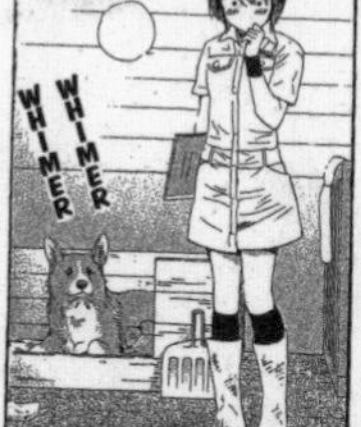

WHIMPER
WHIMPER

⊙TYPE 5

THROUGH CH. 87 TO 100, AND 102 TO 108. SHE WORKED HARD WHILE COVERED IN DIRT.

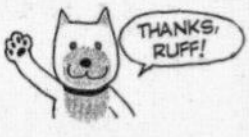

THANKS, RUFF!

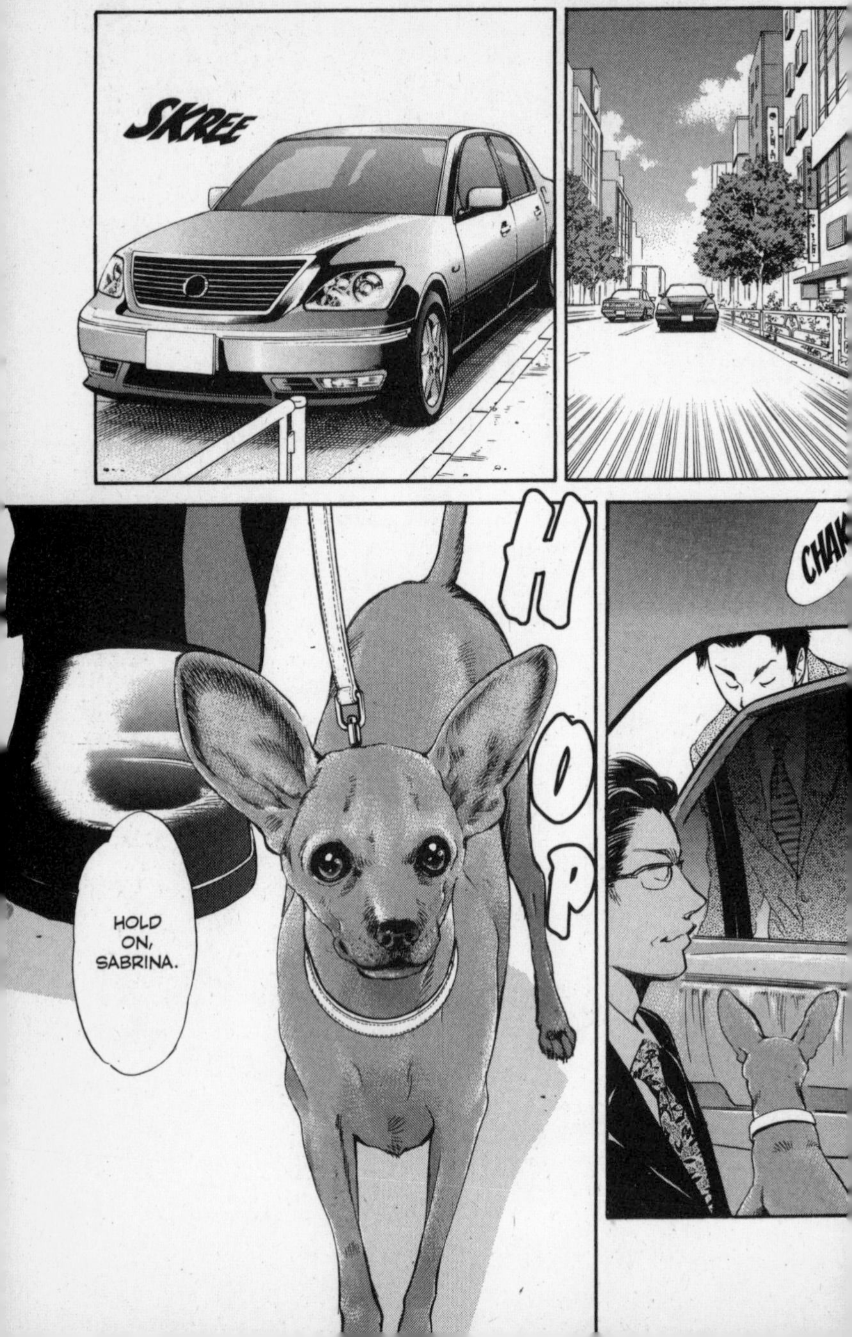
SKREE
CHAK
HOP
HOLD ON, SABRINA.

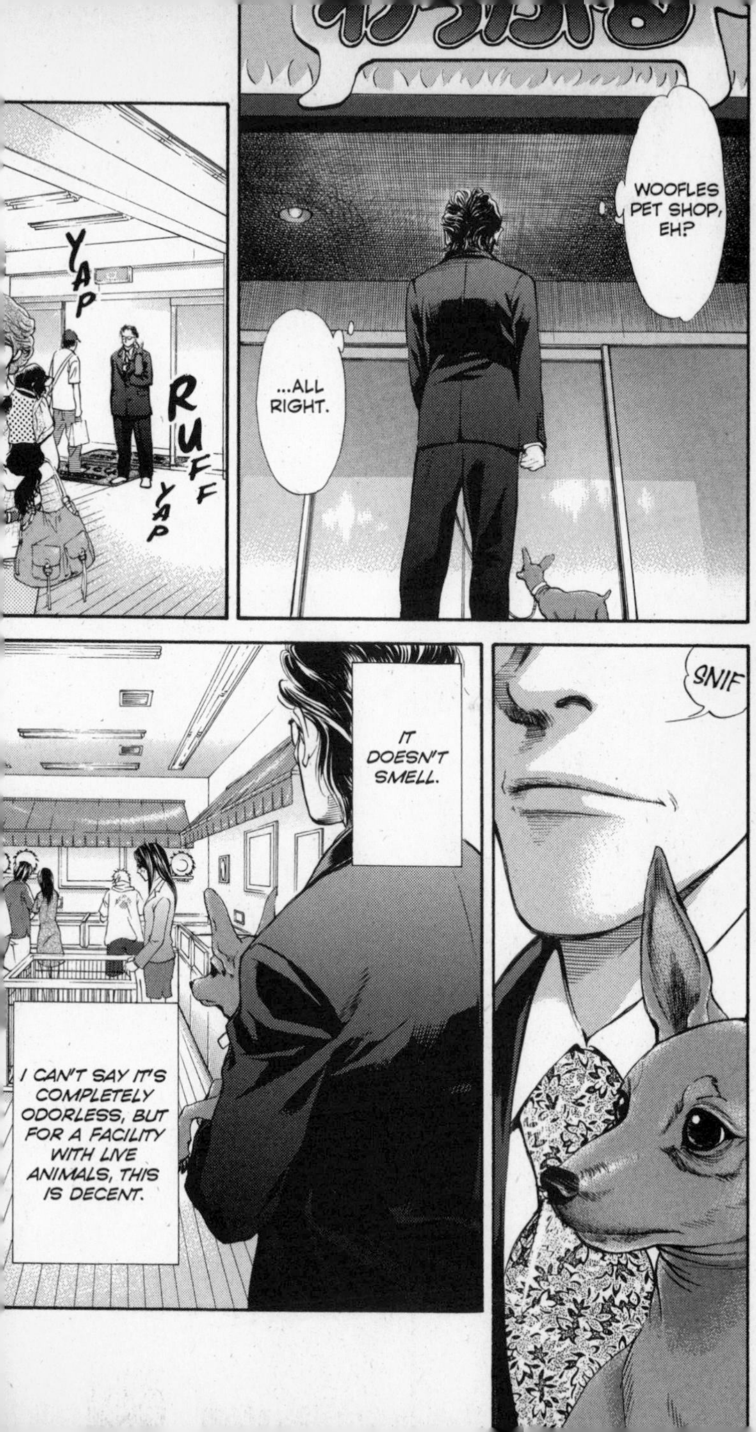
WOOFLES PET SHOP, EH?
...ALL RIGHT.
YAP
RUFF
YAP
SNIF
IT DOESN'T SMELL.
I CAN'T SAY IT'S COMPLETELY ODORLESS, BUT FOR A FACILITY WITH LIVE ANIMALS, THIS IS DECENT.

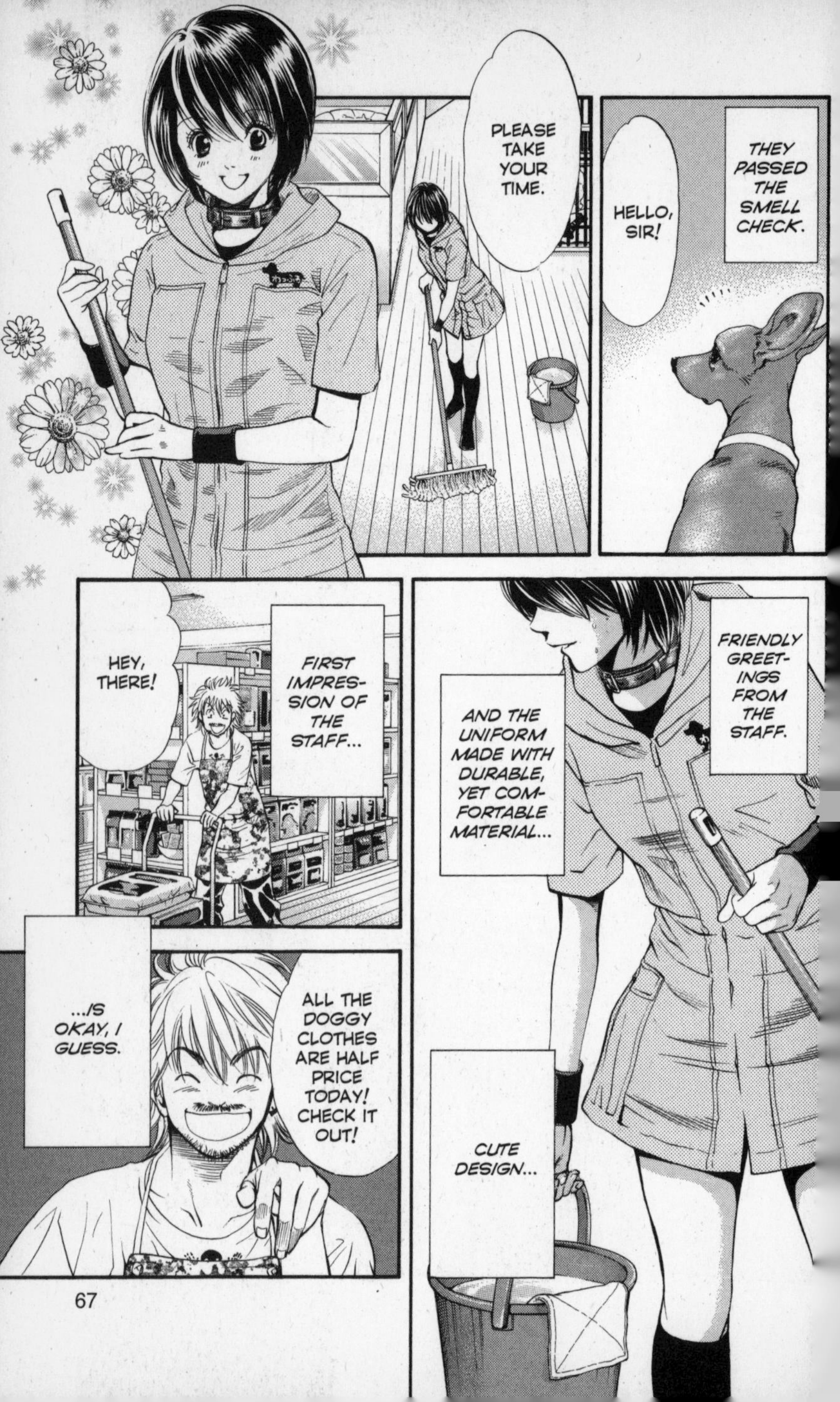
THEY PASSED THE SMELL CHECK.
HELLO, SIR!
PLEASE TAKE YOUR TIME.
FRIENDLY GREET-INGS FROM THE STAFF.
AND THE UNIFORM MADE WITH DURABLE, YET COM-FORTABLE MATERIAL...
CUTE DESIGN...
FIRST IMPRES-SION OF THE STAFF...
HEY, THERE!
ALL THE DOGGY CLOTHES ARE HALF PRICE TODAY! CHECK IT OUT!
...IS OKAY, I GUESS.

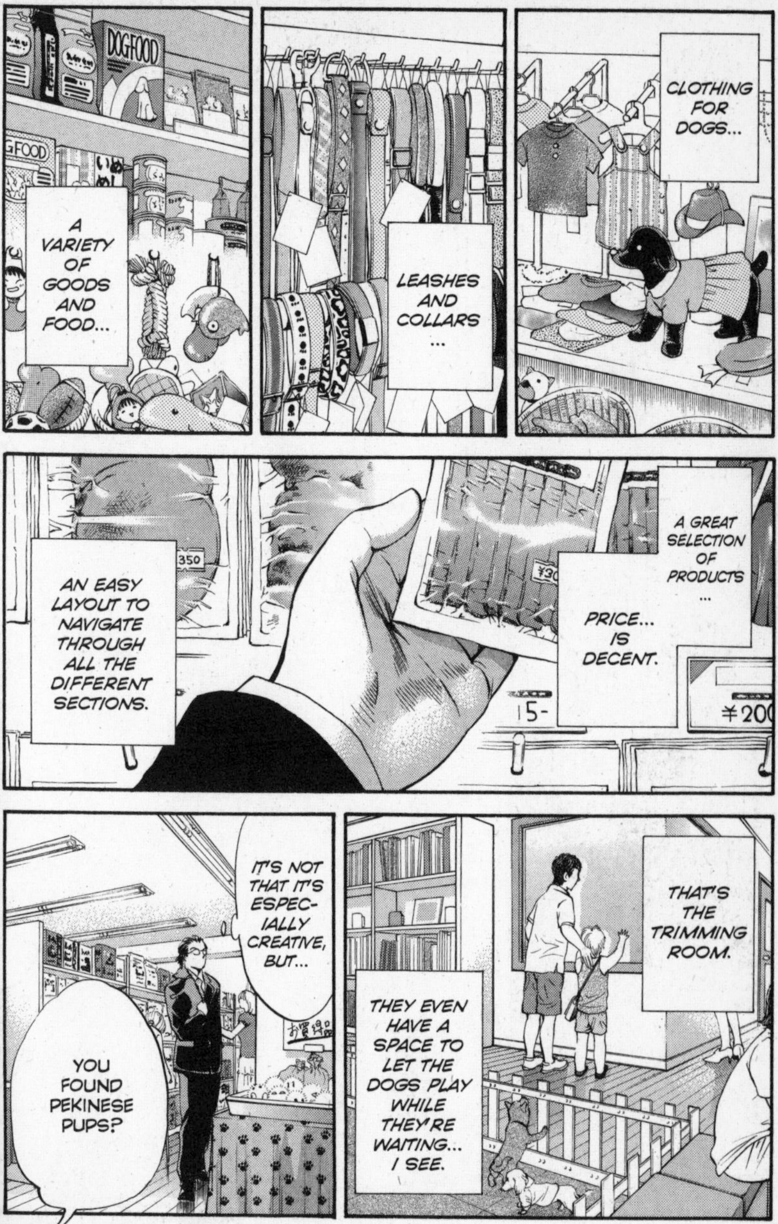
CLOTHING FOR DOGS...
LEASHES AND COLLARS ...
DOGFOOD
A VARIETY OF GOODS AND FOOD...
A GREAT SELECTION OF PRODUCTS ...
PRICE... IS DECENT.
AN EASY LAYOUT TO NAVIGATE THROUGH ALL THE DIFFERENT SECTIONS.
THAT'S THE TRIMMING ROOM.
THEY EVEN HAVE A SPACE TO LET THE DOGS PLAY WHILE THEY'RE WAITING... I SEE.
IT'S NOT THAT IT'S ESPEC-IALLY CREATIVE, BUT...
YOU FOUND PEKINESE PUPS?

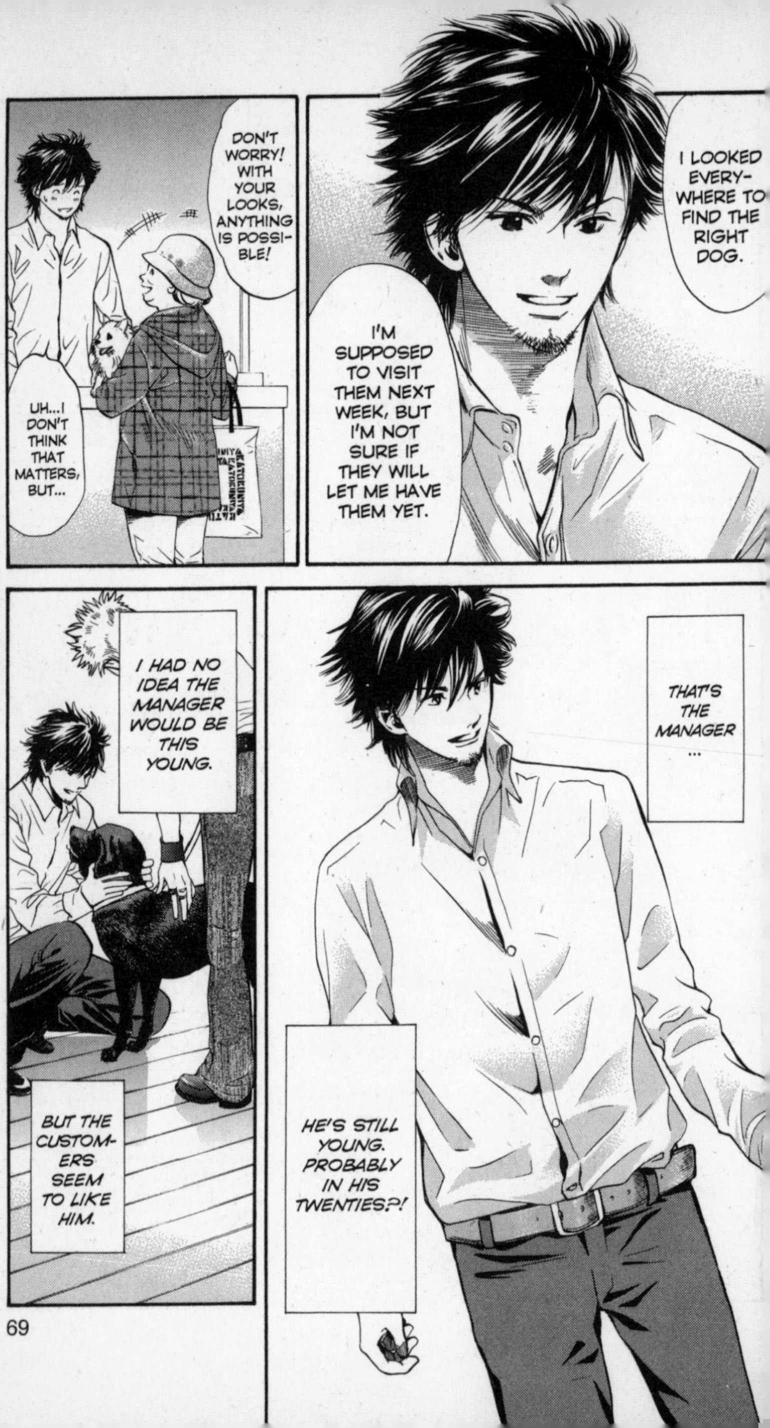
I LOOKED EVERYWHERE TO FIND THE RIGHT DOG.
I'M SUPPOSED TO VISIT THEM NEXT WEEK, BUT I'M NOT SURE IF THEY WILL LET ME HAVE THEM YET.
DON'T WORRY! WITH YOUR LOOKS, ANYTHING IS POSSIBLE!
UH...I DON'T THINK THAT MATTERS, BUT...
THAT'S THE MANAGER...
HE'S STILL YOUNG. PROBABLY IN HIS TWENTIES?!
I HAD NO IDEA THE MANAGER WOULD BE THIS YOUNG.
BUT THE CUSTOMERS SEEM TO LIKE HIM.

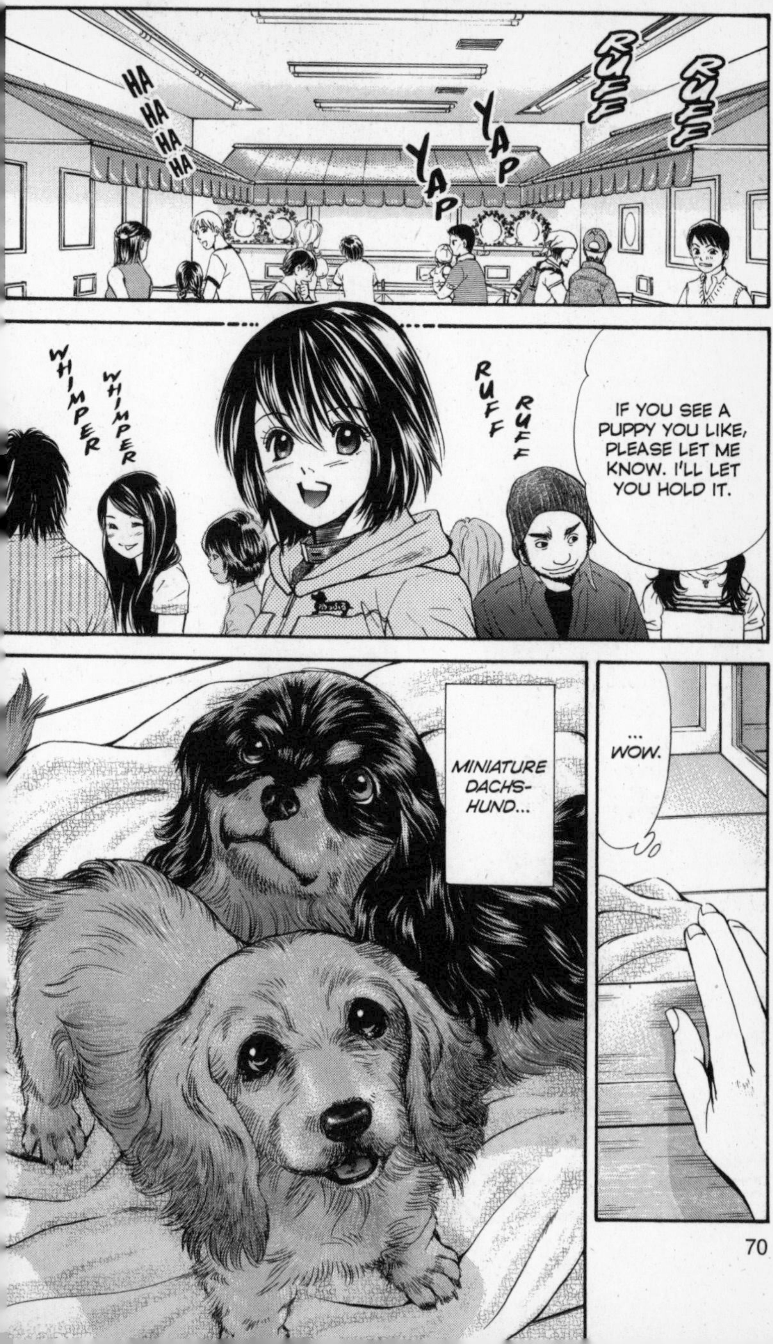
RUFF
RUFF
YAP
YAP
HA HA HA HA
IF YOU SEE A PUPPY YOU LIKE, PLEASE LET ME KNOW. I'LL LET YOU HOLD IT.
RUFF
RUFF
WHIMPER
WHIMPER
... WOW.
MINIATURE DACHS-HUND...

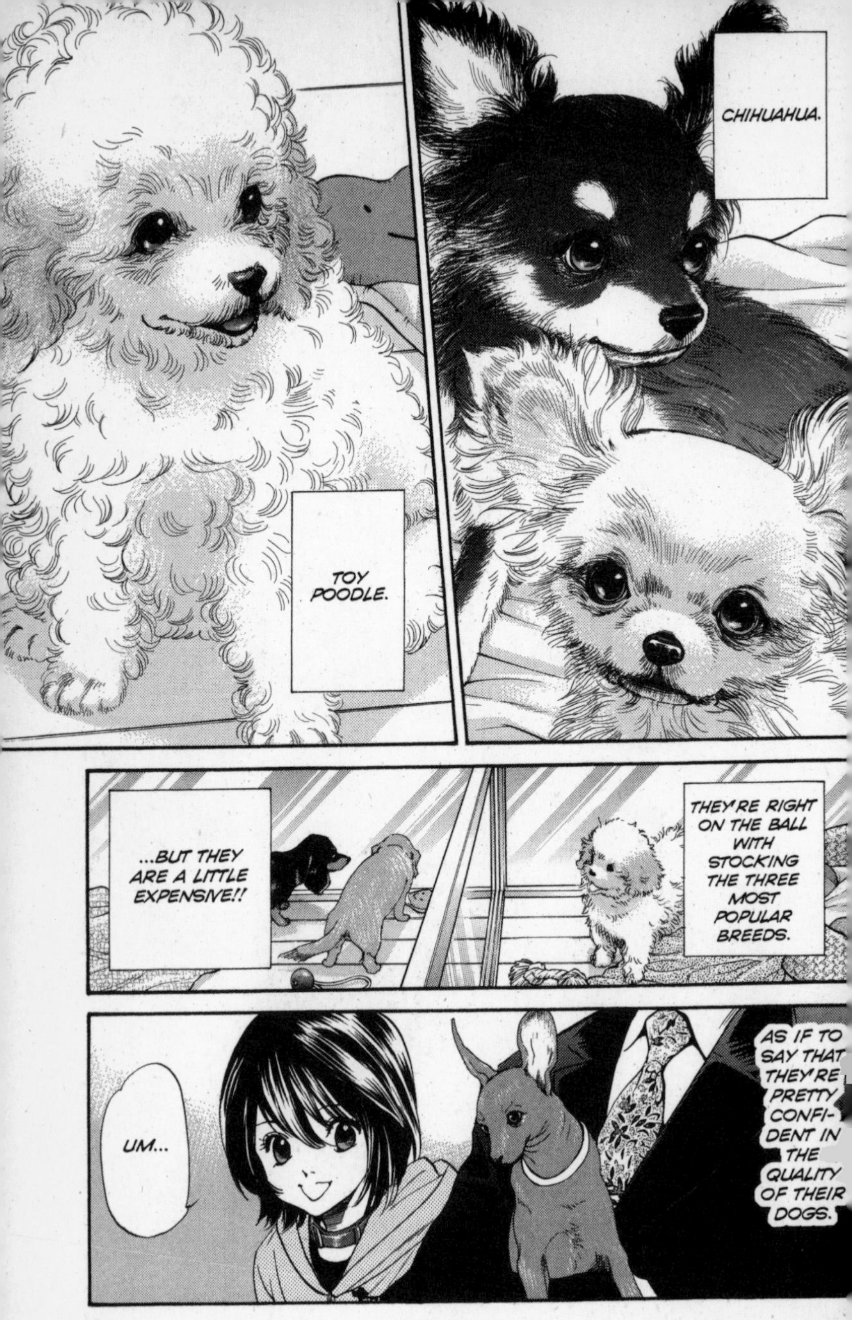
CHIHUAHUA.
TOY POODLE.
THEY'RE RIGHT ON THE BALL WITH STOCKING THE THREE MOST POPULAR BREEDS.
...BUT THEY ARE A LITTLE EXPENSIVE!!
AS IF TO SAY THAT THEY'RE PRETTY CONFI-DENT IN THE QUALITY OF THEIR DOGS.
UM...

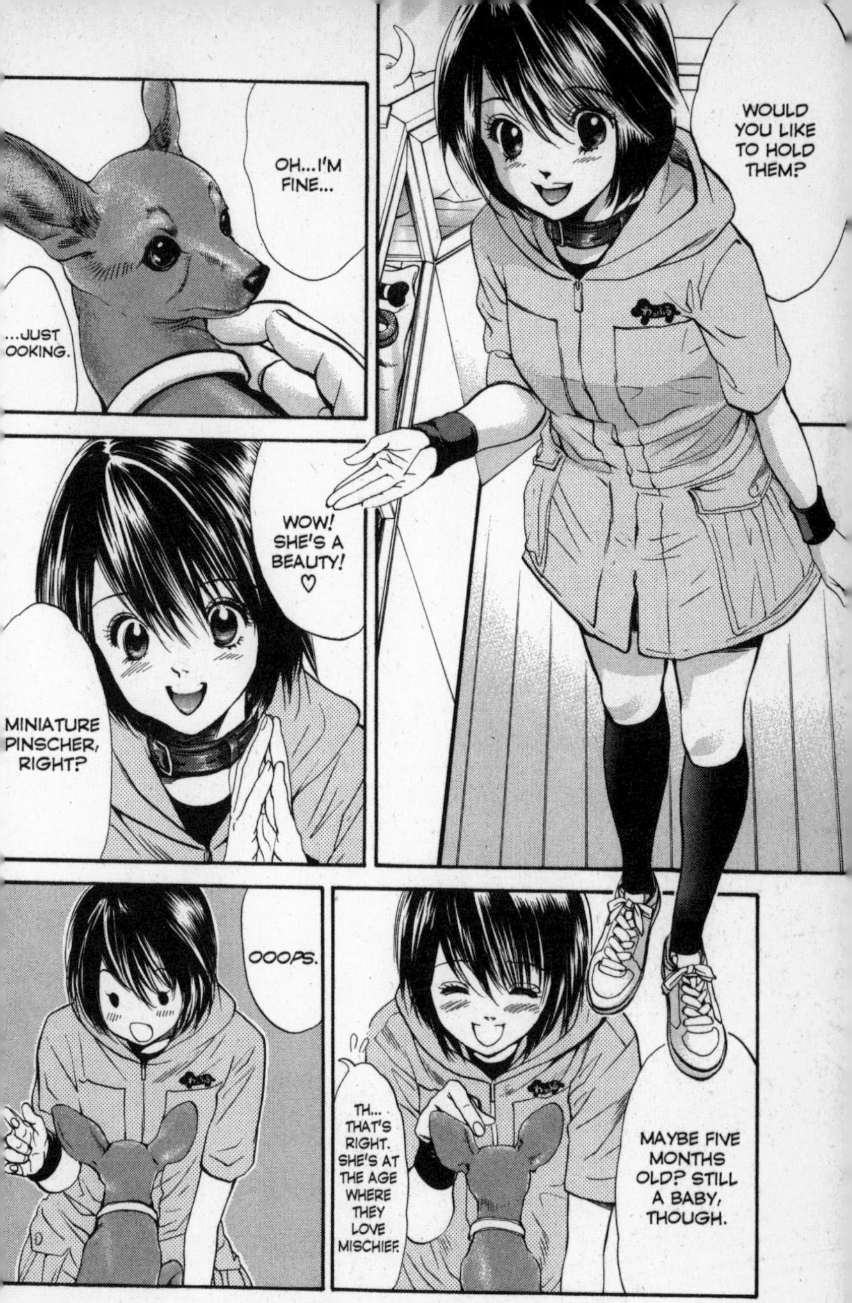
WOULD YOU LIKE TO HOLD THEM?
OH...I'M FINE...
...JUST OOKING.
WOW! SHE'S A BEAUTY! ♡
MINIATURE PINSCHER, RIGHT?
MAYBE FIVE MONTHS OLD? STILL A BABY, THOUGH.
TH... THAT'S RIGHT. SHE'S AT THE AGE WHERE THEY LOVE MISCHIEF.
OOOPS.

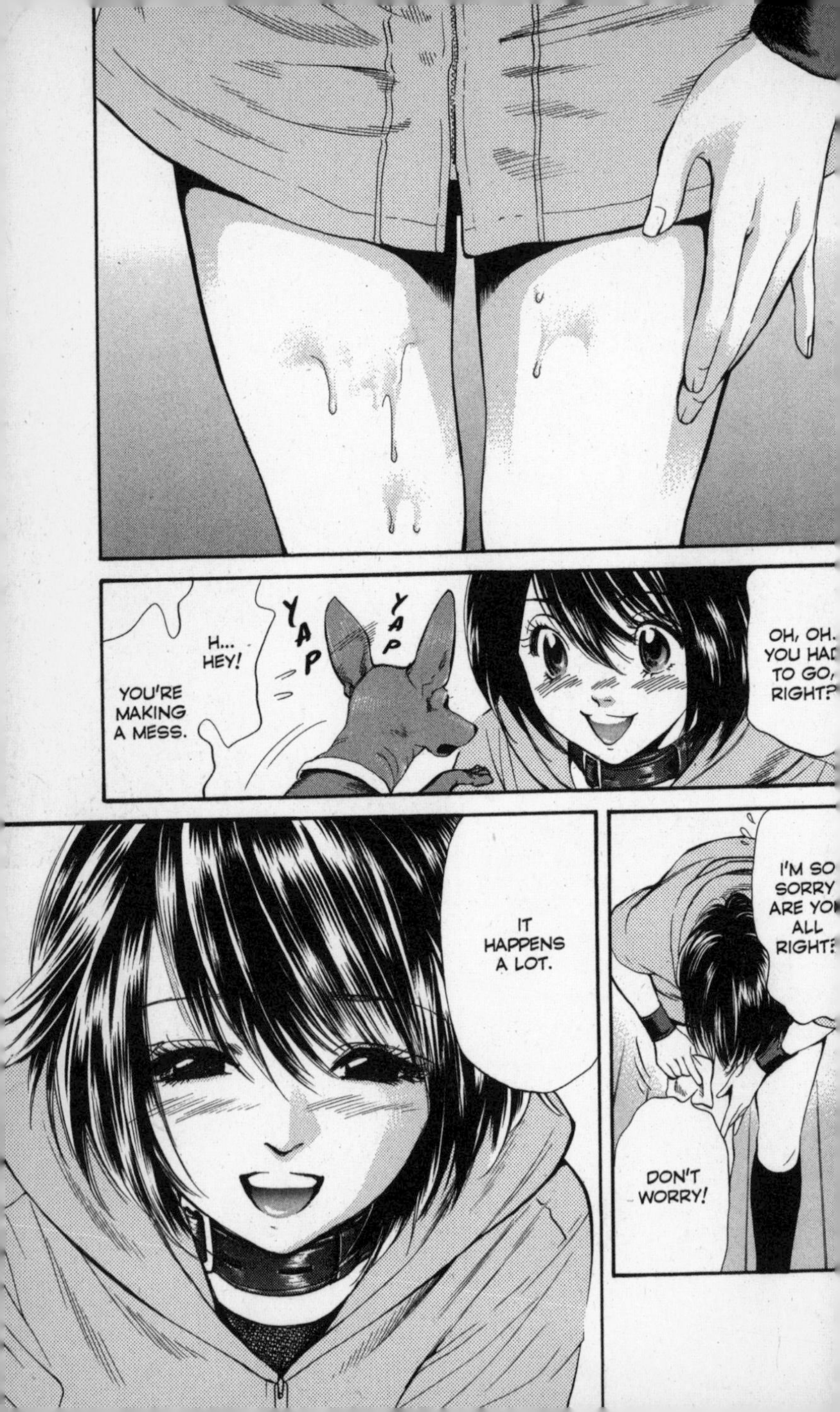
OH, OH. YOU HAD TO GO, RIGHT?
YAP
YAP
H... HEY!
YOU'RE MAKING A MESS.
I'M SO SORRY ARE YOU ALL RIGHT?
DON'T WORRY!
IT HAPPENS A LOT.

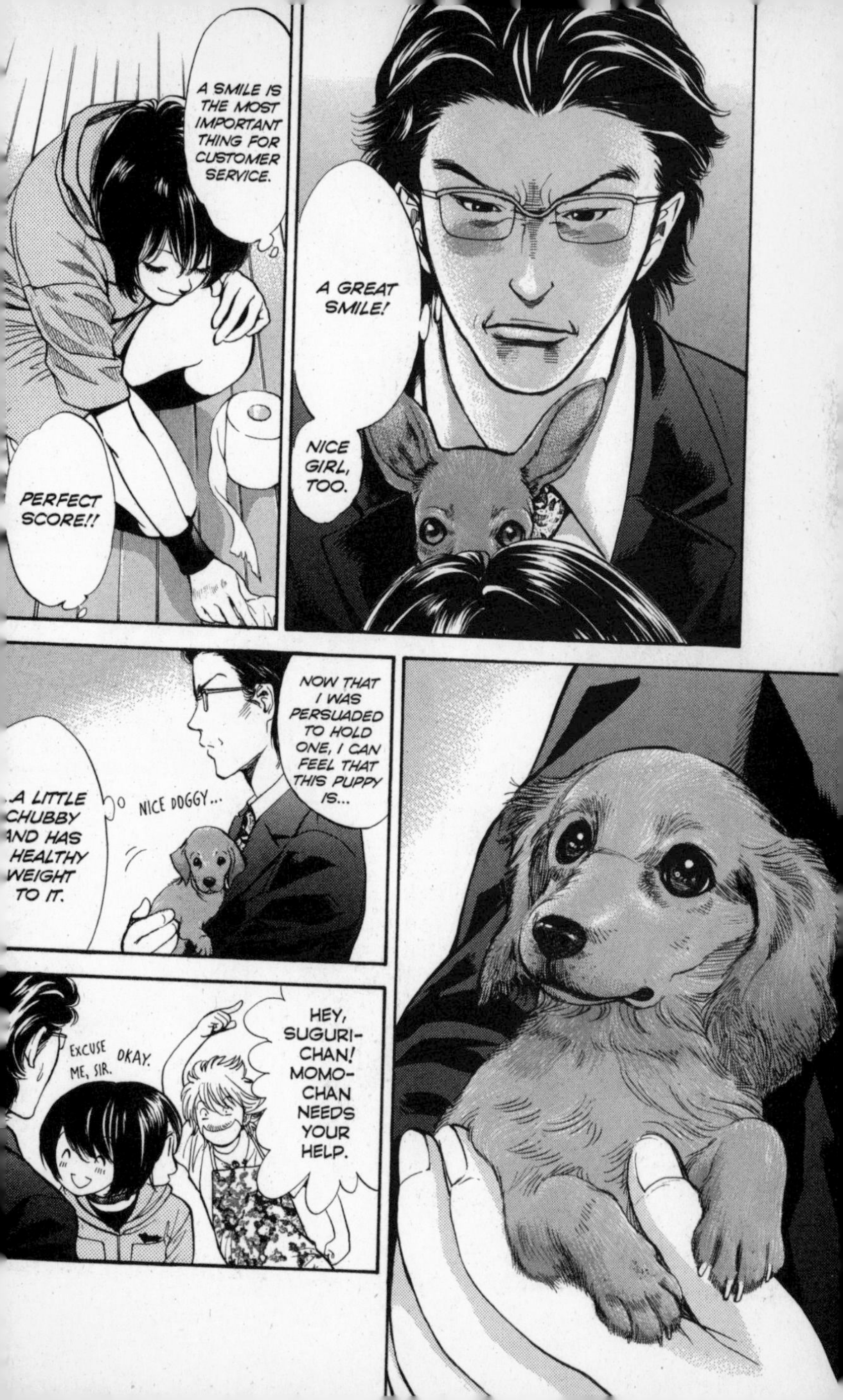
A GREAT SMILE!
NICE GIRL, TOO.
A SMILE IS THE MOST IMPORTANT THING FOR CUSTOMER SERVICE.
PERFECT SCORE!!
NOW THAT I WAS PERSUADED TO HOLD ONE, I CAN FEEL THAT THIS PUPPY IS...
NICE DOGGY...
.A LITTLE CHUBBY AND HAS HEALTHY WEIGHT TO IT.
HEY, SUGURI-CHAN! MOMO-CHAN NEEDS YOUR HELP.
OKAY.
EXCUSE ME, SIR.

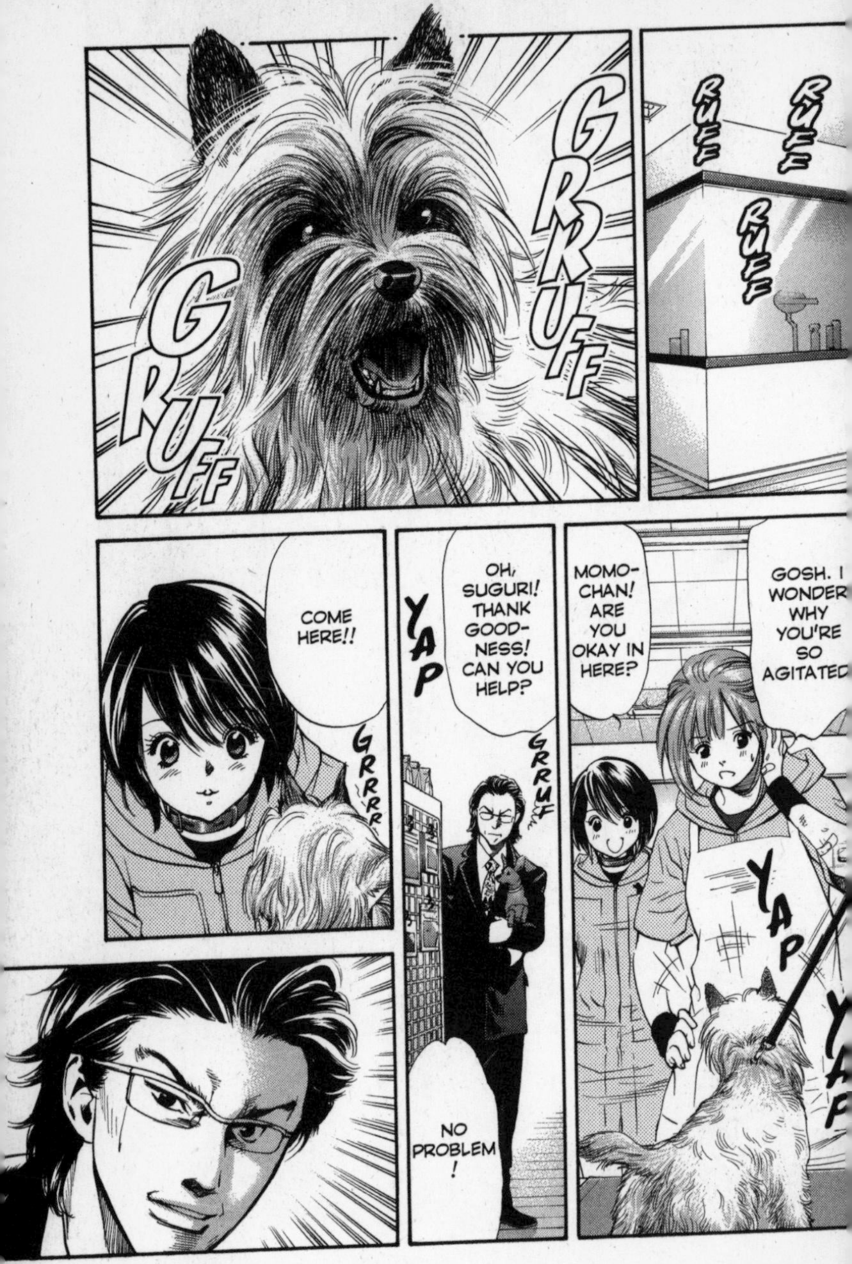
RUFF
RUFF
RUFF
GRRUFF
GRRUFF
GOSH. I WONDER WHY YOU'RE SO AGITATED
MOMO-CHAN! ARE YOU OKAY IN HERE?
YAP YAP
YAP YAP
OH, SUGURI! THANK GOODNESS! CAN YOU HELP?
YAP
GRRUF
NO PROBLEM!
COME HERE!!
GRRRRR

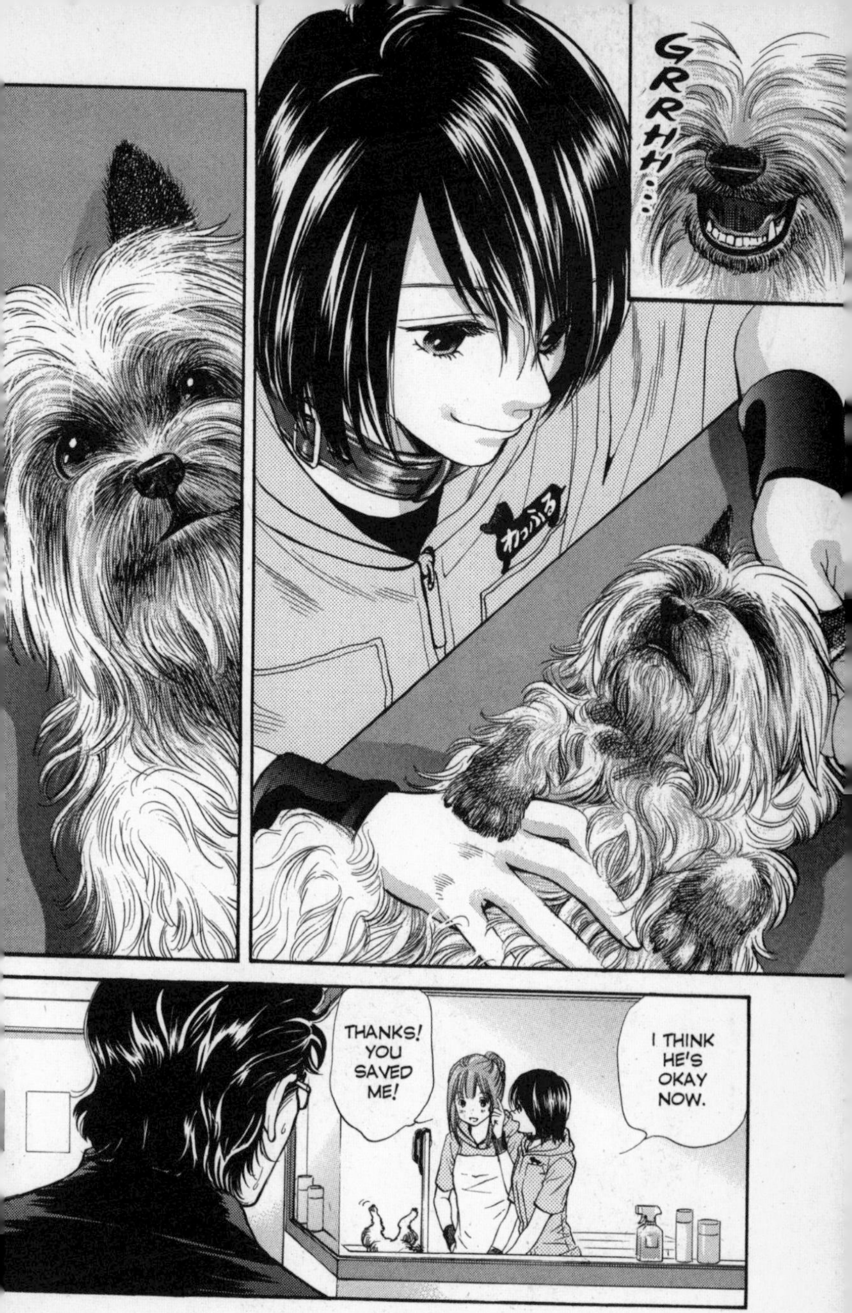
GRRHH...
わっふる
I THINK HE'S OKAY NOW.
THANKS! YOU SAVED ME!

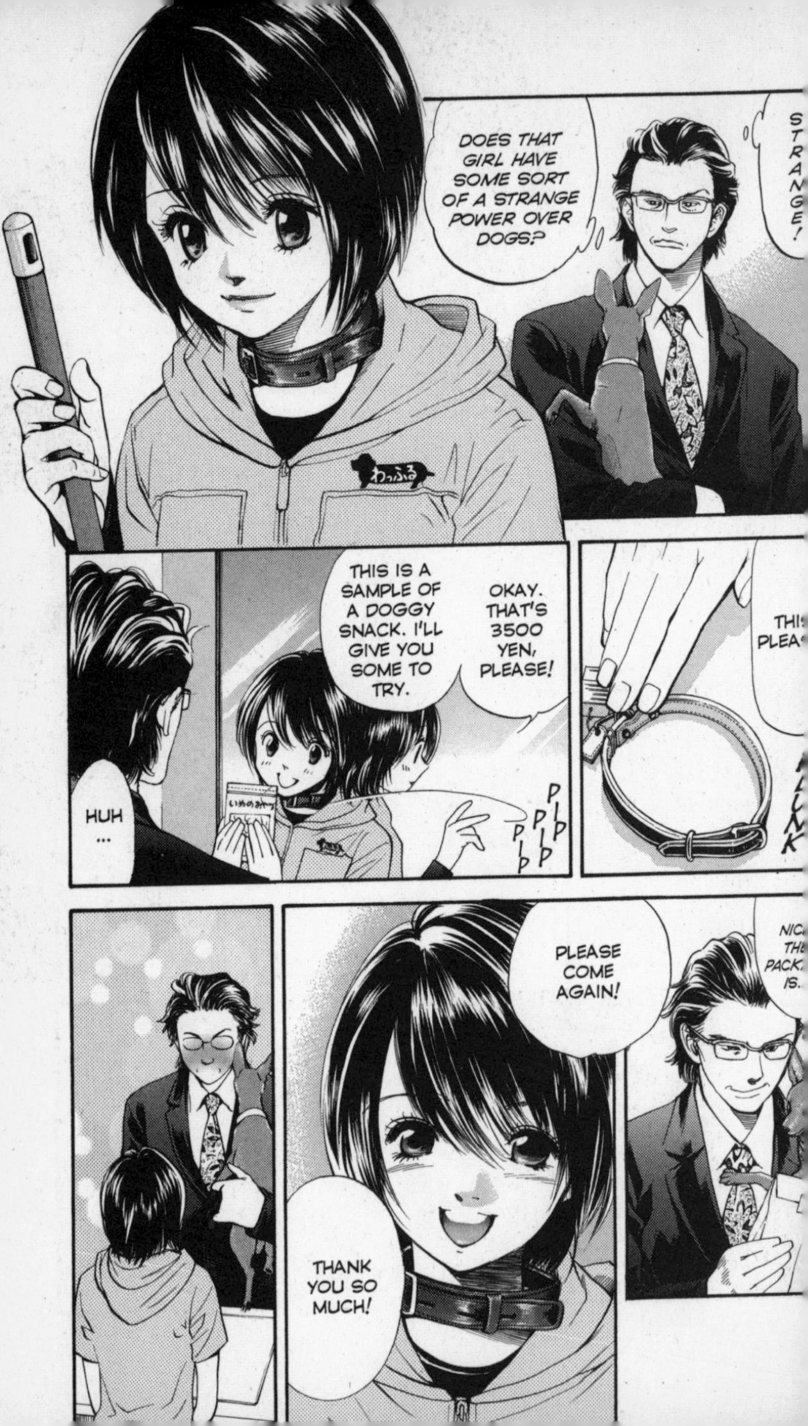
STRANGE!
DOES THAT GIRL HAVE SOME SORT OF A STRANGE POWER OVER DOGS?
OKAY. THAT'S 3500 YEN, PLEASE!
THIS IS A SAMPLE OF A DOGGY SNACK. I'LL GIVE YOU SOME TO TRY.
PIP PIP PIP PIP
HUH ...
PLEASE COME AGAIN!
THANK YOU SO MUCH!

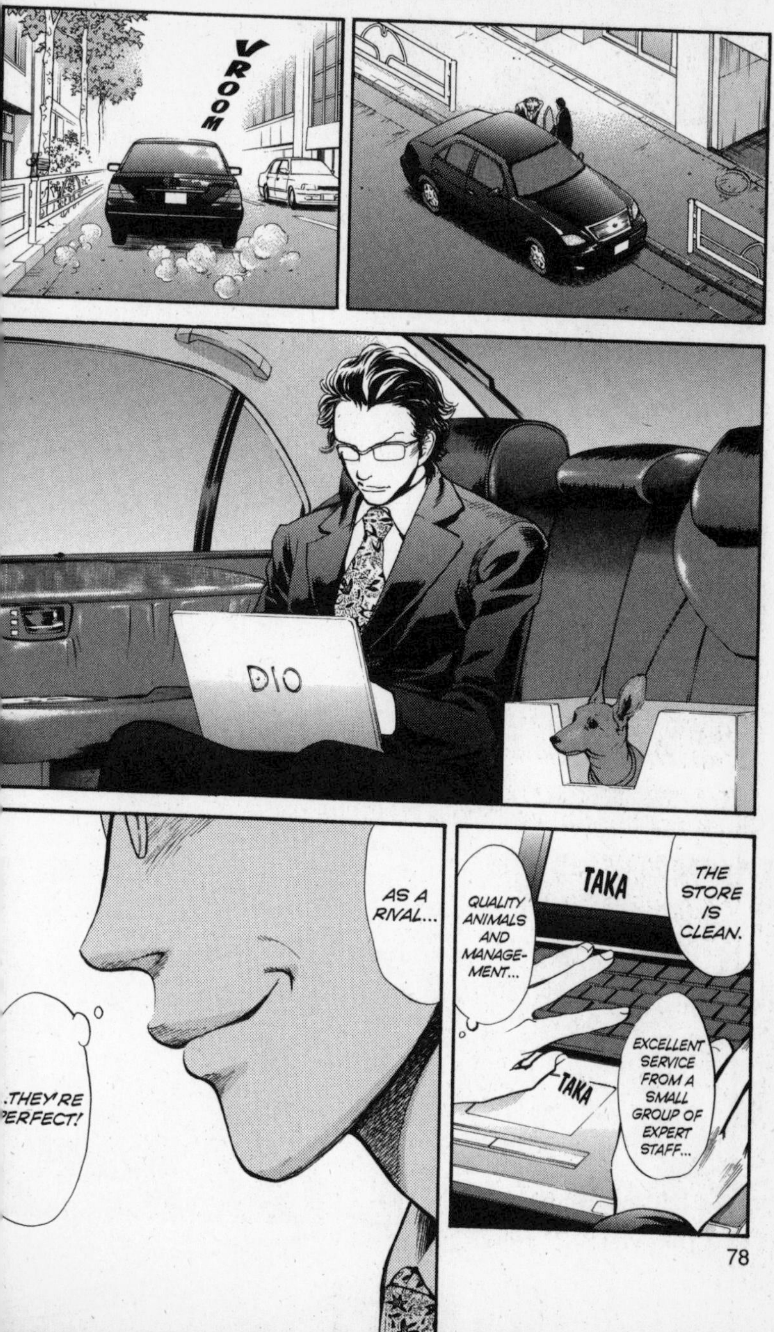
VROOM
DIO
THE STORE IS CLEAN.
TAKA
QUALITY ANIMALS AND MANAGE-MENT...
EXCELLENT SERVICE FROM A SMALL GROUP OF EXPERT STAFF...
TAKA
AS A RIVAL...
.THEY'RE PERFECT!

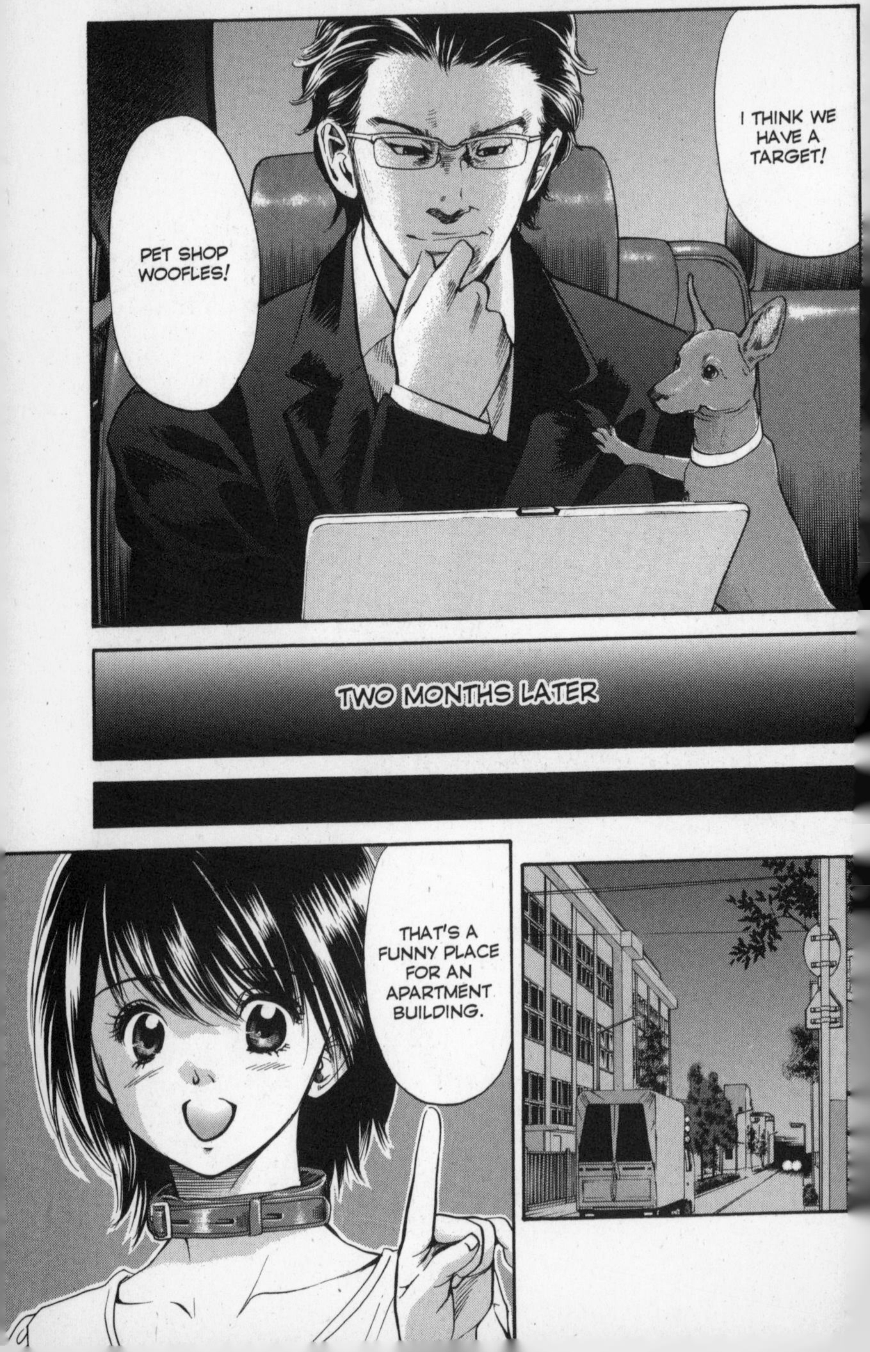
I THINK WE HAVE A TARGET!
PET SHOP WOOFLES!
TWO MONTHS LATER
THAT'S A FUNNY PLACE FOR AN APARTMENT BUILDING.

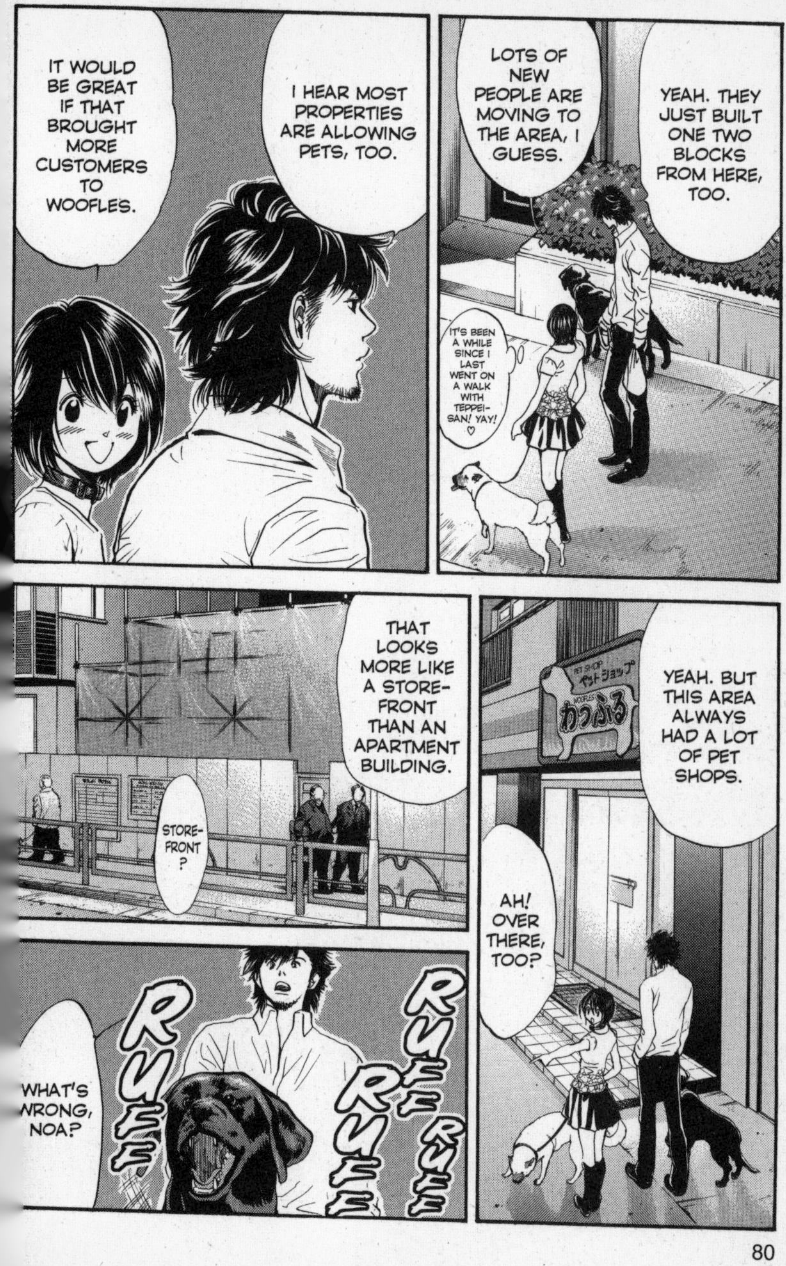
YEAH. THEY JUST BUILT ONE TWO BLOCKS FROM HERE, TOO.
LOTS OF NEW PEOPLE ARE MOVING TO THE AREA, I GUESS.
IT'S BEEN A WHILE SINCE I LAST WENT ON A WALK WITH TEPPEI-SAN! YAY! ♡
I HEAR MOST PROPERTIES ARE ALLOWING PETS, TOO.
IT WOULD BE GREAT IF THAT BROUGHT MORE CUSTOMERS TO WOOFLES.
PET SHOP ペットショップ
WOOFLES わっふる
YEAH. BUT THIS AREA ALWAYS HAD A LOT OF PET SHOPS.
AH! OVER THERE, TOO?
THAT LOOKS MORE LIKE A STORE-FRONT THAN AN APARTMENT BUILDING.
STORE-FRONT?
RUFF RUFF
RUFF
RUFF
WHAT'S WRONG, NOA?

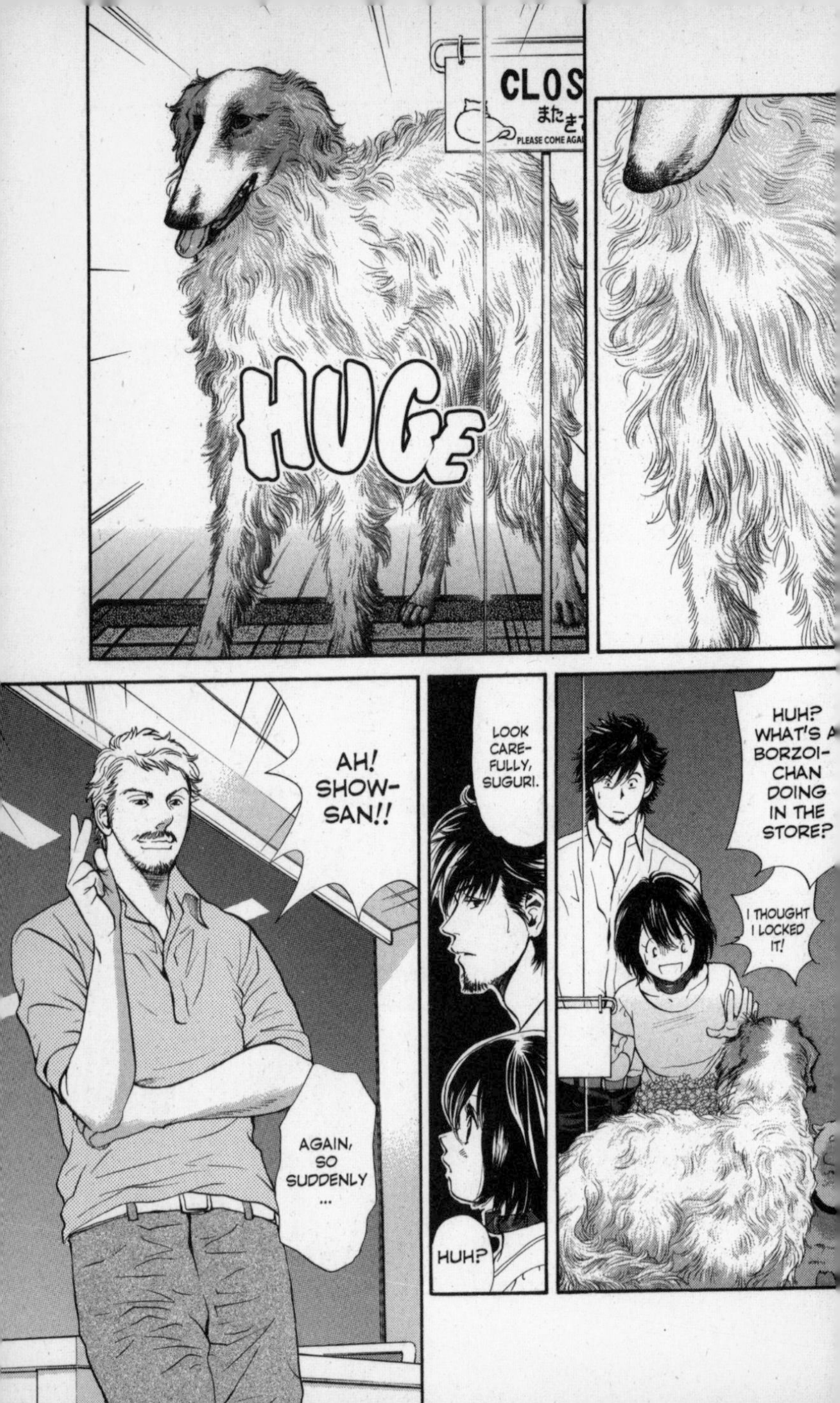

CLOS
HUGE
HUH? WHAT'S A BORZOI-CHAN DOING IN THE STORE?
I THOUGHT I LOCKED IT!
LOOK CARE-FULLY, SUGURI.
HUH?
AH! SHOW-SAN!!
AGAIN, SO SUDDENLY ...

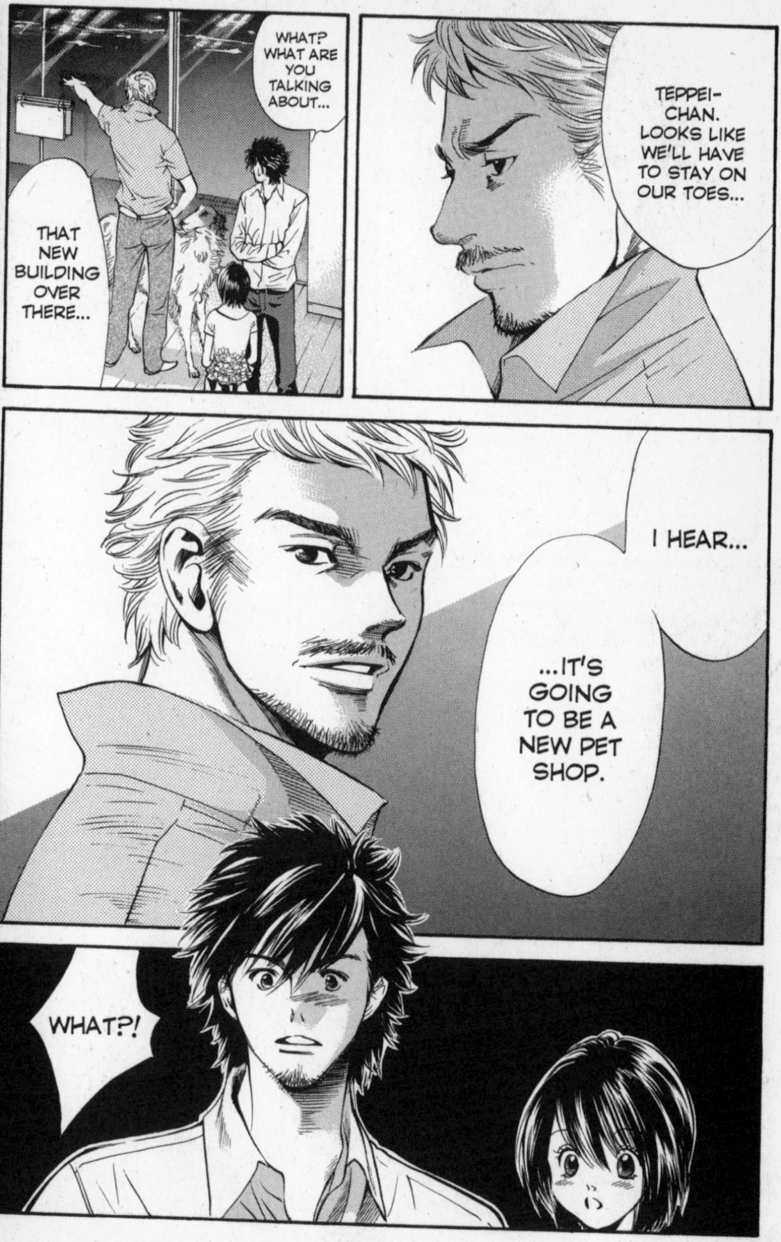
TEPPEI-CHAN. LOOKS LIKE WE'LL HAVE TO STAY ON OUR TOES...
WHAT? WHAT ARE YOU TALKING ABOUT...
THAT NEW BUILDING OVER THERE...
I HEAR...
...IT'S GOING TO BE A NEW PET SHOP.
WHAT?!

CHAPTER 102: ROOKIE

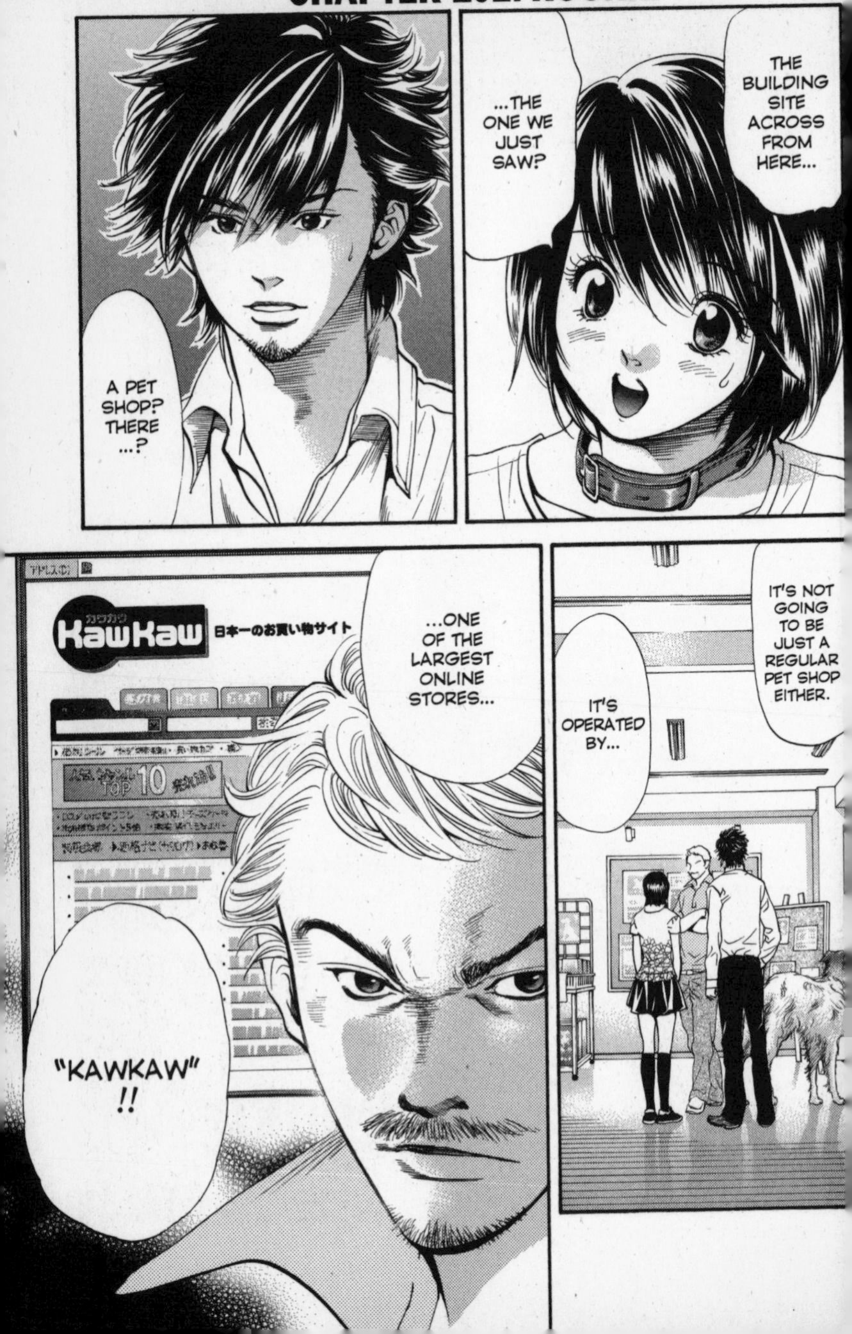
THE BUILDING SITE ACROSS FROM HERE...
...THE ONE WE JUST SAW?
A PET SHOP? THERE ...?
IT'S NOT GOING TO BE JUST A REGULAR PET SHOP EITHER.
IT'S OPERATED BY...
...ONE OF THE LARGEST ONLINE STORES...
KawKaw
日本一のお買い物サイト
"KAWKAW" !!

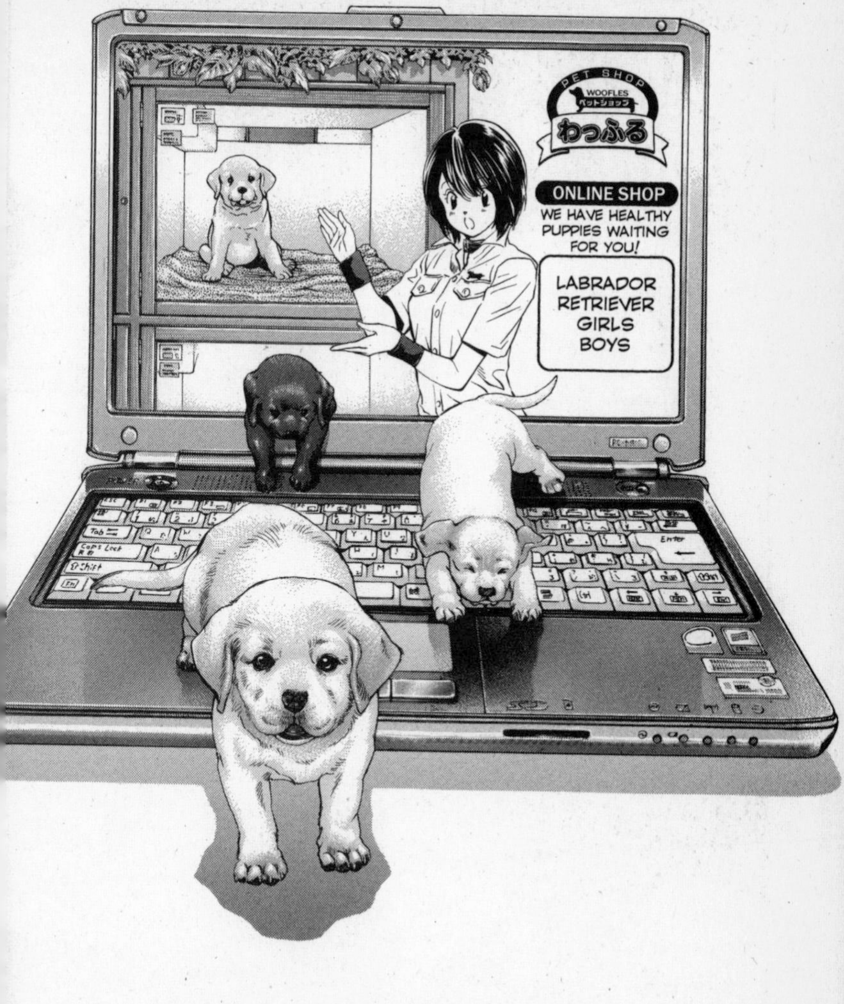
PET SHOP
WOOFLES
ペットショップ
わっふる
ONLINE SHOP
WE HAVE HEALTHY PUPPIES WAITING FOR YOU!
LABRADOR RETRIEVER
GIRLS
BOYS

CHAPTER 102: ROOKIE

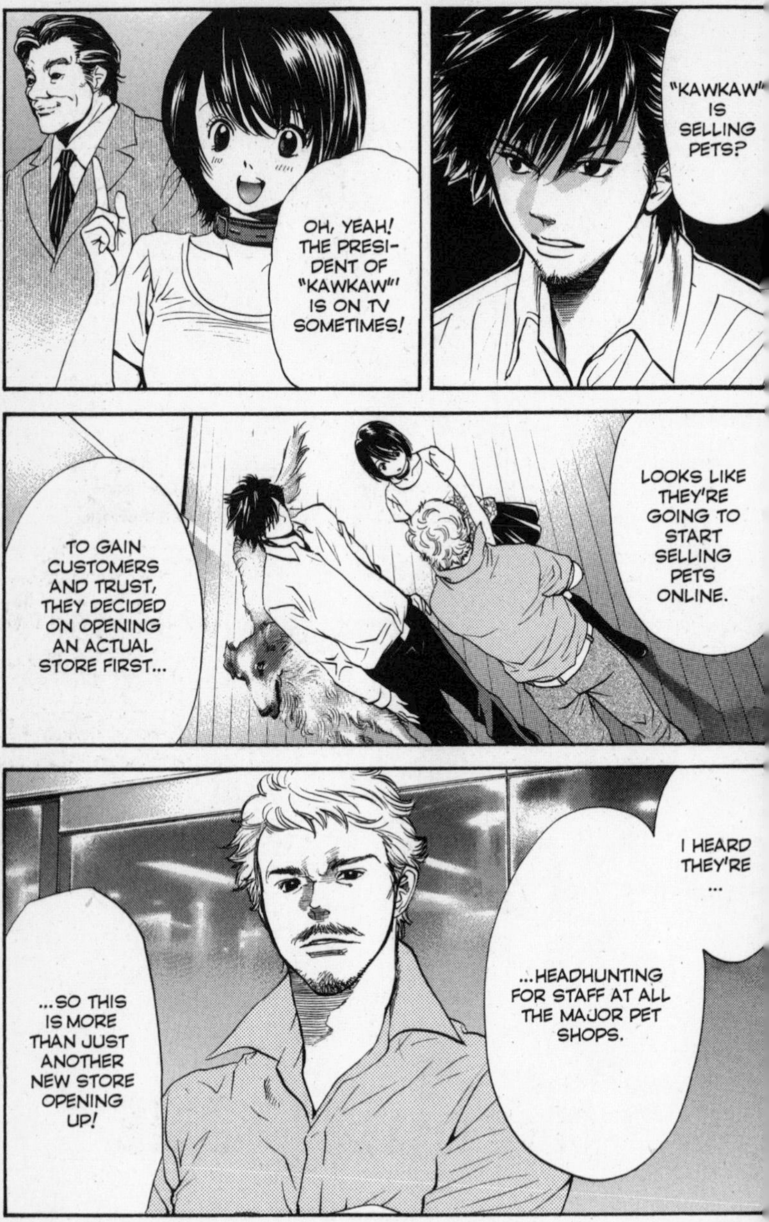
"KAWKAW" IS SELLING PETS?
OH, YEAH! THE PRESIDENT OF "KAWKAW"! IS ON TV SOMETIMES!
LOOKS LIKE THEY'RE GOING TO START SELLING PETS ONLINE.
TO GAIN CUSTOMERS AND TRUST, THEY DECIDED ON OPENING AN ACTUAL STORE FIRST...
I HEARD THEY'RE ...
...HEADHUNTING FOR STAFF AT ALL THE MAJOR PET SHOPS.
...SO THIS IS MORE THAN JUST ANOTHER NEW STORE OPENING UP!

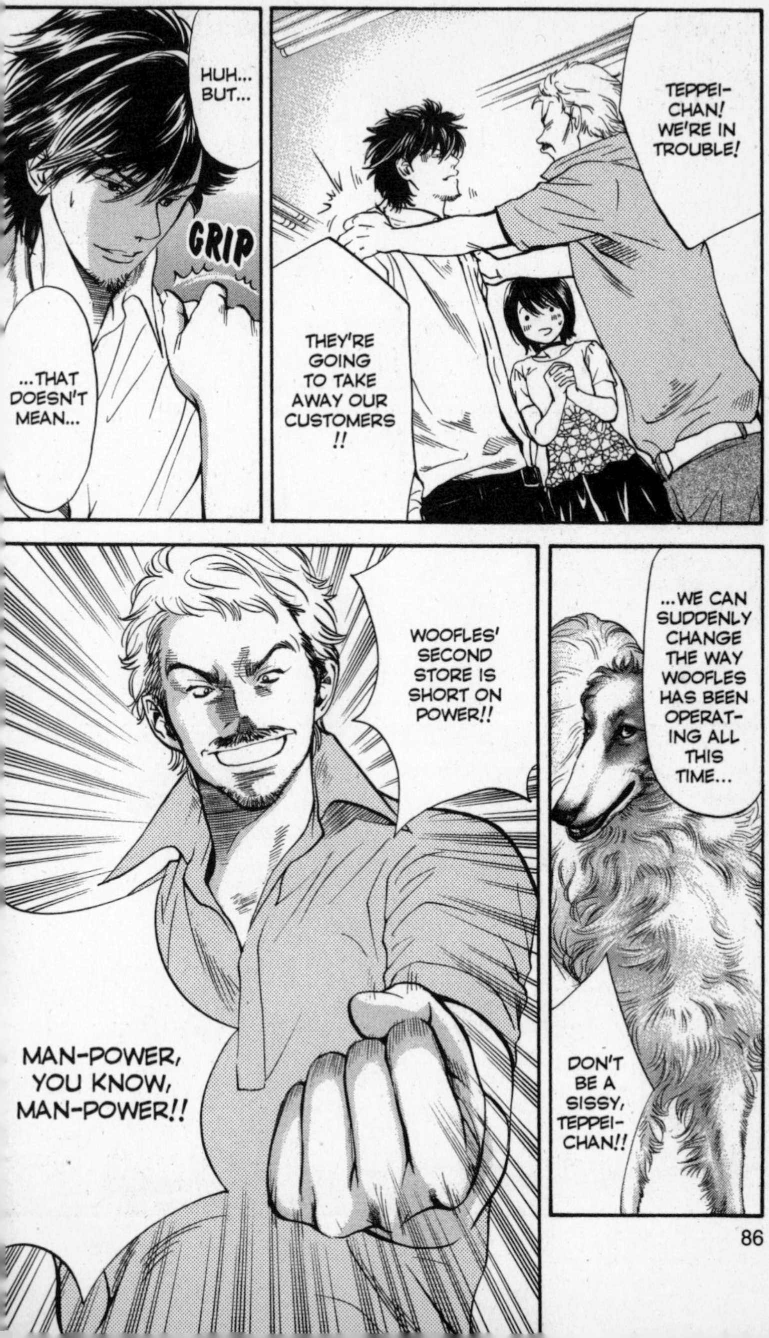
TEPPEI-CHAN! WE'RE IN TROUBLE!
THEY'RE GOING TO TAKE AWAY OUR CUSTOMERS!!
HUH... BUT...
GRIP
...THAT DOESN'T MEAN...
...WE CAN SUDDENLY CHANGE THE WAY WOOFLES HAS BEEN OPERATING ALL THIS TIME...
DON'T BE A SISSY, TEPPEI-CHAN!!
WOOFLES' SECOND STORE IS SHORT ON POWER!!
MAN-POWER, YOU KNOW, MAN-POWER!!

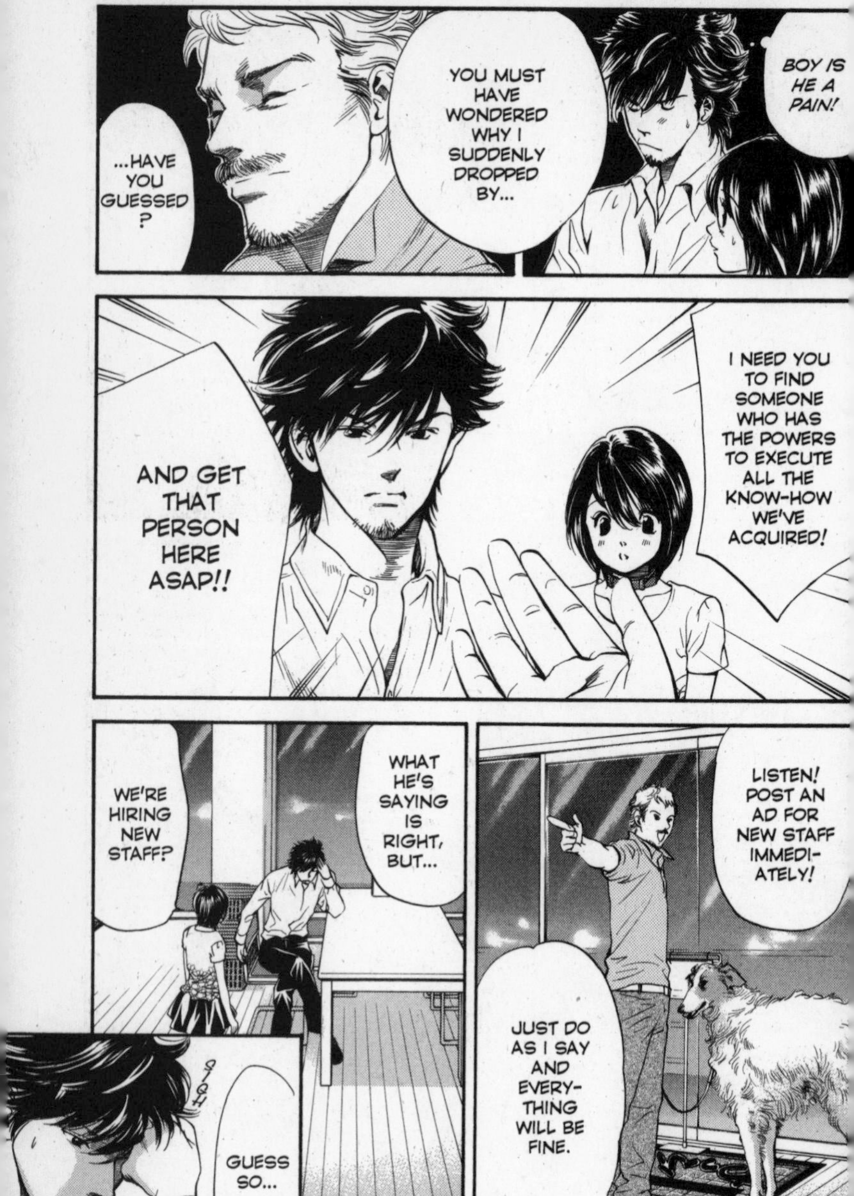
BOY IS HE A PAIN!
YOU MUST HAVE WONDERED WHY I SUDDENLY DROPPED BY...
...HAVE YOU GUESSED?
I NEED YOU TO FIND SOMEONE WHO HAS THE POWERS TO EXECUTE ALL THE KNOW-HOW WE'VE ACQUIRED!
AND GET THAT PERSON HERE ASAP!!
LISTEN! POST AN AD FOR NEW STAFF IMMEDI-ATELY!
JUST DO AS I SAY AND EVERY-THING WILL BE FINE.
WHAT HE'S SAYING IS RIGHT, BUT...
WE'RE HIRING NEW STAFF?
SIGH
GUESS SO...

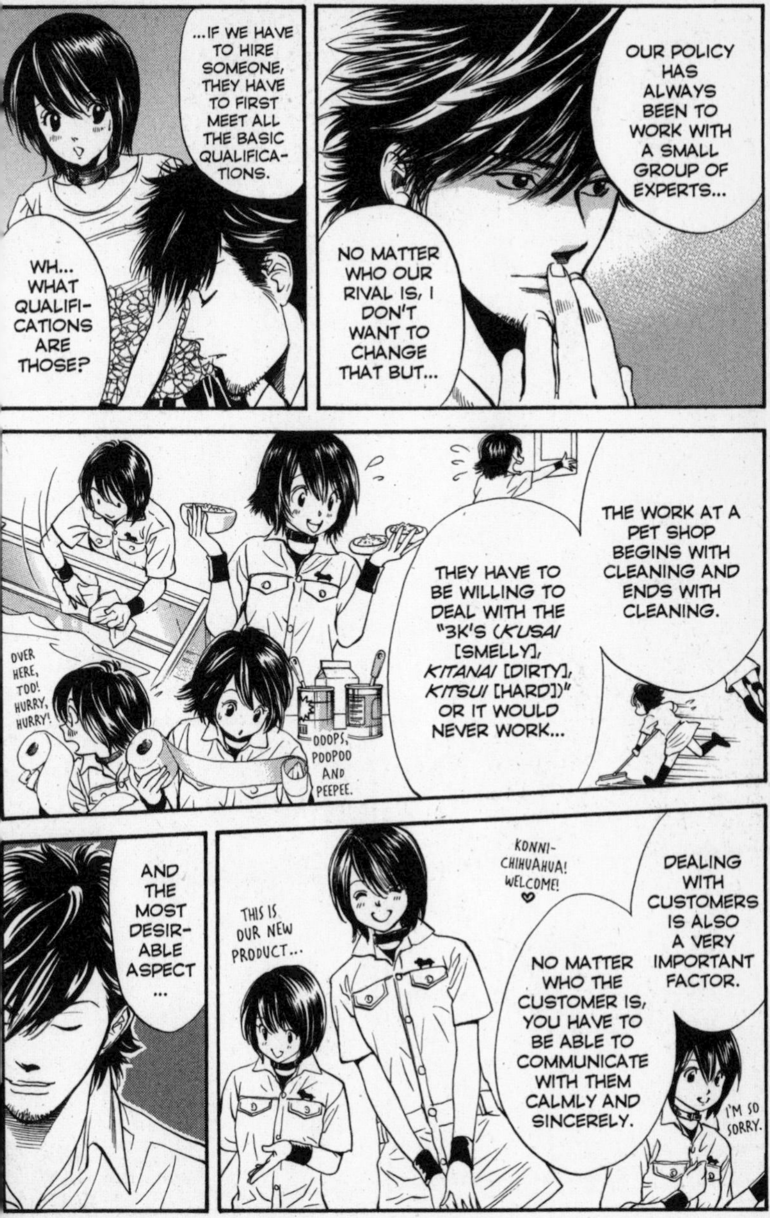
OUR POLICY HAS ALWAYS BEEN TO WORK WITH A SMALL GROUP OF EXPERTS...
NO MATTER WHO OUR RIVAL IS, I DON'T WANT TO CHANGE THAT BUT...
...IF WE HAVE TO HIRE SOMEONE, THEY HAVE TO FIRST MEET ALL THE BASIC QUALIFICATIONS.
WH... WHAT QUALIFICATIONS ARE THOSE?
THE WORK AT A PET SHOP BEGINS WITH CLEANING AND ENDS WITH CLEANING.
THEY HAVE TO BE WILLING TO DEAL WITH THE "3K'S (*KUSAI* [SMELLY], *KITANAI* [DIRTY], *KITSUI* [HARD])" OR IT WOULD NEVER WORK...
OOPS, POOPOO AND PEEPEE.
OVER HERE, TOO! HURRY, HURRY!
DEALING WITH CUSTOMERS IS ALSO A VERY IMPORTANT FACTOR.
I'M SO SORRY.
NO MATTER WHO THE CUSTOMER IS, YOU HAVE TO BE ABLE TO COMMUNICATE WITH THEM CALMLY AND SINCERELY.
KONNI-CHIHUAHUA! WELCOME!
THIS IS OUR NEW PRODUCT...
AND THE MOST DESIRABLE ASPECT ...

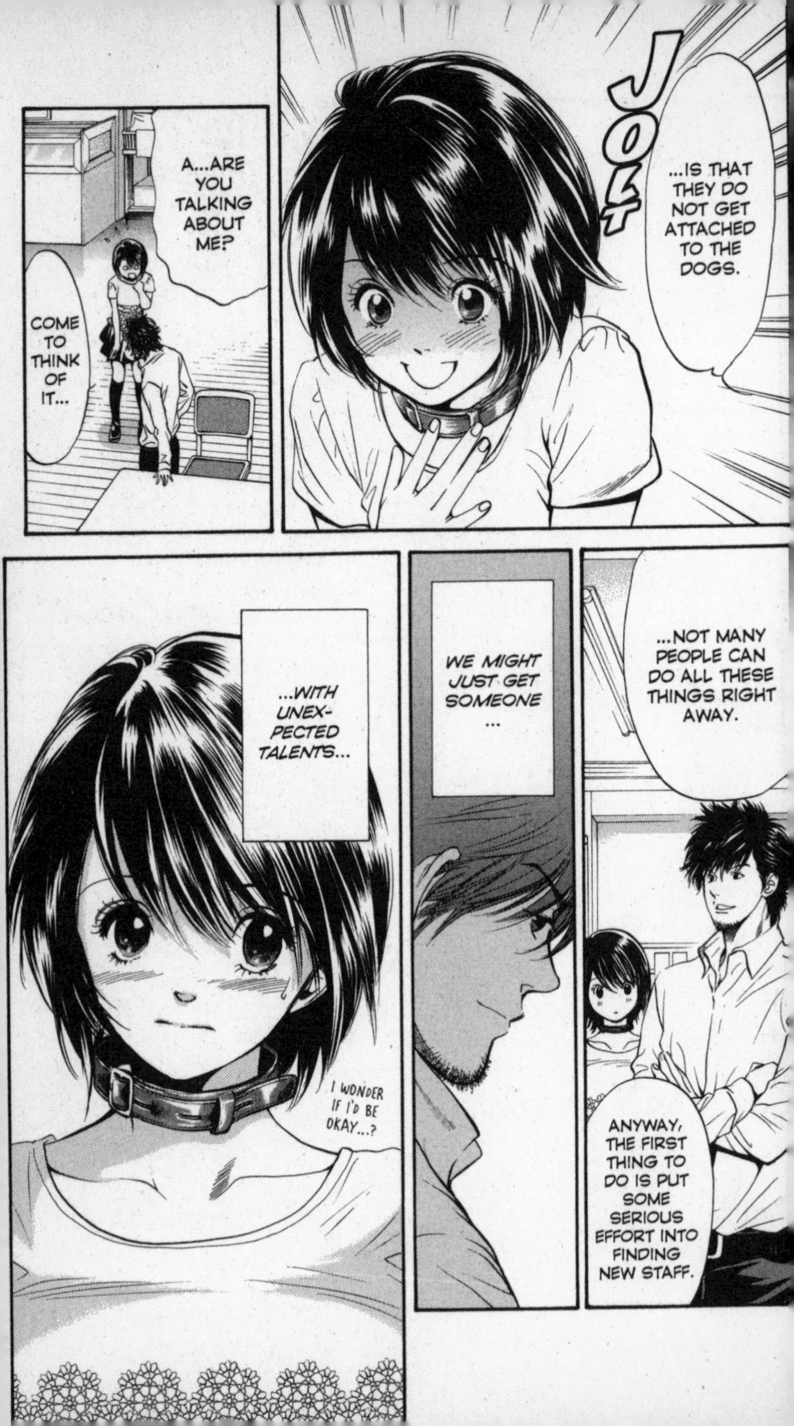
...IS THAT THEY DO NOT GET ATTACHED TO THE DOGS.
JOLT
A...ARE YOU TALKING ABOUT ME?
COME TO THINK OF IT...
...NOT MANY PEOPLE CAN DO ALL THESE THINGS RIGHT AWAY.
ANYWAY, THE FIRST THING TO DO IS PUT SOME SERIOUS EFFORT INTO FINDING NEW STAFF.
WE MIGHT JUST GET SOMEONE ...
...WITH UNEX-PECTED TALENTS...
I WONDER IF I'D BE OKAY...?

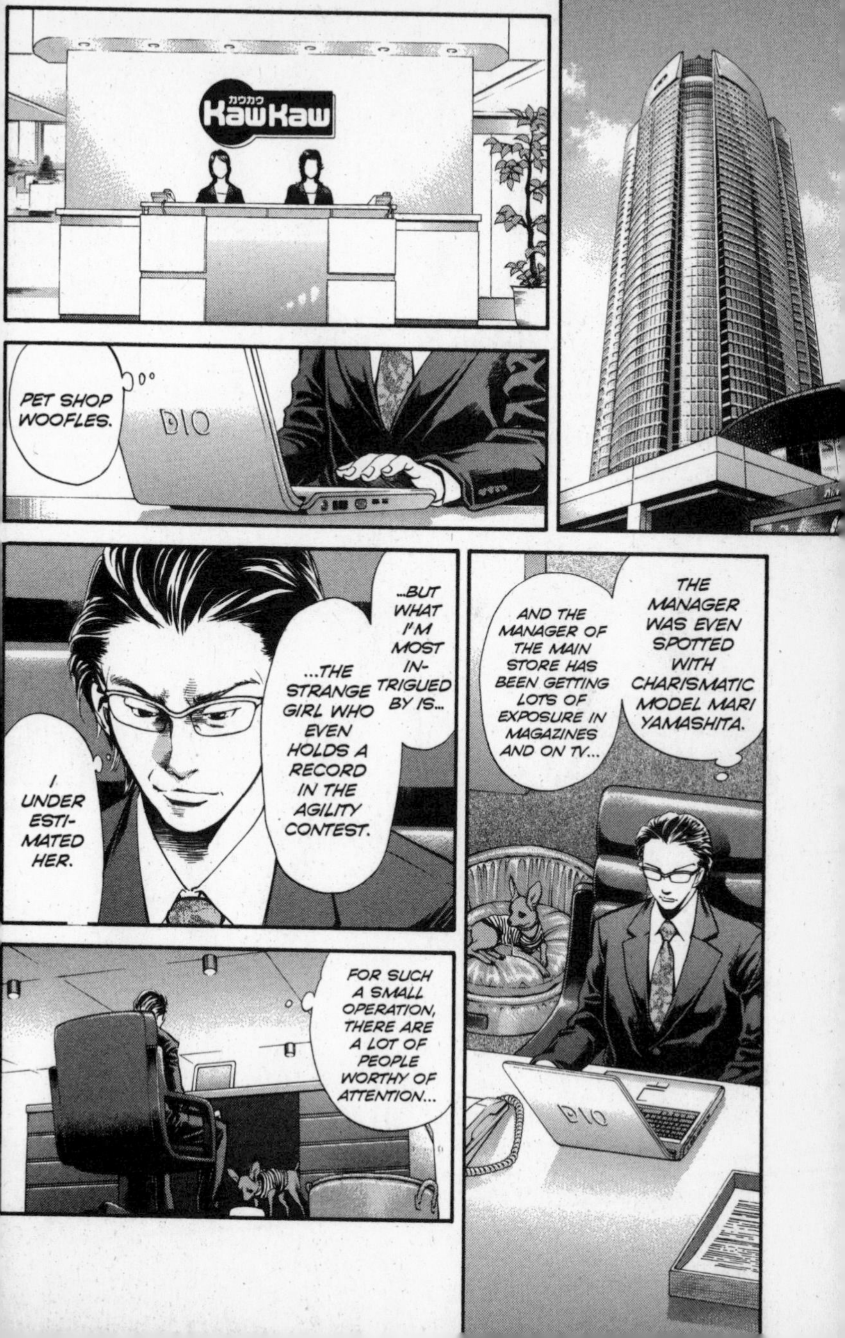

カウカウ
KawKaw
PET SHOP WOOFLES.
DIO
THE MANAGER WAS EVEN SPOTTED WITH CHARISMATIC MODEL MARI YAMASHITA.
AND THE MANAGER OF THE MAIN STORE HAS BEEN GETTING LOTS OF EXPOSURE IN MAGAZINES AND ON TV...
DIO
...BUT WHAT I'M MOST IN-TRIGUED BY IS...
...THE STRANGE GIRL WHO EVEN HOLDS A RECORD IN THE AGILITY CONTEST.
I UNDER ESTI-MATED HER.
FOR SUCH A SMALL OPERATION, THERE ARE A LOT OF PEOPLE WORTHY OF ATTENTION...

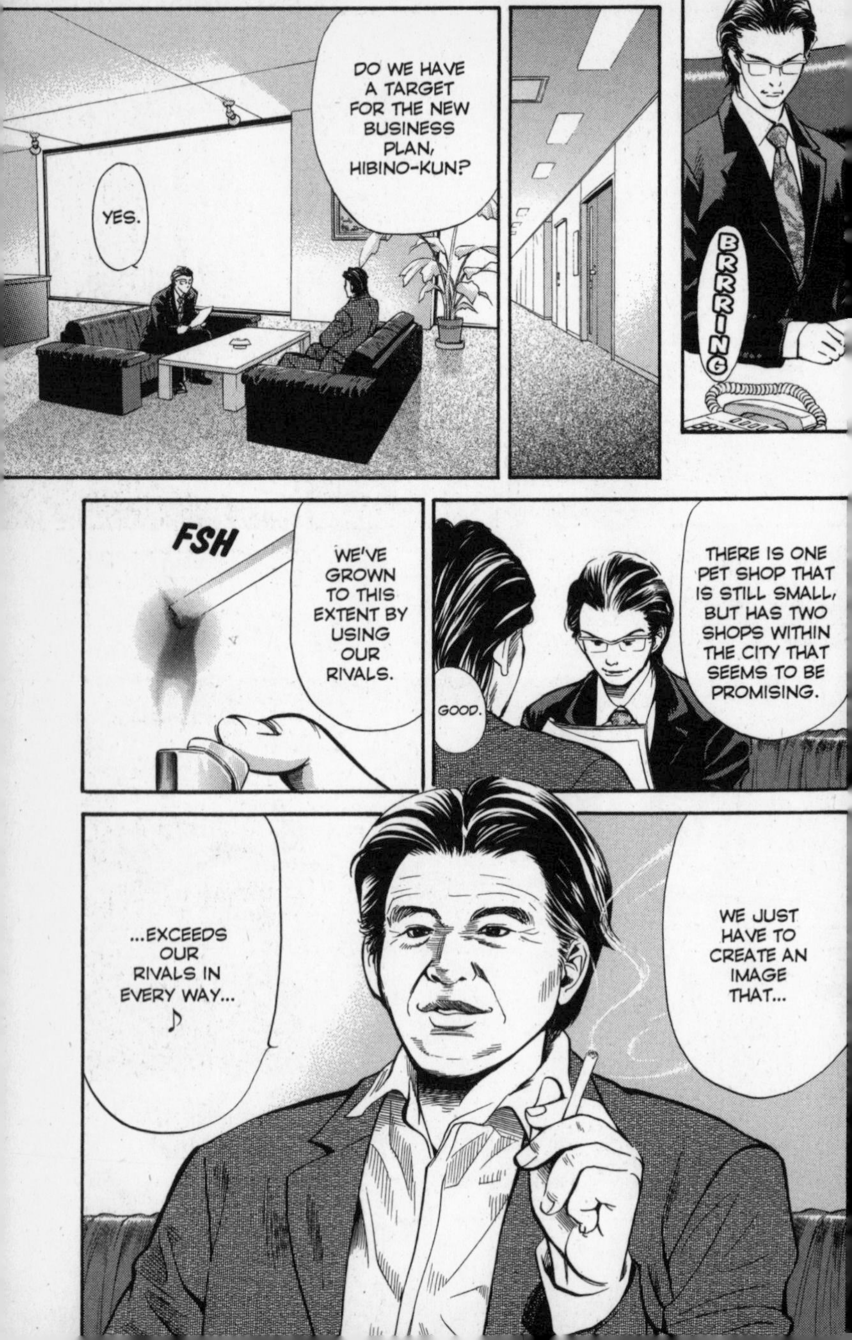
BRRRING
DO WE HAVE A TARGET FOR THE NEW BUSINESS PLAN, HIBINO-KUN?
YES.
THERE IS ONE PET SHOP THAT IS STILL SMALL, BUT HAS TWO SHOPS WITHIN THE CITY THAT SEEMS TO BE PROMISING.
GOOD.
FSH
WE'VE GROWN TO THIS EXTENT BY USING OUR RIVALS.
WE JUST HAVE TO CREATE AN IMAGE THAT...
...EXCEEDS OUR RIVALS IN EVERY WAY... ♪

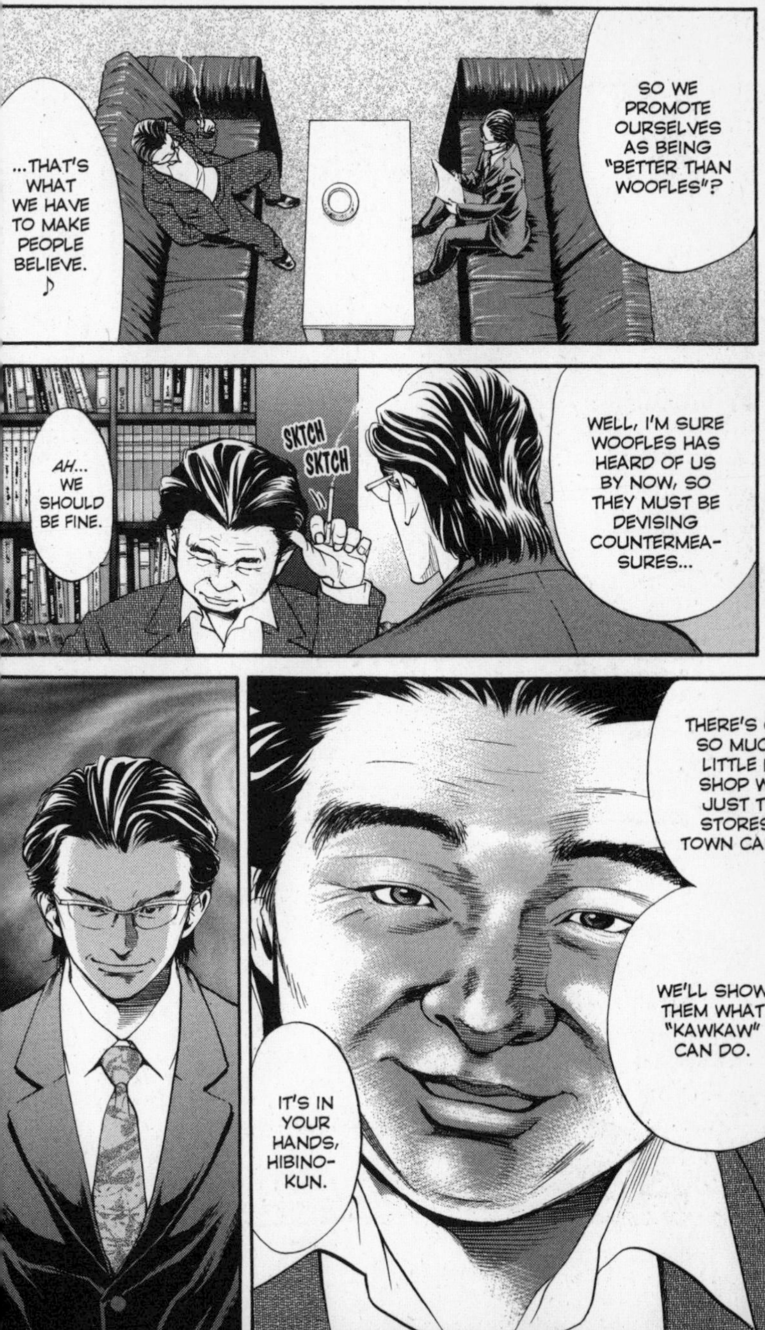
SO WE PROMOTE OURSELVES AS BEING "BETTER THAN WOOFLES"?
...THAT'S WHAT WE HAVE TO MAKE PEOPLE BELIEVE. ♪
WELL, I'M SURE WOOFLES HAS HEARD OF US BY NOW, SO THEY MUST BE DEVISING COUNTERMEA-SURES...
SKTCH SKTCH
AH... WE SHOULD BE FINE.
THERE'S ONLY SO MUCH A LITTLE PET SHOP WITH JUST TWO STORES IN TOWN CAN DO.
WE'LL SHOW THEM WHAT "KAWKAW" CAN DO.
IT'S IN YOUR HANDS, HIBINO-KUN.

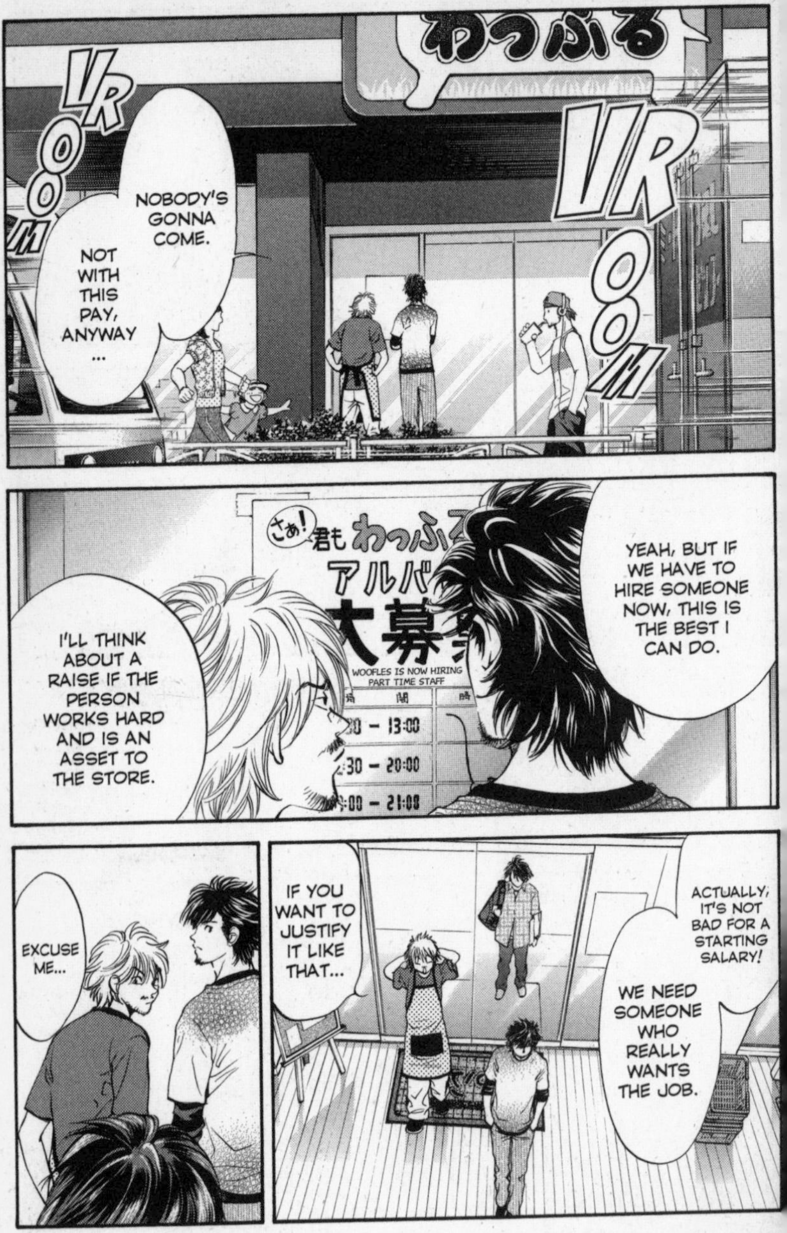
わっふる
VROOM
NOBODY'S GONNA COME.
NOT WITH THIS PAY, ANYWAY ...
VROOM
YEAH, BUT IF WE HAVE TO HIRE SOMEONE NOW, THIS IS THE BEST I CAN DO.
さぁ!
君も
WOOFLES IS NOW HIRING PART TIME STAFF
I'LL THINK ABOUT A RAISE IF THE PERSON WORKS HARD AND IS AN ASSET TO THE STORE.
ACTUALLY, IT'S NOT BAD FOR A STARTING SALARY!
WE NEED SOMEONE WHO REALLY WANTS THE JOB.
IF YOU WANT TO JUSTIFY IT LIKE THAT...
EXCUSE ME...

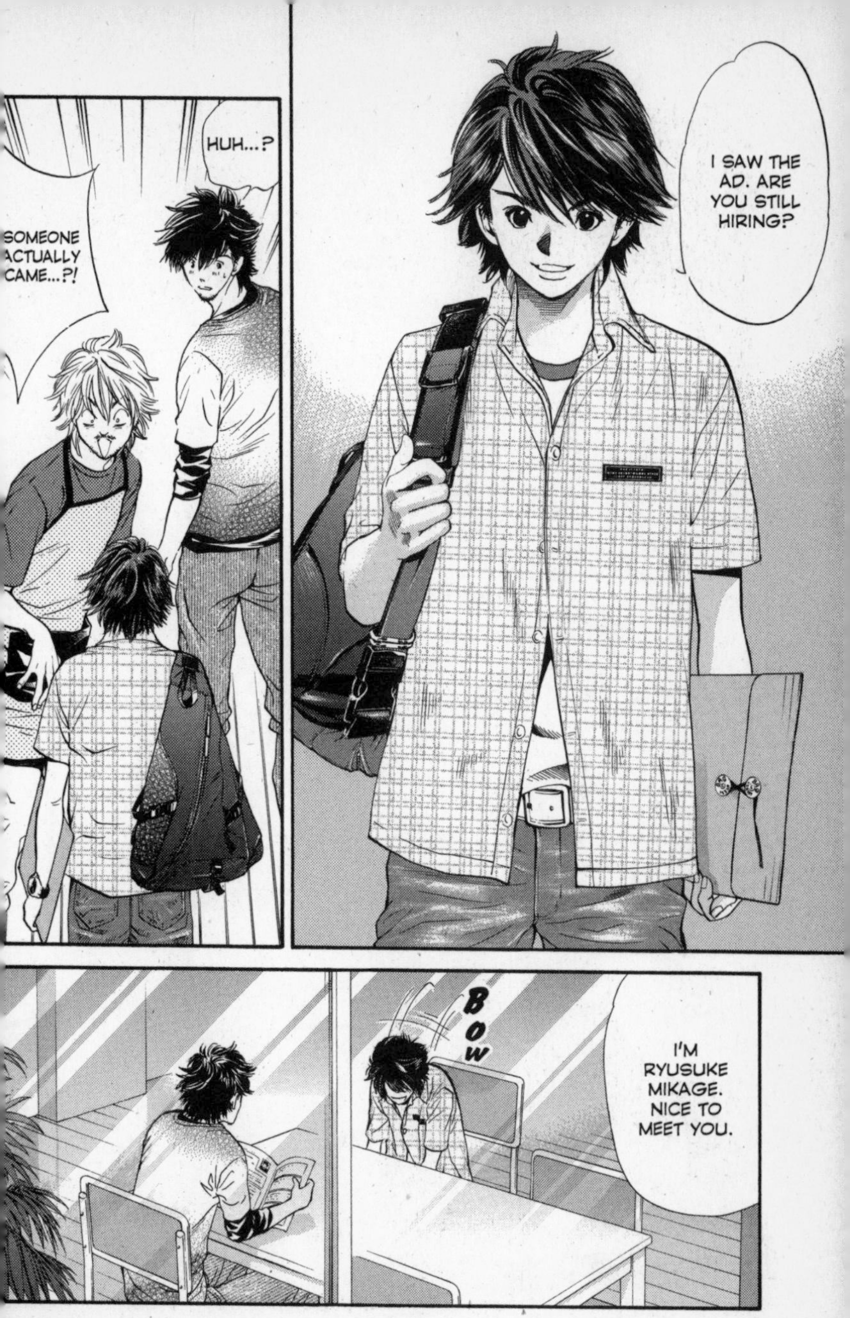
I SAW THE AD. ARE YOU STILL HIRING?
HUH...?
SOMEONE ACTUALLY CAME...?!
I'M RYUSUKE MIKAGE. NICE TO MEET YOU.
BOW

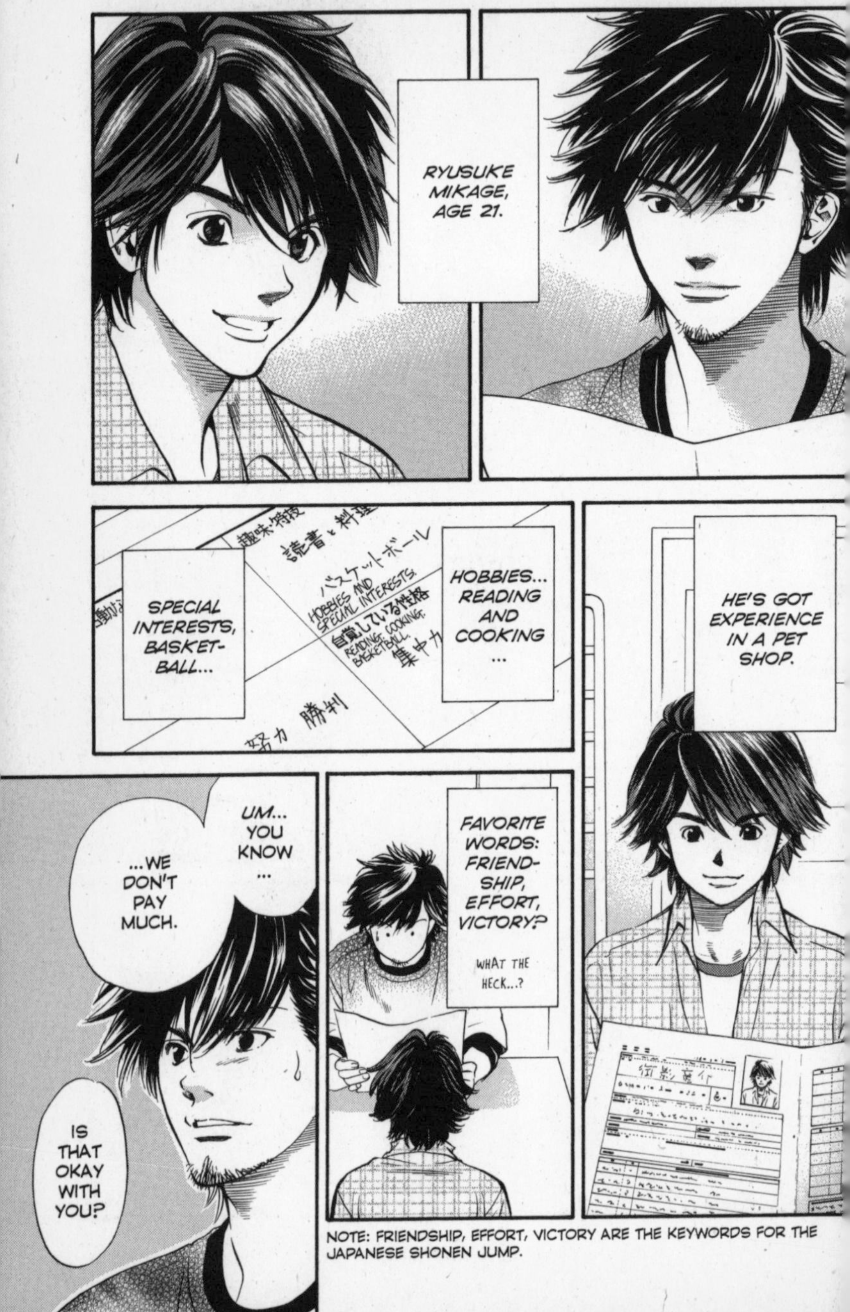
RYUSUKE MIKAGE, AGE 21.
HE'S GOT EXPERIENCE IN A PET SHOP.
HOBBIES... READING AND COOKING ...
趣味特技
読書と料理
バスケットボール
HOBBIES AND SPECIAL INTERESTS
自覚している性格
READING, COOKING, BASKETBALL.
集中力
努力 勝利
SPECIAL INTERESTS, BASKET-BALL...
FAVORITE WORDS: FRIEND-SHIP, EFFORT, VICTORY?
WHAT THE HECK...?
UM... YOU KNOW ...
...WE DON'T PAY MUCH.
IS THAT OKAY WITH YOU?

NOTE: FRIENDSHIP, EFFORT, VICTORY ARE THE KEYWORDS FOR THE JAPANESE SHONEN JUMP.

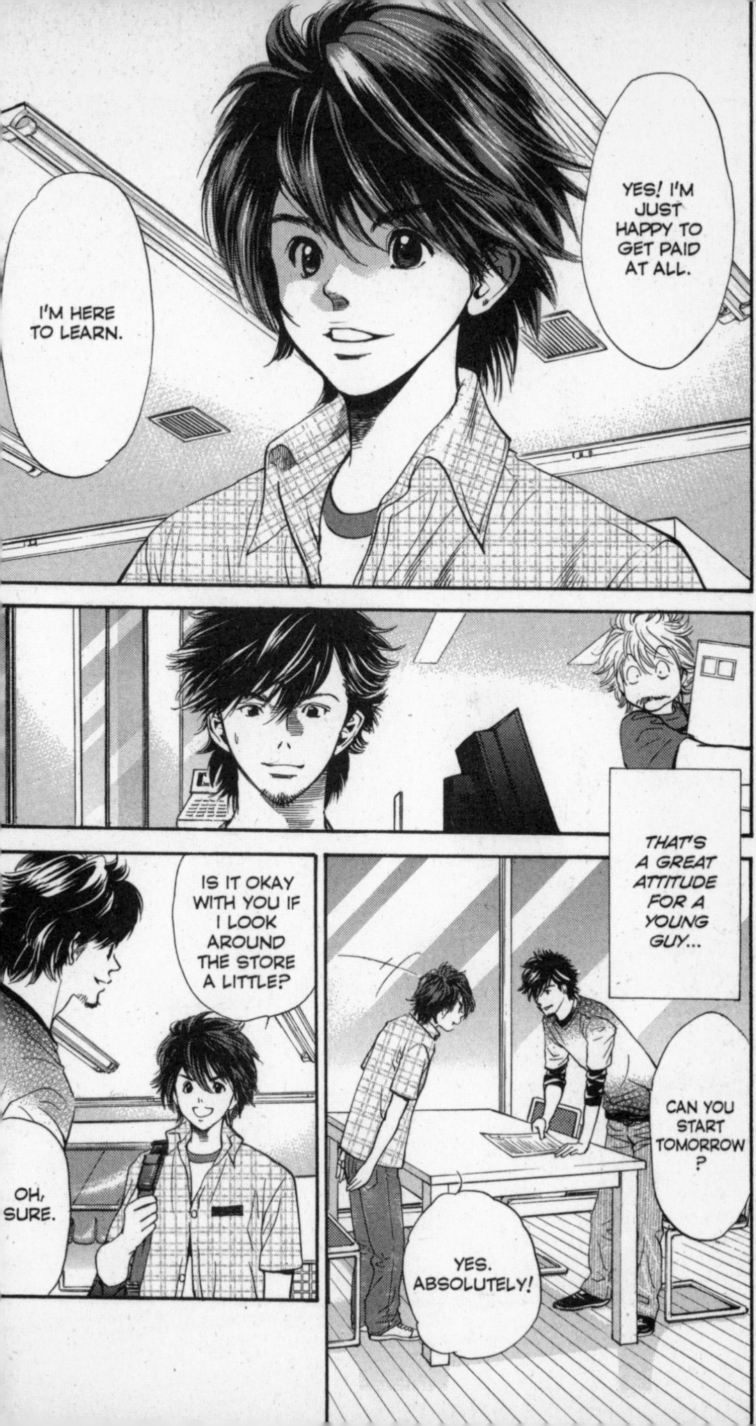
YES! I'M JUST HAPPY TO GET PAID AT ALL.
I'M HERE TO LEARN.
THAT'S A GREAT ATTITUDE FOR A YOUNG GUY...
CAN YOU START TOMORROW?
YES. ABSOLUTELY!
IS IT OKAY WITH YOU IF I LOOK AROUND THE STORE A LITTLE?
OH, SURE.

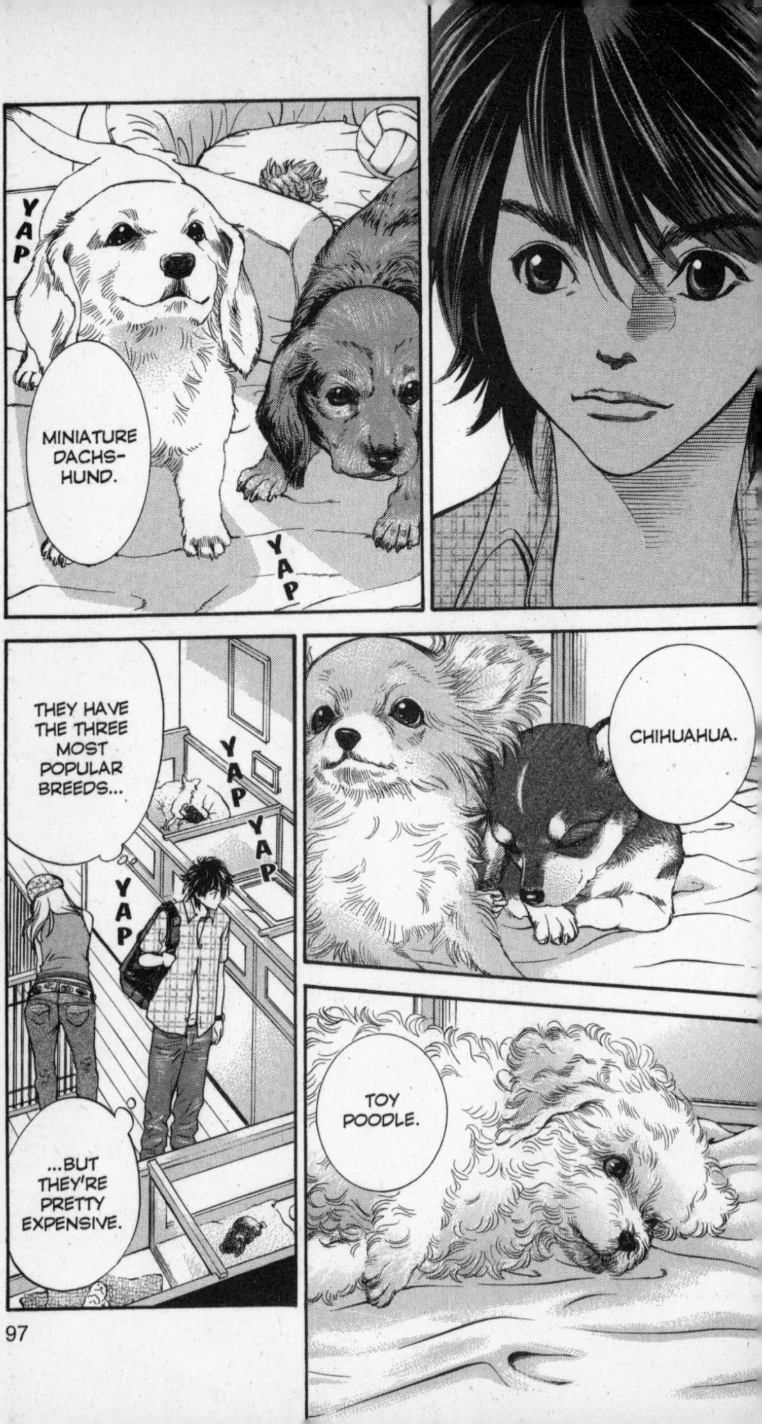
YAP
MINIATURE DACHS-HUND.
YAP
CHIHUAHUA.
TOY POODLE.
THEY HAVE THE THREE MOST POPULAR BREEDS...
YAP
YAP
YAP
YAP
...BUT THEY'RE PRETTY EXPENSIVE.

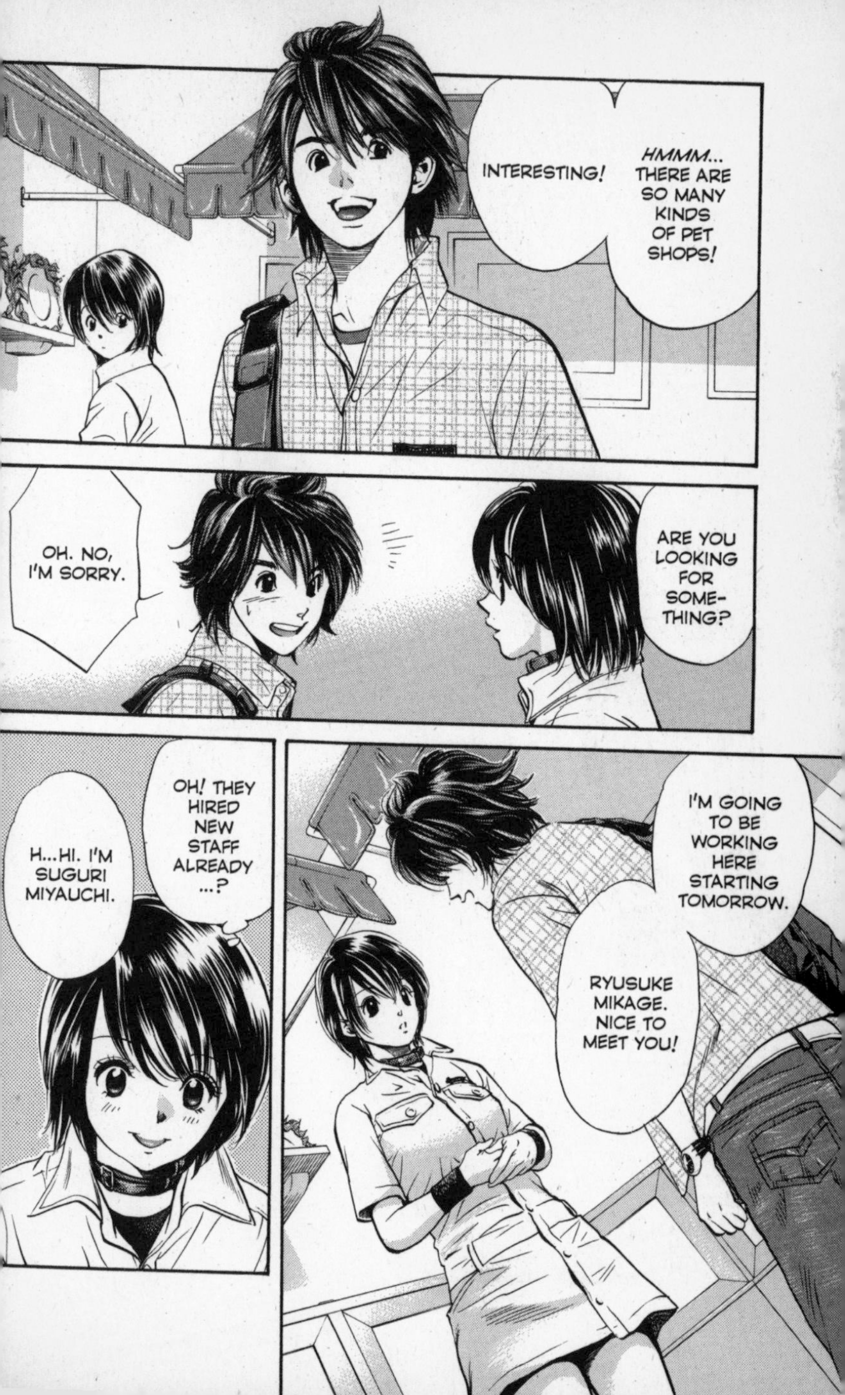
HMMM... THERE ARE SO MANY KINDS OF PET SHOPS!
INTERESTING!
ARE YOU LOOKING FOR SOME-THING?
OH. NO, I'M SORRY.
I'M GOING TO BE WORKING HERE STARTING TOMORROW.
RYUSUKE MIKAGE. NICE TO MEET YOU!
OH! THEY HIRED NEW STAFF ALREADY...?
H...HI. I'M SUGURI MIYAUCHI.

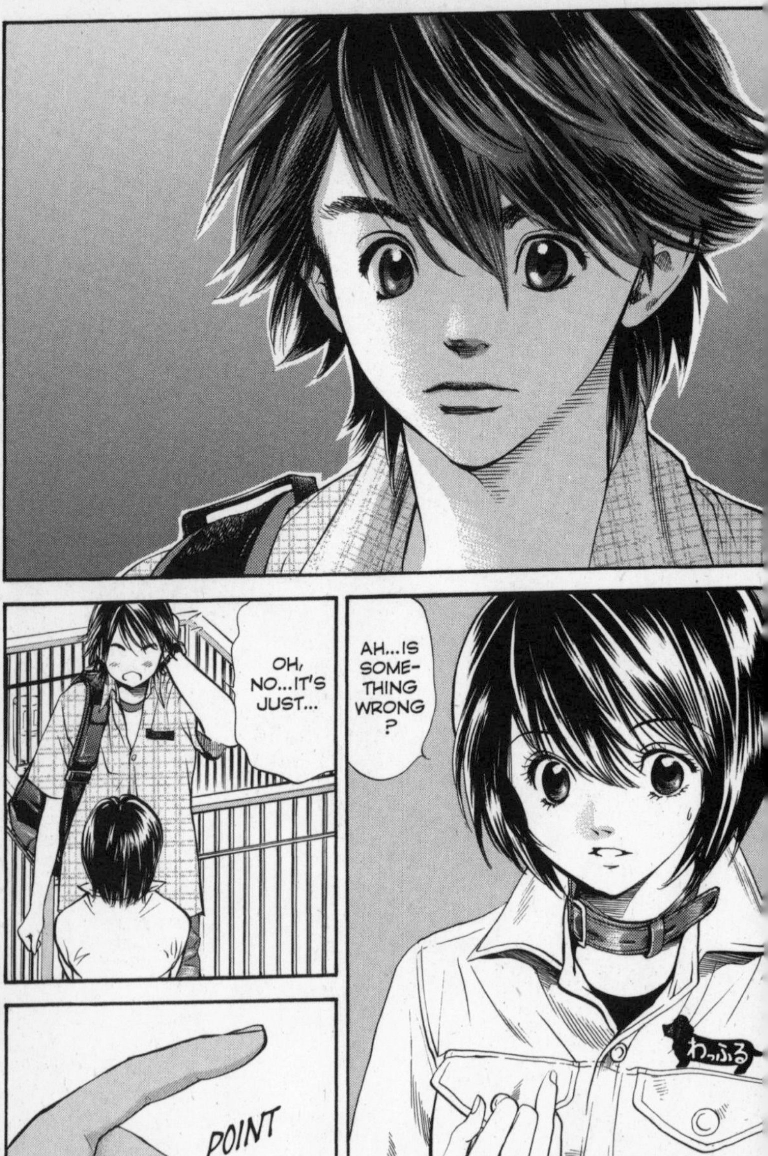
AH...IS SOME-THING WRONG?
わっふる
OH, NO...IT'S JUST...
POINT

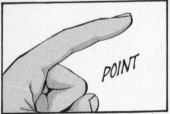

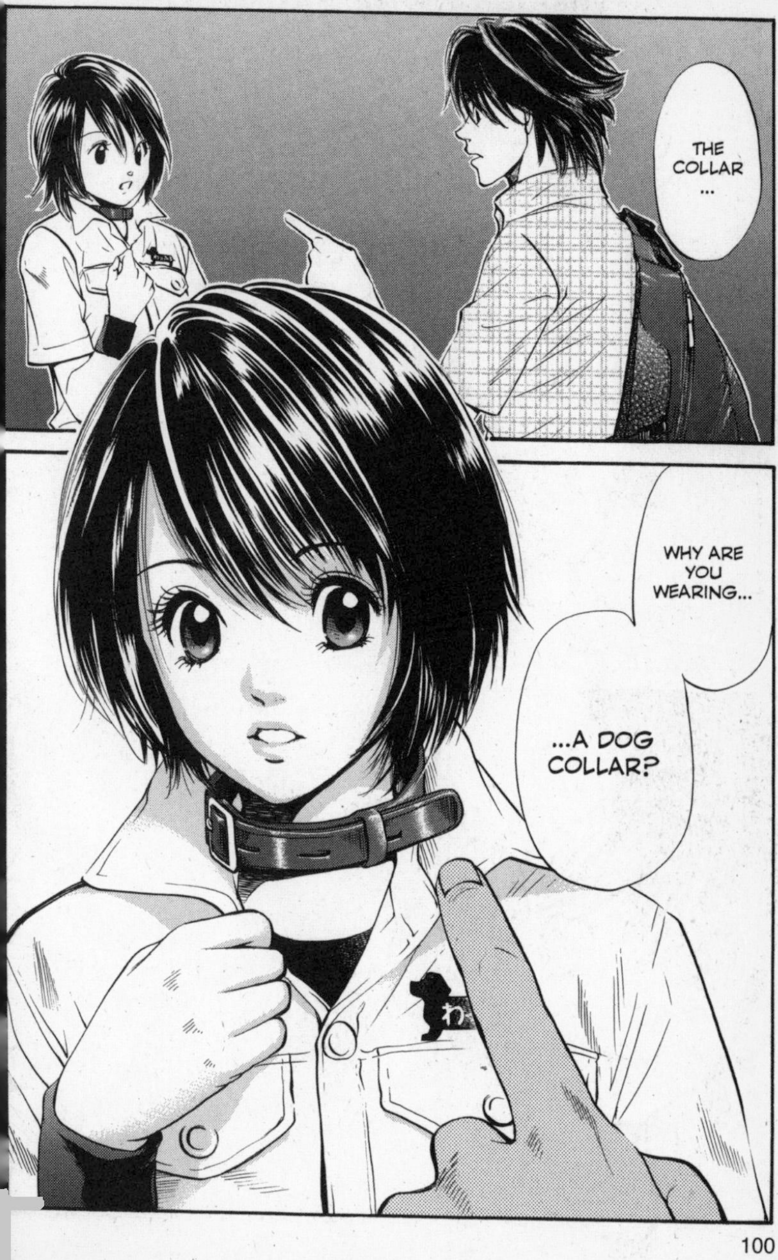
THE COLLAR ...
WHY ARE YOU WEARING...
...A DOG COLLAR?

CHAPTER 103: WIND OF SENIORITY

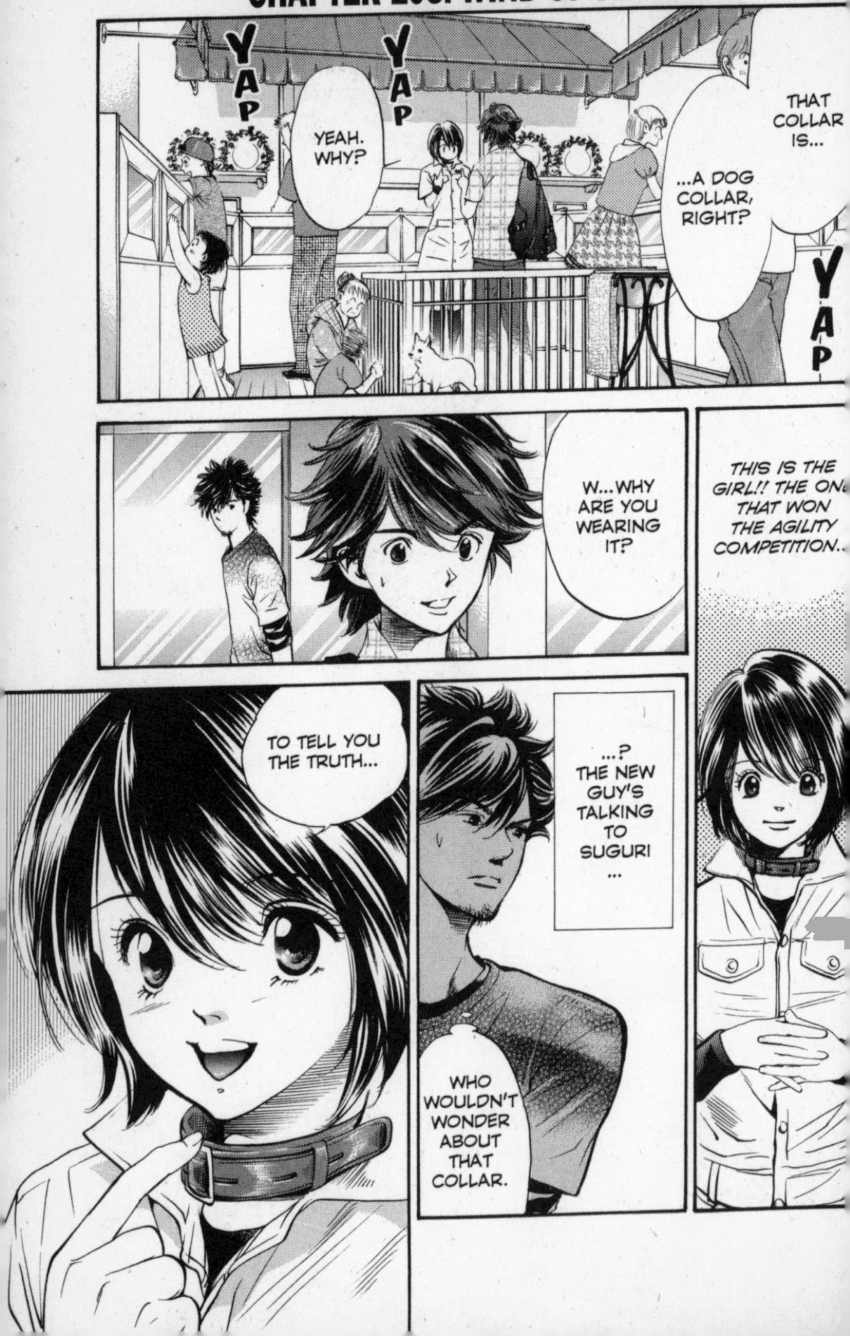
THAT COLLAR IS...
...A DOG COLLAR, RIGHT?
YAP
YAP
YEAH. WHY?
YAP
THIS IS THE GIRL!! THE ON
THAT WON THE AGILITY COMPETITION..
W...WHY ARE YOU WEARING IT?
...? THE NEW GUY'S TALKING TO SUGURI ...
WHO WOULDN'T WONDER ABOUT THAT COLLAR.
TO TELL YOU THE TRUTH...

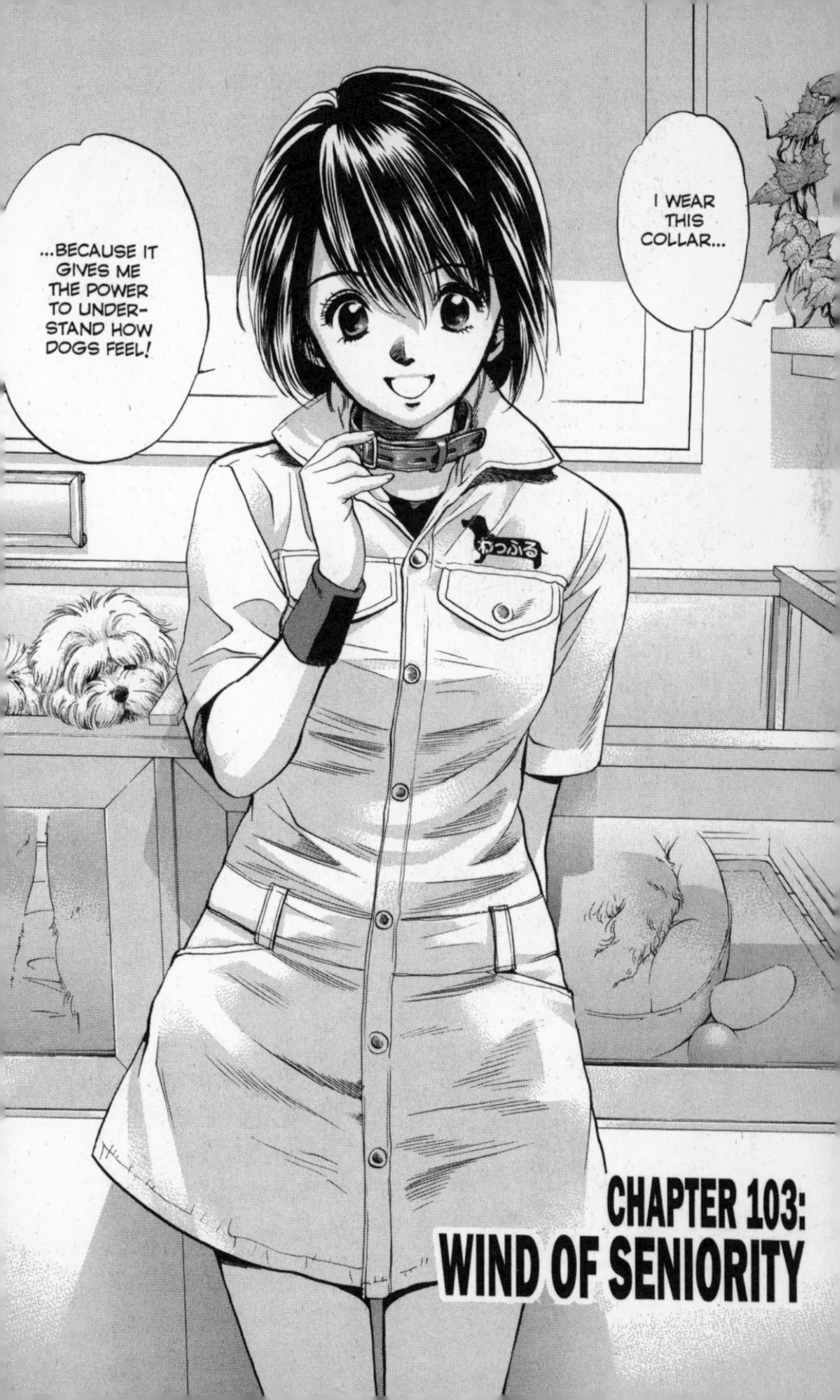
I WEAR THIS COLLAR...
...BECAUSE IT GIVES ME THE POWER TO UNDER-STAND HOW DOGS FEEL!
わっふる

CHAPTER 103: WIND OF SENIORITY

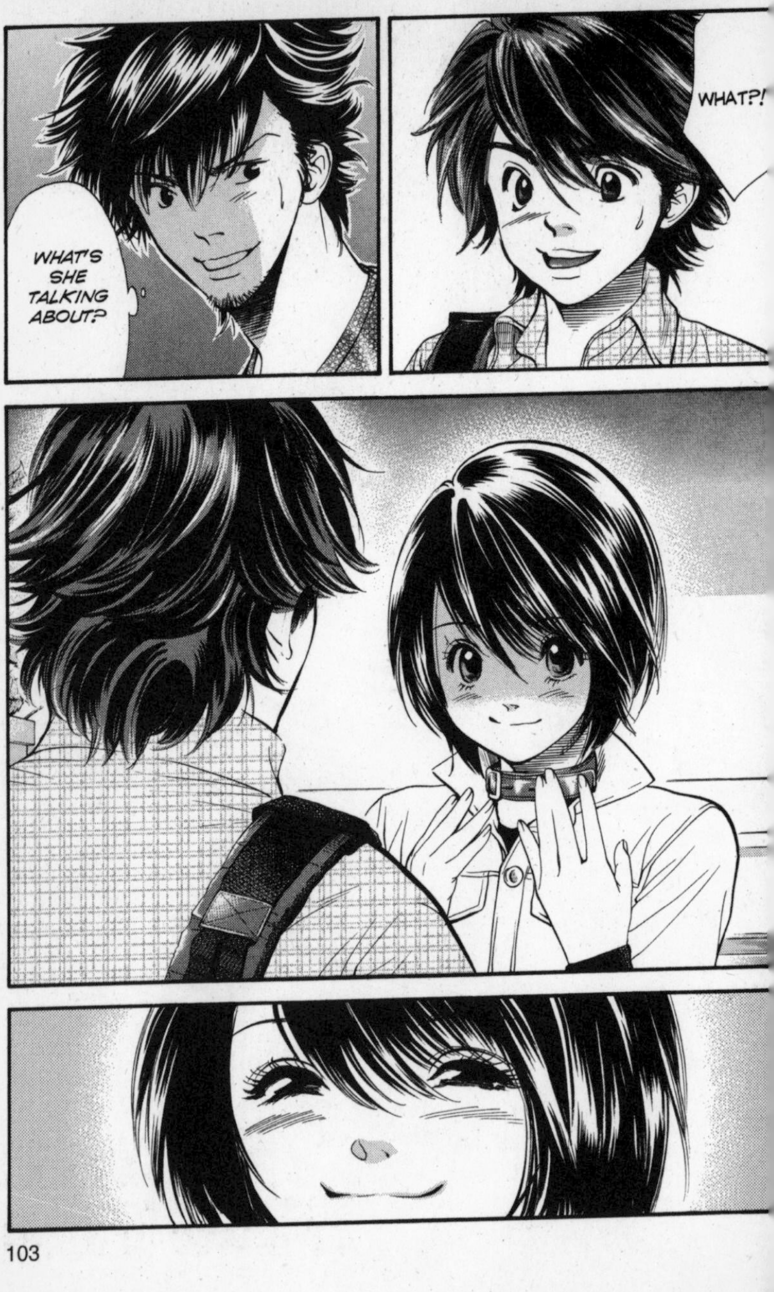
WHAT?!
WHAT'S SHE TALKING ABOUT?

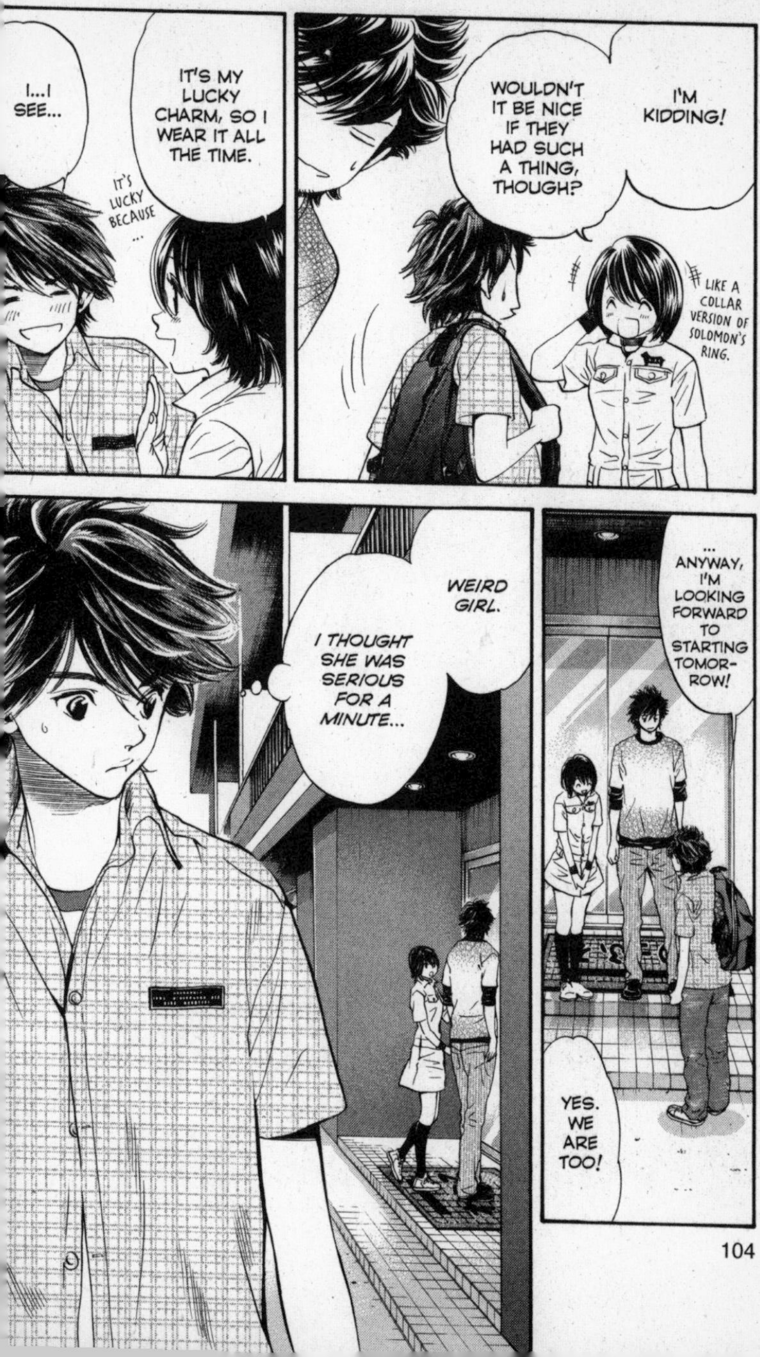
I'M KIDDING!
WOULDN'T IT BE NICE IF THEY HAD SUCH A THING, THOUGH?
LIKE A COLLAR VERSION OF SOLOMON'S RING.
IT'S MY LUCKY CHARM, SO I WEAR IT ALL THE TIME.
IT'S LUCKY BECAUSE ...
I...I SEE...
... ANYWAY, I'M LOOKING FORWARD TO STARTING TOMOR-ROW!
YES. WE ARE TOO!
WEIRD GIRL.
I THOUGHT SHE WAS SERIOUS FOR A MINUTE...

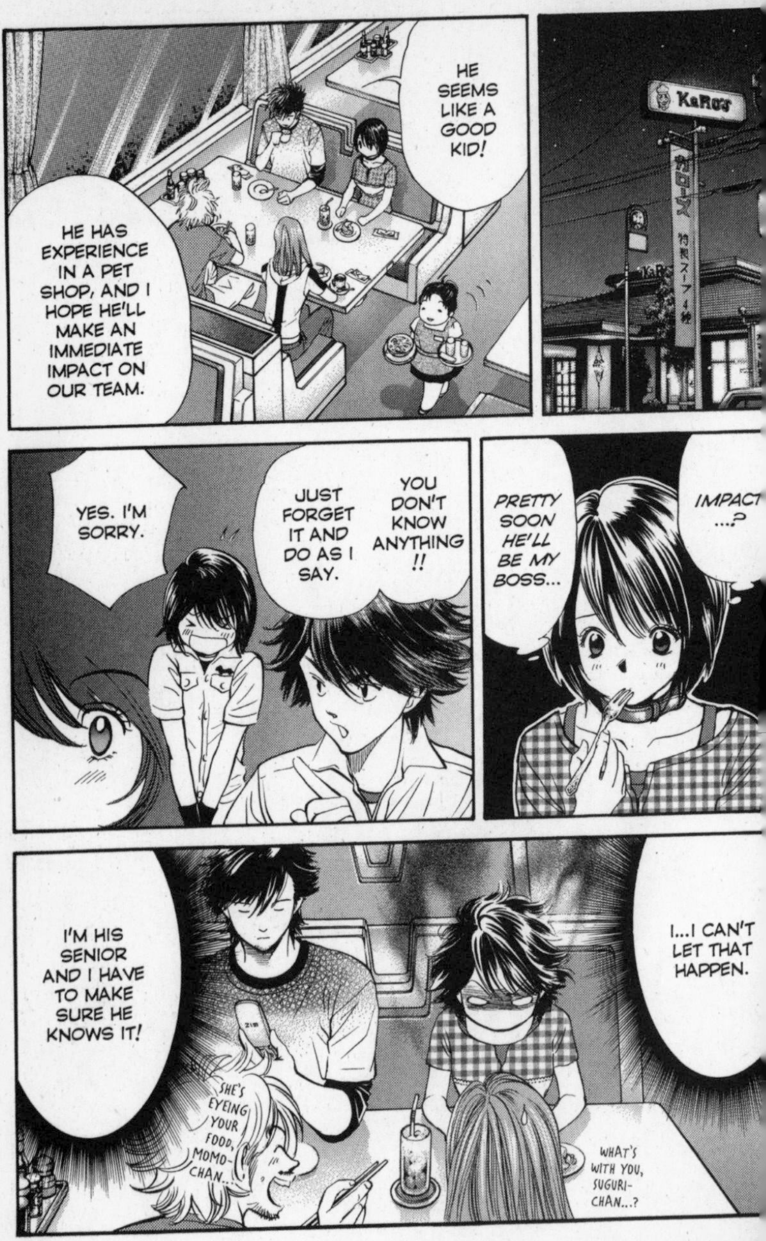
KaRO'S
HE SEEMS LIKE A GOOD KID!
HE HAS EXPERIENCE IN A PET SHOP, AND I HOPE HE'LL MAKE AN IMMEDIATE IMPACT ON OUR TEAM.
IMPACT ...?
PRETTY SOON HE'LL BE MY BOSS...
YOU DON'T KNOW ANYTHING !!
JUST FORGET IT AND DO AS I SAY.
YES. I'M SORRY.
I...I CAN'T LET THAT HAPPEN.
WHAT'S WITH YOU, SUGURI-CHAN...?
I'M HIS SENIOR AND I HAVE TO MAKE SURE HE KNOWS IT!
SHE'S EYEING YOUR FOOD, MOMO-CHAN...

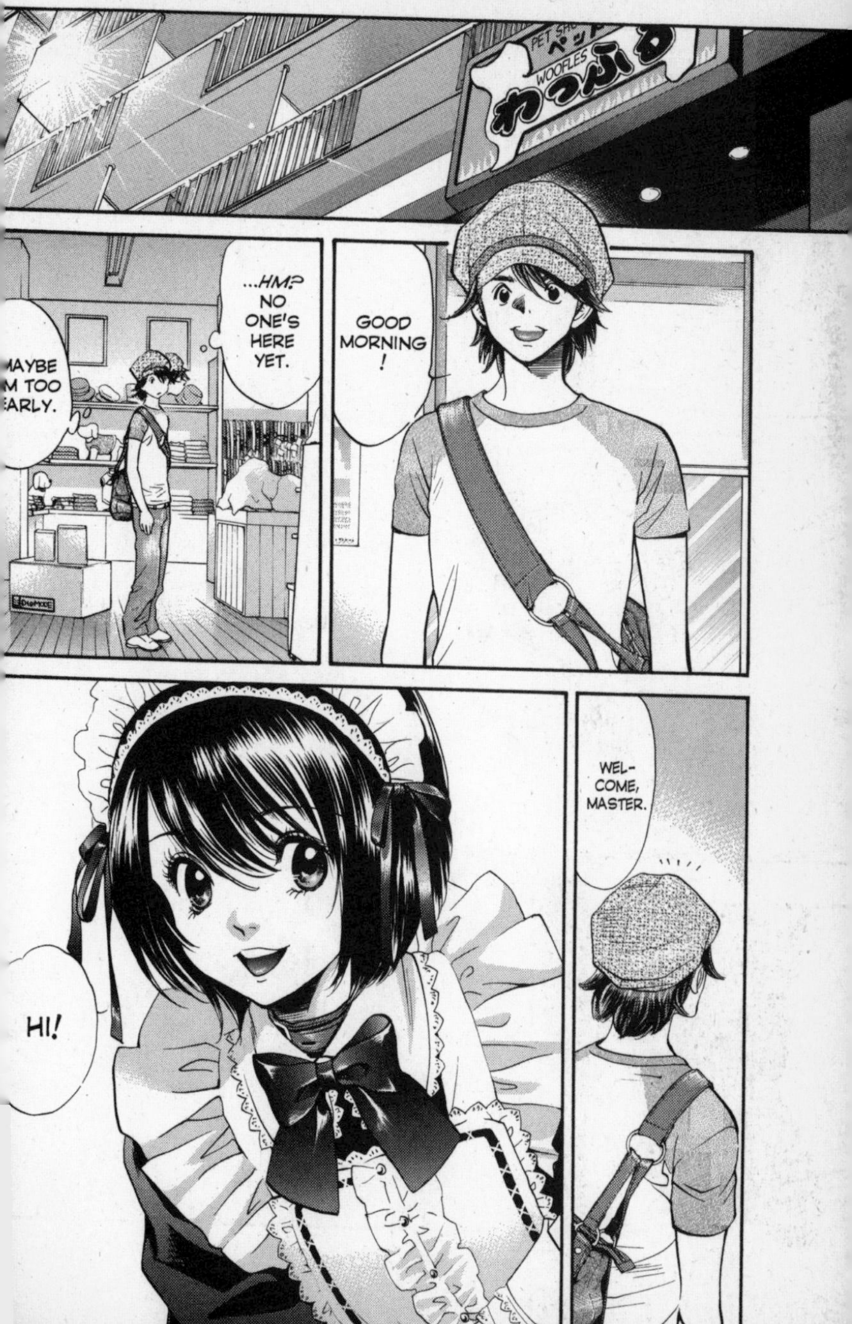
WOOFLES
GOOD MORNING!
...HM? NO ONE'S HERE YET.
MAYBE M TOO EARLY.
WEL-COME, MASTER.
HI!

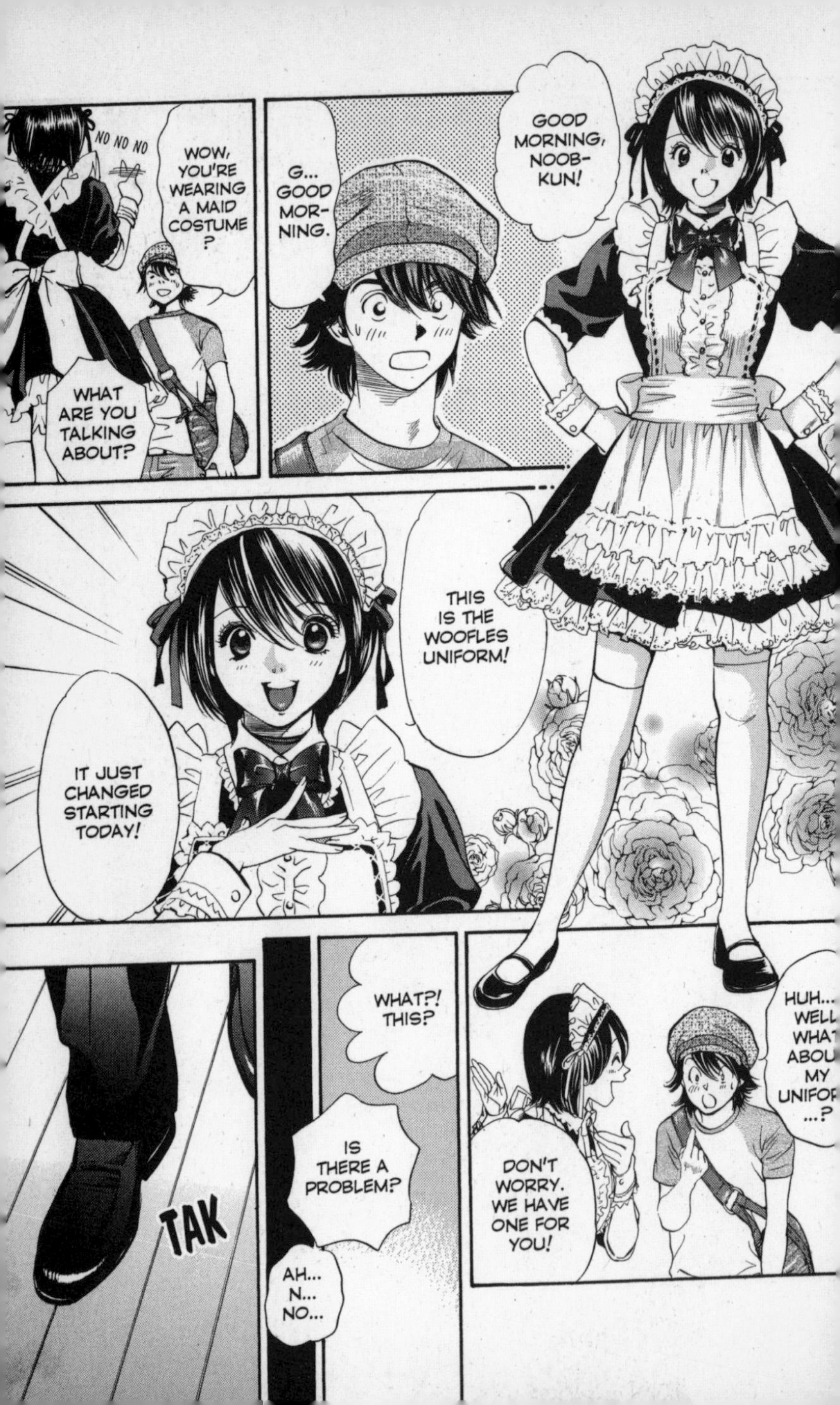
GOOD MORNING, NOOB-KUN!
G... GOOD MOR-NING.
WOW, YOU'RE WEARING A MAID COSTUME?
NO NO NO
WHAT ARE YOU TALKING ABOUT?
THIS IS THE WOOFLES UNIFORM!
IT JUST CHANGED STARTING TODAY!
HUH... WELL WHA ABOU MY UNIFO ...?
DON'T WORRY. WE HAVE ONE FOR YOU!
WHAT?! THIS?
IS THERE A PROBLEM?
AH... N... NO...
TAK

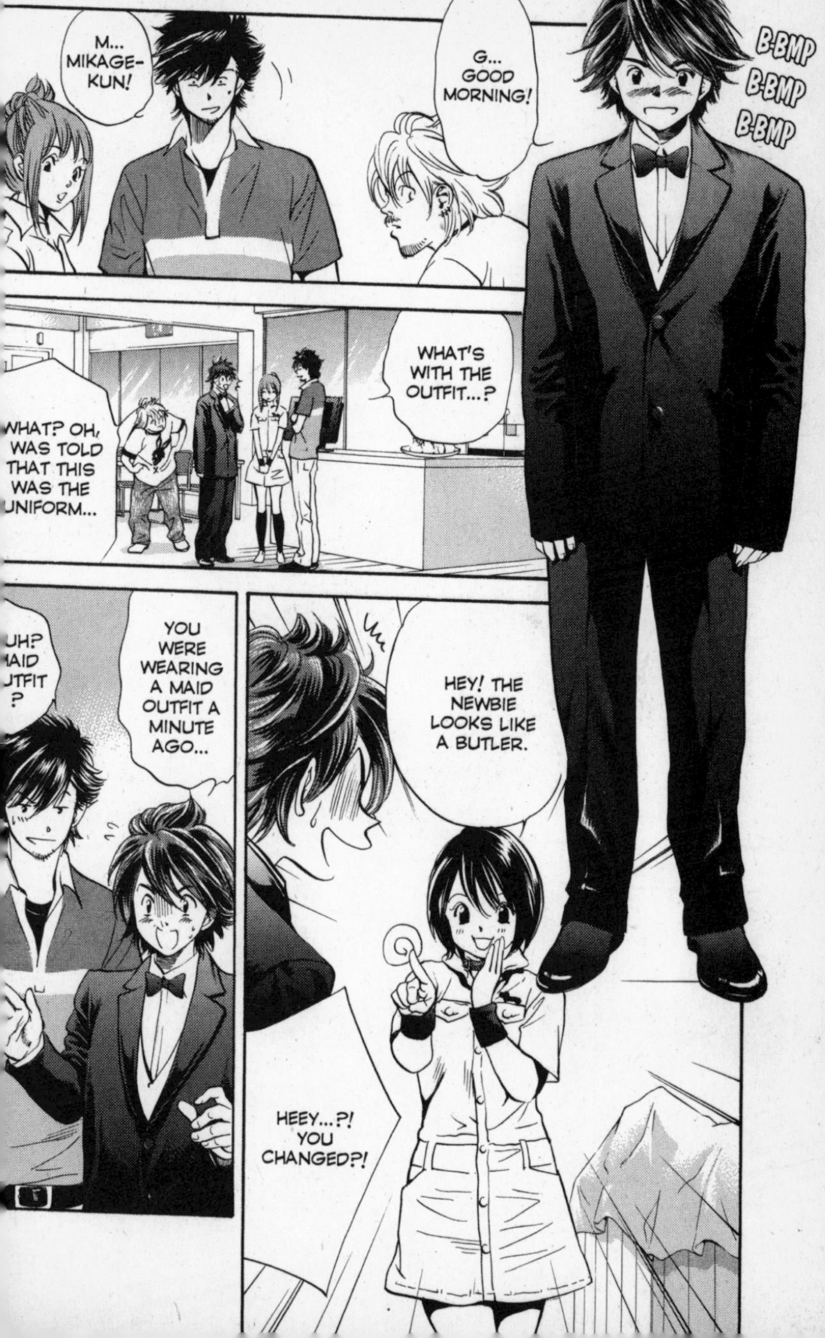
B-BMP
B-BMP
B-BMP
G... GOOD MORNING!
M... MIKAGE-KUN!
WHAT'S WITH THE OUTFIT...?
WHAT? OH, WAS TOLD THAT THIS WAS THE UNIFORM...
HEY! THE NEWBIE LOOKS LIKE A BUTLER.
HEEY...?! YOU CHANGED?!
YOU WERE WEARING A MAID OUTFIT A MINUTE AGO...
UH? AID UTFIT ?

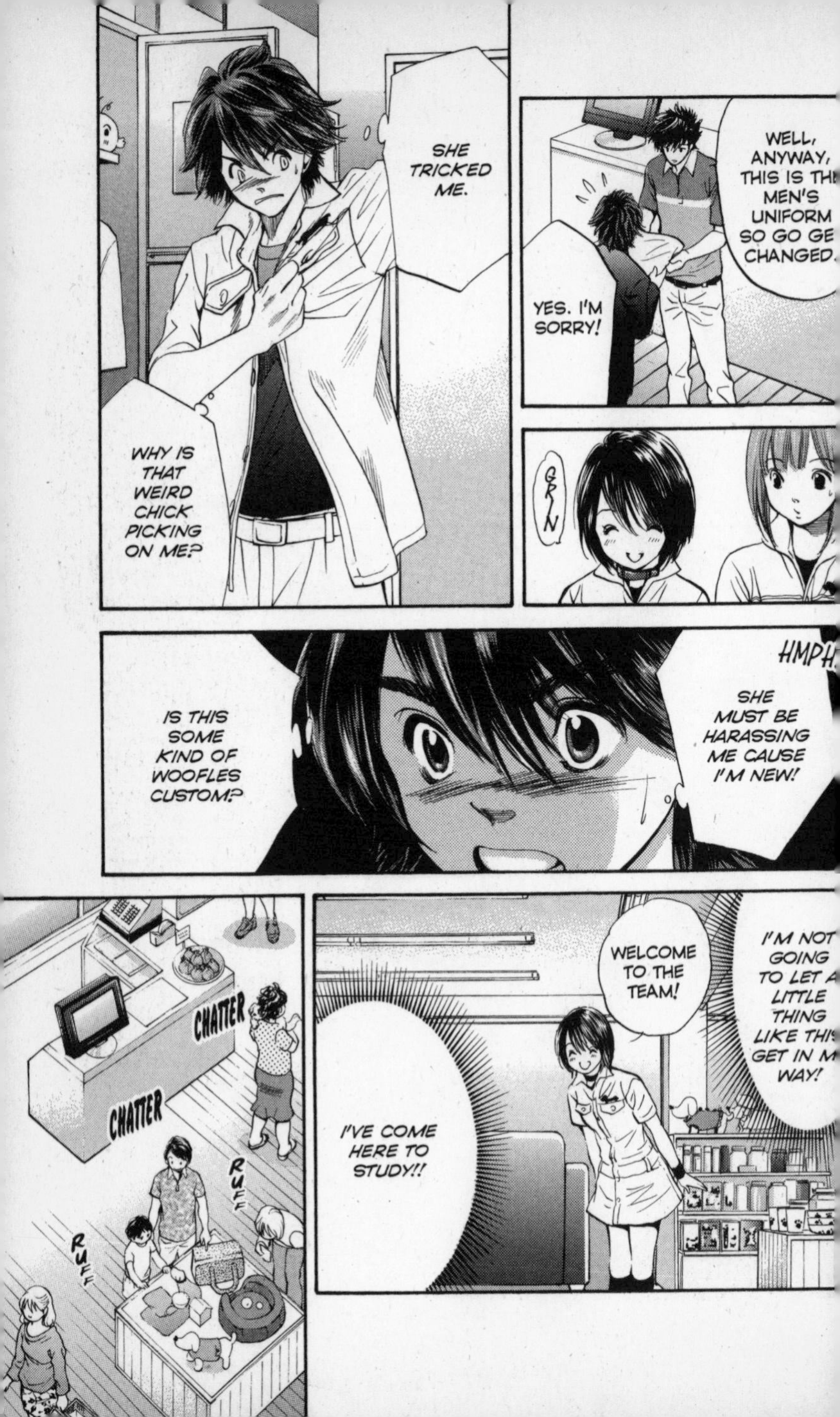
WELL, ANYWAY, THIS IS TH MEN'S UNIFORM SO GO GE CHANGED.
YES. I'M SORRY!
GRIN
SHE TRICKED ME.
WHY IS THAT WEIRD CHICK PICKING ON ME?
HMPH
SHE MUST BE HARASSING ME CAUSE I'M NEW!
IS THIS SOME KIND OF WOOFLES CUSTOM?
I'M NOT GOING TO LET A LITTLE THING LIKE THIS GET IN M WAY!
WELCOME TO THE TEAM!
I'VE COME HERE TO STUDY!!
CHATTER
CHATTER
RUFF
RUFF

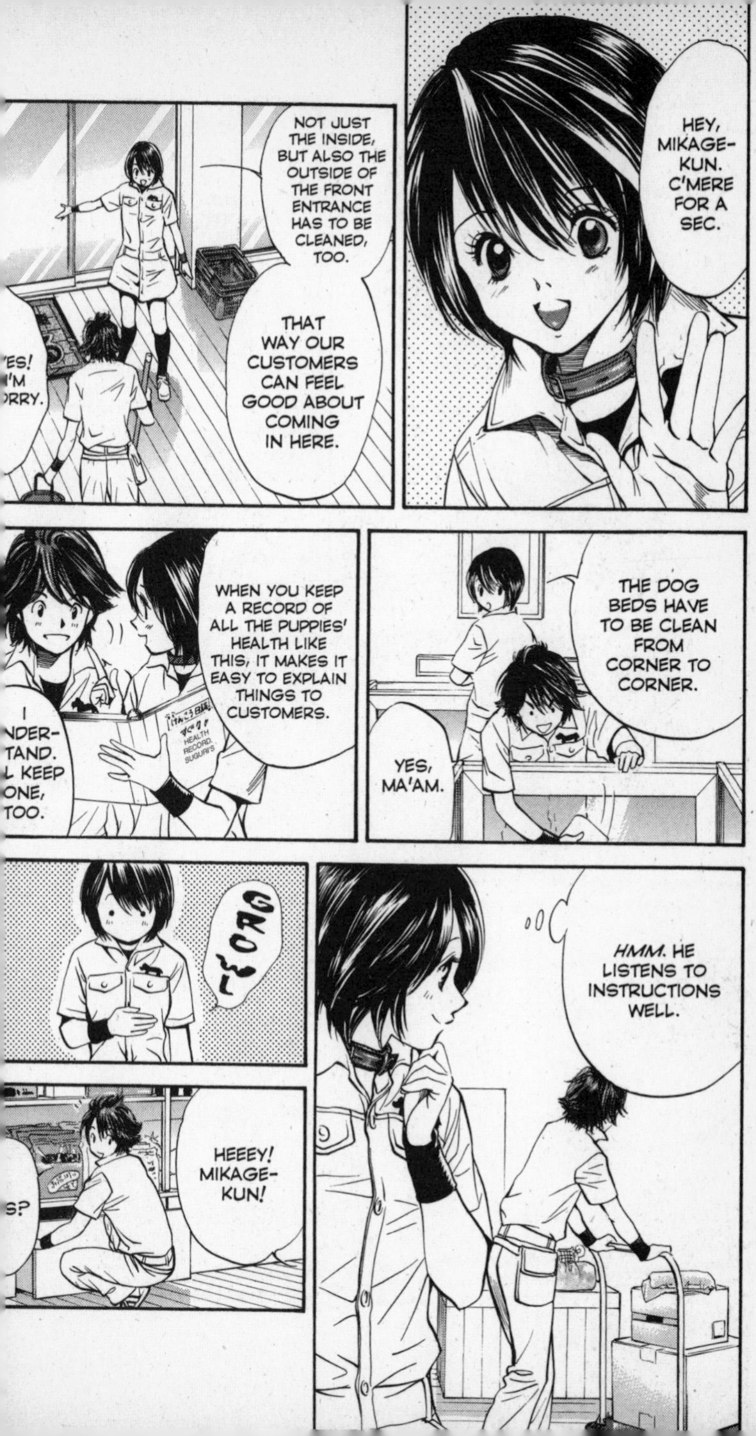
HEY, MIKAGE-KUN. C'MERE FOR A SEC.
NOT JUST THE INSIDE, BUT ALSO THE OUTSIDE OF THE FRONT ENTRANCE HAS TO BE CLEANED, TOO.
THAT WAY OUR CUSTOMERS CAN FEEL GOOD ABOUT COMING IN HERE.
THE DOG BEDS HAVE TO BE CLEAN FROM CORNER TO CORNER.
YES, MA'AM.
WHEN YOU KEEP A RECORD OF ALL THE PUPPIES' HEALTH LIKE THIS, IT MAKES IT EASY TO EXPLAIN THINGS TO CUSTOMERS.
HEALTH RECORD: SUGURI'S
HMM. HE LISTENS TO INSTRUCTIONS WELL.
GROWL
HEEEY! MIKAGE-KUN!

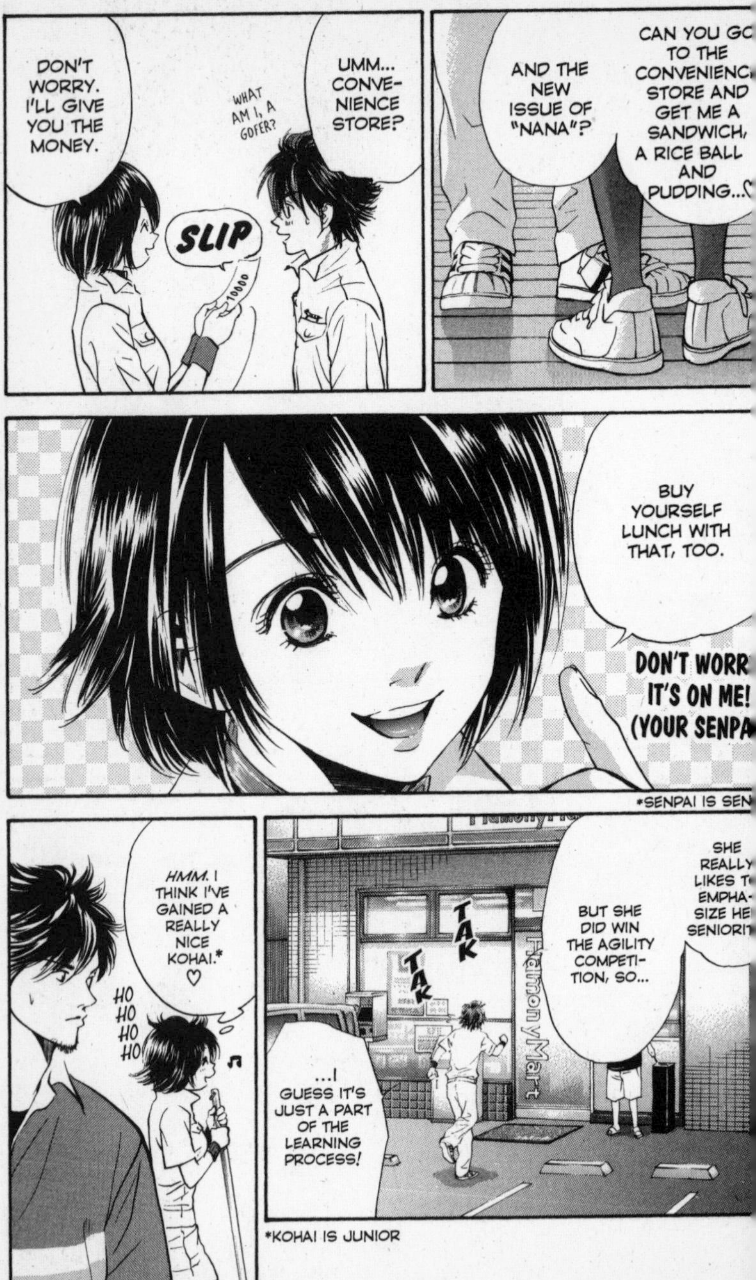
CAN YOU GO TO THE CONVENIENC STORE AND GET ME A SANDWICH, A RICE BALL AND PUDDING...
AND THE NEW ISSUE OF "NANA"?
UMM... CONVE-NIENCE STORE?
WHAT AM I, A GOFER?
SLIP
10000
DON'T WORRY. I'LL GIVE YOU THE MONEY.
BUY YOURSELF LUNCH WITH THAT, TOO.
DON'T WORR IT'S ON ME! (YOUR SENPA
SHE REALLY LIKES T EMPHA-SIZE HE SENIORIT
BUT SHE DID WIN THE AGILITY COMPETI-TION, SO...
TAK
TAK
...I GUESS IT'S JUST A PART OF THE LEARNING PROCESS!
HMM. I THINK I'VE GAINED A REALLY NICE KOHAI.* ♡
HO HO HO HO

*SENPAI IS SEN

*KOHAI IS JUNIOR

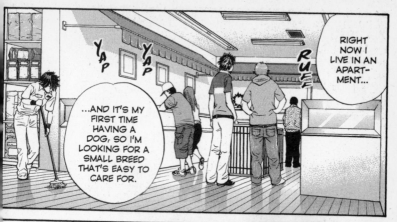

YAP YAP RUFF

RIGHT NOW I LIVE IN AN APARTMENT...

...AND IT'S MY FIRST TIME HAVING A DOG, SO I'M LOOKING FOR A SMALL BREED THAT'S EASY TO CARE FOR.

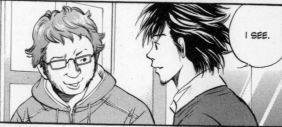

BUT THE DACHSHUNDS AND CHIHUAHUAS SO POPULAR NOWADAYS ARE BORING TO ME SO...

I SEE.

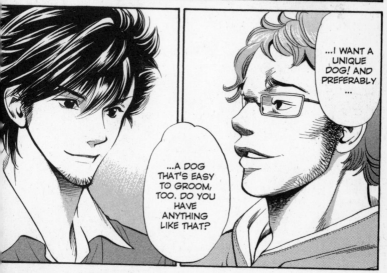

...I WANT A UNIQUE DOG! AND PREFERABLY...

...A DOG THAT'S EASY TO GROOM, TOO. DO YOU HAVE ANYTHING LIKE THAT?

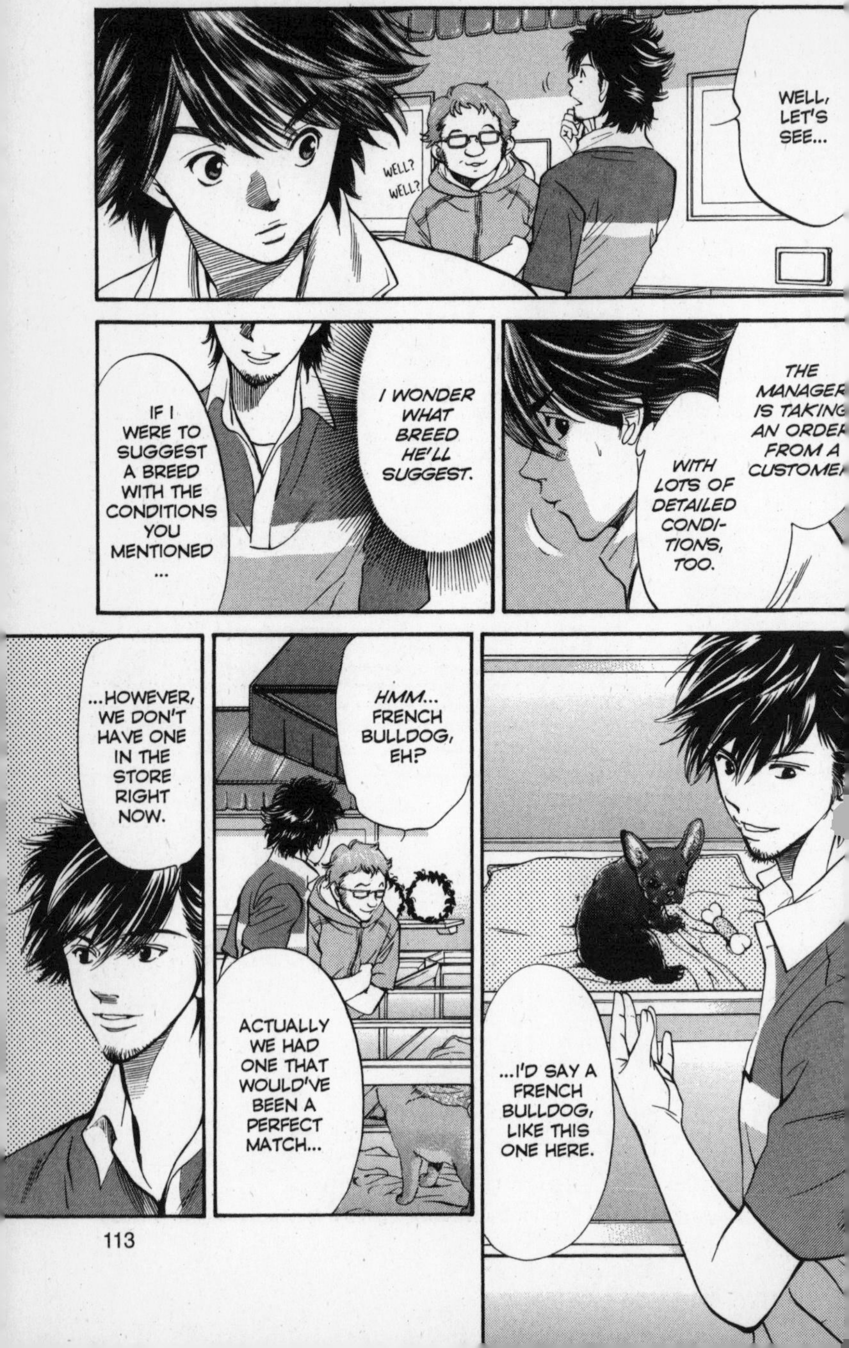
WELL, LET'S SEE...
WELL? WELL?
THE MANAGER IS TAKING AN ORDER FROM A CUSTOMER
WITH LOTS OF DETAILED CONDITIONS, TOO.
I WONDER WHAT BREED HE'LL SUGGEST.
IF I WERE TO SUGGEST A BREED WITH THE CONDITIONS YOU MENTIONED ...
...I'D SAY A FRENCH BULLDOG, LIKE THIS ONE HERE.
HMM... FRENCH BULLDOG, EH?
ACTUALLY WE HAD ONE THAT WOULD'VE BEEN A PERFECT MATCH...
...HOWEVER, WE DON'T HAVE ONE IN THE STORE RIGHT NOW.

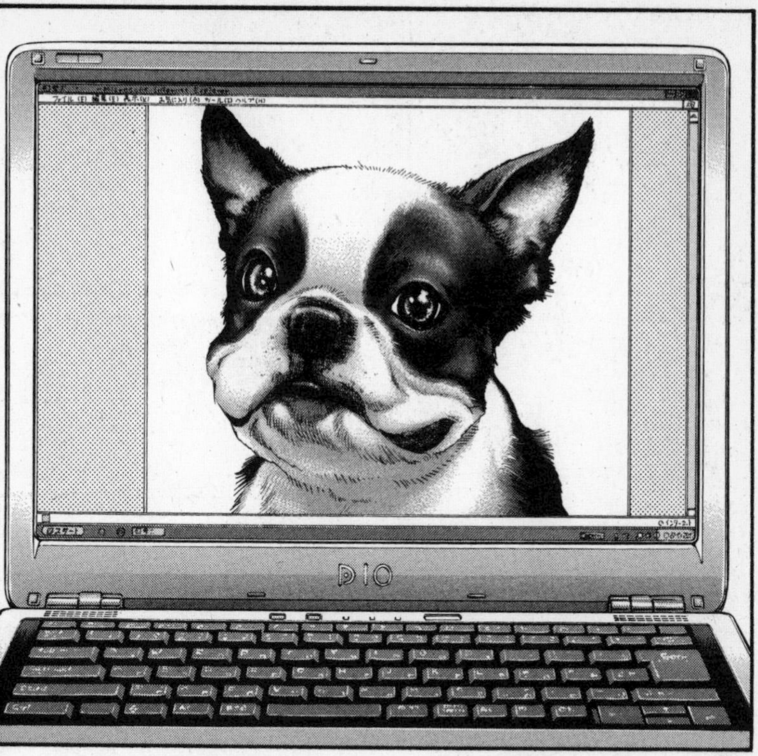
DIO

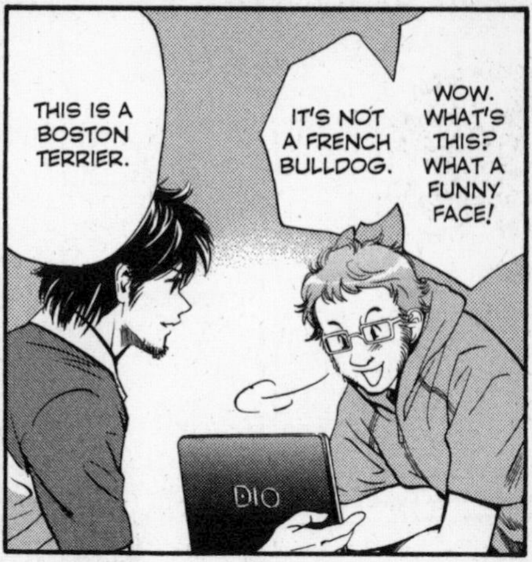
WOW. WHAT'S THIS? WHAT A FUNNY FACE!
IT'S NOT A FRENCH BULLDOG.
THIS IS A BOSTON TERRIER.
DIO

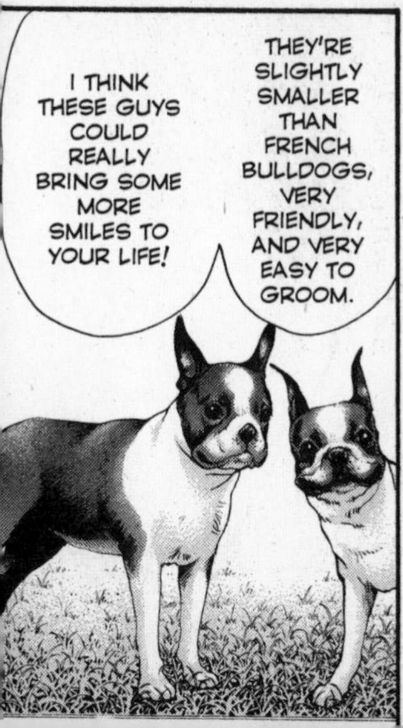
THEY'RE SLIGHTLY SMALLER THAN FRENCH BULLDOGS, VERY FRIENDLY, AND VERY EASY TO GROOM.
I THINK THESE GUYS COULD REALLY BRING SOME MORE SMILES TO YOUR LIFE!

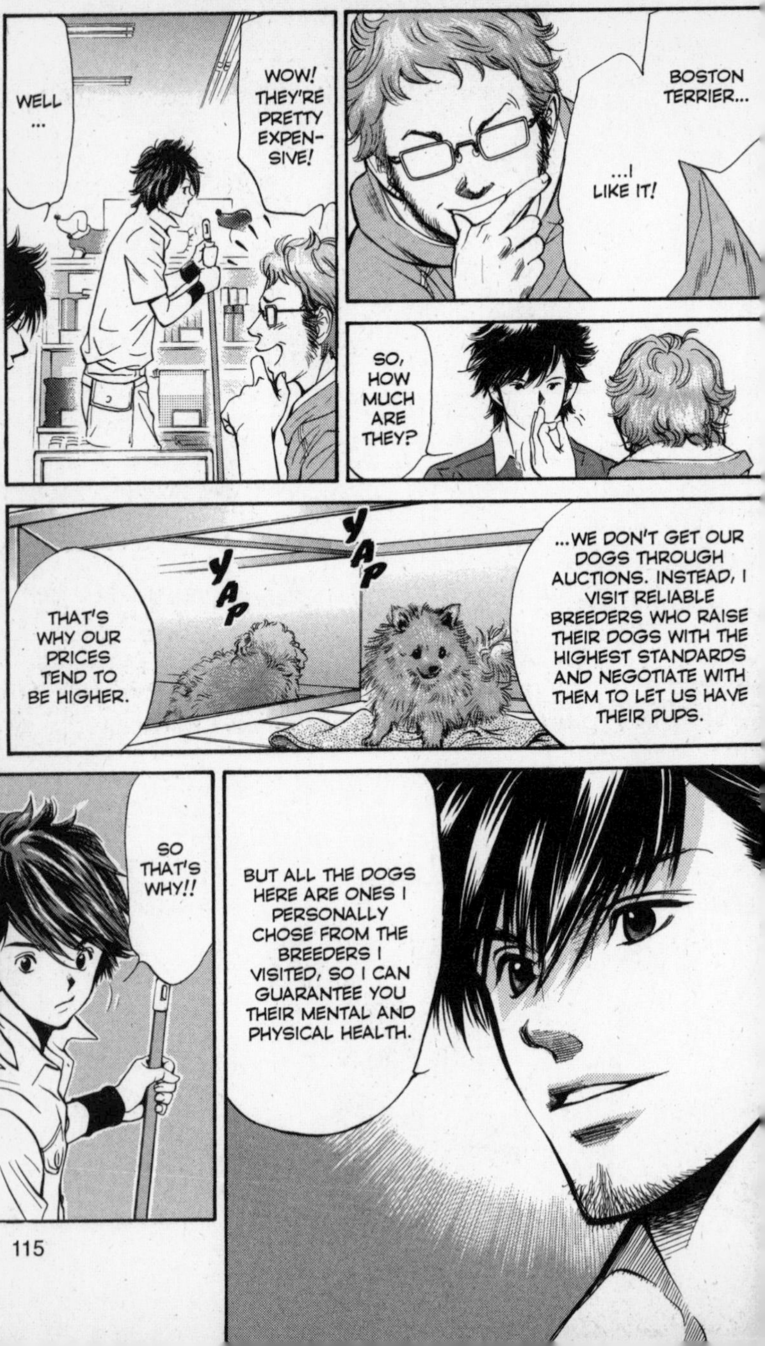
BOSTON TERRIER...
...I LIKE IT!
SO, HOW MUCH ARE THEY?
WOW! THEY'RE PRETTY EXPENSIVE!
WELL ...
...WE DON'T GET OUR DOGS THROUGH AUCTIONS. INSTEAD, I VISIT RELIABLE BREEDERS WHO RAISE THEIR DOGS WITH THE HIGHEST STANDARDS AND NEGOTIATE WITH THEM TO LET US HAVE THEIR PUPS.
YAP
YAP
THAT'S WHY OUR PRICES TEND TO BE HIGHER.
BUT ALL THE DOGS HERE ARE ONES I PERSONALLY CHOSE FROM THE BREEDERS I VISITED, SO I CAN GUARANTEE YOU THEIR MENTAL AND PHYSICAL HEALTH.
SO THAT'S WHY!!

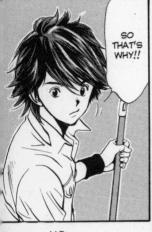

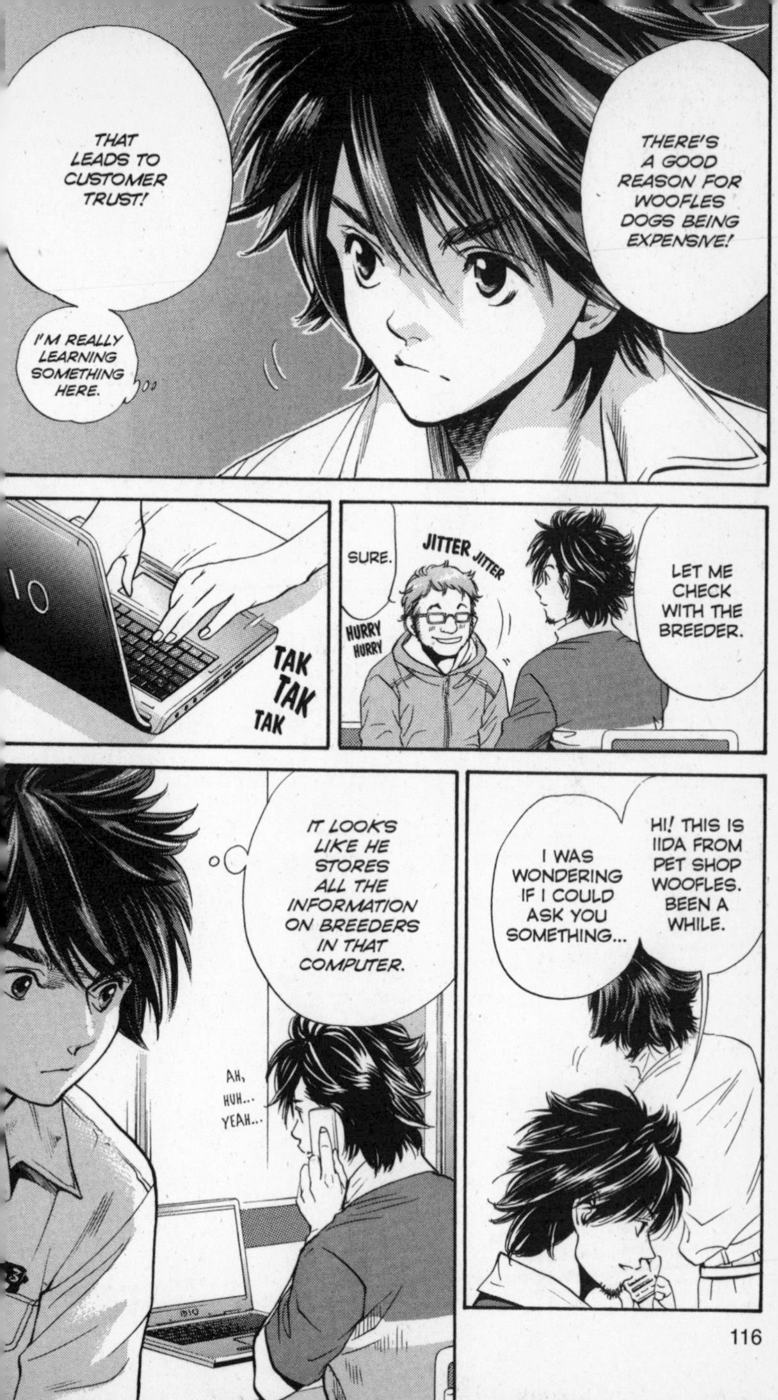
THERE'S A GOOD REASON FOR WOOFLES DOGS BEING EXPENSIVE!
THAT LEADS TO CUSTOMER TRUST!
I'M REALLY LEARNING SOMETHING HERE.
LET ME CHECK WITH THE BREEDER.
JITTER JITTER
SURE.
HURRY HURRY
TAK TAK TAK
HI! THIS IS IIDA FROM PET SHOP WOOFLES. BEEN A WHILE.
I WAS WONDERING IF I COULD ASK YOU SOMETHING...
IT LOOKS LIKE HE STORES ALL THE INFORMATION ON BREEDERS IN THAT COMPUTER.
AH, HUH... YEAH...

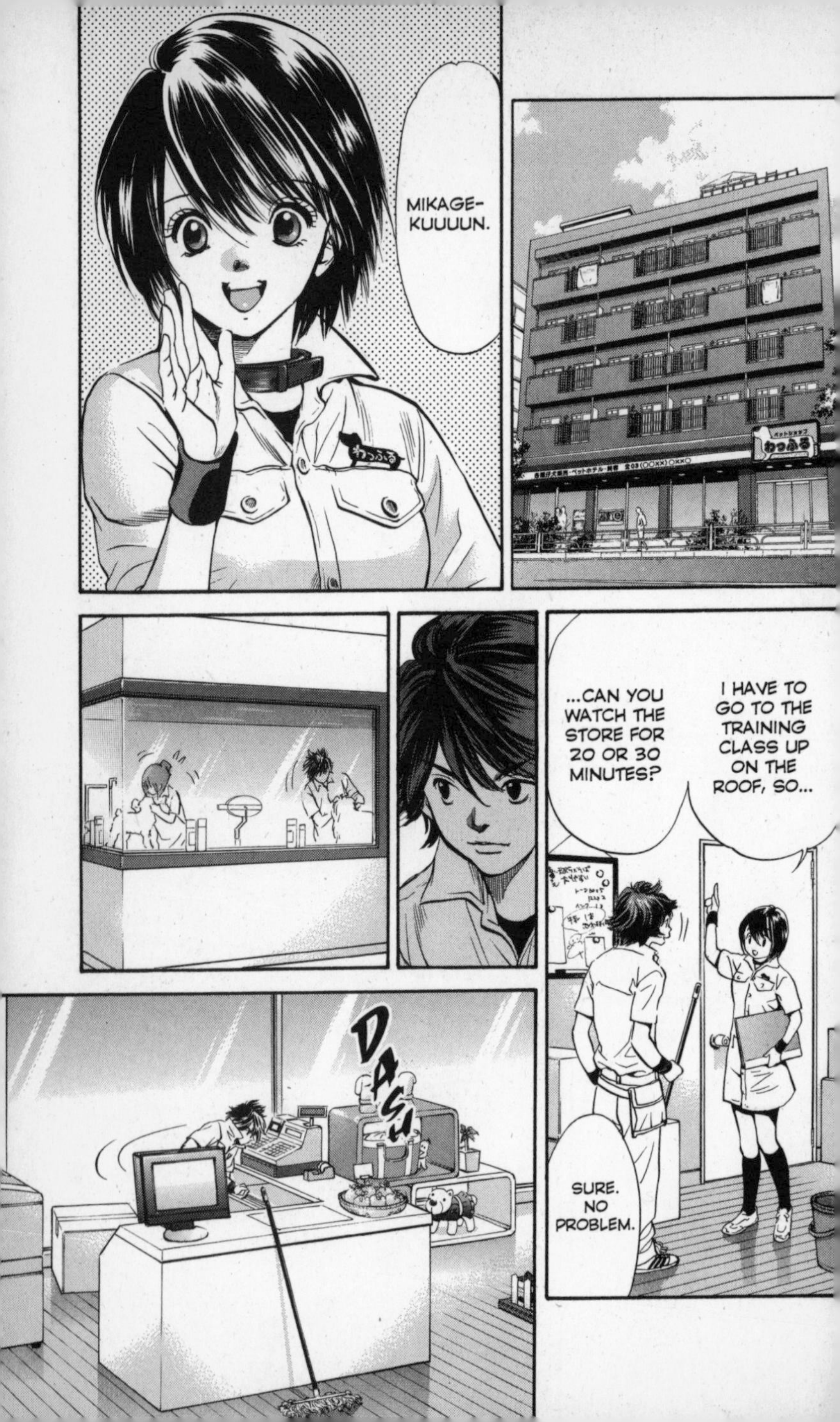
MIKAGE-KUUUUN.
I HAVE TO GO TO THE TRAINING CLASS UP ON THE ROOF, SO...
...CAN YOU WATCH THE STORE FOR 20 OR 30 MINUTES?
SURE. NO PROBLEM.
DASH

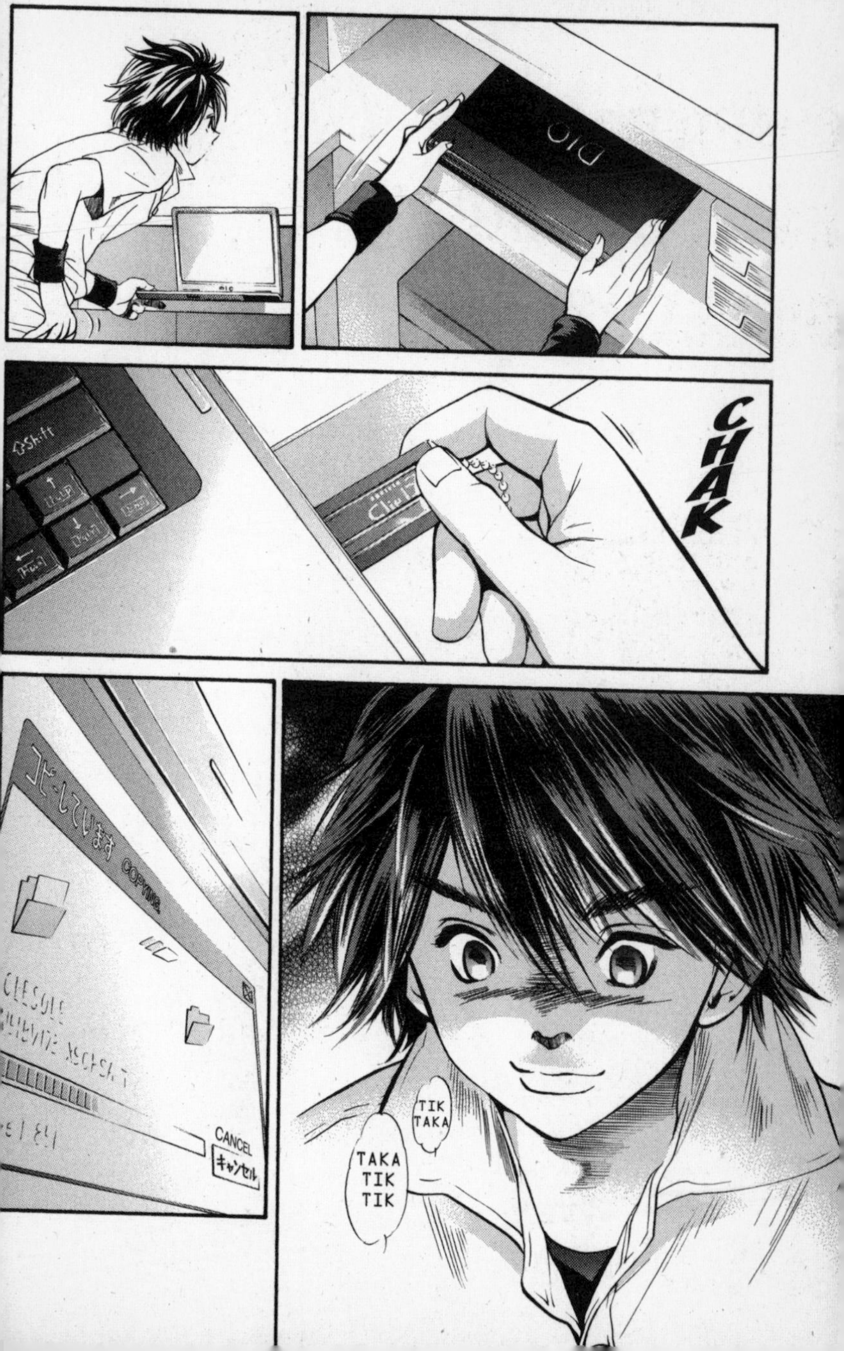
CHAK
TIK TAKA
TAKA TIK TIK
コピーしています
CANCEL
キャンセル

CHAPTER 104: INDESCRIBABLE SMELL...?!

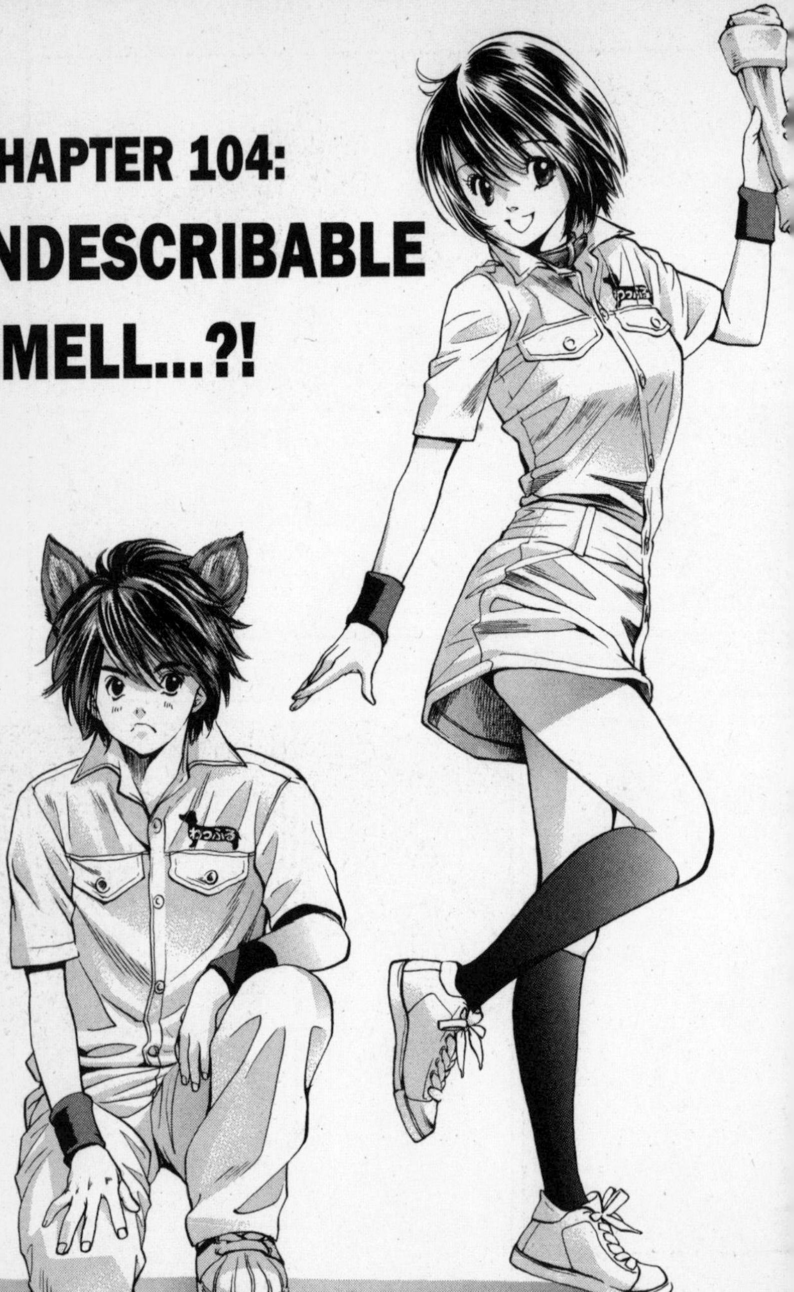

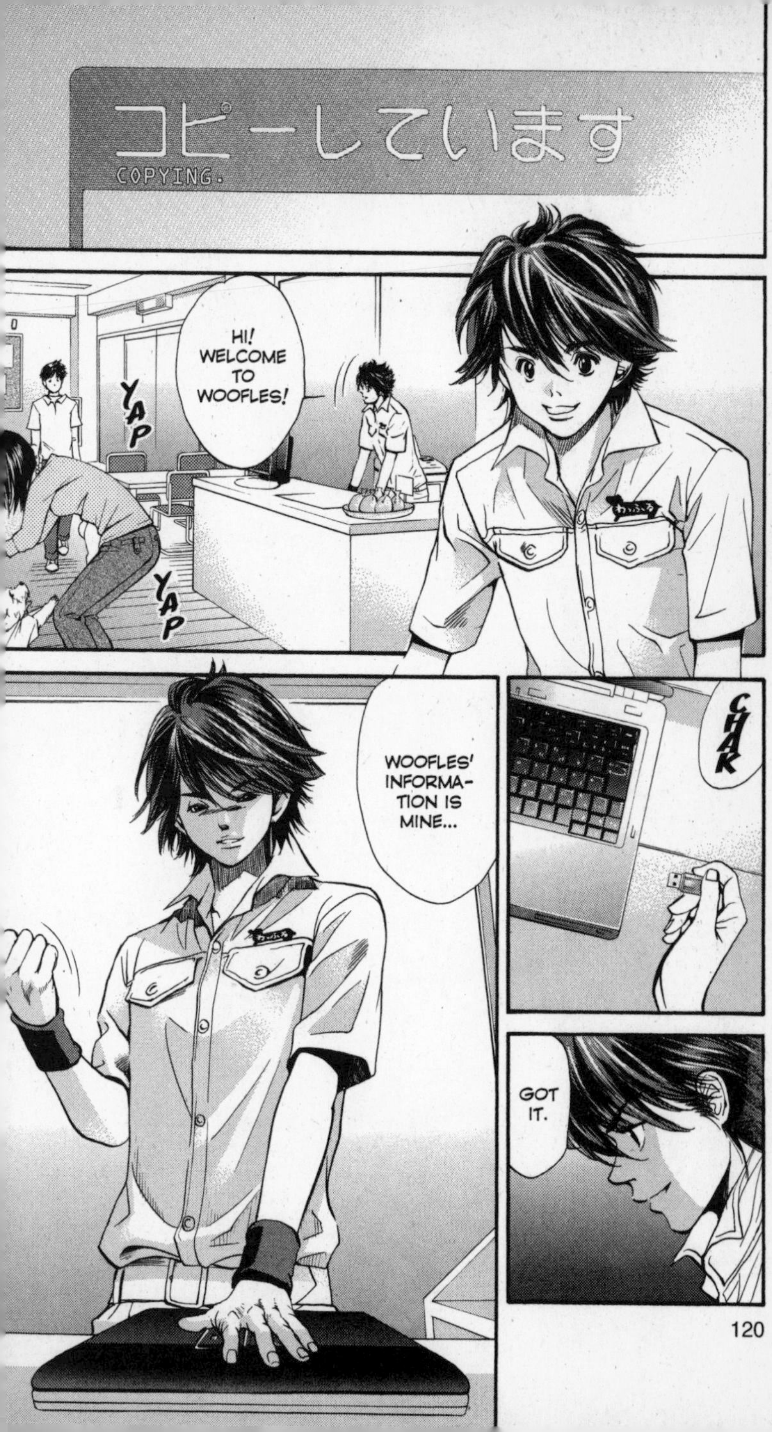
コピーしています
COPYING.
HI! WELCOME TO WOOFLES!
YAP
YAP
CHAK
GOT IT.
WOOFLES' INFORMATION IS MINE...

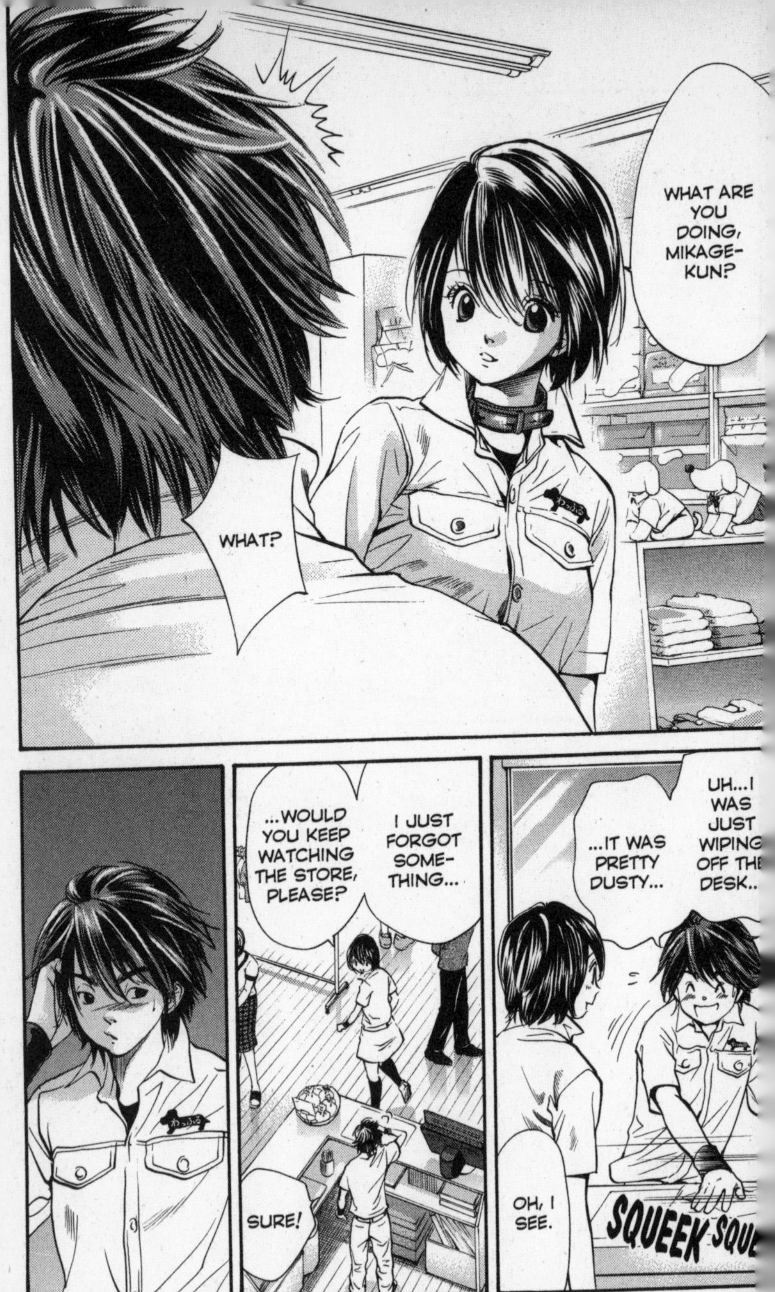
WHAT ARE YOU DOING, MIKAGE-KUN?
WHAT?
UH...I WAS JUST WIPING OFF THE DESK..
...IT WAS PRETTY DUSTY...
OH, I SEE.
SQUEEK SQUE
I JUST FORGOT SOME-THING...
...WOULD YOU KEEP WATCHING THE STORE, PLEASE?
SURE!

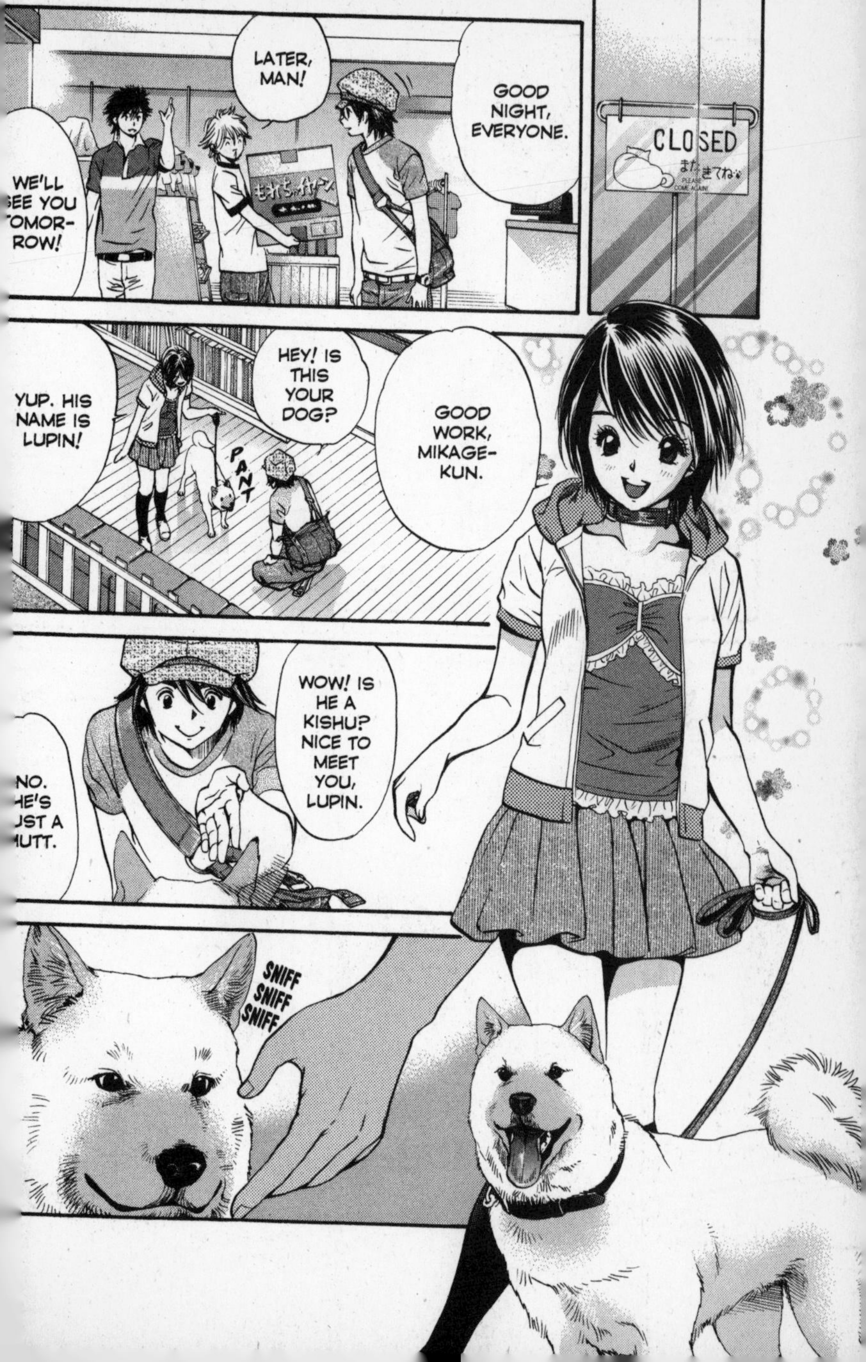
CLOSED
またきてね
PLEASE COME AGAIN
GOOD NIGHT, EVERYONE.
LATER, MAN!
WE'LL SEE YOU TOMOR-ROW!
GOOD WORK, MIKAGE-KUN.
HEY! IS THIS YOUR DOG?
YUP. HIS NAME IS LUPIN!
PANT
WOW! IS HE A KISHU? NICE TO MEET YOU, LUPIN.
NO. HE'S JUST A MUTT.
SNIFF SNIFF SNIFF

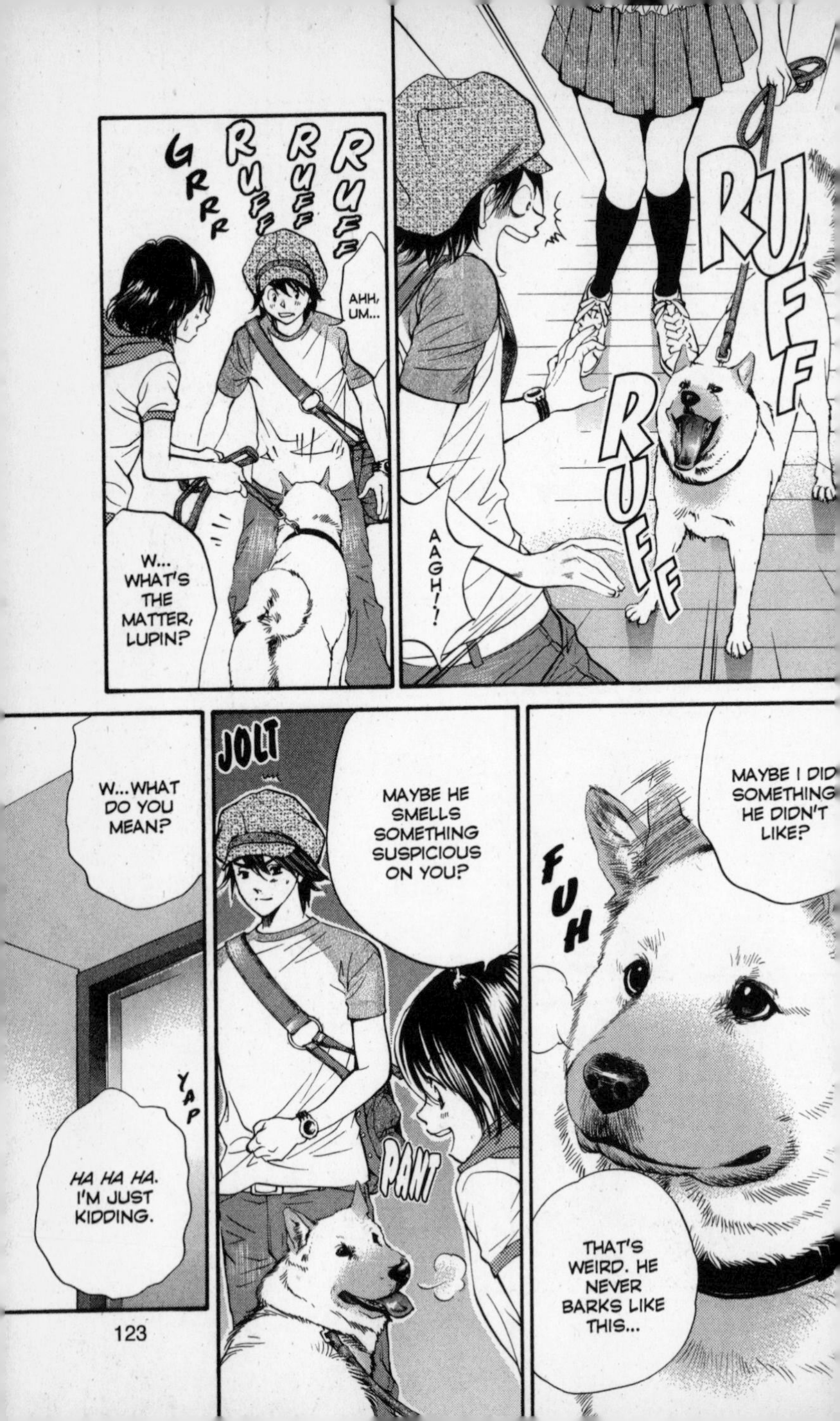
RUFF
RUFF
AAGH!!
GRRR
RUFF
RUFF
RUFF
AHH, UM...
W... WHAT'S THE MATTER, LUPIN?
MAYBE I DID SOMETHING HE DIDN'T LIKE?
FUH
THAT'S WEIRD. HE NEVER BARKS LIKE THIS...
JOLT
MAYBE HE SMELLS SOMETHING SUSPICIOUS ON YOU?
PANT
W...WHAT DO YOU MEAN?
YAP
HA HA HA. I'M JUST KIDDING.

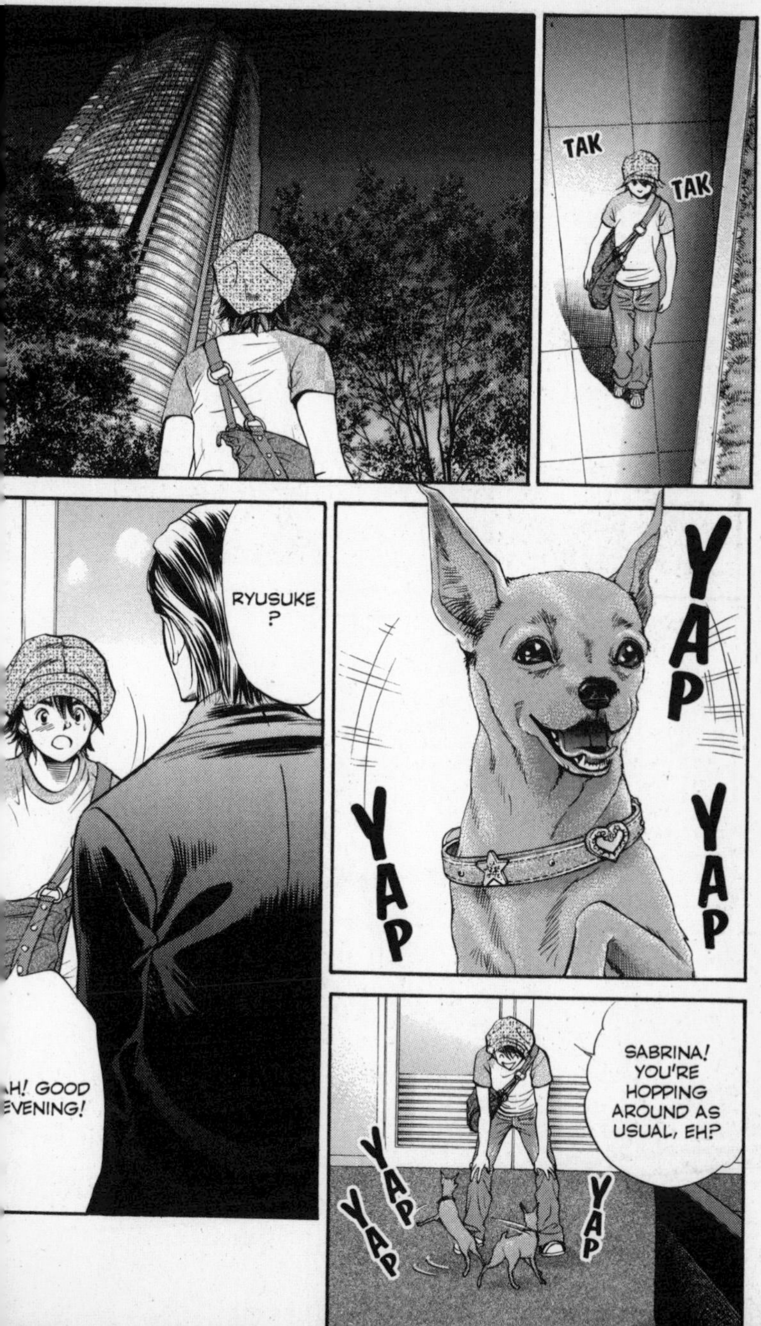
TAK
TAK
YAP YAP
YAP YAP
YAP YAP
SABRINA! YOU'RE HOPPING AROUND AS USUAL, EH?
YAP YAP
YAP YAP
YAP
RYUSUKE?
H! GOOD EVENING!

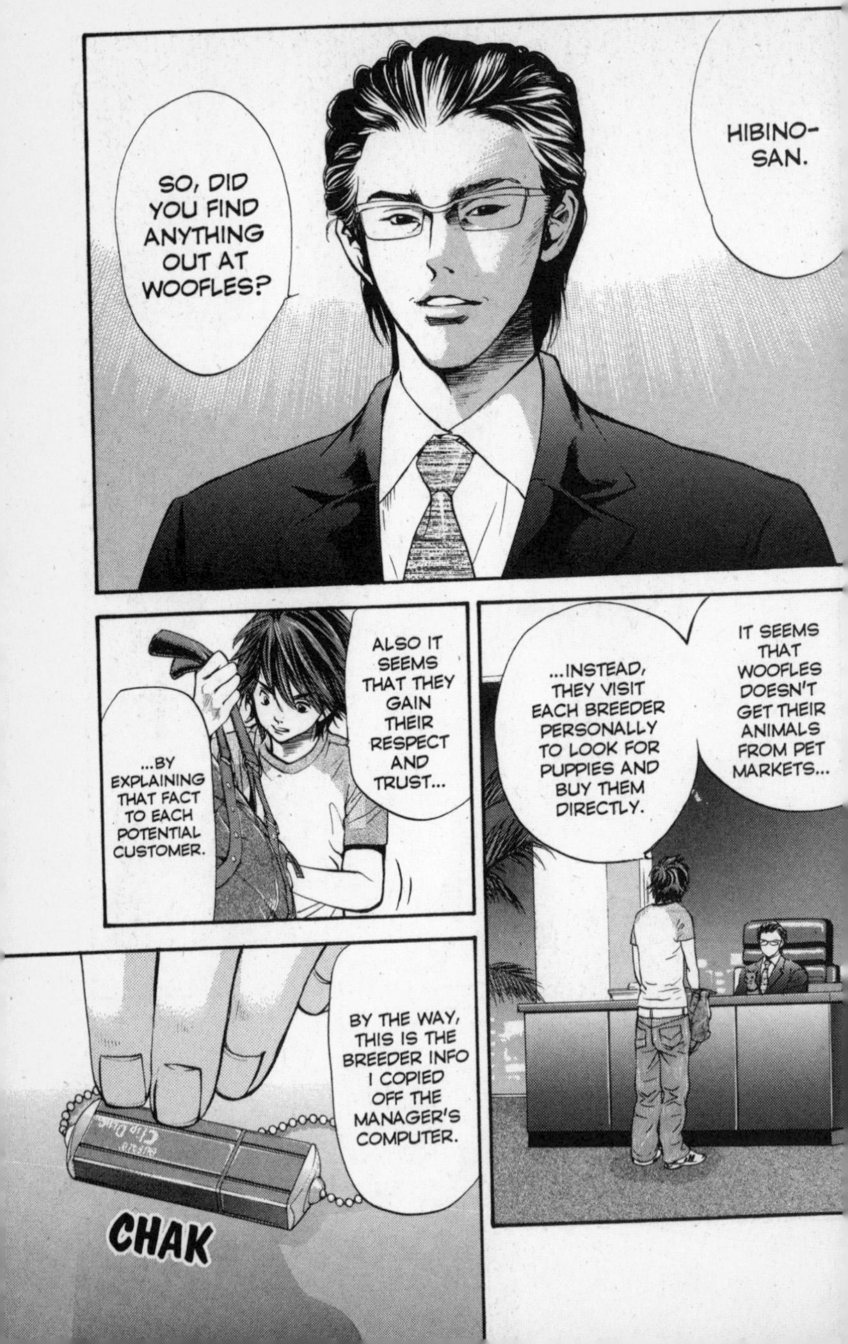
HIBINO-SAN.
SO, DID YOU FIND ANYTHING OUT AT WOOFLES?
IT SEEMS THAT WOOFLES DOESN'T GET THEIR ANIMALS FROM PET MARKETS...
...INSTEAD, THEY VISIT EACH BREEDER PERSONALLY TO LOOK FOR PUPPIES AND BUY THEM DIRECTLY.
ALSO IT SEEMS THAT THEY GAIN THEIR RESPECT AND TRUST...
...BY EXPLAINING THAT FACT TO EACH POTENTIAL CUSTOMER.
BY THE WAY, THIS IS THE BREEDER INFO I COPIED OFF THE MANAGER'S COMPUTER.
CHAK

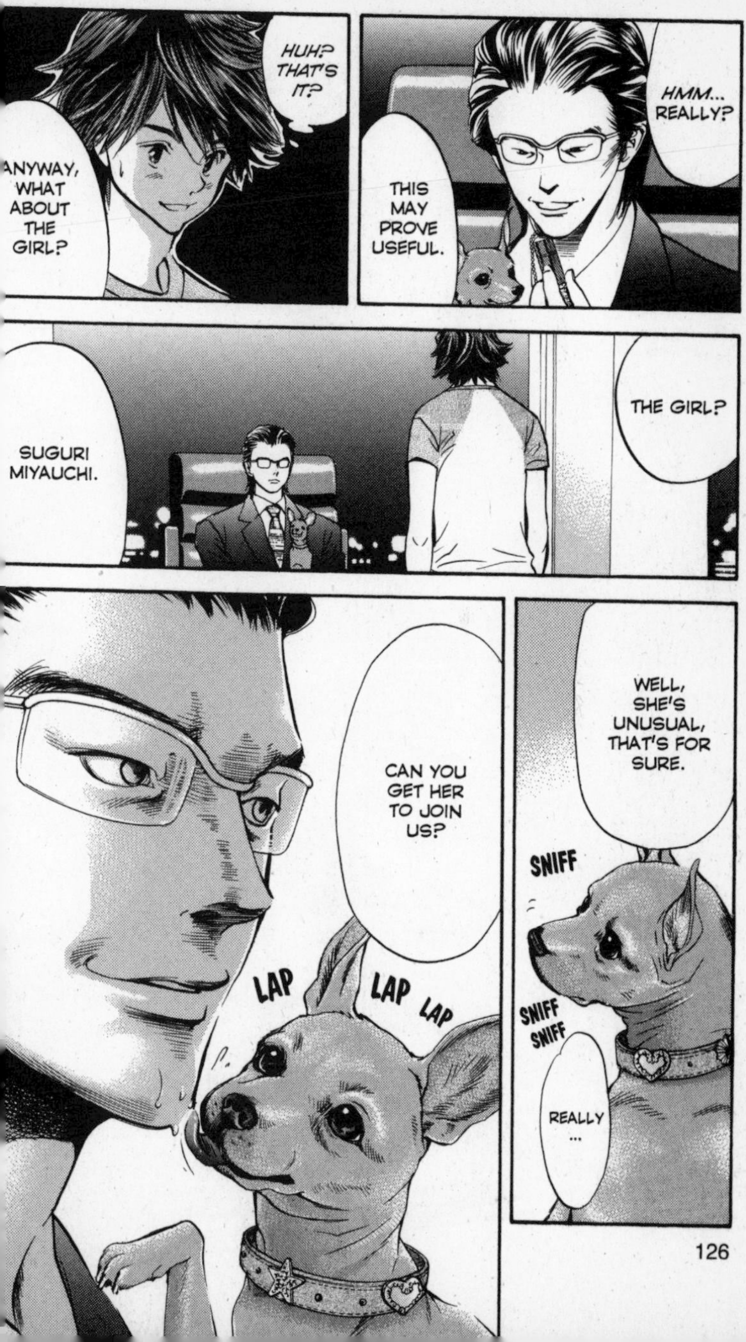
HMM... REALLY?
THIS MAY PROVE USEFUL.
HUH? THAT'S IT?
ANYWAY, WHAT ABOUT THE GIRL?
THE GIRL?
SUGURI MIYAUCHI.
WELL, SHE'S UNUSUAL, THAT'S FOR SURE.
SNIFF
SNIFF SNIFF
REALLY ...
CAN YOU GET HER TO JOIN US?
LAP
LAP
LAP

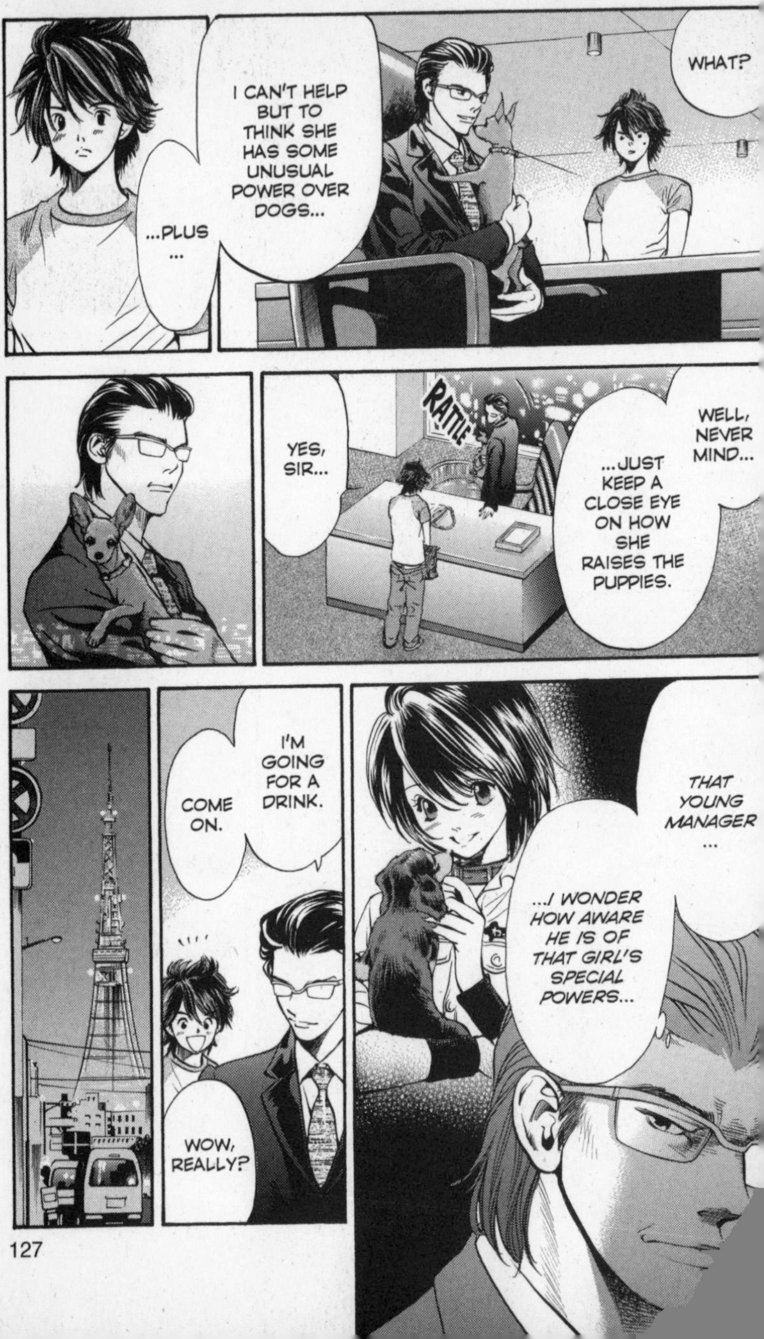
WHAT?
I CAN'T HELP BUT TO THINK SHE HAS SOME UNUSUAL POWER OVER DOGS...
...PLUS ...
WELL, NEVER MIND...
...JUST KEEP A CLOSE EYE ON HOW SHE RAISES THE PUPPIES.
RATTLE
YES, SIR...
THAT YOUNG MANAGER ...
...I WONDER HOW AWARE HE IS OF THAT GIRL'S SPECIAL POWERS...
I'M GOING FOR A DRINK.
COME ON.
WOW, REALLY?

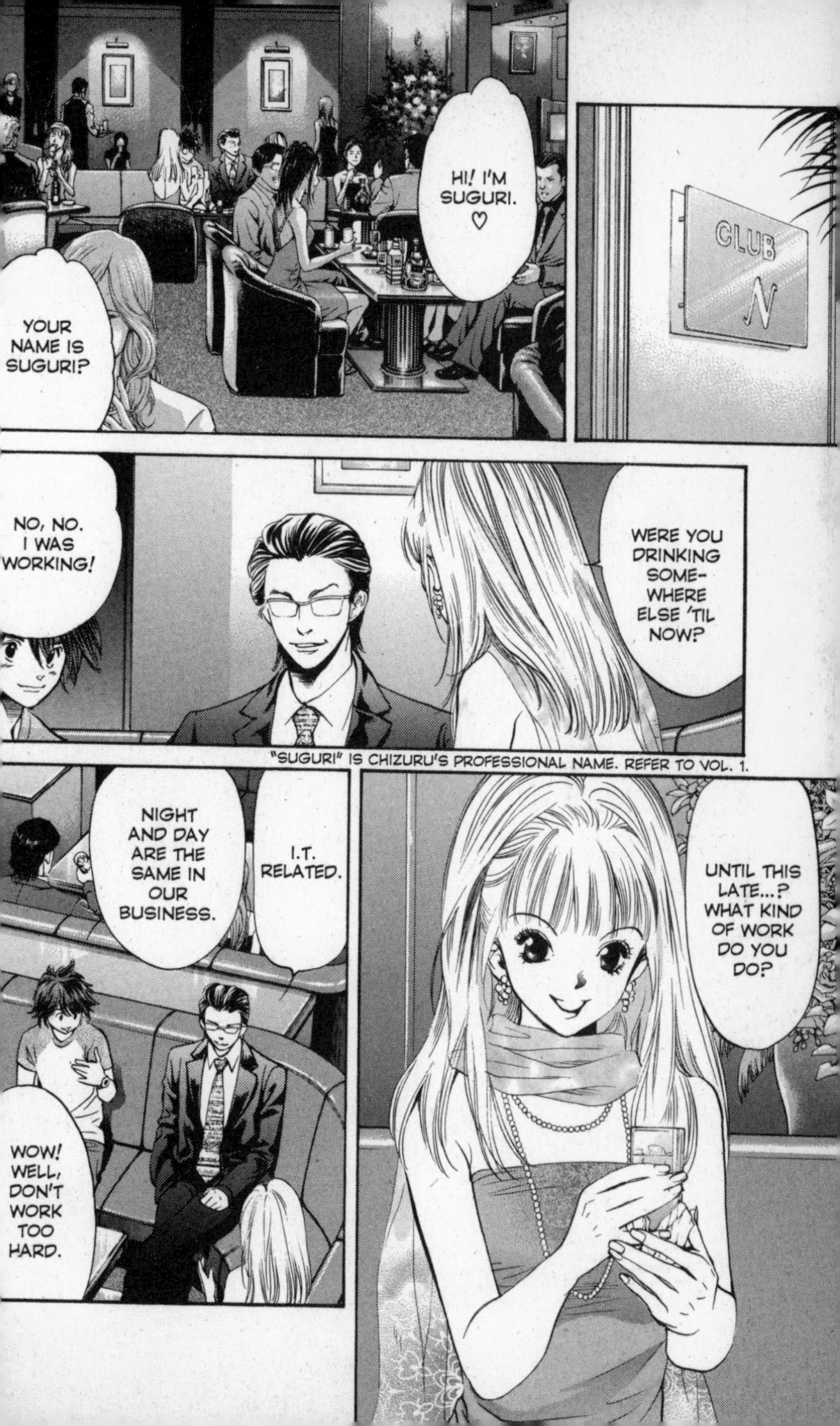
CLUB N
HI! I'M SUGURI. ♡
YOUR NAME IS SUGURI?
WERE YOU DRINKING SOMEWHERE ELSE 'TIL NOW?
NO, NO. I WAS WORKING!
"SUGURI" IS CHIZURU'S PROFESSIONAL NAME. REFER TO VOL. 1.
UNTIL THIS LATE...? WHAT KIND OF WORK DO YOU DO?
I.T. RELATED.
NIGHT AND DAY ARE THE SAME IN OUR BUSINESS.
WOW! WELL, DON'T WORK TOO HARD.

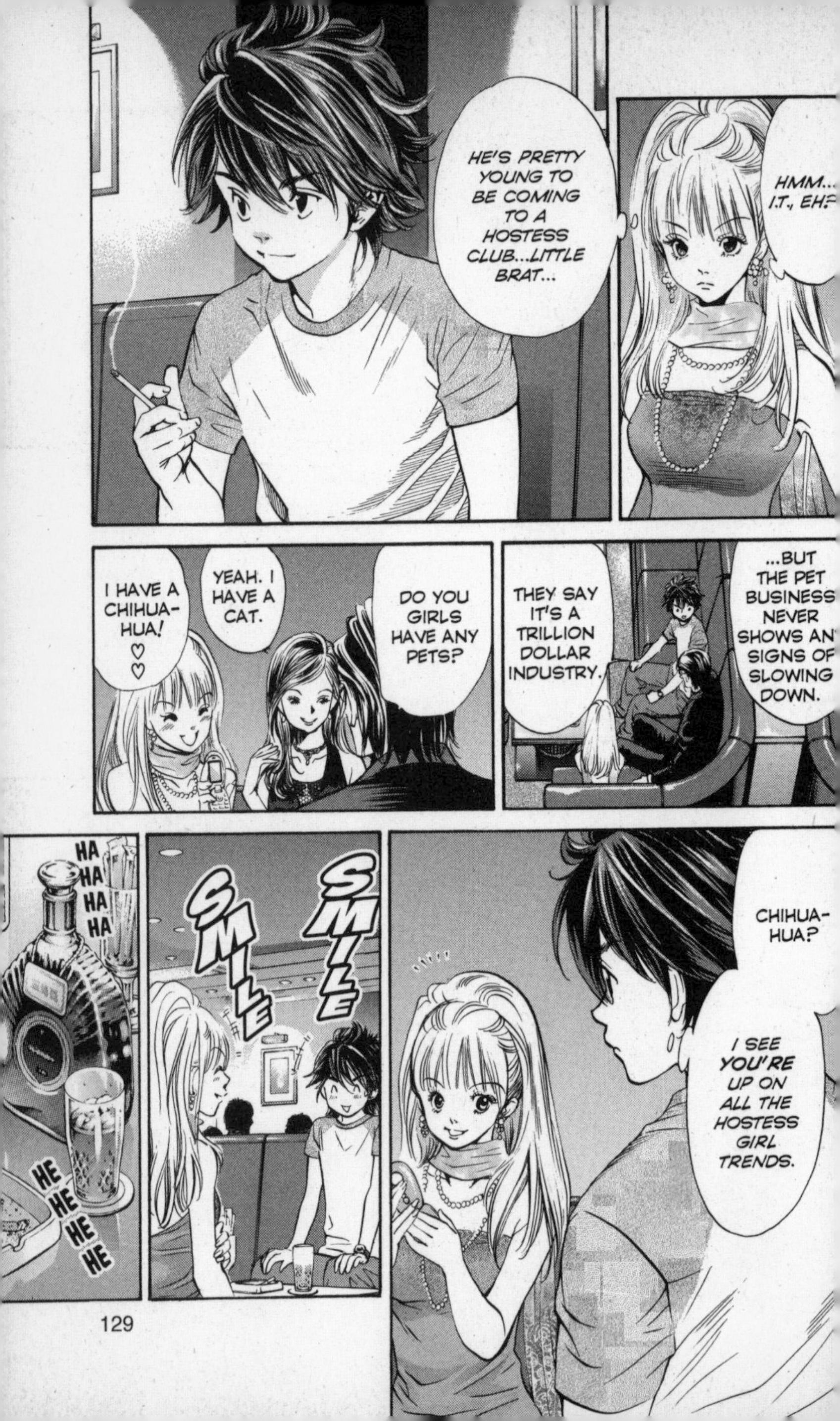
HMM... I.T., EH?
HE'S PRETTY YOUNG TO BE COMING TO A HOSTESS CLUB...LITTLE BRAT...
...BUT THE PET BUSINESS NEVER SHOWS AN SIGNS OF SLOWING DOWN.
THEY SAY IT'S A TRILLION DOLLAR INDUSTRY.
DO YOU GIRLS HAVE ANY PETS?
YEAH. I HAVE A CAT.
I HAVE A CHIHUAHUA! ♡ ♡
CHIHUAHUA?
I SEE YOU'RE UP ON ALL THE HOSTESS GIRL TRENDS.
SMILE
SMILE
HA HA HA HA
HE HE HE HE

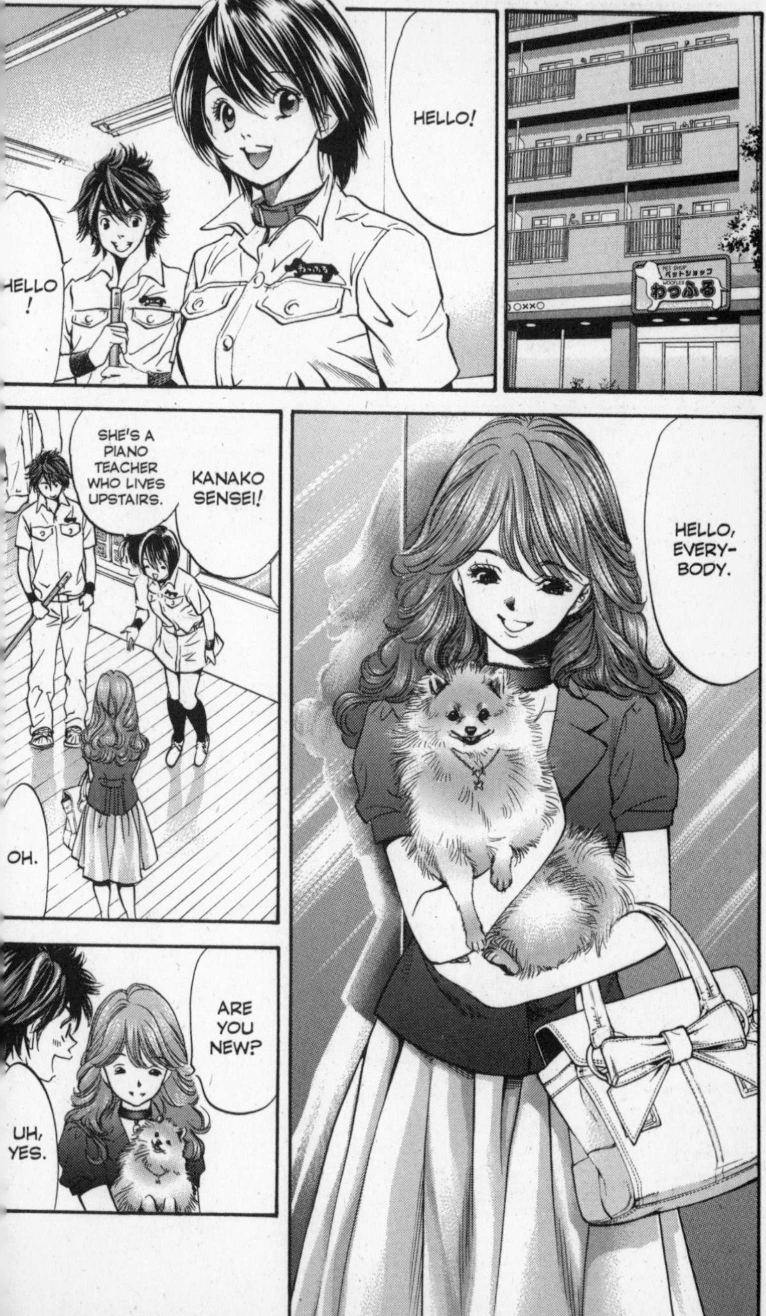
PET SHOP
ペットショップ
WOOFLES
わっふる
HELLO!
HELLO!
HELLO, EVERY-BODY.
KANAKO SENSEI!
SHE'S A PIANO TEACHER WHO LIVES UPSTAIRS.
OH.
ARE YOU NEW?
UH, YES.

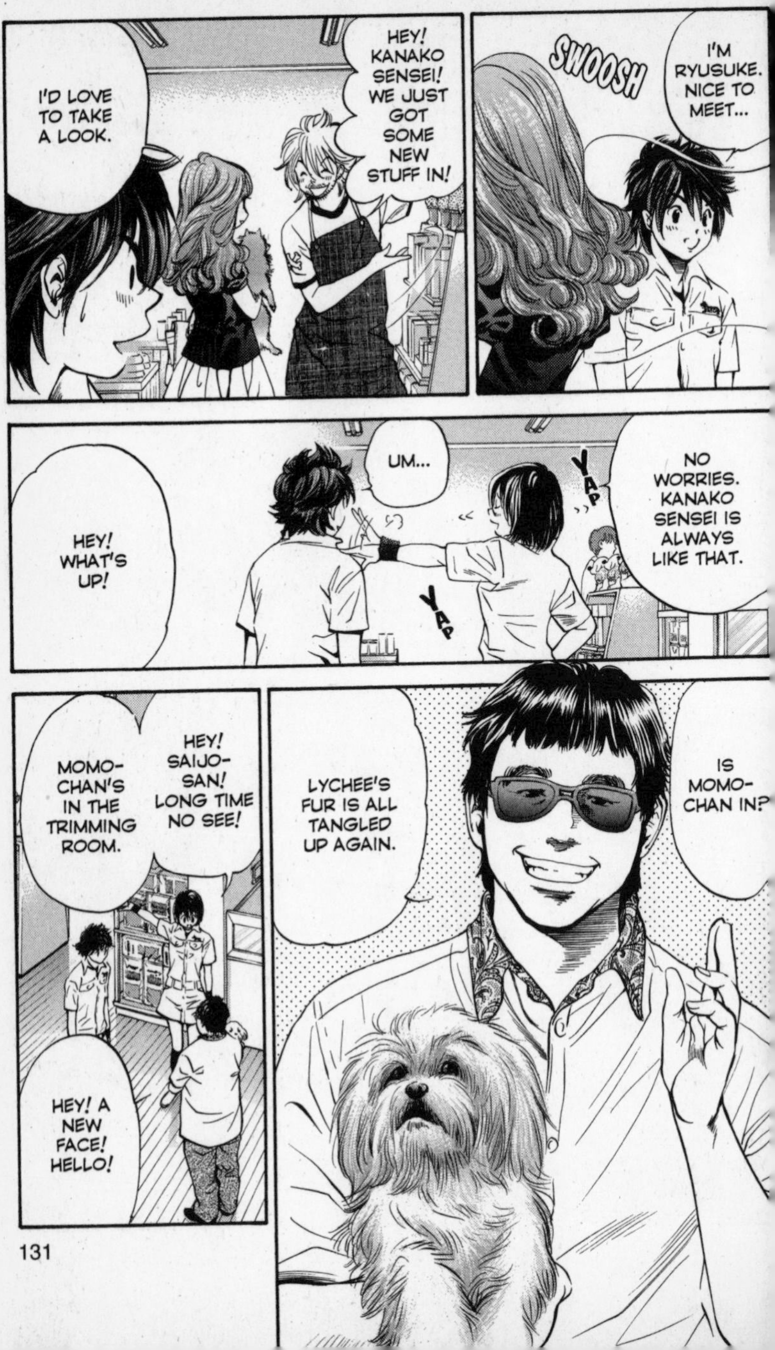
I'M RYUSUKE. NICE TO MEET...
SWOOSH
HEY! KANAKO SENSEI! WE JUST GOT SOME NEW STUFF IN!
I'D LOVE TO TAKE A LOOK.
NO WORRIES. KANAKO SENSEI IS ALWAYS LIKE THAT.
YAP
UM...
YAP
HEY! WHAT'S UP!
IS MOMO-CHAN IN?
LYCHEE'S FUR IS ALL TANGLED UP AGAIN.
HEY! SAIJO-SAN! LONG TIME NO SEE!
MOMO-CHAN'S IN THE TRIMMING ROOM.
HEY! A NEW FACE! HELLO!

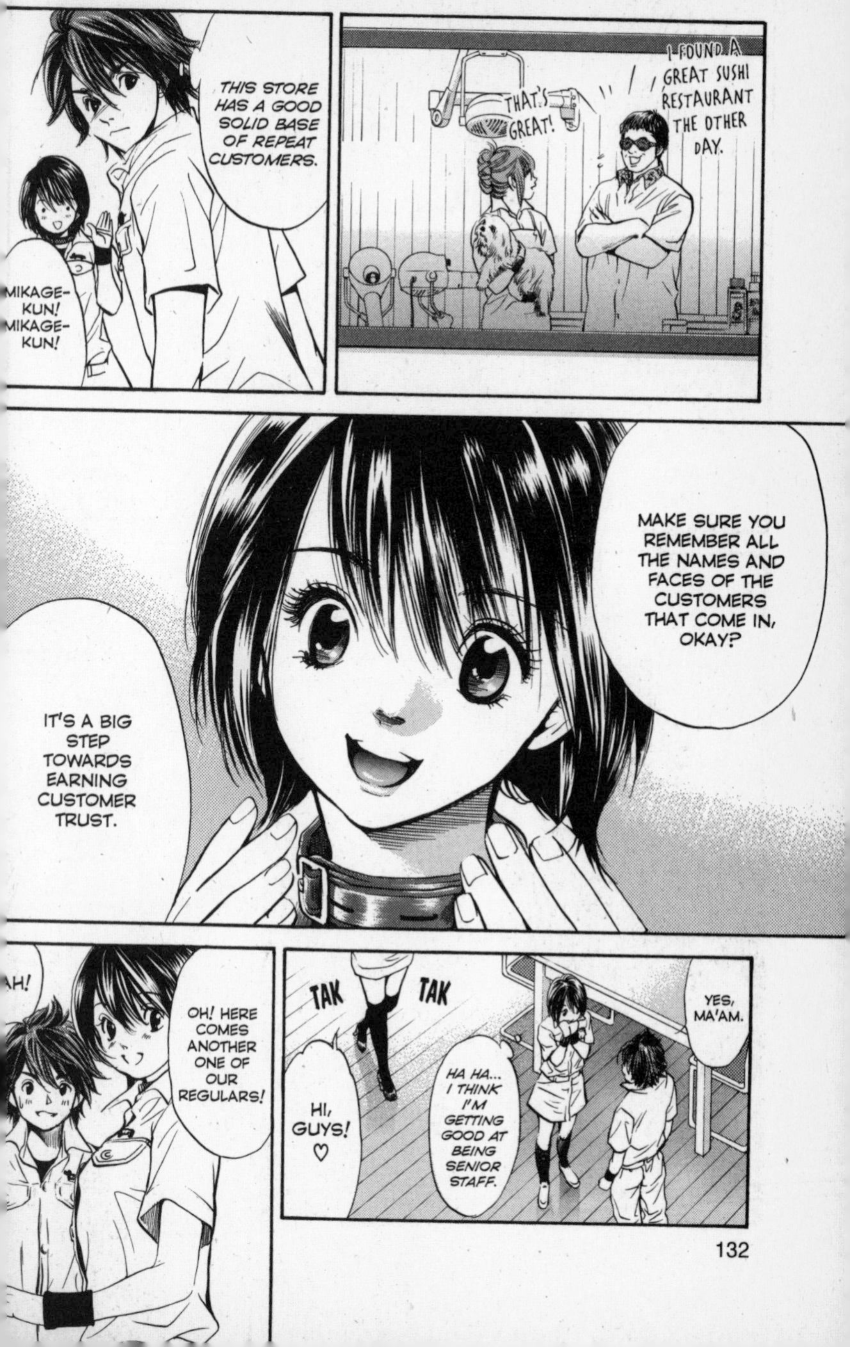
I FOUND A GREAT SUSHI RESTAURANT THE OTHER DAY.
THAT'S GREAT!
THIS STORE HAS A GOOD SOLID BASE OF REPEAT CUSTOMERS.
MIKAGE-KUN! MIKAGE-KUN!
MAKE SURE YOU REMEMBER ALL THE NAMES AND FACES OF THE CUSTOMERS THAT COME IN, OKAY?
IT'S A BIG STEP TOWARDS EARNING CUSTOMER TRUST.
YES, MA'AM.
HA HA... I THINK I'M GETTING GOOD AT BEING SENIOR STAFF.
TAK TAK
HI, GUYS! ♡
H!
OH! HERE COMES ANOTHER ONE OF OUR REGULARS!

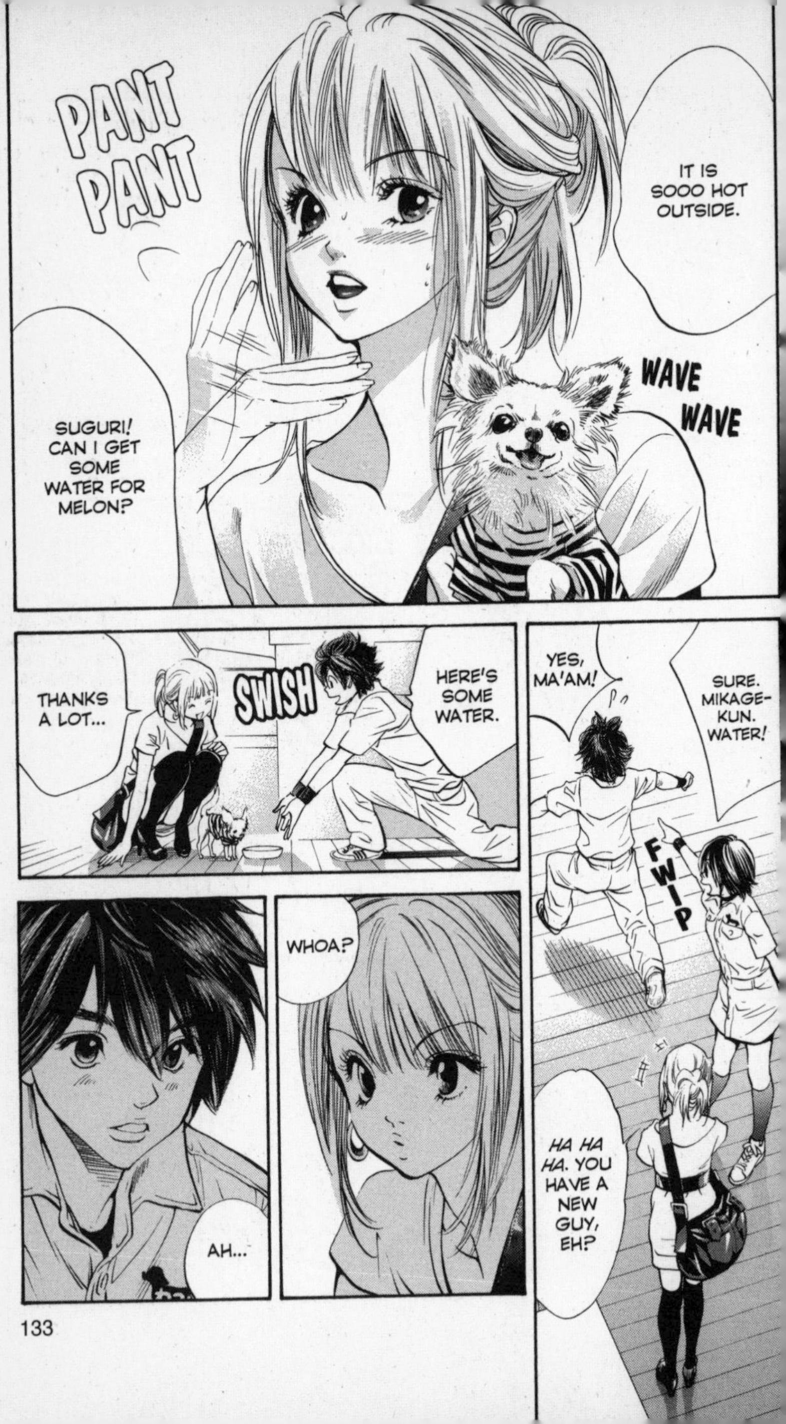
IT IS SOOO HOT OUTSIDE.
PANT PANT
WAVE WAVE
SUGURI! CAN I GET SOME WATER FOR MELON?
SURE. MIKAGE-KUN. WATER!
YES, MA'AM!
FWIP
HA HA HA. YOU HAVE A NEW GUY, EH?
HERE'S SOME WATER.
SWISH
THANKS A LOT...
WHOA?
AH...

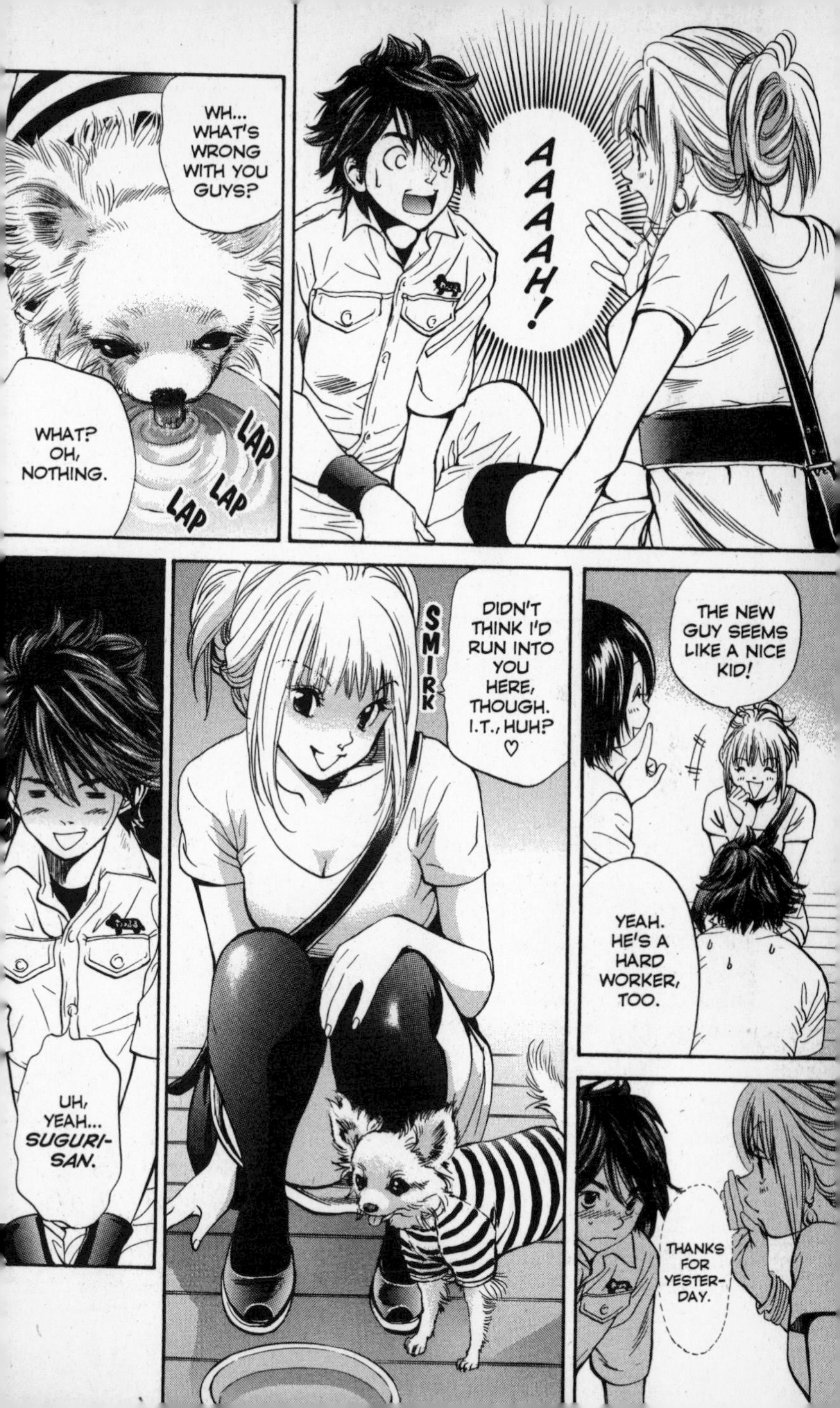
AAAAAH!
WH... WHAT'S WRONG WITH YOU GUYS?
WHAT? OH, NOTHING.
LAP
LAP
LAP
THE NEW GUY SEEMS LIKE A NICE KID!
YEAH. HE'S A HARD WORKER, TOO.
THANKS FOR YESTER-DAY.
SMIRK
DIDN'T THINK I'D RUN INTO YOU HERE, THOUGH. I.T., HUH? ♡
UH, YEAH... SUGURI-SAN.

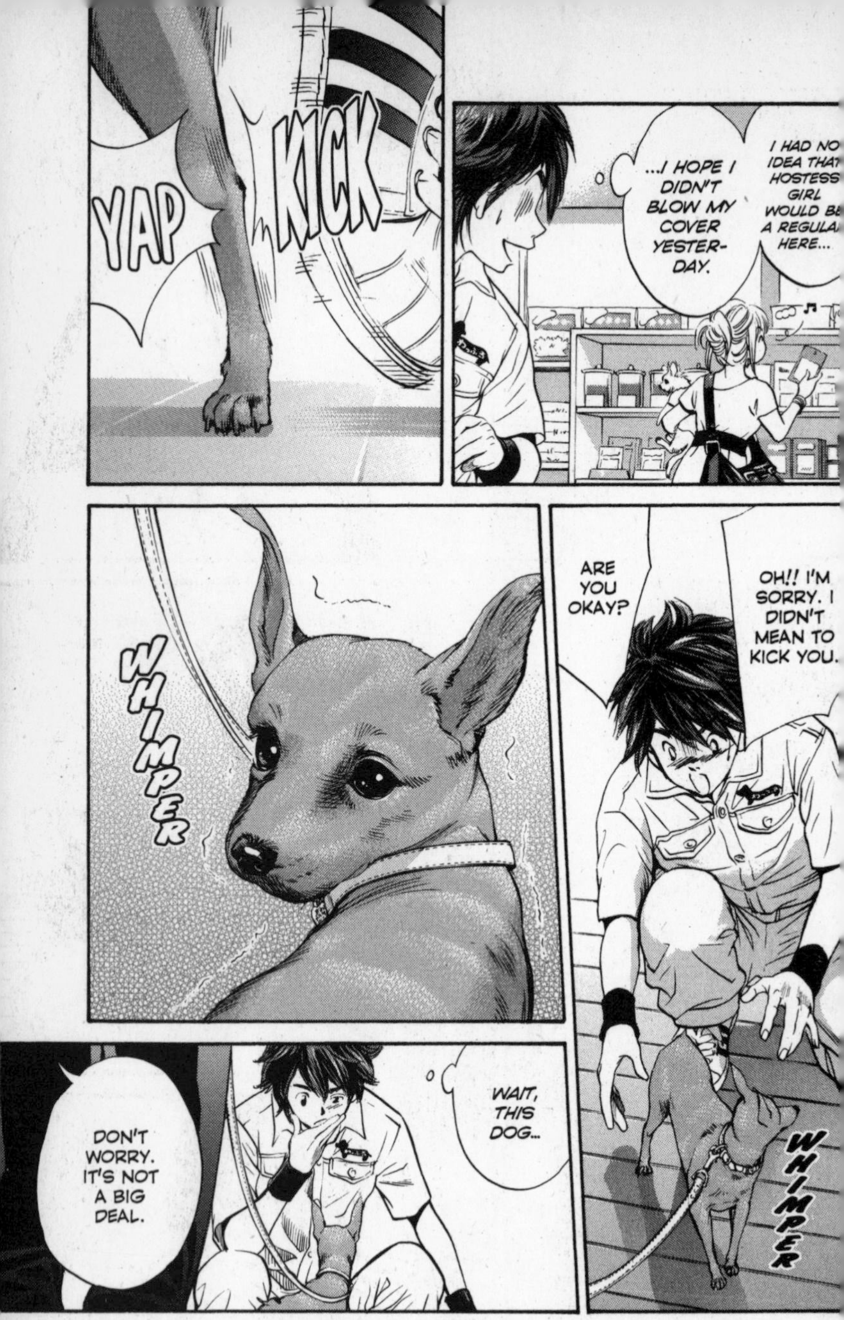
I HAD NO IDEA THAT HOSTESS GIRL WOULD BE A REGULA HERE...
...I HOPE I DIDN'T BLOW MY COVER YESTER-DAY.
KICK
YAP
OH!! I'M SORRY. I DIDN'T MEAN TO KICK YOU.
ARE YOU OKAY?
WHIMPER
WHIMPER
WAIT, THIS DOG...
DON'T WORRY. IT'S NOT A BIG DEAL.

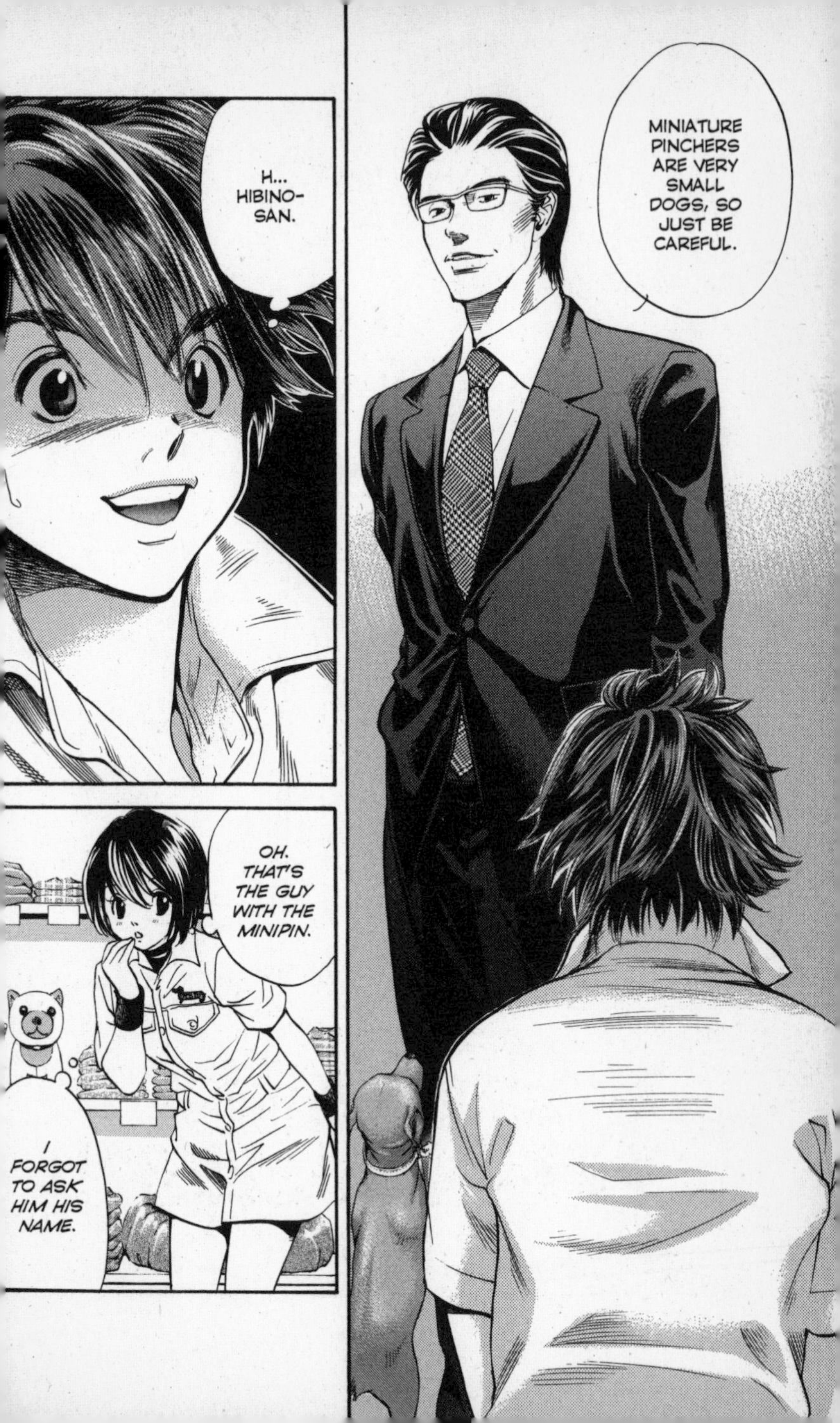
MINIATURE PINCHERS ARE VERY SMALL DOGS, SO JUST BE CAREFUL.
H... HIBINO-SAN.
OH. THAT'S THE GUY WITH THE MINIPIN.
I FORGOT TO ASK HIM HIS NAME.

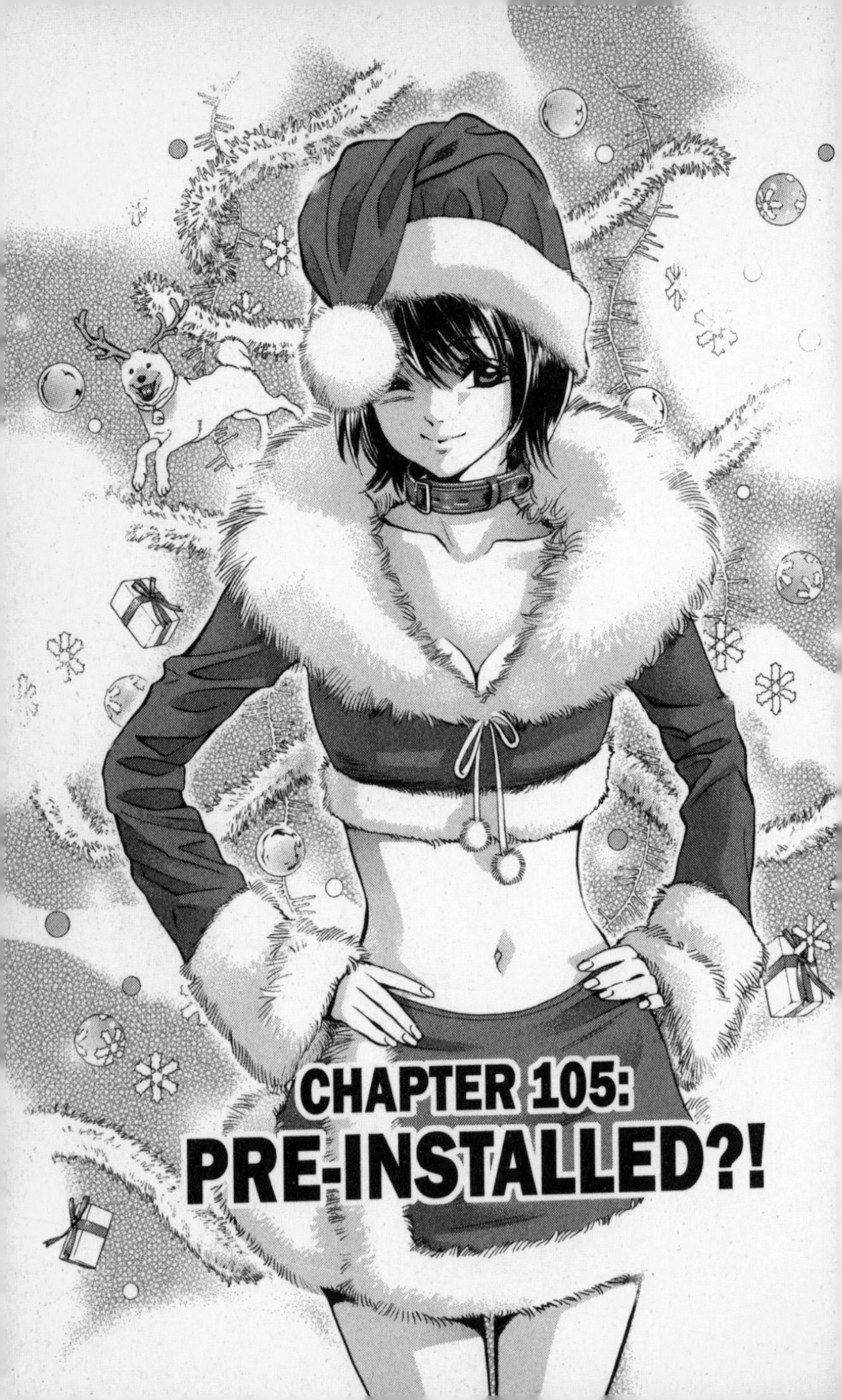
CHAPTER 105:
PRE-INSTALLED?!

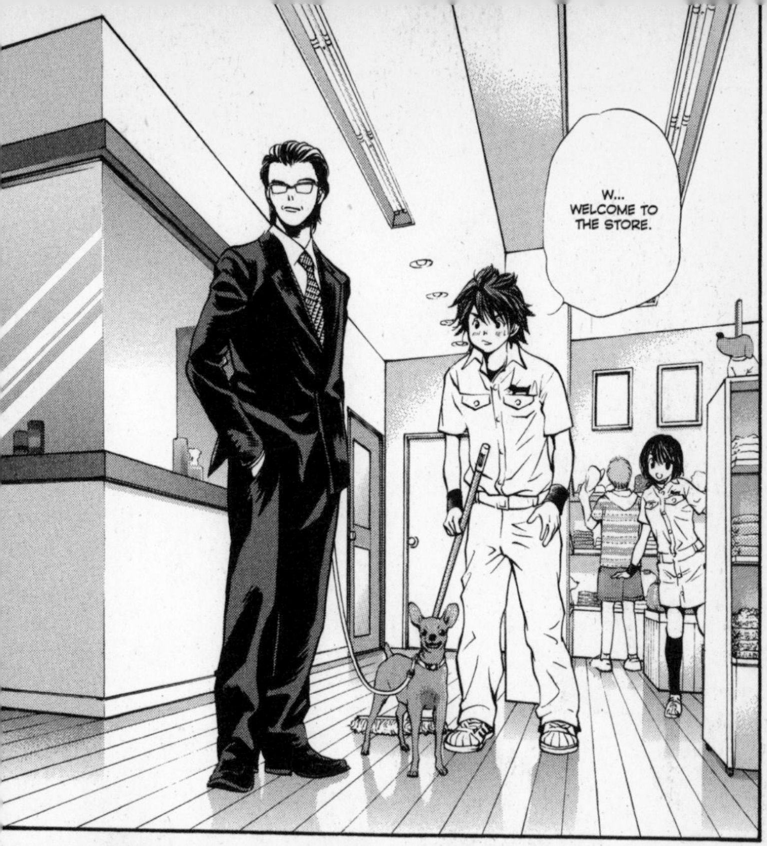
W... WELCOME TO THE STORE.

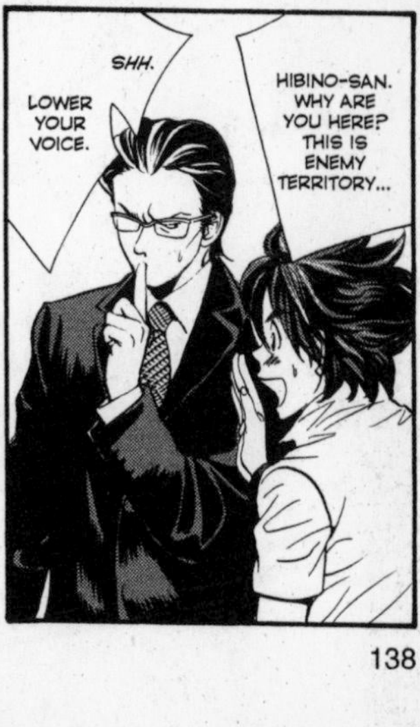
HIBINO-SAN. WHY ARE YOU HERE? THIS IS ENEMY TERRITORY...
SHH.
LOWER YOUR VOICE.

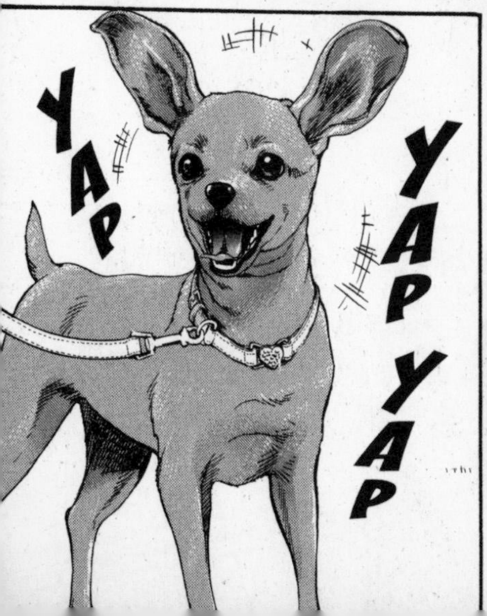
YAP
YAP
YAP
YAP

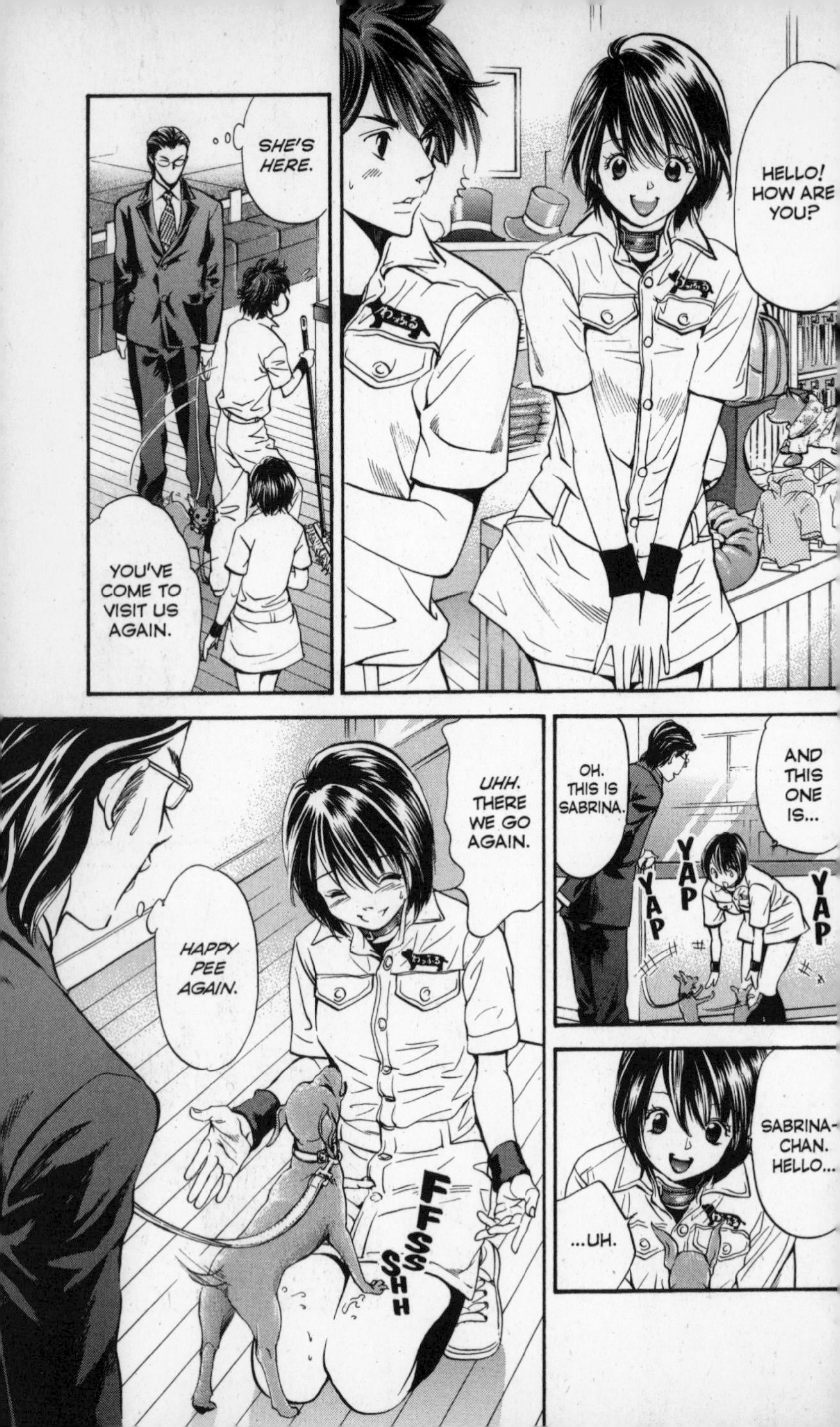
HELLO! HOW ARE YOU?
SHE'S HERE.
YOU'VE COME TO VISIT US AGAIN.
AND THIS ONE IS...
OH. THIS IS SABRINA.
YAP
YAP
YAP
SABRINA-CHAN. HELLO...
...UH.
UHH. THERE WE GO AGAIN.
HAPPY PEE AGAIN.
FFSS
SHH

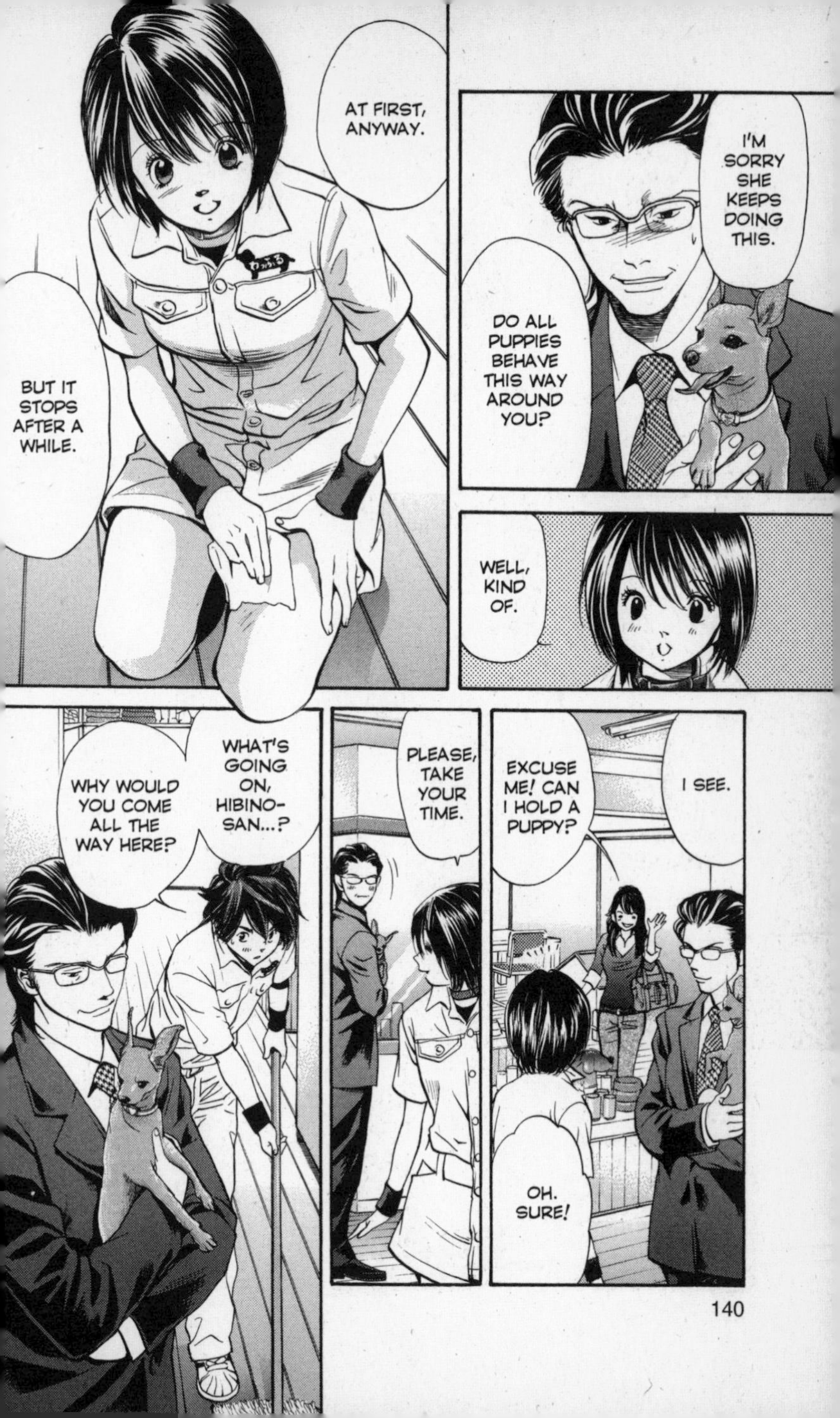
I'M SORRY SHE KEEPS DOING THIS.
DO ALL PUPPIES BEHAVE THIS WAY AROUND YOU?
WELL, KIND OF.
AT FIRST, ANYWAY.
BUT IT STOPS AFTER A WHILE.
I SEE.
EXCUSE ME! CAN I HOLD A PUPPY?
OH. SURE!
PLEASE, TAKE YOUR TIME.
WHAT'S GOING ON, HIBINO-SAN...?
WHY WOULD YOU COME ALL THE WAY HERE?

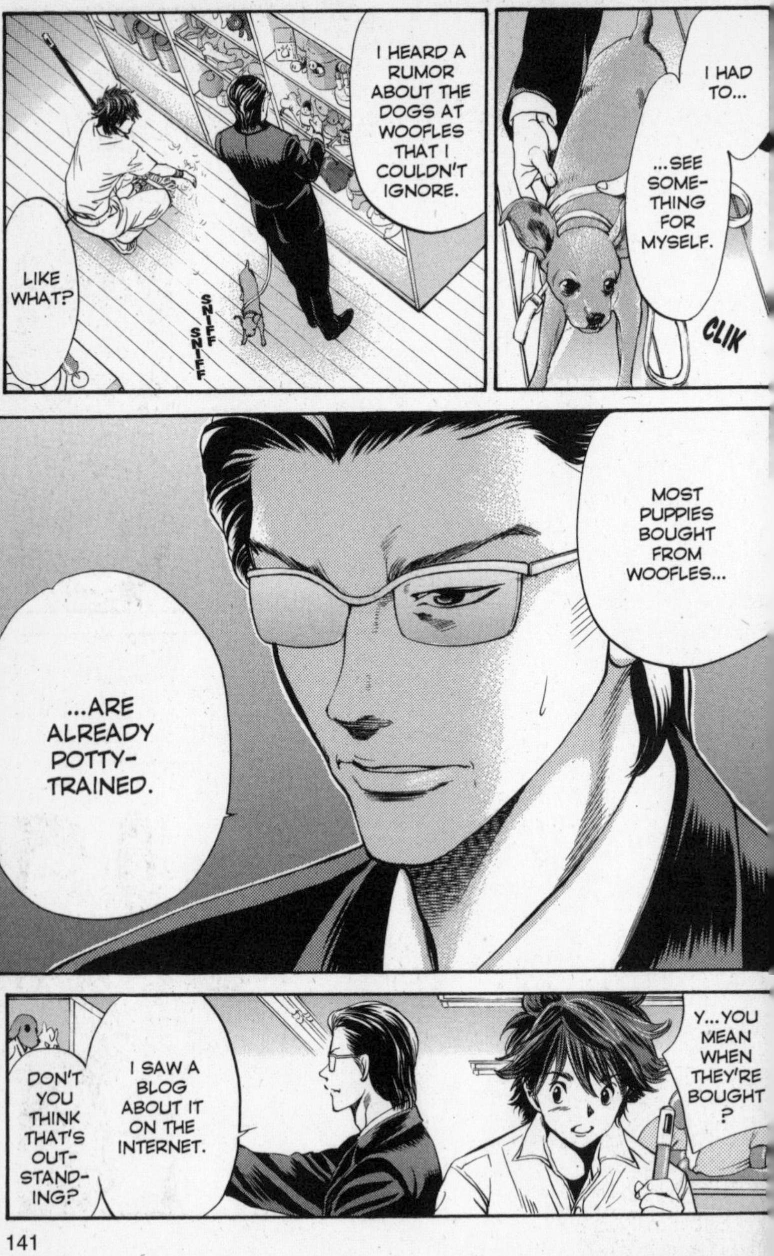
I HAD TO...
...SEE SOMETHING FOR MYSELF.
CLIK
I HEARD A RUMOR ABOUT THE DOGS AT WOOFLES THAT I COULDN'T IGNORE.
LIKE WHAT?
SNIFF SNIFF
MOST PUPPIES BOUGHT FROM WOOFLES...
...ARE ALREADY POTTY-TRAINED.
Y...YOU MEAN WHEN THEY'RE BOUGHT?
I SAW A BLOG ABOUT IT ON THE INTERNET.
DON'T YOU THINK THAT'S OUTSTANDING?

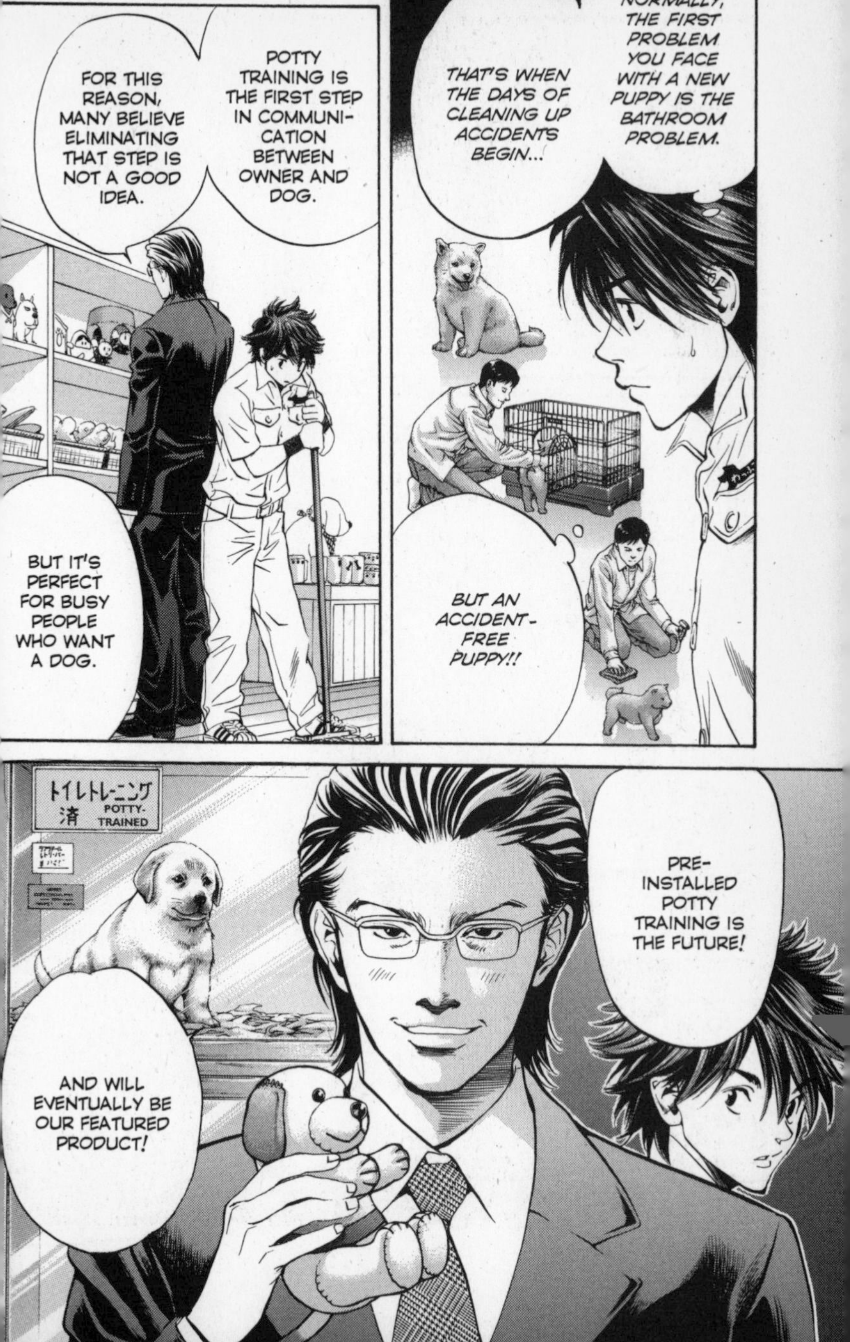
NORMALLY, THE FIRST PROBLEM YOU FACE WITH A NEW PUPPY IS THE BATHROOM PROBLEM.
THAT'S WHEN THE DAYS OF CLEANING UP ACCIDENTS BEGIN...
BUT AN ACCIDENT-FREE PUPPY!!
POTTY TRAINING IS THE FIRST STEP IN COMMUNICATION BETWEEN OWNER AND DOG.
FOR THIS REASON, MANY BELIEVE ELIMINATING THAT STEP IS NOT A GOOD IDEA.
BUT IT'S PERFECT FOR BUSY PEOPLE WHO WANT A DOG.
トイレトレーニング済
POTTY-TRAINED
PRE-INSTALLED POTTY TRAINING IS THE FUTURE!
AND WILL EVENTUALLY BE OUR FEATURED PRODUCT!

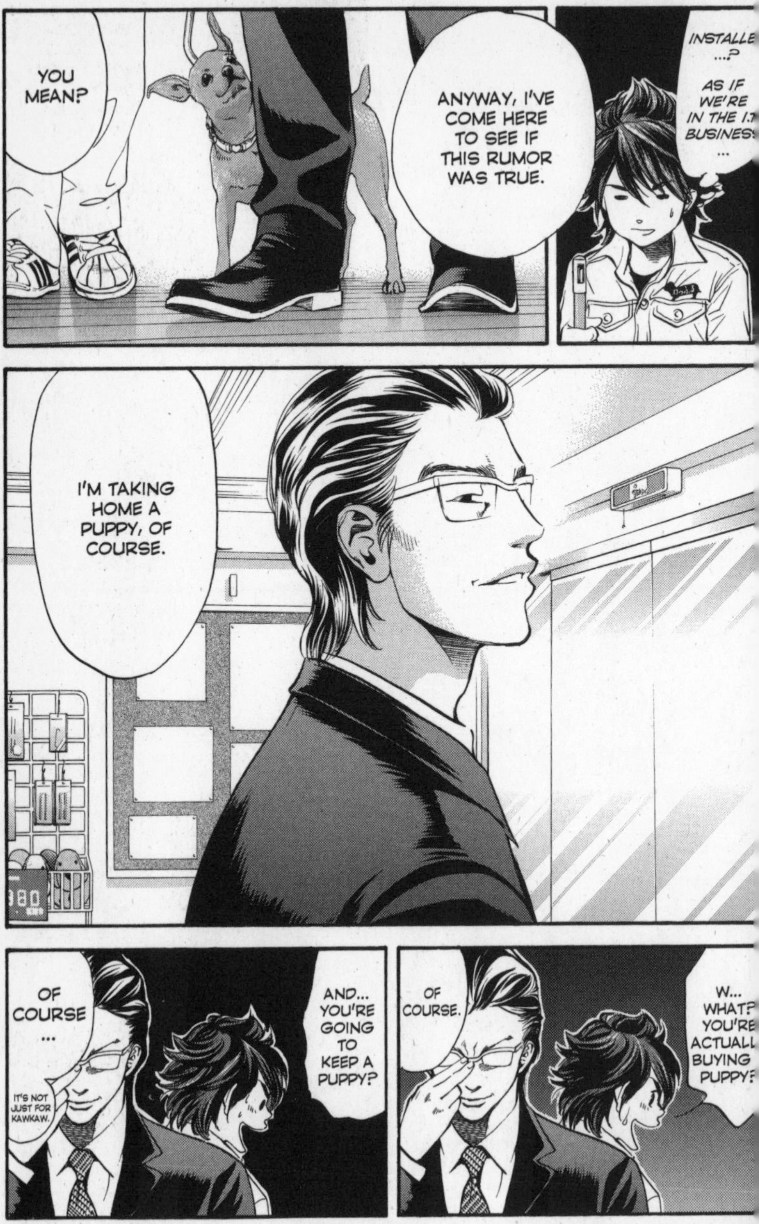
INSTALLE ...?
AS IF WE'RE IN THE I.T BUSINES ...
ANYWAY, I'VE COME HERE TO SEE IF THIS RUMOR WAS TRUE.
YOU MEAN?
I'M TAKING HOME A PUPPY, OF COURSE.
W... WHAT? YOU'RE ACTUALL BUYING PUPPY?
OF COURSE.
AND... YOU'RE GOING TO KEEP A PUPPY?
OF COURSE ...
IT'S NOT JUST FOR KAWKAW.

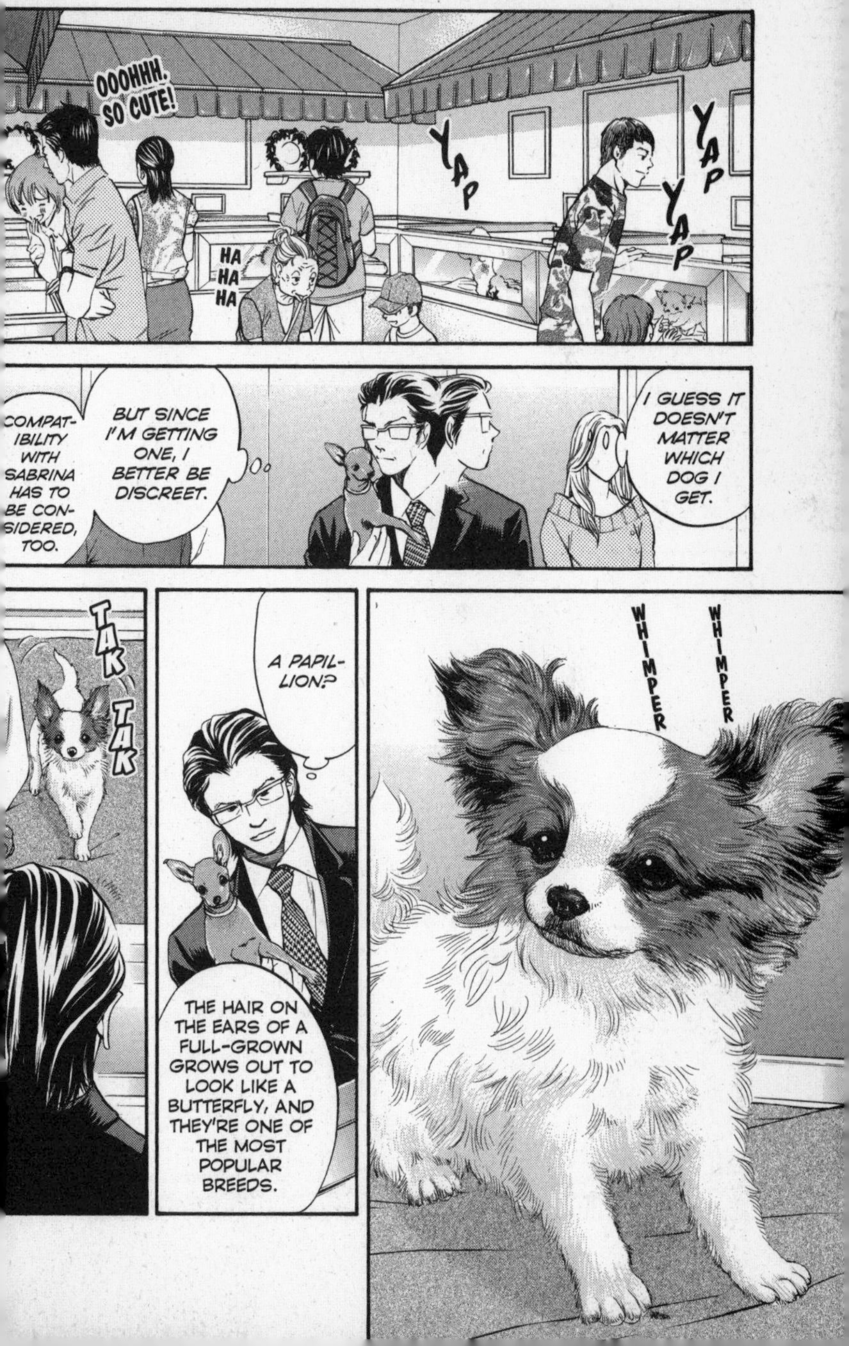
YAP YAP
YAP
YAP
HA HA HA
OOOHHH. SO CUTE!
I GUESS IT DOESN'T MATTER WHICH DOG I GET.
BUT SINCE I'M GETTING ONE, I BETTER BE DISCREET.
COMPATIBILITY WITH SABRINA HAS TO BE CONSIDERED, TOO.
WHIMPER
WHIMPER
A PAPILLION?
THE HAIR ON THE EARS OF A FULL-GROWN GROWS OUT TO LOOK LIKE A BUTTERFLY, AND THEY'RE ONE OF THE MOST POPULAR BREEDS.
TAK TAK

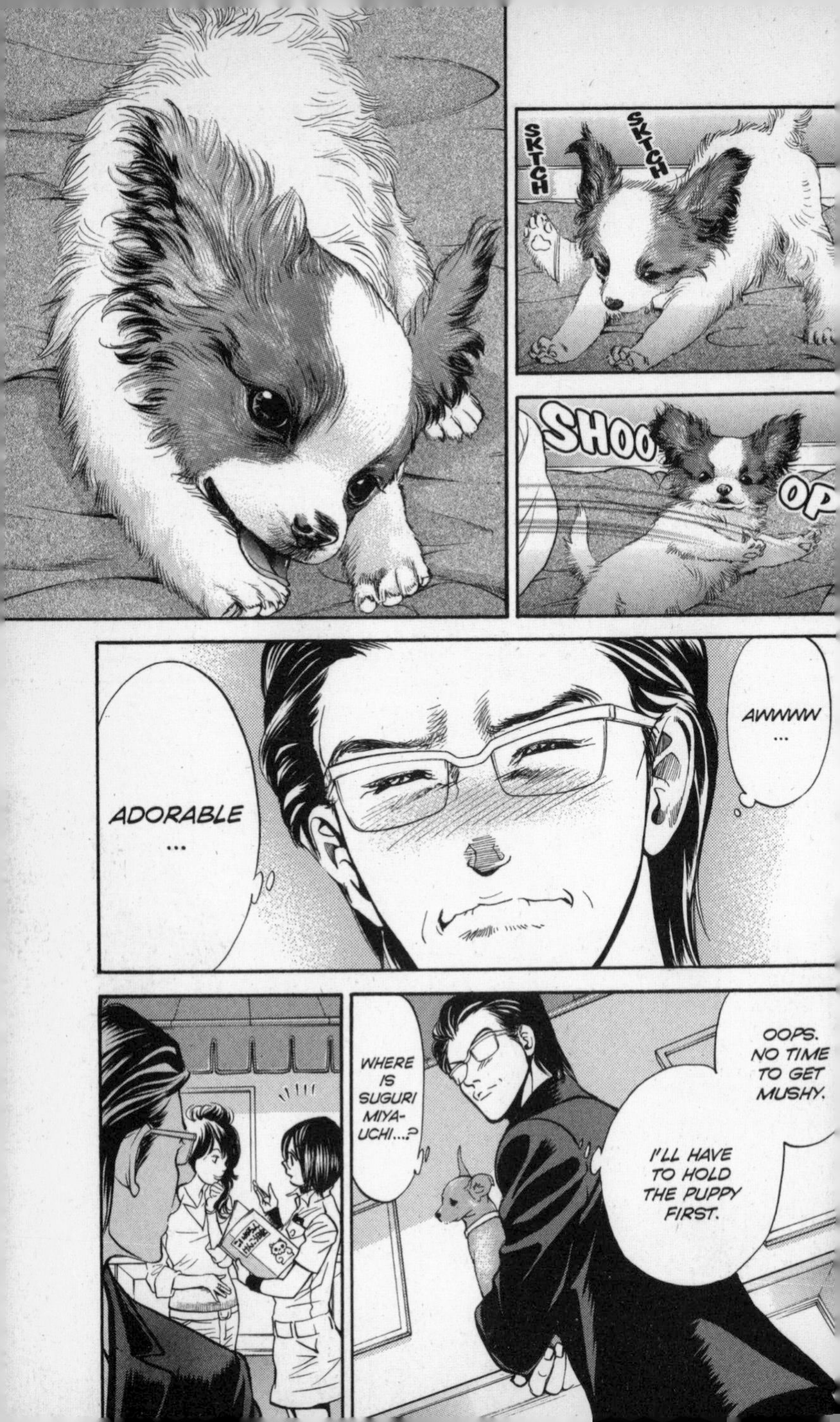
SKTCH SKTCH
SHOOOP
AWWWW...
ADORABLE...
OOPS. NO TIME TO GET MUSHY.
I'LL HAVE TO HOLD THE PUPPY FIRST.
WHERE IS SUGURI MIYA-UCHI...?

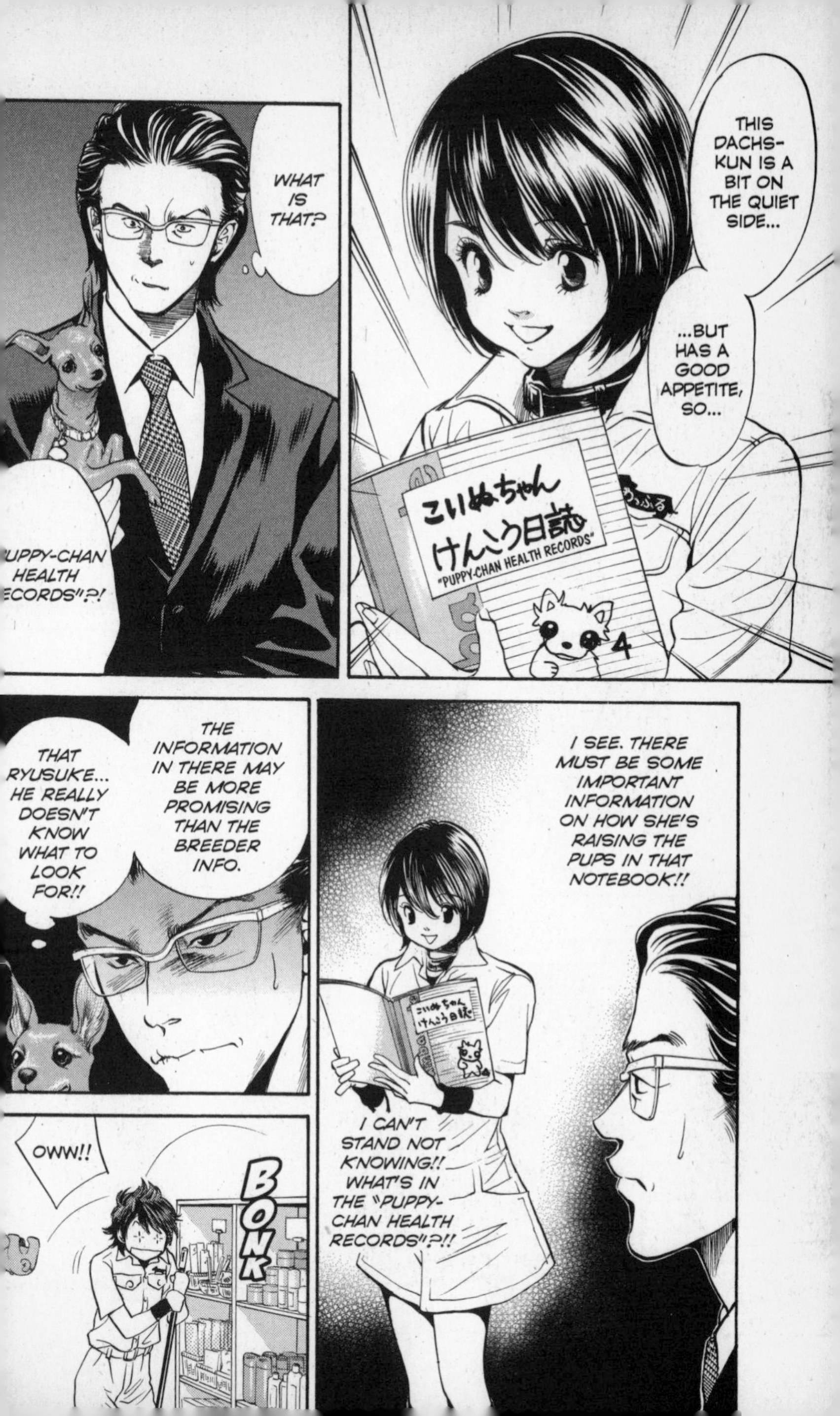
THIS DACHS-KUN IS A BIT ON THE QUIET SIDE...
...BUT HAS A GOOD APPETITE, SO...
こいぬちゃん けんこう日誌
"PUPPY-CHAN HEALTH RECORDS"
4
WHAT IS THAT?
UPPY-CHAN HEALTH ECORDS"?!
I SEE. THERE MUST BE SOME IMPORTANT INFORMATION ON HOW SHE'S RAISING THE PUPS IN THAT NOTEBOOK!!
I CAN'T STAND NOT KNOWING!! WHAT'S IN THE "PUPPY-CHAN HEALTH RECORDS"?!!
THE INFORMATION IN THERE MAY BE MORE PROMISING THAN THE BREEDER INFO.
THAT RYUSUKE... HE REALLY DOESN'T KNOW WHAT TO LOOK FOR!!
BONK
OWW!!

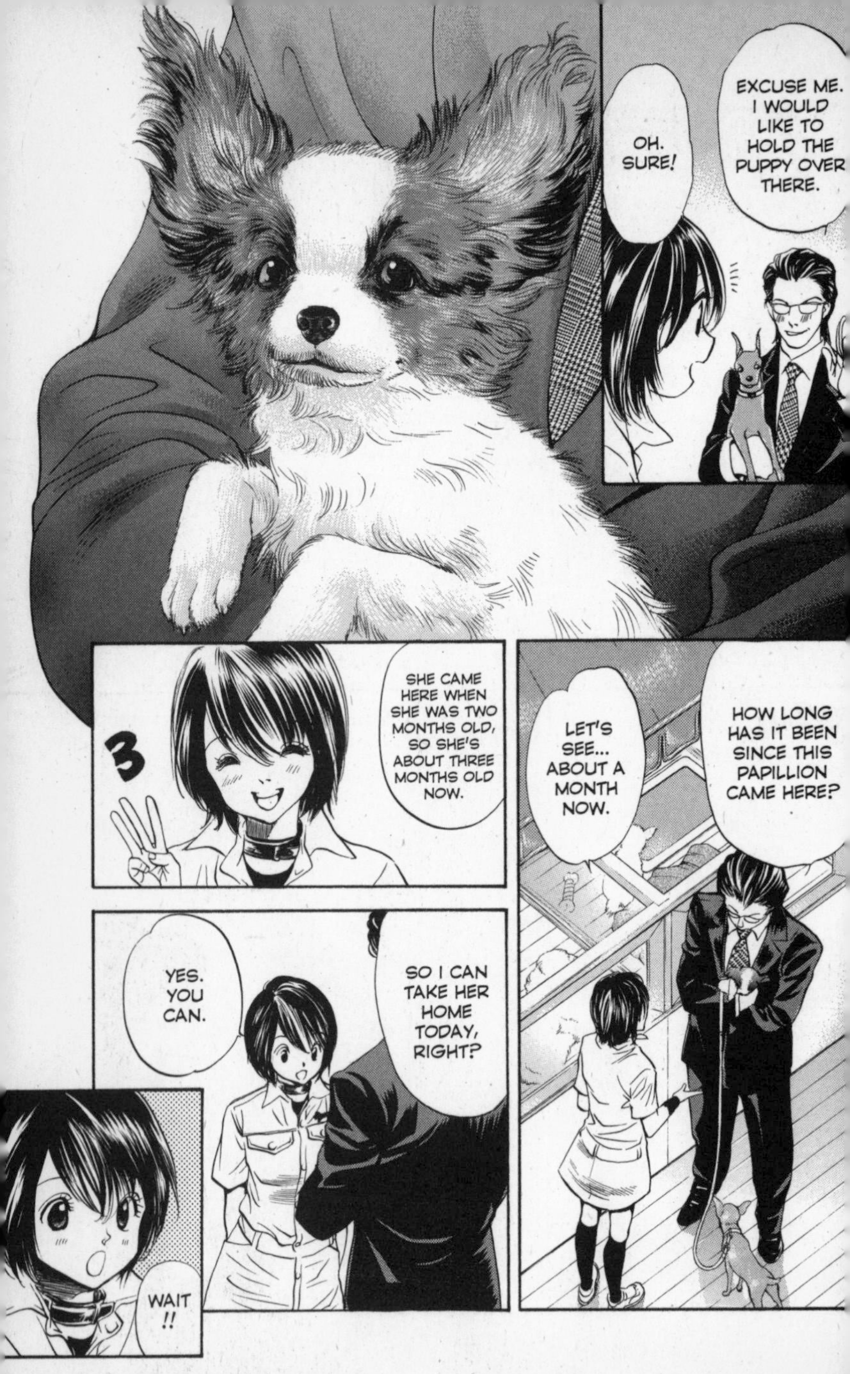
EXCUSE ME. I WOULD LIKE TO HOLD THE PUPPY OVER THERE.
OH. SURE!
HOW LONG HAS IT BEEN SINCE THIS PAPILLION CAME HERE?
LET'S SEE... ABOUT A MONTH NOW.
SHE CAME HERE WHEN SHE WAS TWO MONTHS OLD, SO SHE'S ABOUT THREE MONTHS OLD NOW.
3
SO I CAN TAKE HER HOME TODAY, RIGHT?
YES. YOU CAN.
WAIT !!

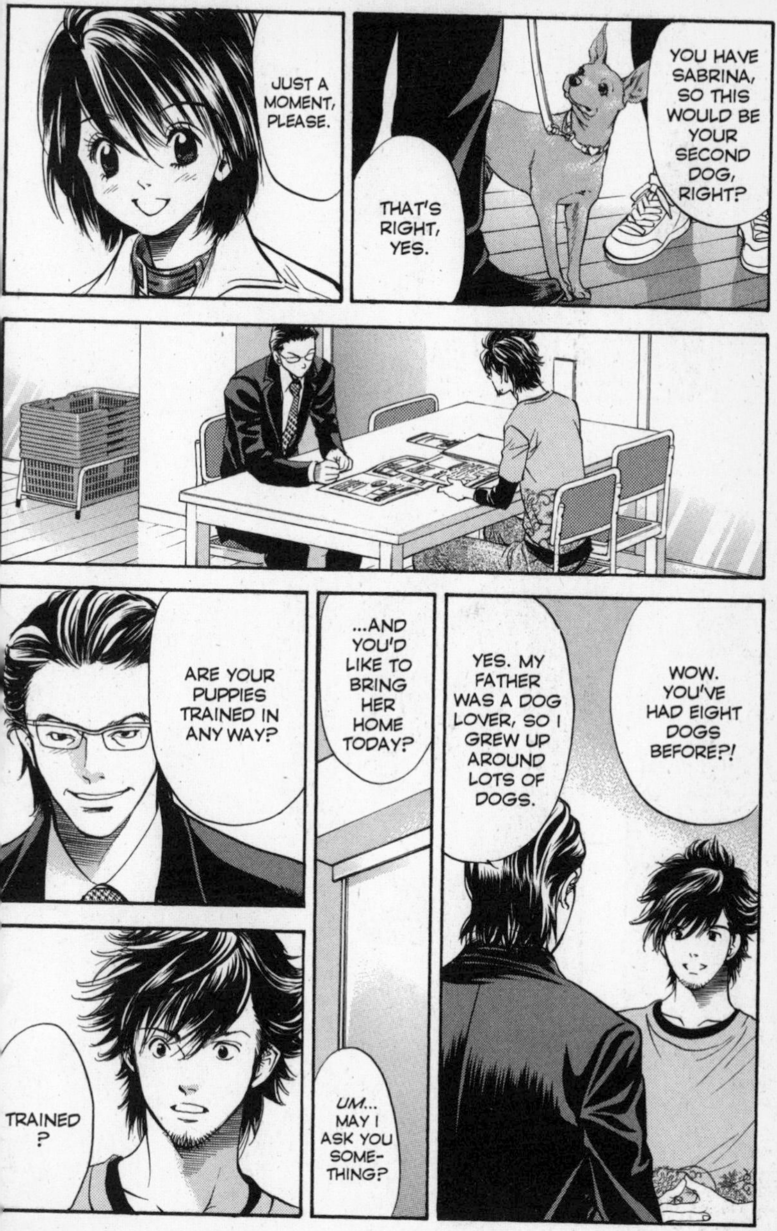
YOU HAVE SABRINA, SO THIS WOULD BE YOUR SECOND DOG, RIGHT?
THAT'S RIGHT, YES.
JUST A MOMENT, PLEASE.
WOW. YOU'VE HAD EIGHT DOGS BEFORE?!
YES. MY FATHER WAS A DOG LOVER, SO I GREW UP AROUND LOTS OF DOGS.
...AND YOU'D LIKE TO BRING HER HOME TODAY?
UM... MAY I ASK YOU SOMETHING?
ARE YOUR PUPPIES TRAINED IN ANY WAY?
TRAINED?

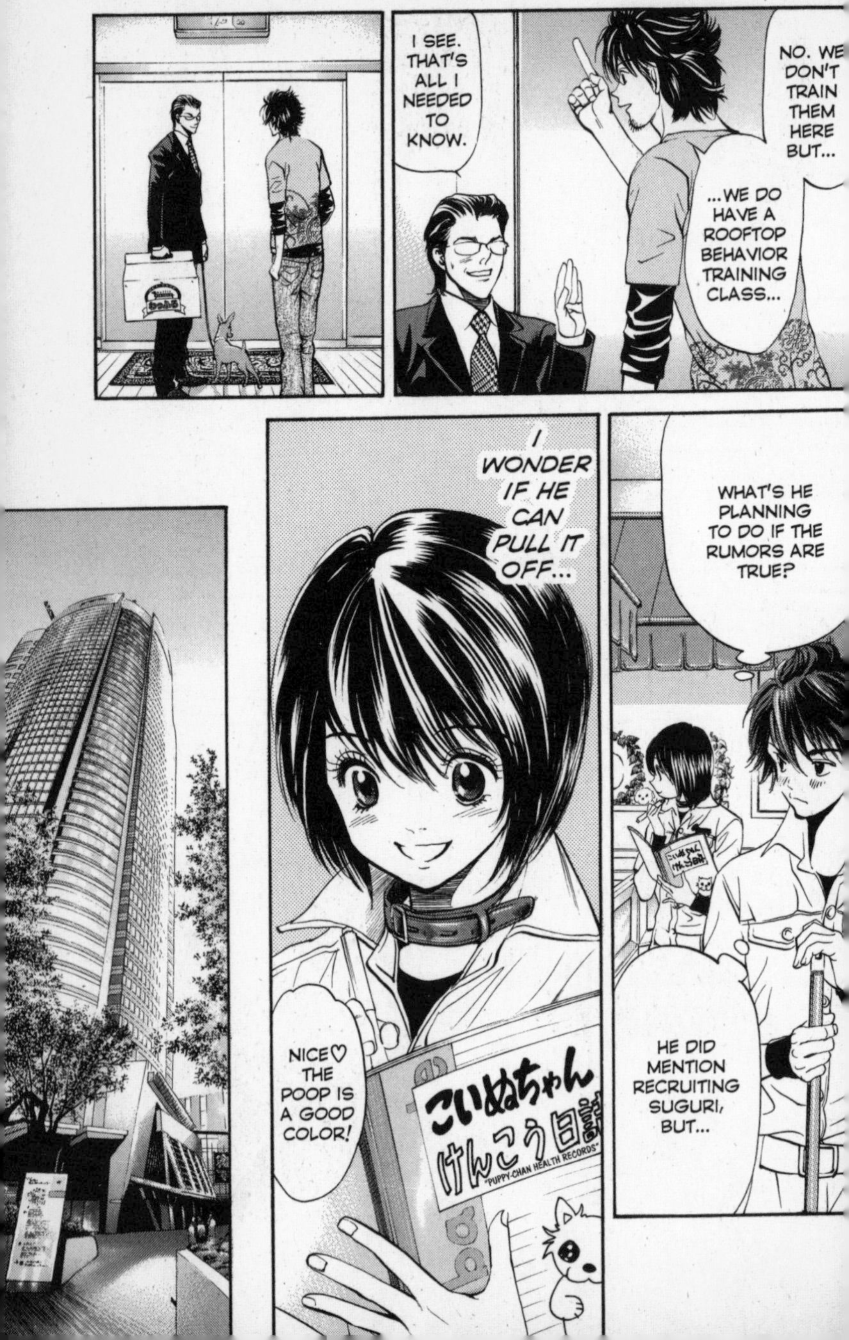
NO. WE DON'T TRAIN THEM HERE BUT...
...WE DO HAVE A ROOFTOP BEHAVIOR TRAINING CLASS...
I SEE. THAT'S ALL I NEEDED TO KNOW.
WHAT'S HE PLANNING TO DO IF THE RUMORS ARE TRUE?
HE DID MENTION RECRUITING SUGURI, BUT...
I WONDER IF HE CAN PULL IT OFF...
こいぬちゃん けんこう日誌
"PUPPY-CHAN HEALTH RECORDS"
NICE♡ THE POOP IS A GOOD COLOR!

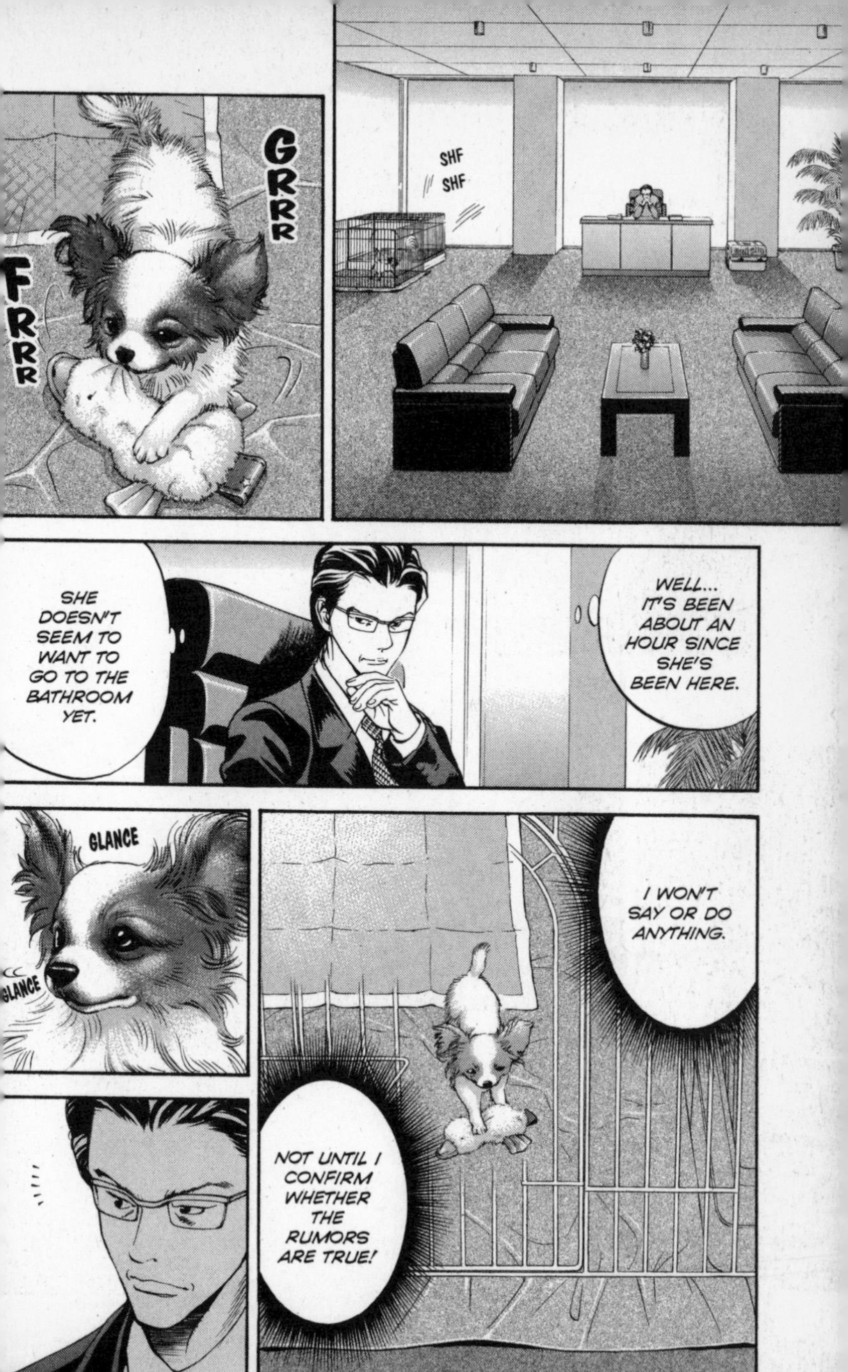
SHF
SHF
GRRR
FRRR
WELL... IT'S BEEN ABOUT AN HOUR SINCE SHE'S BEEN HERE.
SHE DOESN'T SEEM TO WANT TO GO TO THE BATHROOM YET.
I WON'T SAY OR DO ANYTHING.
NOT UNTIL I CONFIRM WHETHER THE RUMORS ARE TRUE!
GLANCE
GLANCE

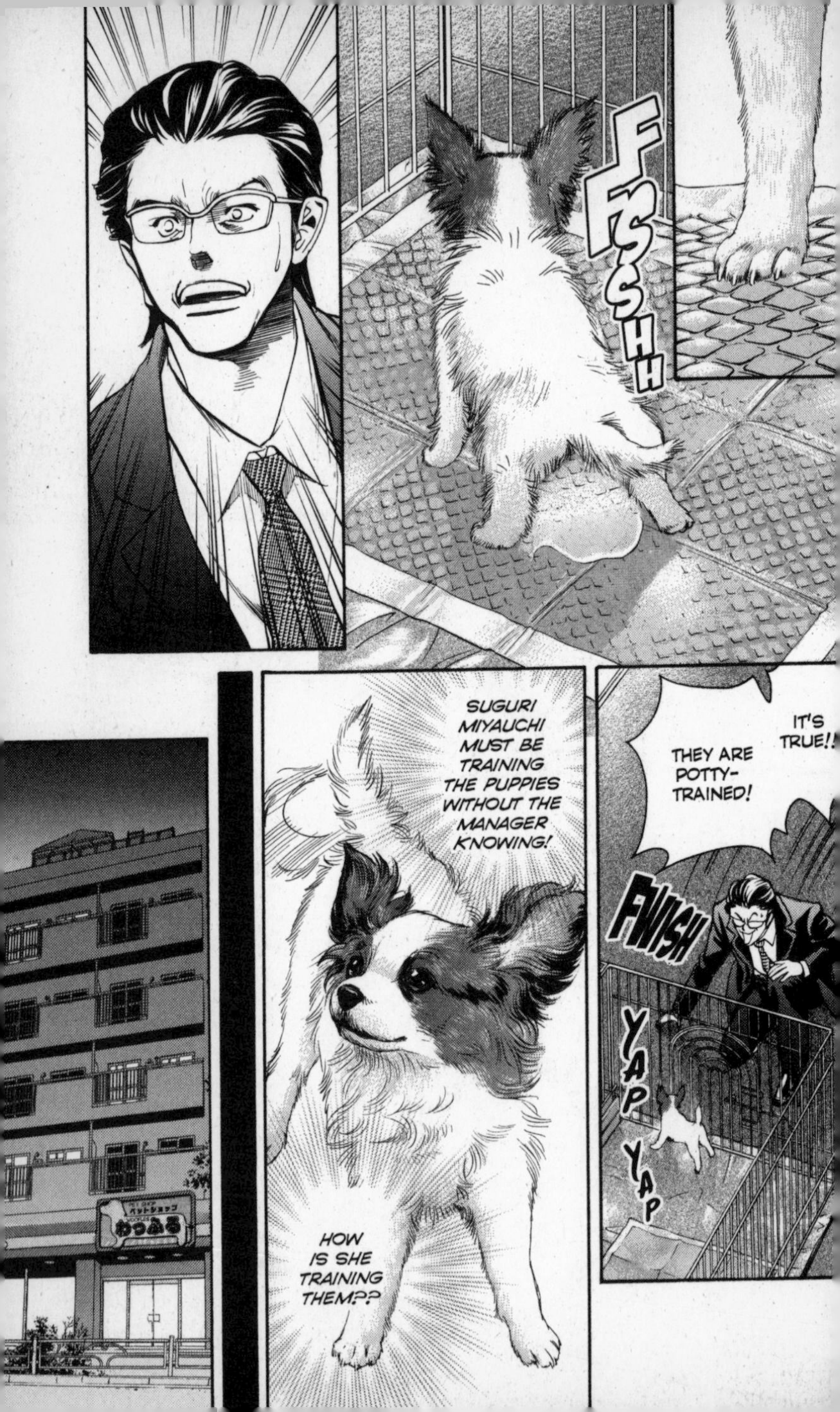
FSSHH
IT'S TRUE!!
THEY ARE POTTY-TRAINED!
FWISH
YAP YAP
SUGURI MIYAUCHI MUST BE TRAINING THE PUPPIES WITHOUT THE MANAGER KNOWING!
HOW IS SHE TRAINING THEM??

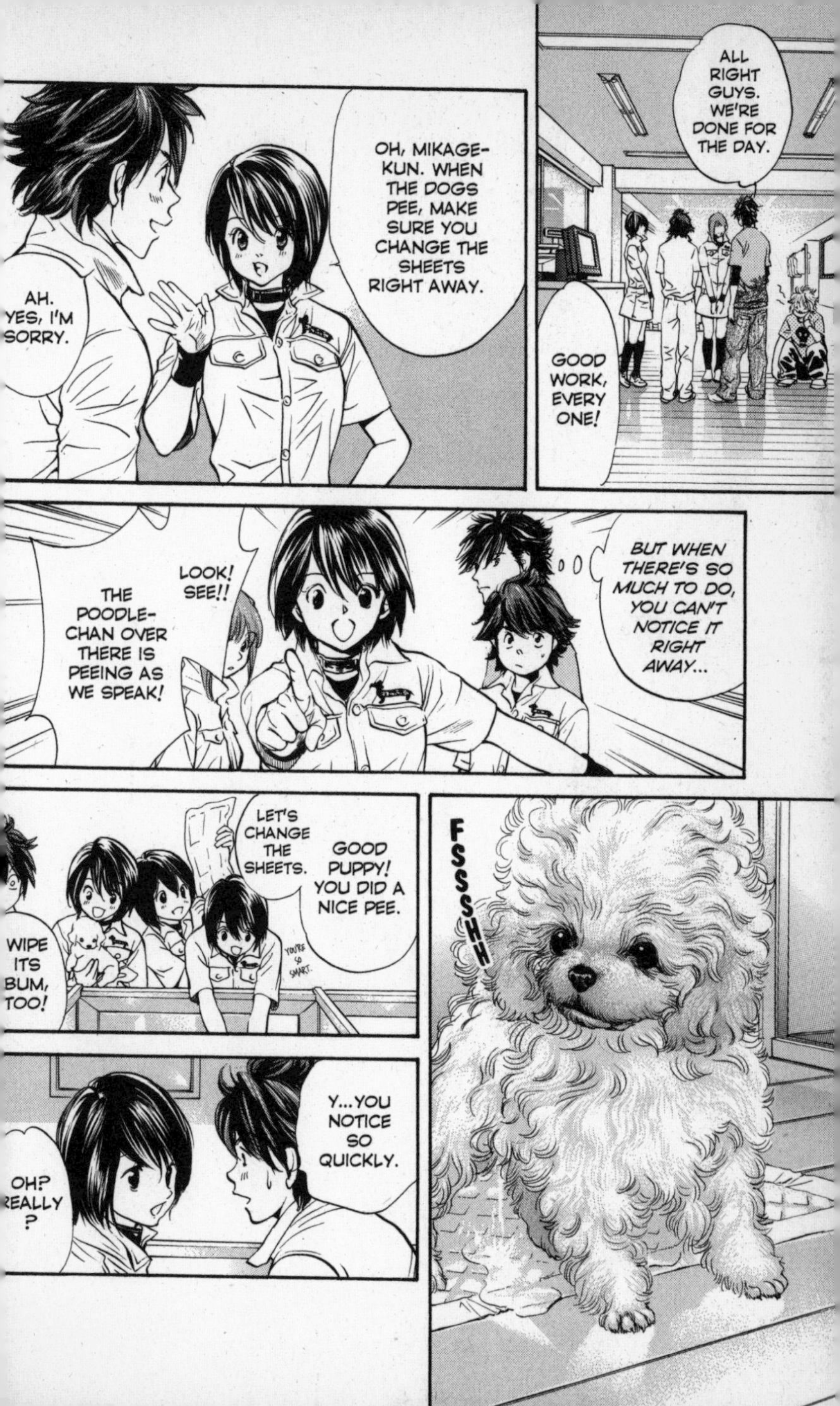
ALL RIGHT GUYS. WE'RE DONE FOR THE DAY.
GOOD WORK, EVERY ONE!
OH, MIKAGE-KUN. WHEN THE DOGS PEE, MAKE SURE YOU CHANGE THE SHEETS RIGHT AWAY.
AH. YES, I'M SORRY.
BUT WHEN THERE'S SO MUCH TO DO, YOU CAN'T NOTICE IT RIGHT AWAY...
LOOK! SEE!!
THE POODLE-CHAN OVER THERE IS PEEING AS WE SPEAK!
FSSSHH
GOOD PUPPY! YOU DID A NICE PEE.
LET'S CHANGE THE SHEETS.
YOU'RE SO SMART.
WIPE ITS BUM, TOO!
Y...YOU NOTICE SO QUICKLY.
OH? EALLY?

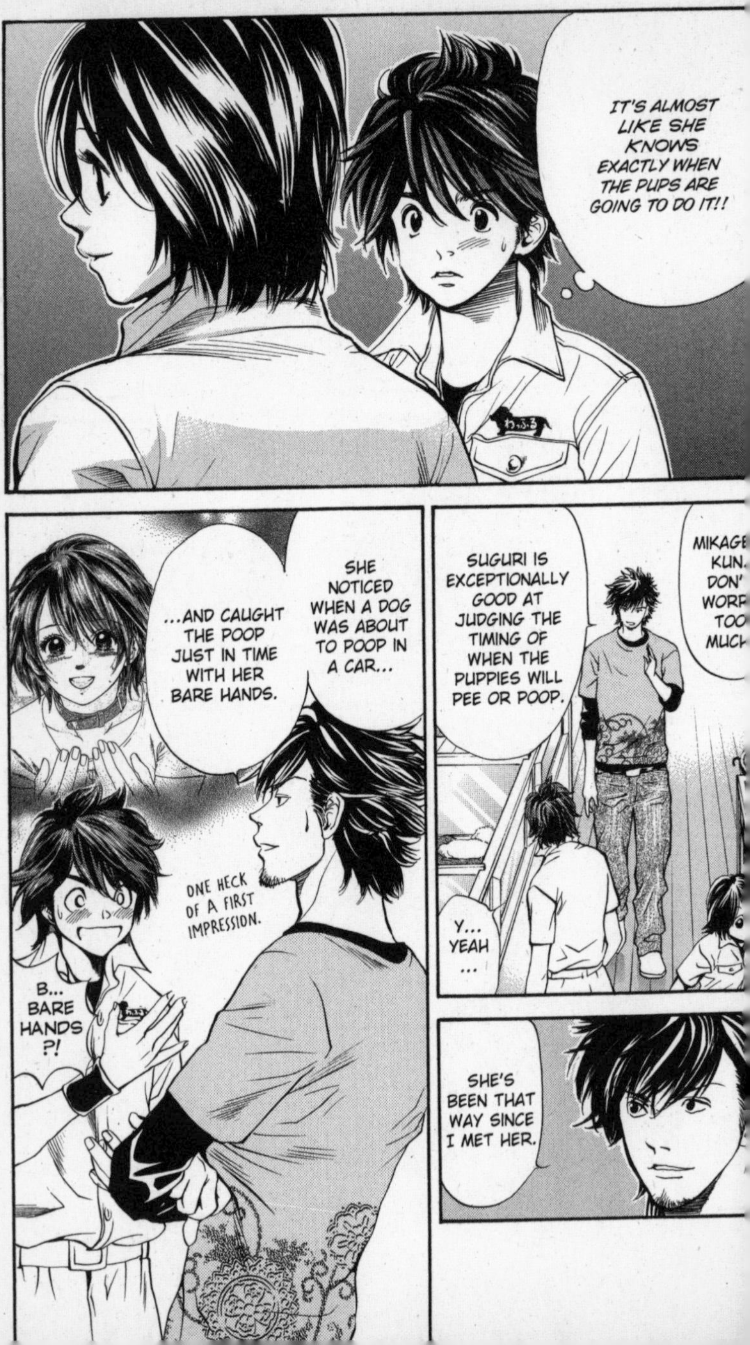
IT'S ALMOST LIKE SHE KNOWS EXACTLY WHEN THE PUPS ARE GOING TO DO IT!!
MIKAGE KUN. DON' WORR TOO MUC
SUGURI IS EXCEPTIONALLY GOOD AT JUDGING THE TIMING OF WHEN THE PUPPIES WILL PEE OR POOP.
Y... YEAH ...
SHE'S BEEN THAT WAY SINCE I MET HER.
SHE NOTICED WHEN A DOG WAS ABOUT TO POOP IN A CAR...
...AND CAUGHT THE POOP JUST IN TIME WITH HER BARE HANDS.
ONE HECK OF A FIRST IMPRESSION.
B... BARE HANDS ?!

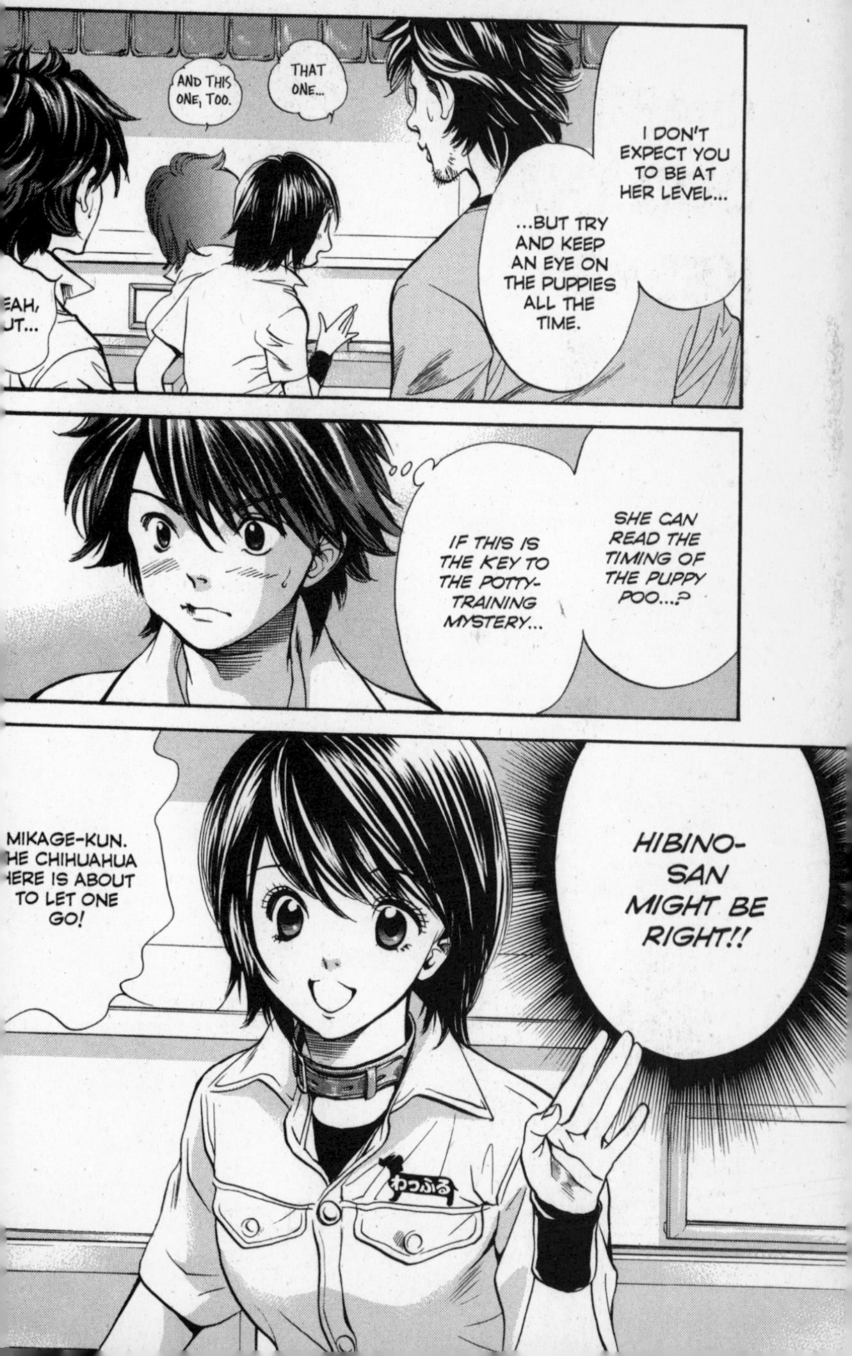
I DON'T EXPECT YOU TO BE AT HER LEVEL...
...BUT TRY AND KEEP AN EYE ON THE PUPPIES ALL THE TIME.
THAT ONE...
AND THIS ONE, TOO.
EAH, UT...
SHE CAN READ THE TIMING OF THE PUPPY POO...?
IF THIS IS THE KEY TO THE POTTY-TRAINING MYSTERY...
HIBINO-SAN MIGHT BE RIGHT!!
MIKAGE-KUN. HE CHIHUAHUA HERE IS ABOUT TO LET ONE GO!
わっふる

CHAPTER 106: DOG THAT KEEPS GROWLING

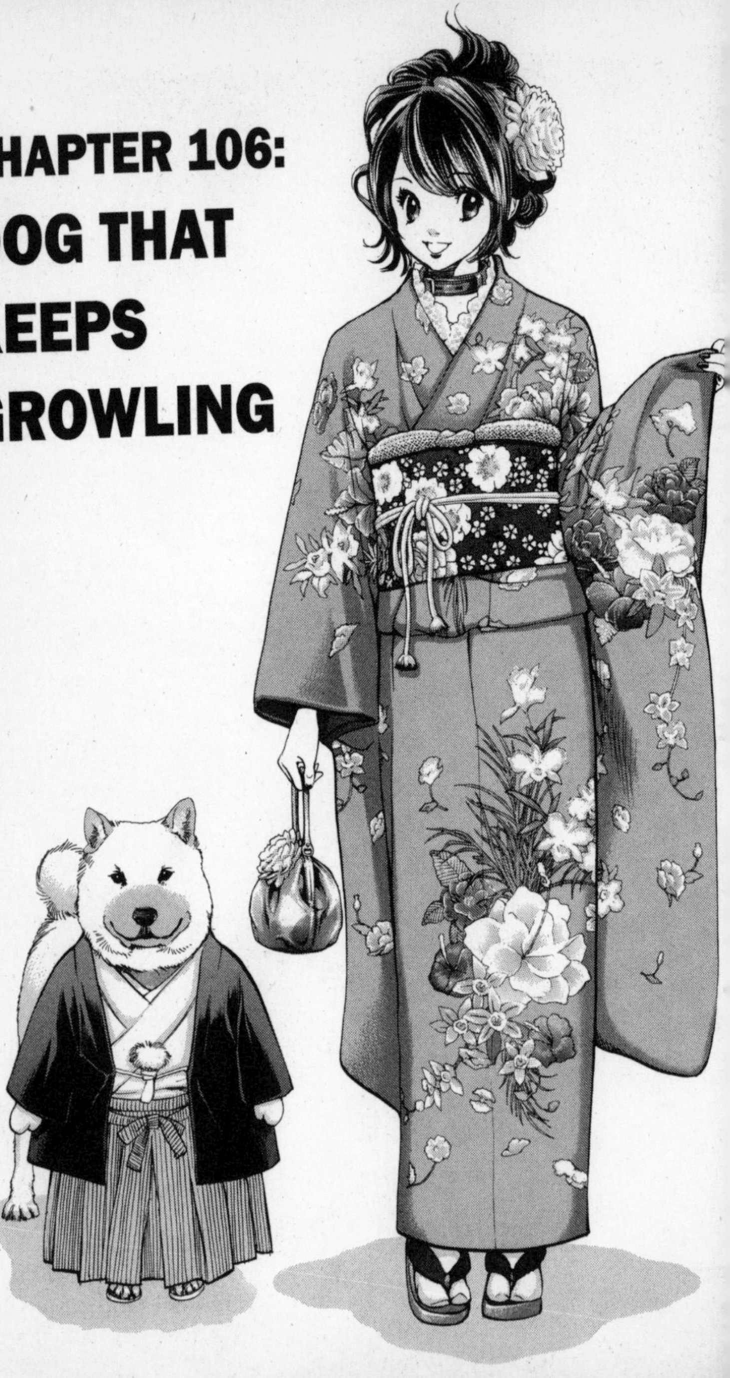

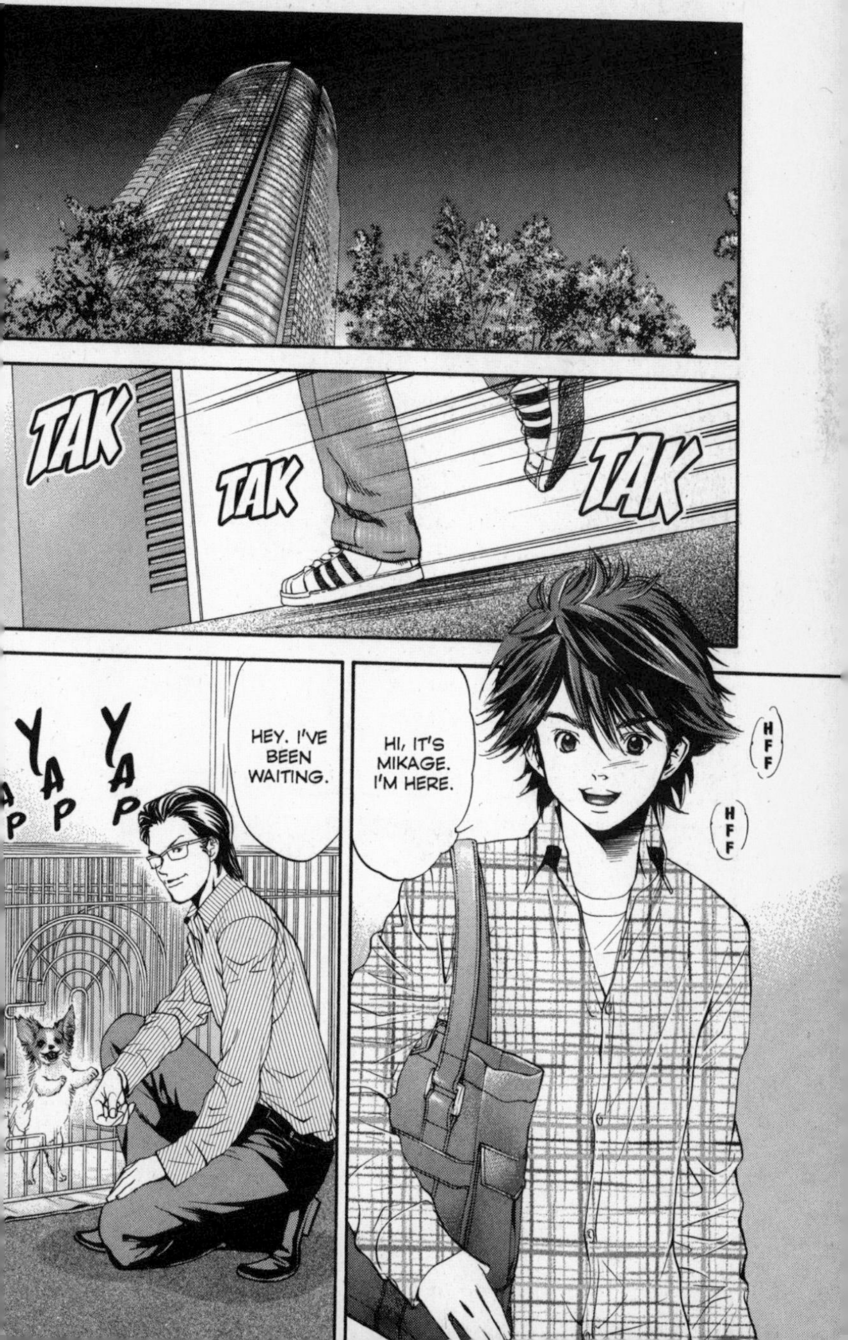
TAK
TAK
TAK
HI, IT'S MIKAGE. I'M HERE.
HFF
HFF
HEY. I'VE BEEN WAITING.
YAP
YAP

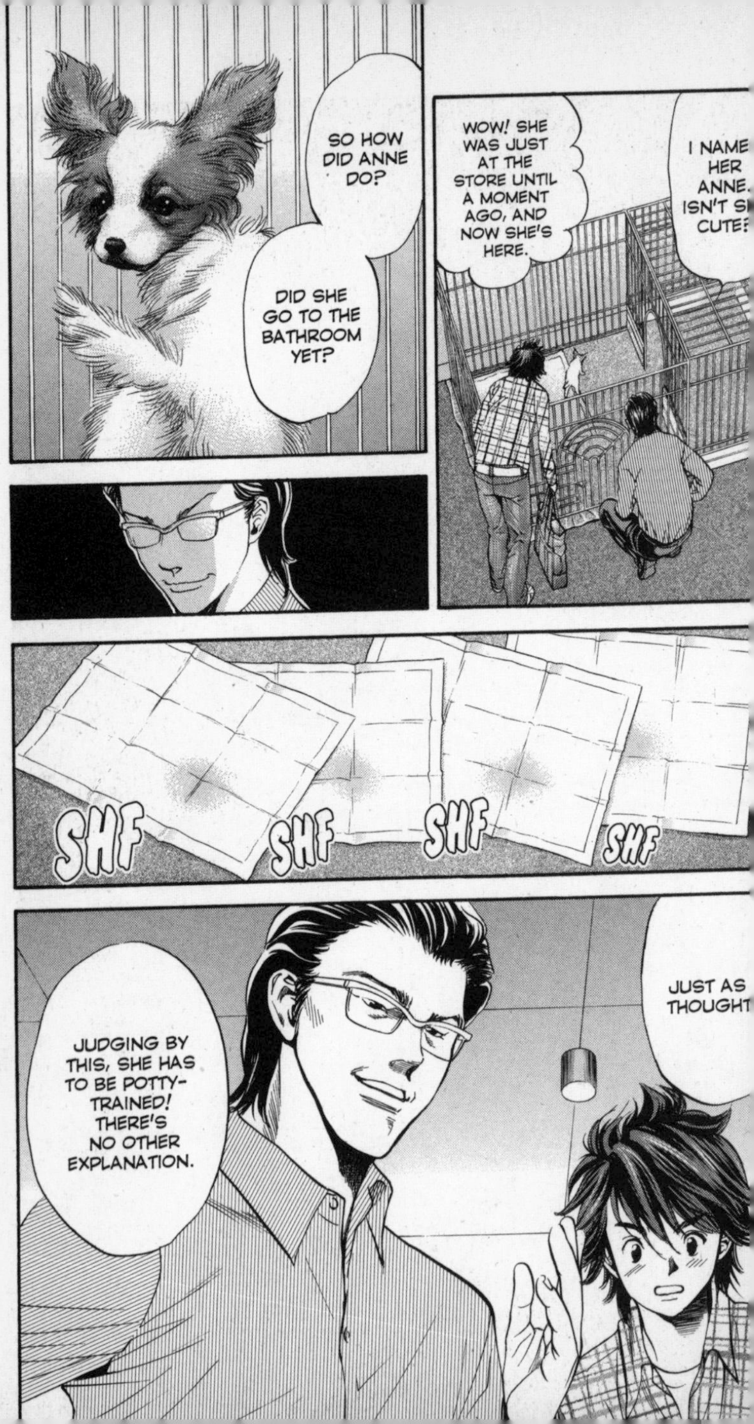
I NAME HER ANNE. ISN'T S CUTE?
WOW! SHE WAS JUST AT THE STORE UNTIL A MOMENT AGO, AND NOW SHE'S HERE.
SO HOW DID ANNE DO?
DID SHE GO TO THE BATHROOM YET?
SHF
SHF
SHF
SHF
JUST AS THOUGHT
JUDGING BY THIS, SHE HAS TO BE POTTY-TRAINED! THERE'S NO OTHER EXPLANATION.

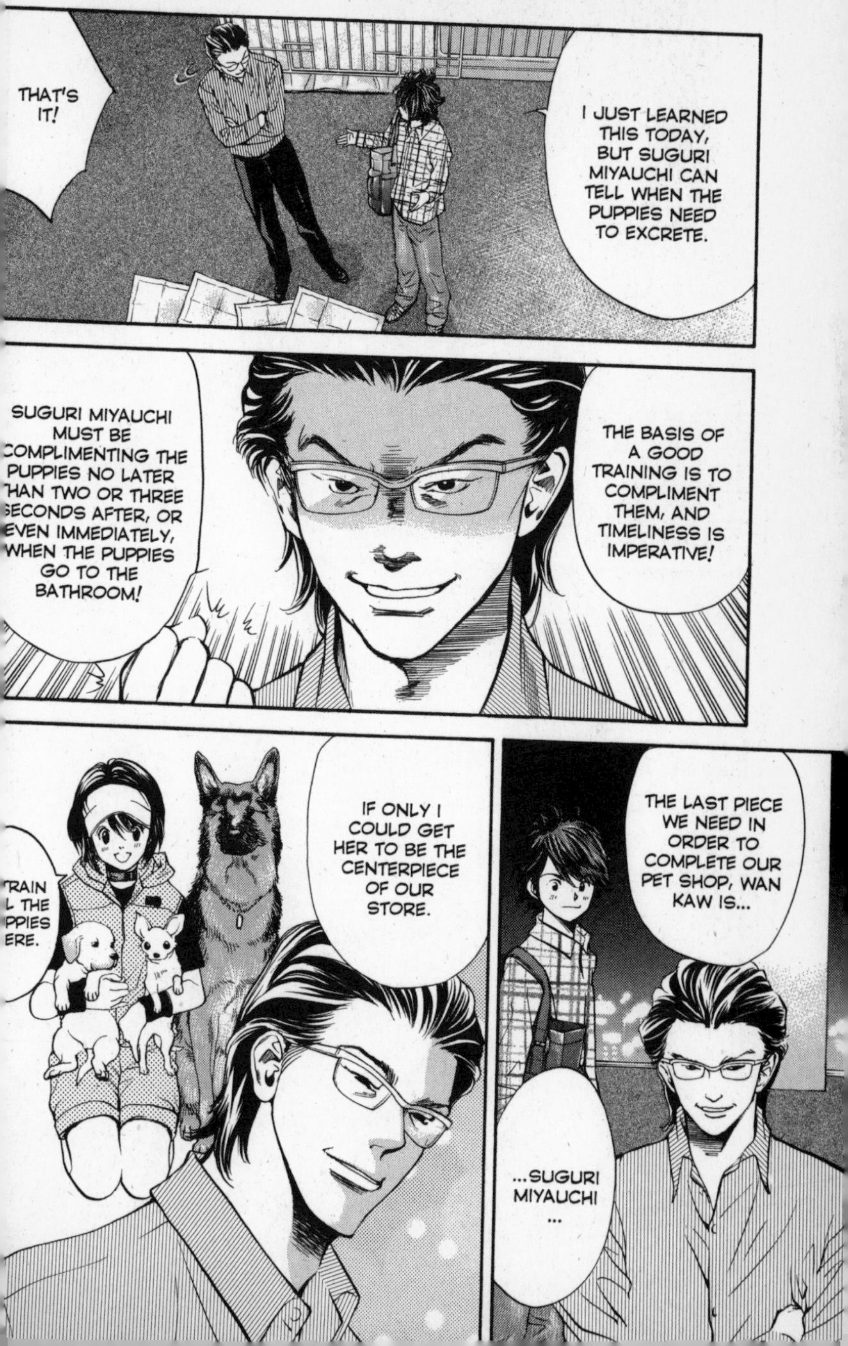
I JUST LEARNED THIS TODAY, BUT SUGURI MIYAUCHI CAN TELL WHEN THE PUPPIES NEED TO EXCRETE.
THAT'S IT!
THE BASIS OF A GOOD TRAINING IS TO COMPLIMENT THEM, AND TIMELINESS IS IMPERATIVE!
SUGURI MIYAUCHI MUST BE COMPLIMENTING THE PUPPIES NO LATER THAN TWO OR THREE SECONDS AFTER, OR EVEN IMMEDIATELY, WHEN THE PUPPIES GO TO THE BATHROOM!
THE LAST PIECE WE NEED IN ORDER TO COMPLETE OUR PET SHOP, WAN KAW IS...
...SUGURI MIYAUCHI ...
IF ONLY I COULD GET HER TO BE THE CENTERPIECE OF OUR STORE.
TRAIN L THE PPIES ERE.

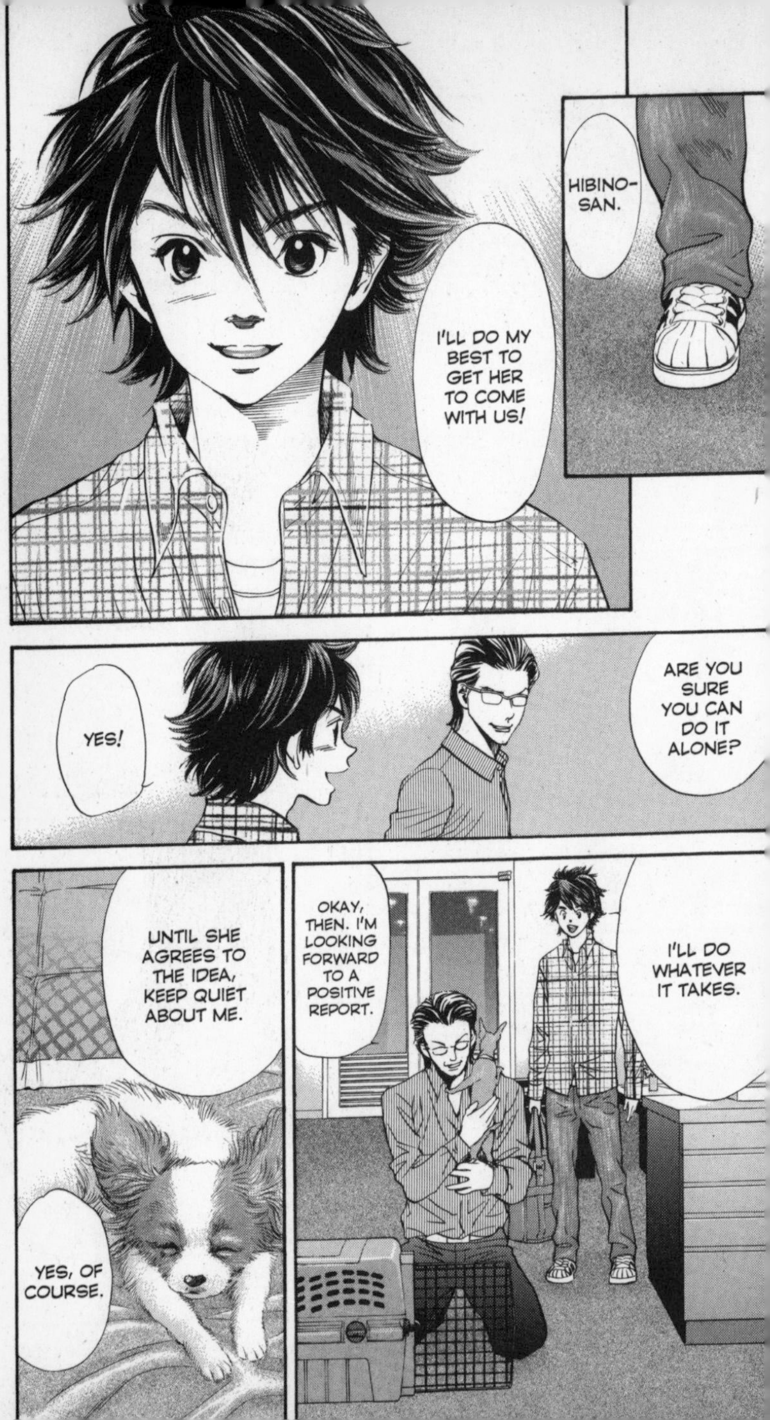
HIBINO-SAN.
I'LL DO MY BEST TO GET HER TO COME WITH US!
ARE YOU SURE YOU CAN DO IT ALONE?
YES!
I'LL DO WHATEVER IT TAKES.
OKAY, THEN. I'M LOOKING FORWARD TO A POSITIVE REPORT.
UNTIL SHE AGREES TO THE IDEA, KEEP QUIET ABOUT ME.
YES, OF COURSE.

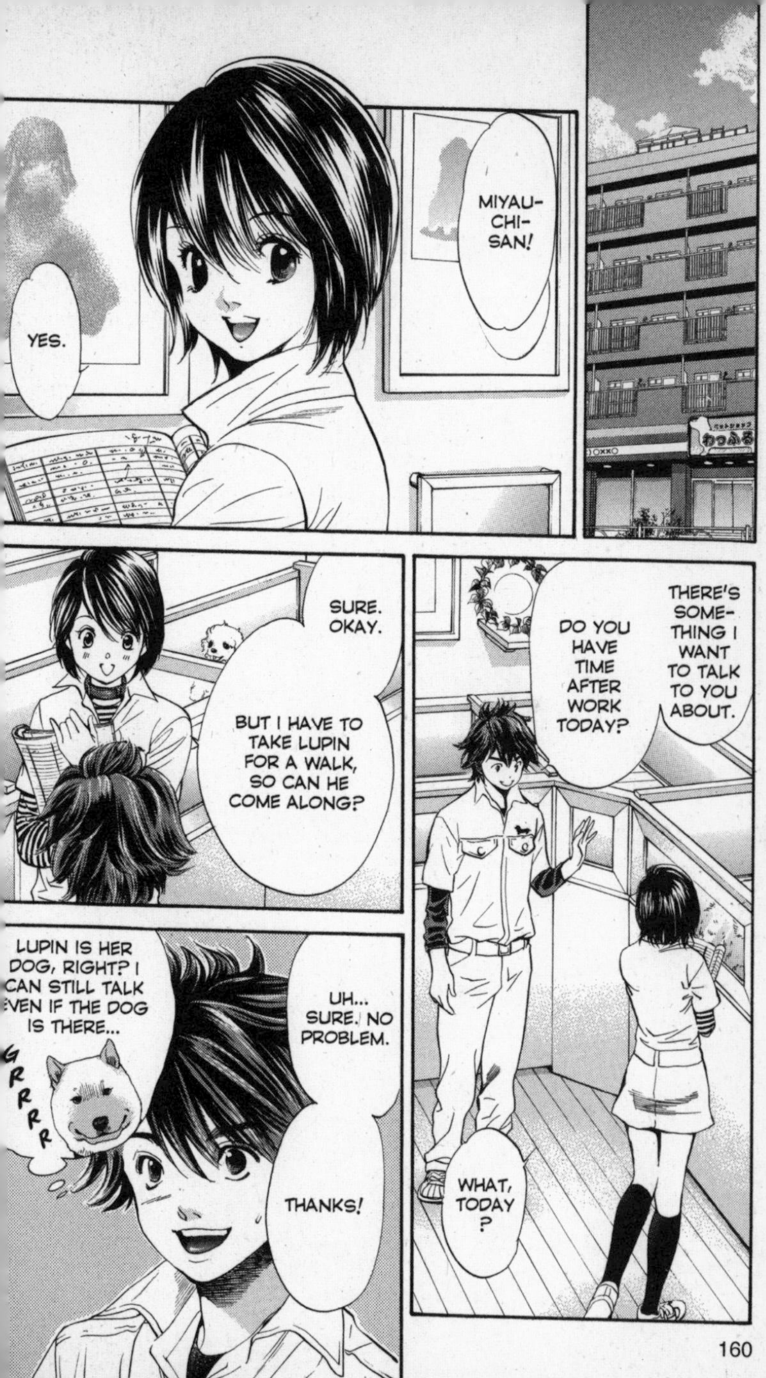
MIYAU-CHI-SAN!
YES.
THERE'S SOME-THING I WANT TO TALK TO YOU ABOUT.
DO YOU HAVE TIME AFTER WORK TODAY?
WHAT, TODAY?
SURE. OKAY.
BUT I HAVE TO TAKE LUPIN FOR A WALK, SO CAN HE COME ALONG?
UH... SURE. NO PROBLEM.
LUPIN IS HER DOG, RIGHT? I CAN STILL TALK EVEN IF THE DOG IS THERE...
GRRRR
THANKS!

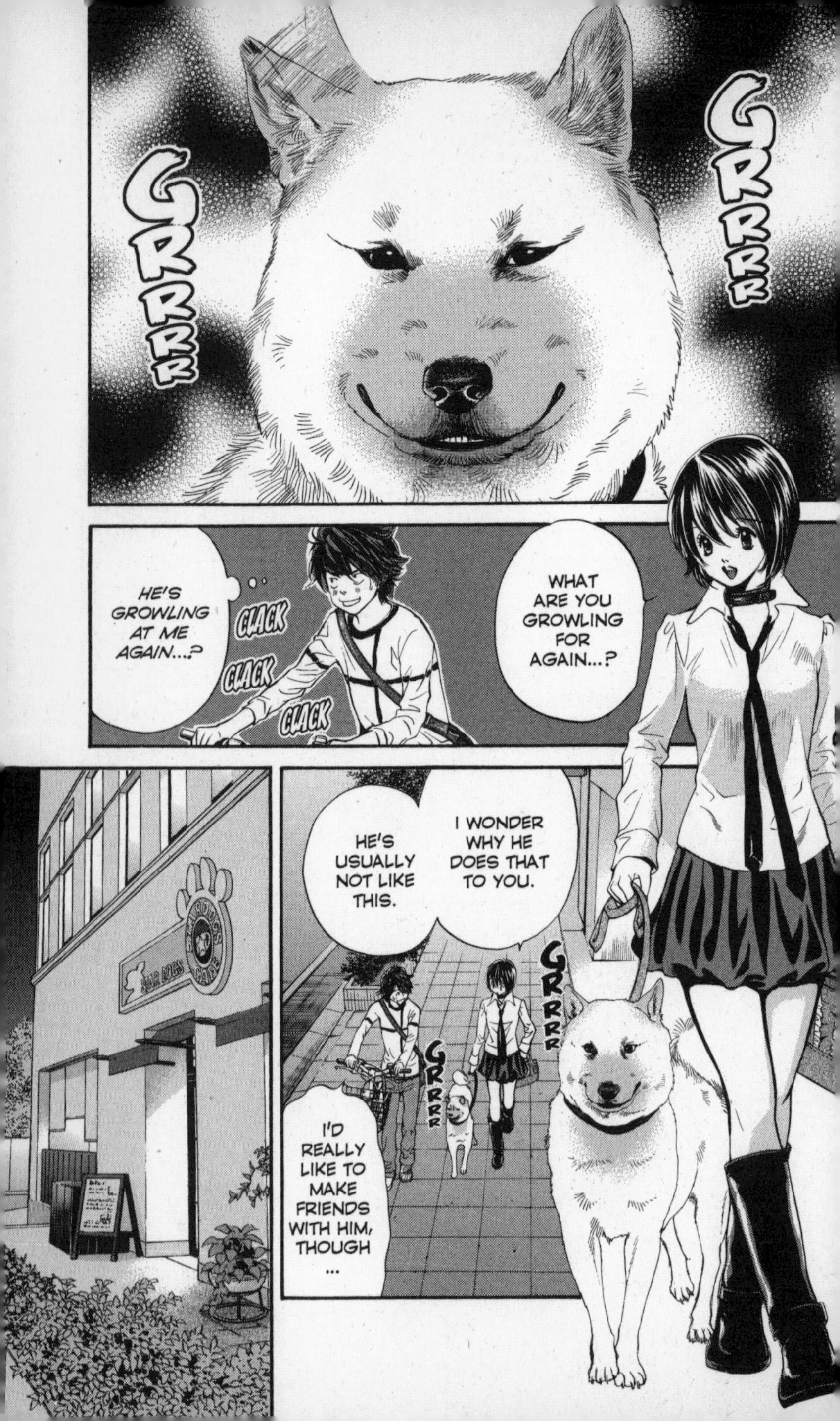
GRRRR
GRRRR
WHAT ARE YOU GROWLING FOR AGAIN...?
HE'S GROWLING AT ME AGAIN...?
CLACK
CLACK
CLACK
I WONDER WHY HE DOES THAT TO YOU.
HE'S USUALLY NOT LIKE THIS.
GRRRR
GRRRR
I'D REALLY LIKE TO MAKE FRIENDS WITH HIM, THOUGH...

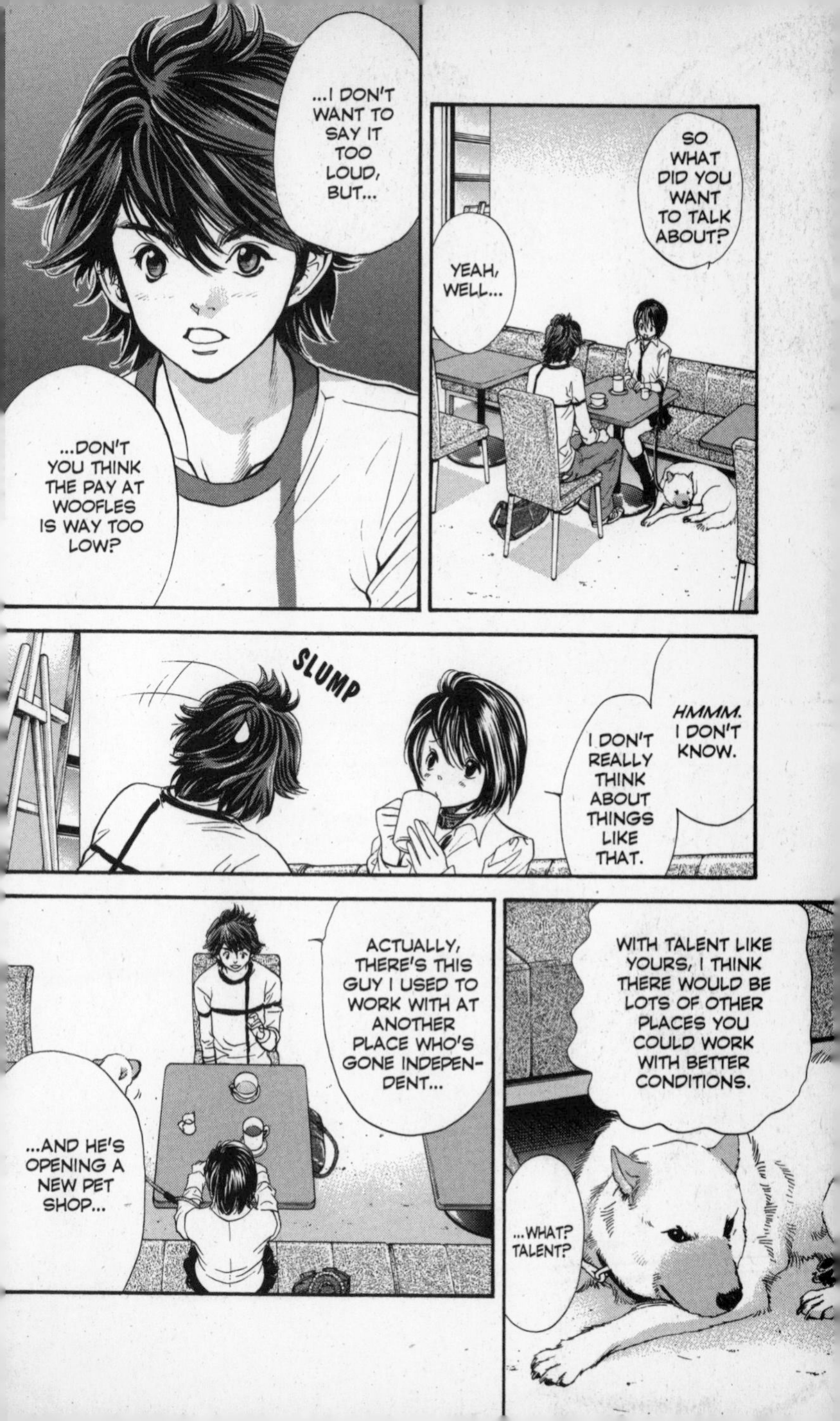
SO WHAT DID YOU WANT TO TALK ABOUT?
YEAH, WELL...
...I DON'T WANT TO SAY IT TOO LOUD, BUT...
...DON'T YOU THINK THE PAY AT WOOFLES IS WAY TOO LOW?
HMMM. I DON'T KNOW.
I DON'T REALLY THINK ABOUT THINGS LIKE THAT.
SLUMP
WITH TALENT LIKE YOURS, I THINK THERE WOULD BE LOTS OF OTHER PLACES YOU COULD WORK WITH BETTER CONDITIONS.
...WHAT? TALENT?
ACTUALLY, THERE'S THIS GUY I USED TO WORK WITH AT ANOTHER PLACE WHO'S GONE INDEPEN-DENT...
...AND HE'S OPENING A NEW PET SHOP...

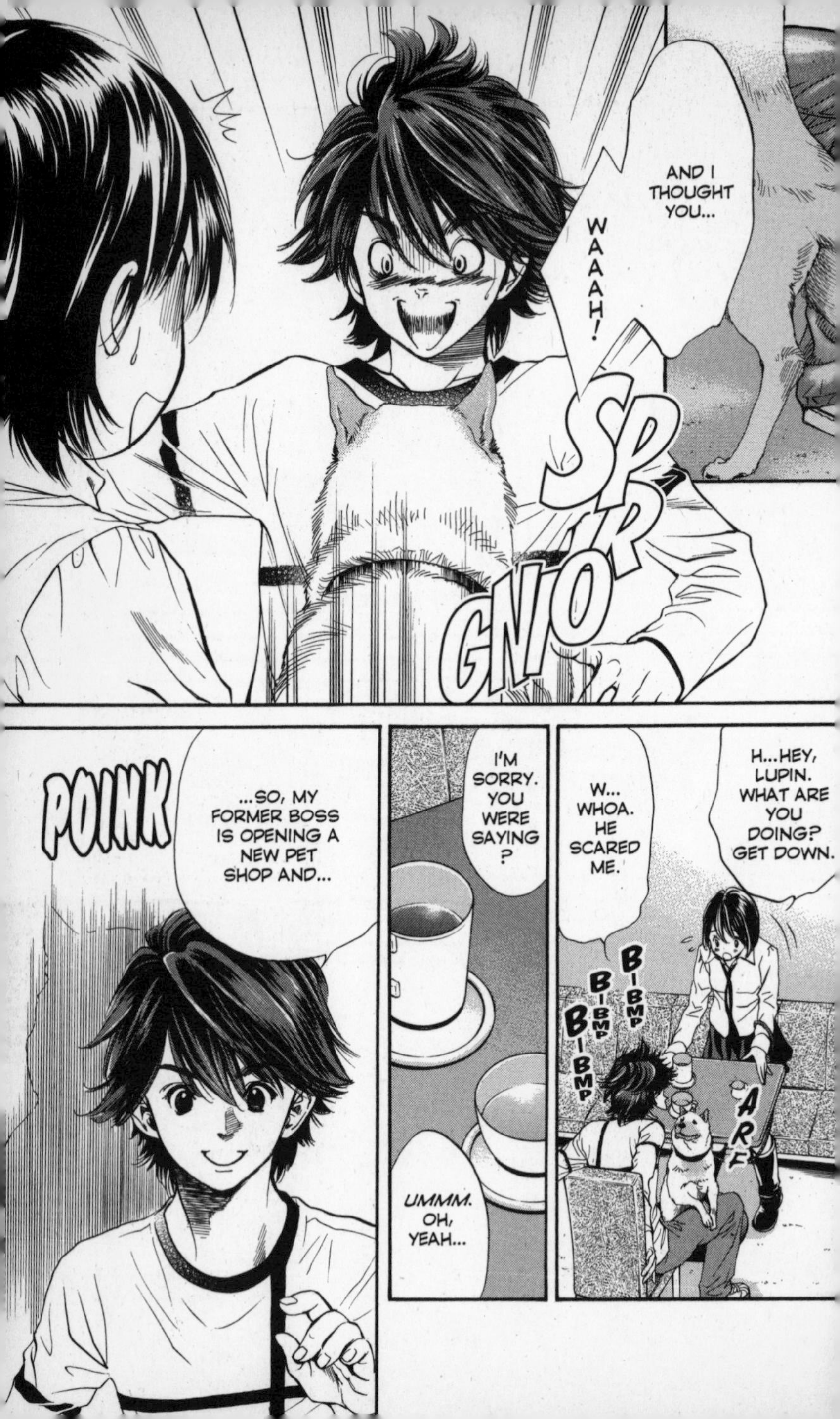
AND I THOUGHT YOU...
WAAAAH!
SPRONG
H...HEY, LUPIN. WHAT ARE YOU DOING? GET DOWN.
W... WHOA. HE SCARED ME.
BIBMP
BIBMP
BIBMP
ARF
I'M SORRY. YOU WERE SAYING?
UMMM. OH, YEAH...
POINK
...SO, MY FORMER BOSS IS OPENING A NEW PET SHOP AND...

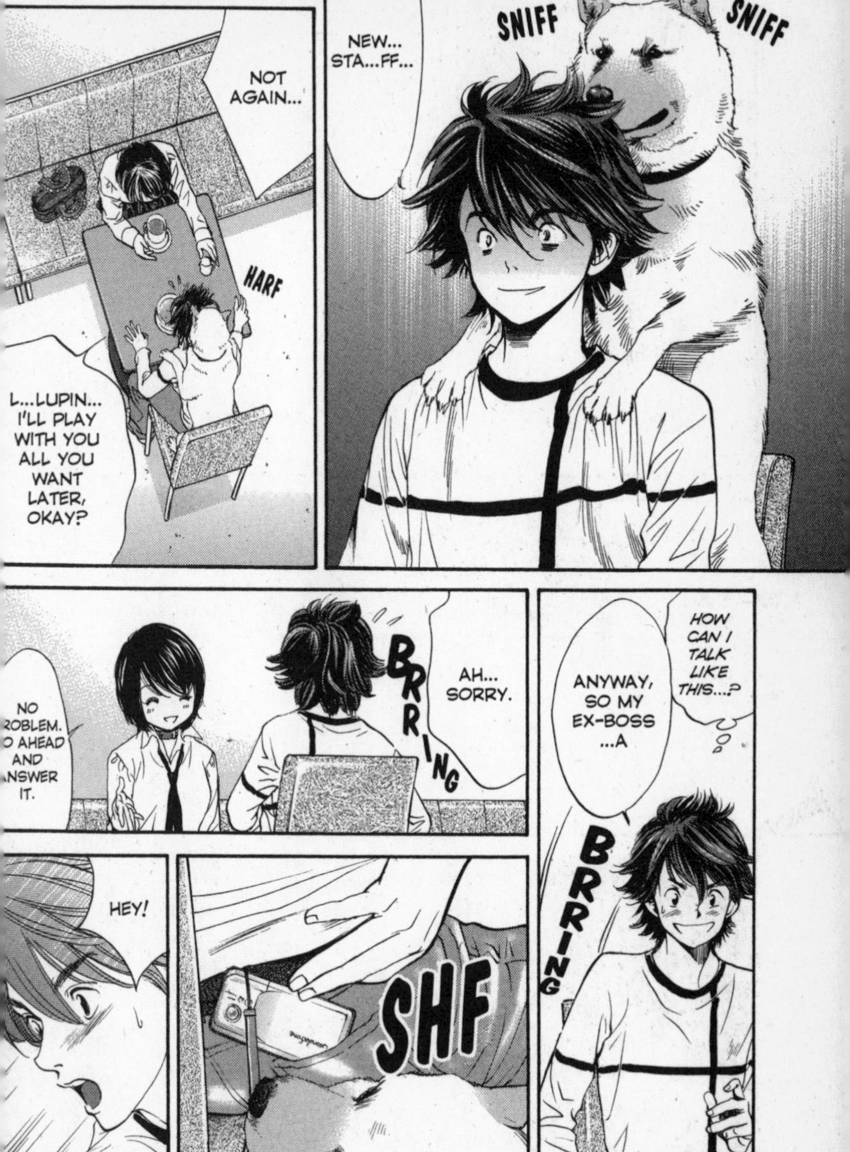
NEW... STA...FF...
SNIFF
SNIFF
NOT AGAIN...
HARF
L...LUPIN... I'LL PLAY WITH YOU ALL YOU WANT LATER, OKAY?
HOW CAN I TALK LIKE THIS...?
ANYWAY, SO MY EX-BOSS ...A
BRRING
AH... SORRY.
BRRING
NO ROBLEM. O AHEAD AND NSWER IT.
SHF
HEY!

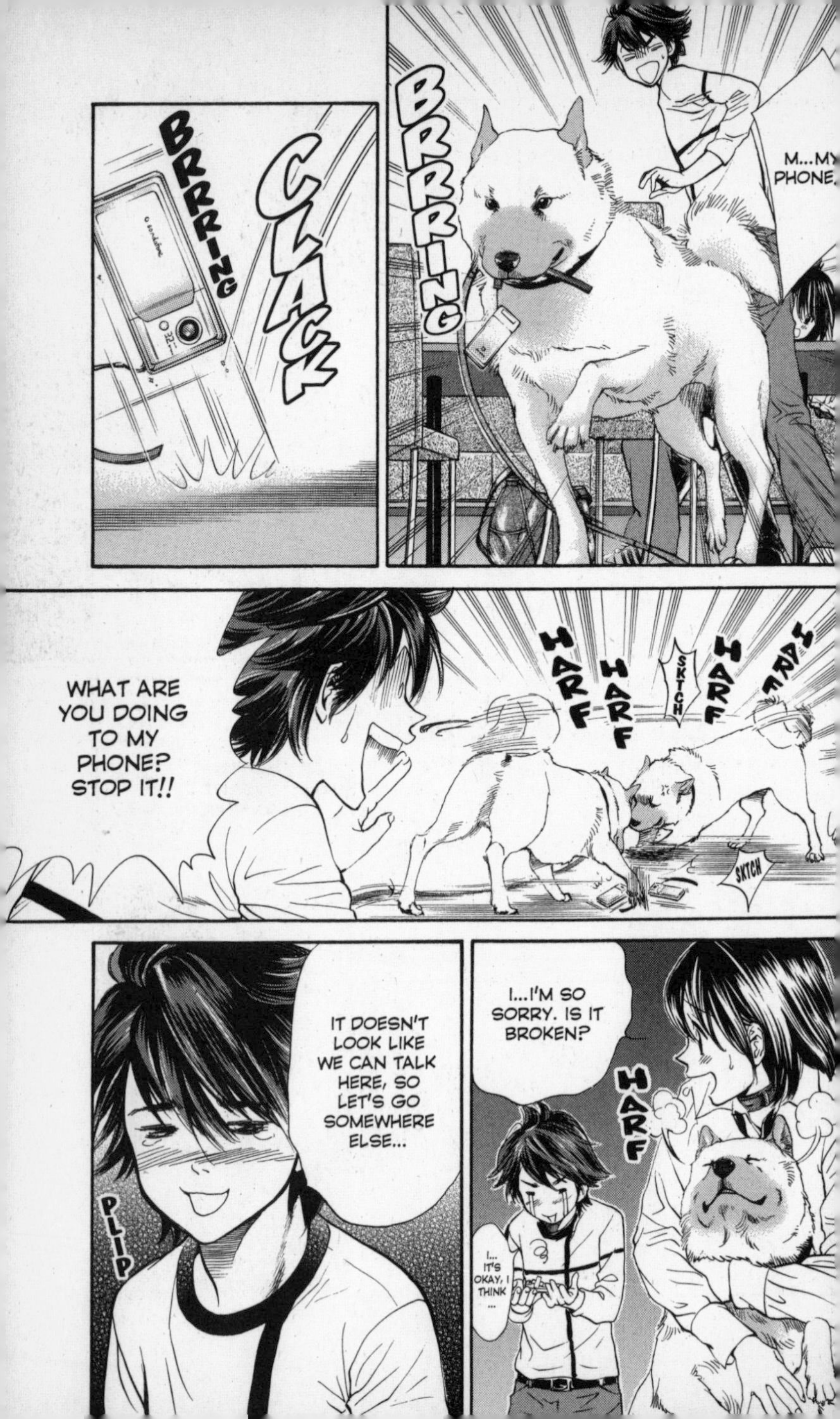
M...MY PHONE.
BRRRING
BRRRING
CLACK
HARF
SKTCH
HARF
HARF
HARF
SKTCH
WHAT ARE YOU DOING TO MY PHONE? STOP IT!!
I...I'M SO SORRY. IS IT BROKEN?
HARF
I... IT'S OKAY, I THINK ...
IT DOESN'T LOOK LIKE WE CAN TALK HERE, SO LET'S GO SOMEWHERE ELSE...
PLIP

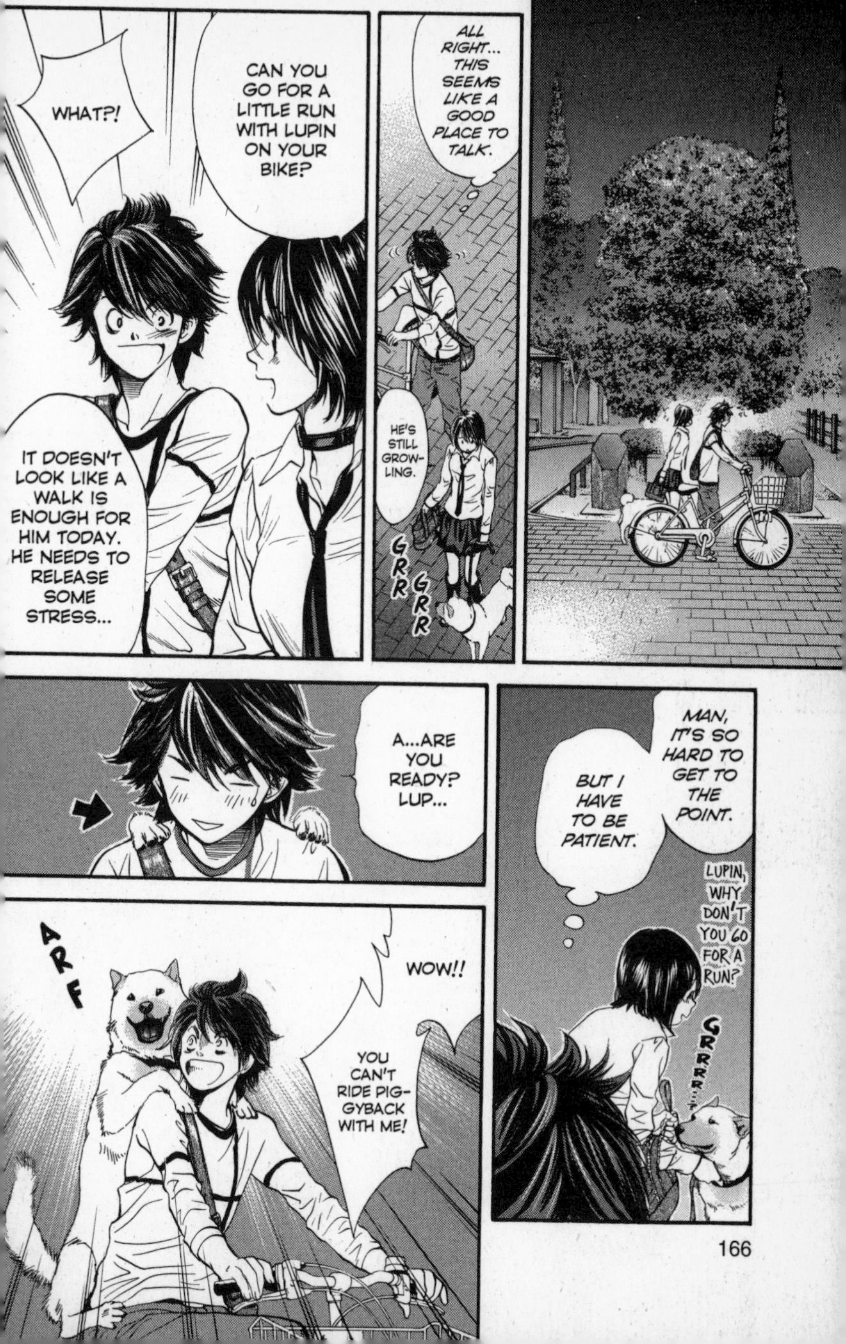
ALL RIGHT... THIS SEEMS LIKE A GOOD PLACE TO TALK.
HE'S STILL GROWLING.
GRR GRR
CAN YOU GO FOR A LITTLE RUN WITH LUPIN ON YOUR BIKE?
WHAT?!
IT DOESN'T LOOK LIKE A WALK IS ENOUGH FOR HIM TODAY. HE NEEDS TO RELEASE SOME STRESS...
MAN, IT'S SO HARD TO GET TO THE POINT.
BUT I HAVE TO BE PATIENT.
LUPIN, WHY DON'T YOU GO FOR A RUN?
GRRRR...?
A...ARE YOU READY? LUP...
WOW!!
ARF
YOU CAN'T RIDE PIGGYBACK WITH ME!

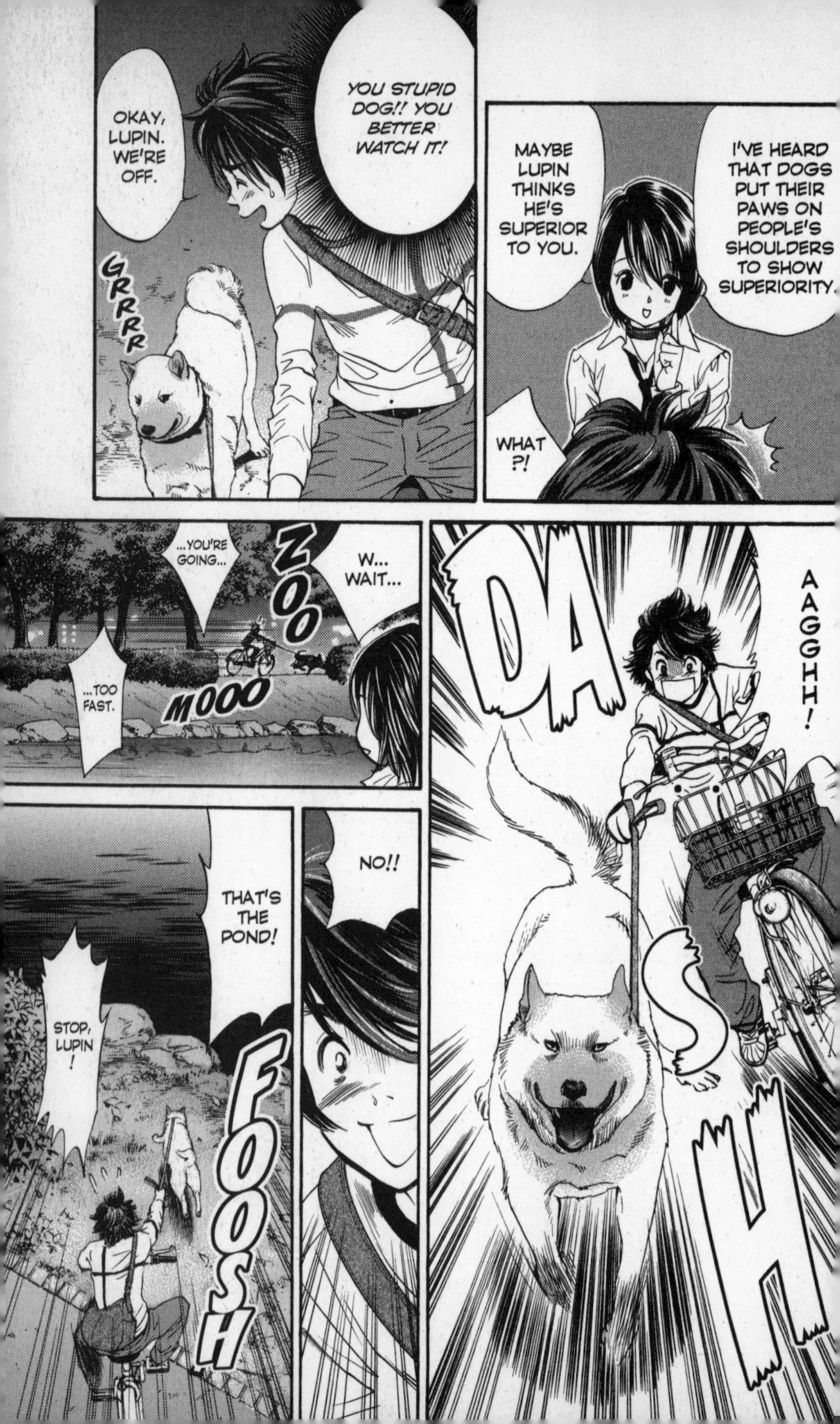
I'VE HEARD THAT DOGS PUT THEIR PAWS ON PEOPLE'S SHOULDERS TO SHOW SUPERIORITY.
MAYBE LUPIN THINKS HE'S SUPERIOR TO YOU.
WHAT?!
YOU STUPID DOG!! YOU BETTER WATCH IT!
OKAY, LUPIN. WE'RE OFF.
GRRRR
AAGGHH!
DASH
W... WAIT...
ZOOO
...YOU'RE GOING...
MOOO
...TOO FAST.
NO!!
THAT'S THE POND!
FOOSH
STOP, LUPIN!

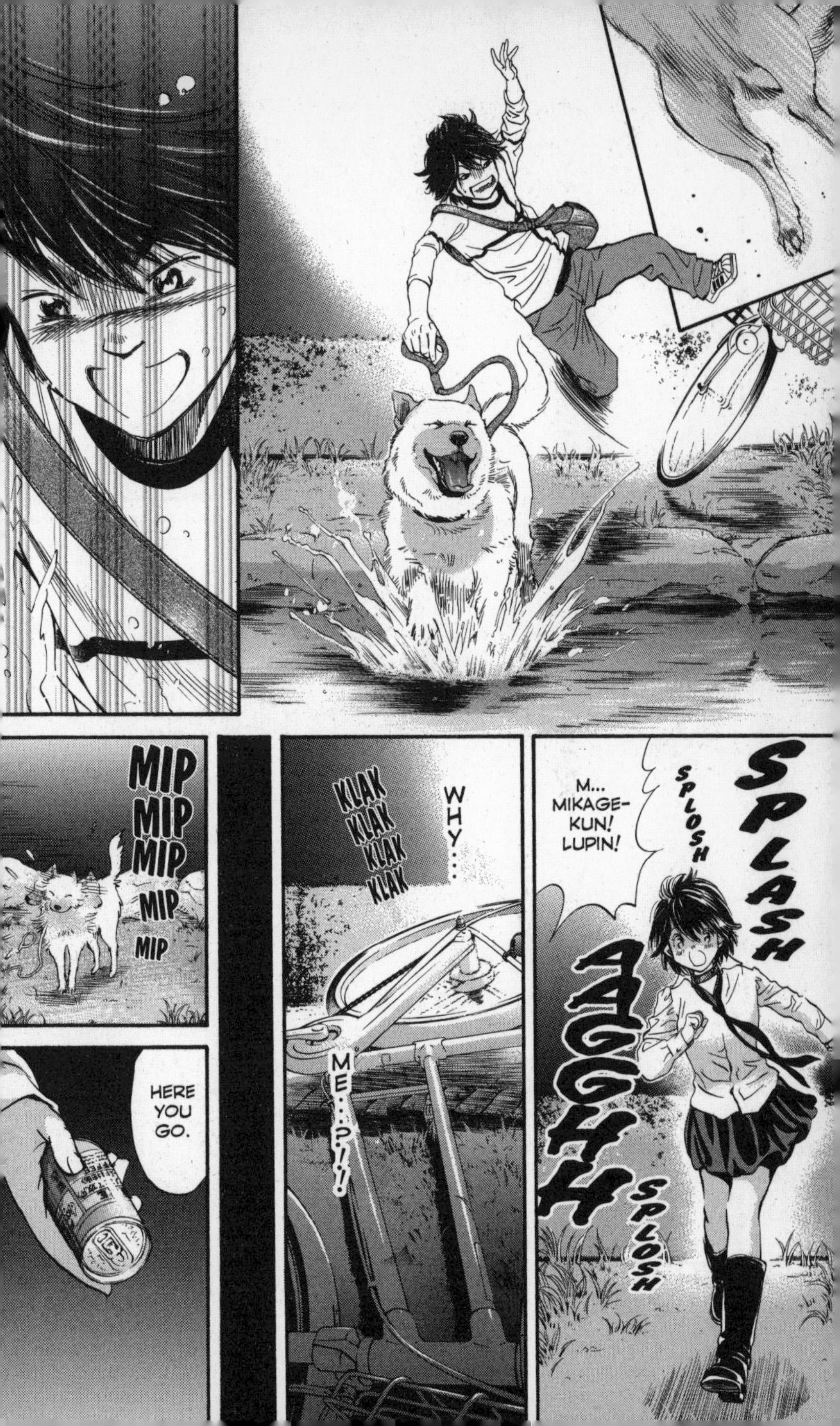
SPLASH
SPLOSH
M... MIKAGE-KUN! LUPIN!
AGGHH
SPLOSH
WHY...
KLAK KLAK KLAK KLAK
ME...?!!
MIP MIP MIP MIP MIP
HERE YOU GO.

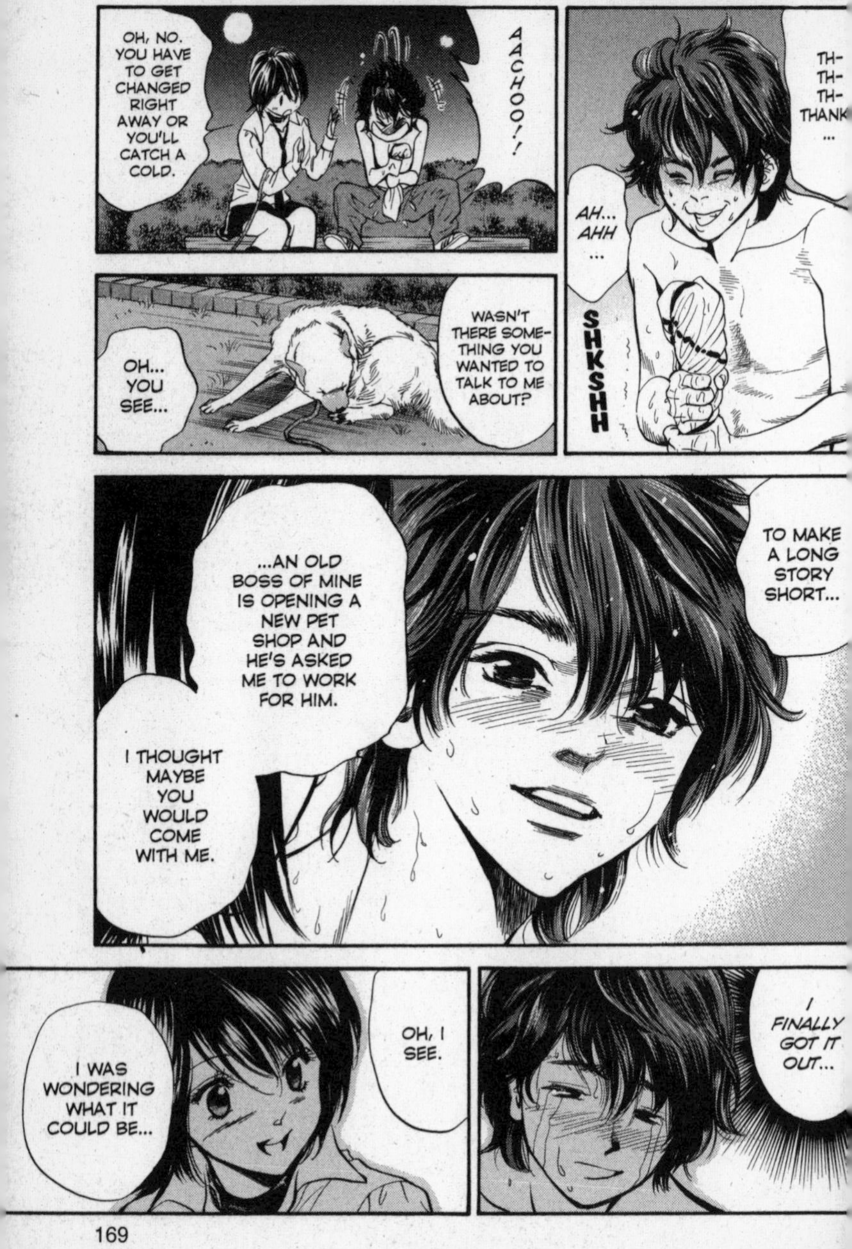
TH-TH-TH-THANK...
AH... AHH...
SHKSHH
AACHOO!!
OH, NO. YOU HAVE TO GET CHANGED RIGHT AWAY OR YOU'LL CATCH A COLD.
WASN'T THERE SOMETHING YOU WANTED TO TALK TO ME ABOUT?
OH... YOU SEE...
TO MAKE A LONG STORY SHORT...
...AN OLD BOSS OF MINE IS OPENING A NEW PET SHOP AND HE'S ASKED ME TO WORK FOR HIM.
I THOUGHT MAYBE YOU WOULD COME WITH ME.
I FINALLY GOT IT OUT...
OH, I SEE.
I WAS WONDERING WHAT IT COULD BE...

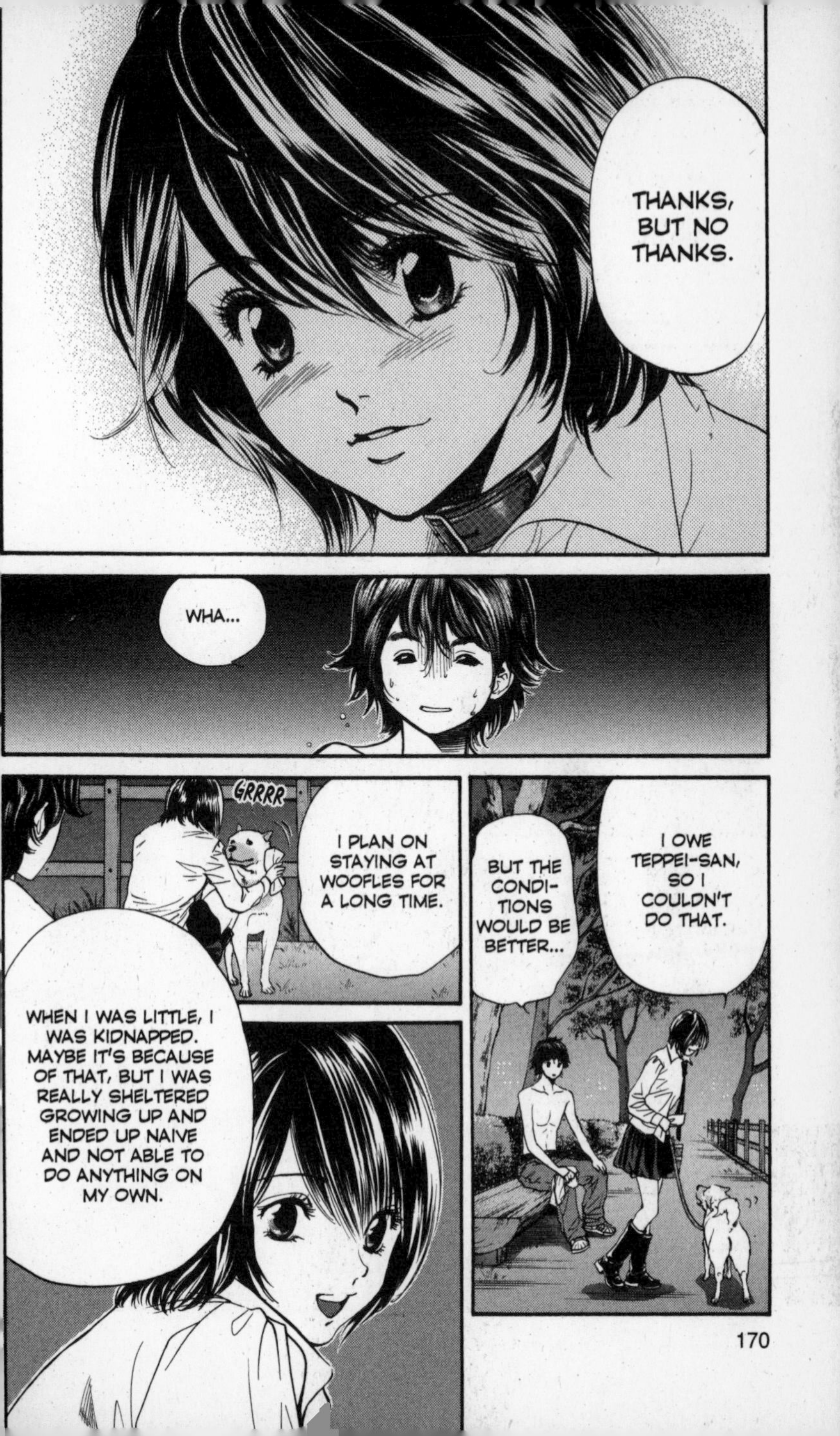
THANKS, BUT NO THANKS.
WHA...
I OWE TEPPEI-SAN, SO I COULDN'T DO THAT.
BUT THE CONDI-TIONS WOULD BE BETTER...
GRRRR
I PLAN ON STAYING AT WOOFLES FOR A LONG TIME.
WHEN I WAS LITTLE, I WAS KIDNAPPED. MAYBE IT'S BECAUSE OF THAT, BUT I WAS REALLY SHELTERED GROWING UP AND ENDED UP NAIVE AND NOT ABLE TO DO ANYTHING ON MY OWN.

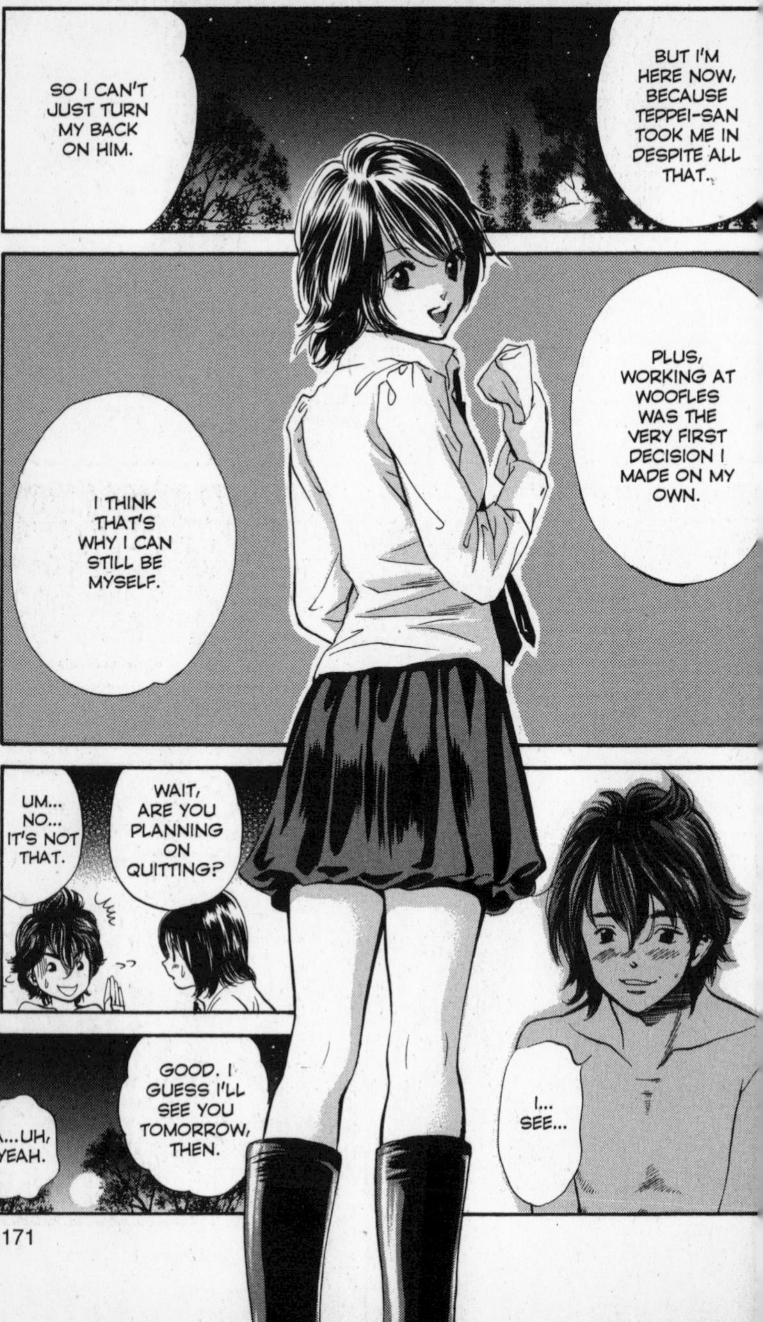
BUT I'M HERE NOW, BECAUSE TEPPEI-SAN TOOK ME IN DESPITE ALL THAT.
SO I CAN'T JUST TURN MY BACK ON HIM.
PLUS, WORKING AT WOOFLES WAS THE VERY FIRST DECISION I MADE ON MY OWN.
I THINK THAT'S WHY I CAN STILL BE MYSELF.
I... SEE...
WAIT, ARE YOU PLANNING ON QUITTING?
UM... NO... IT'S NOT THAT.
GOOD. I GUESS I'LL SEE YOU TOMORROW, THEN.
A...UH, YEAH.

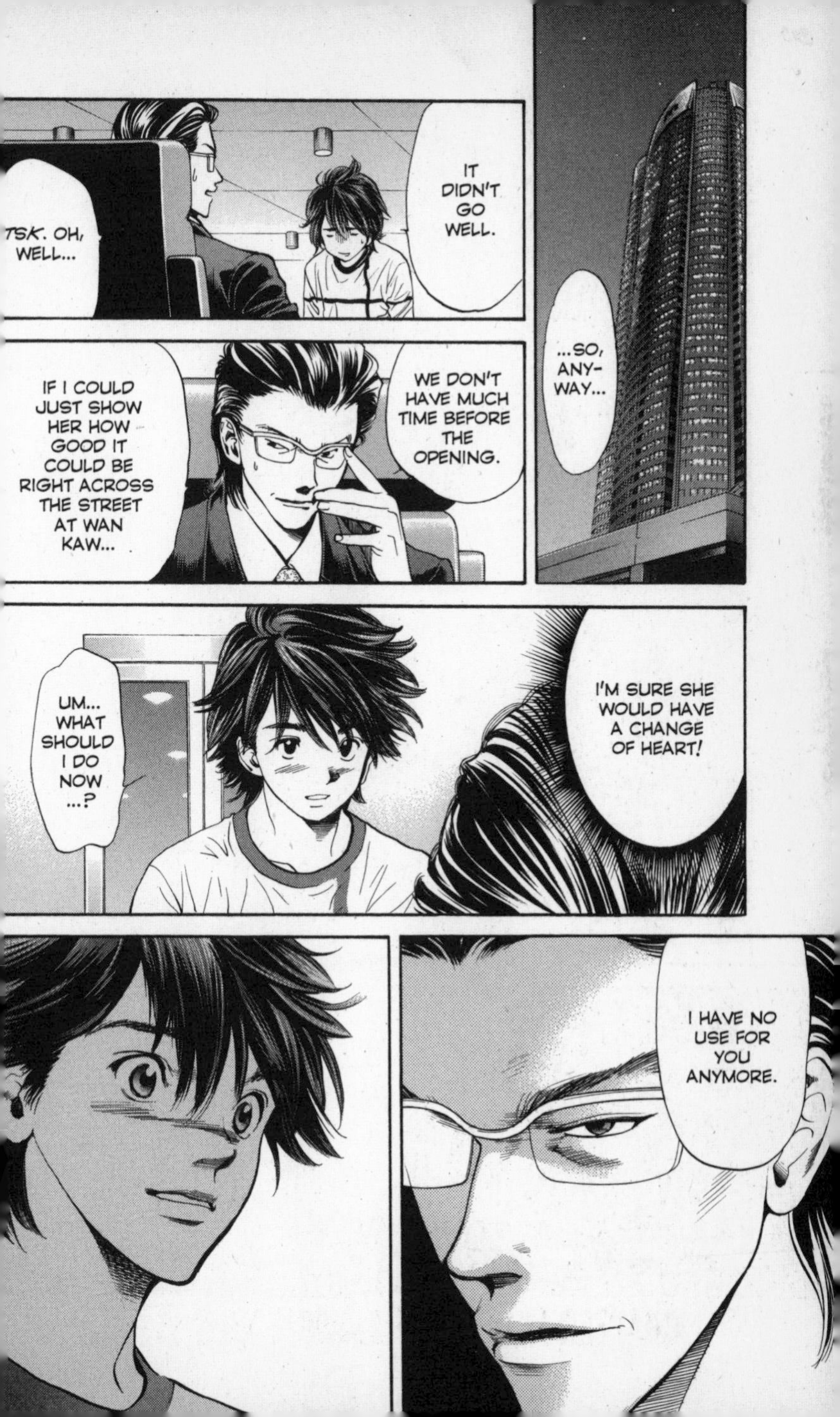
...SO, ANYWAY...
IT DIDN'T GO WELL.
TSK. OH, WELL...
WE DON'T HAVE MUCH TIME BEFORE THE OPENING.
IF I COULD JUST SHOW HER HOW GOOD IT COULD BE RIGHT ACROSS THE STREET AT WAN KAW...
I'M SURE SHE WOULD HAVE A CHANGE OF HEART!
UM... WHAT SHOULD I DO NOW ...?
I HAVE NO USE FOR YOU ANYMORE.

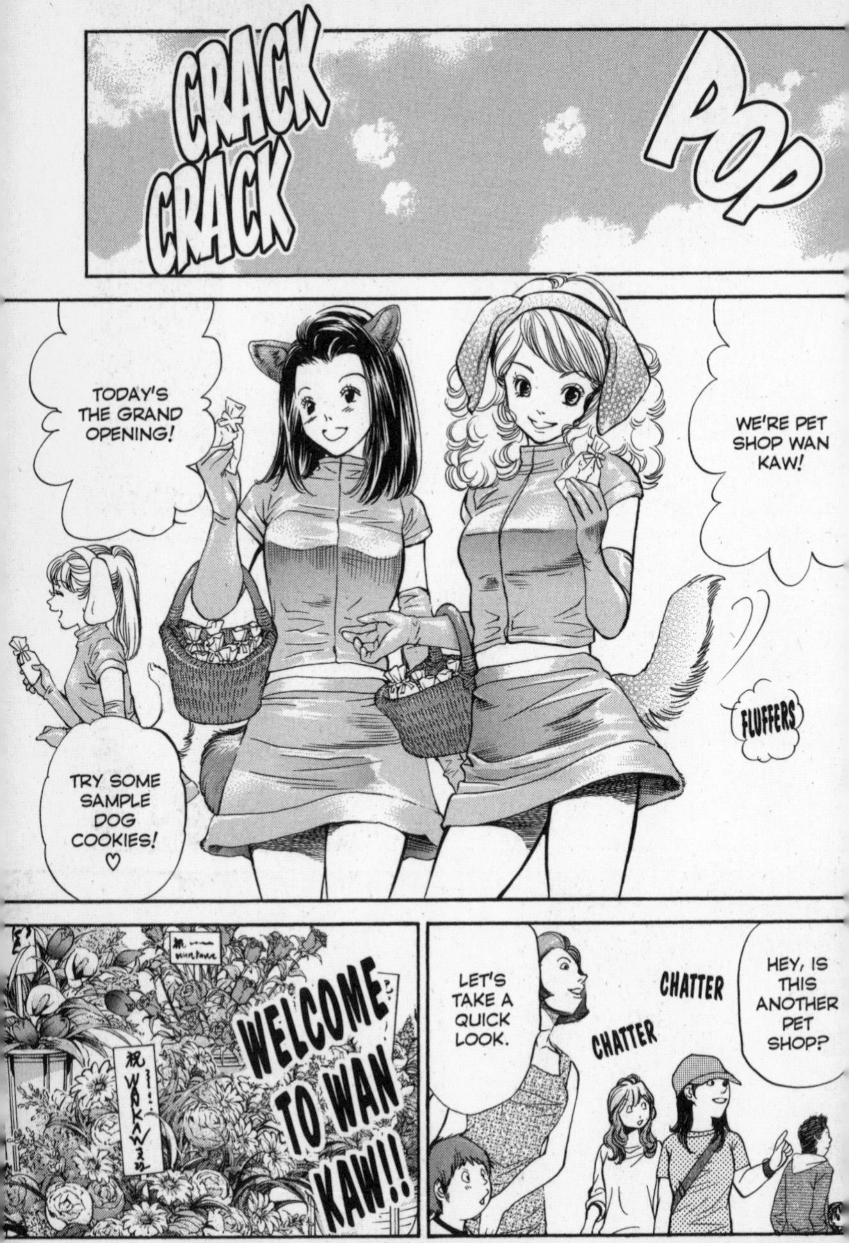
POP
CRACK CRACK
WE'RE PET SHOP WAN KAW!
FLUFFERS
TODAY'S THE GRAND OPENING!
TRY SOME SAMPLE DOG COOKIES! ♡
HEY, IS THIS ANOTHER PET SHOP?
CHATTER
CHATTER
LET'S TAKE A QUICK LOOK.
WELCOME TO WAN KAW!!

CHAPTER 107: THE NEIGHBOR'S YARD IS GREENER

CHAPTER 107:
THE NEIGHBOR'S YARD IS GREENER

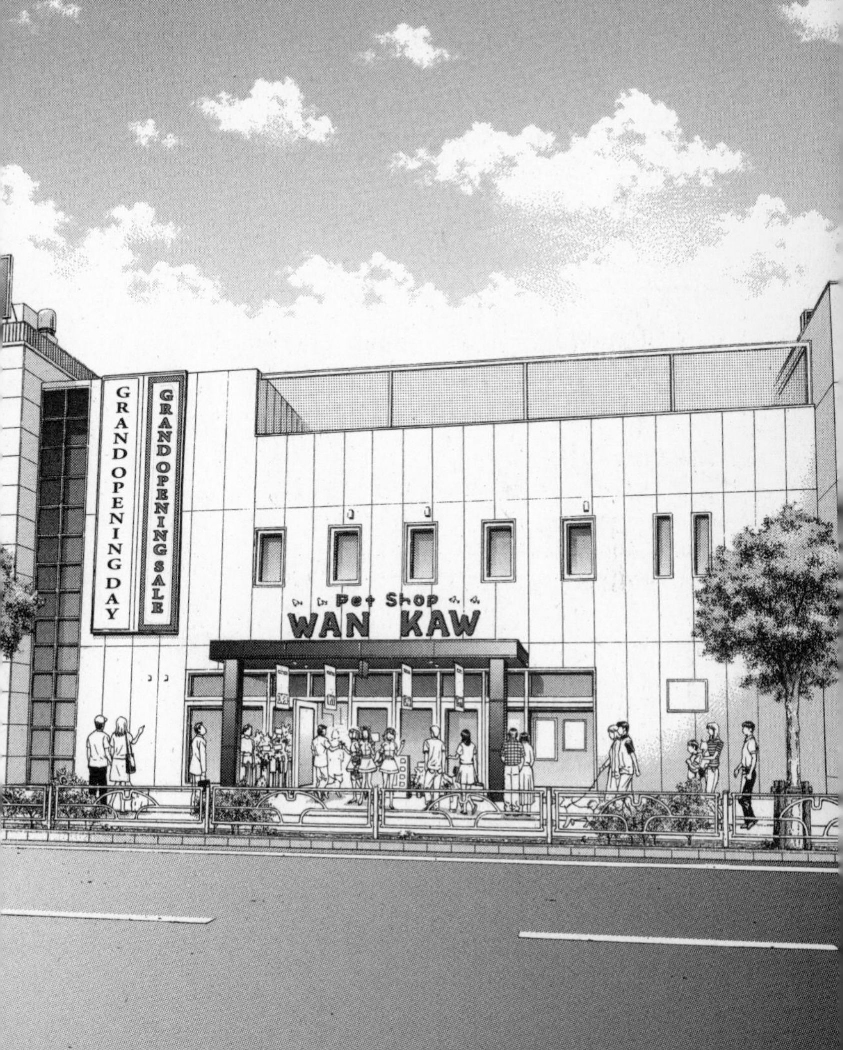
GRAND OPENING SALE
GRAND OPENING DAY
Pet Shop
WAN KAW

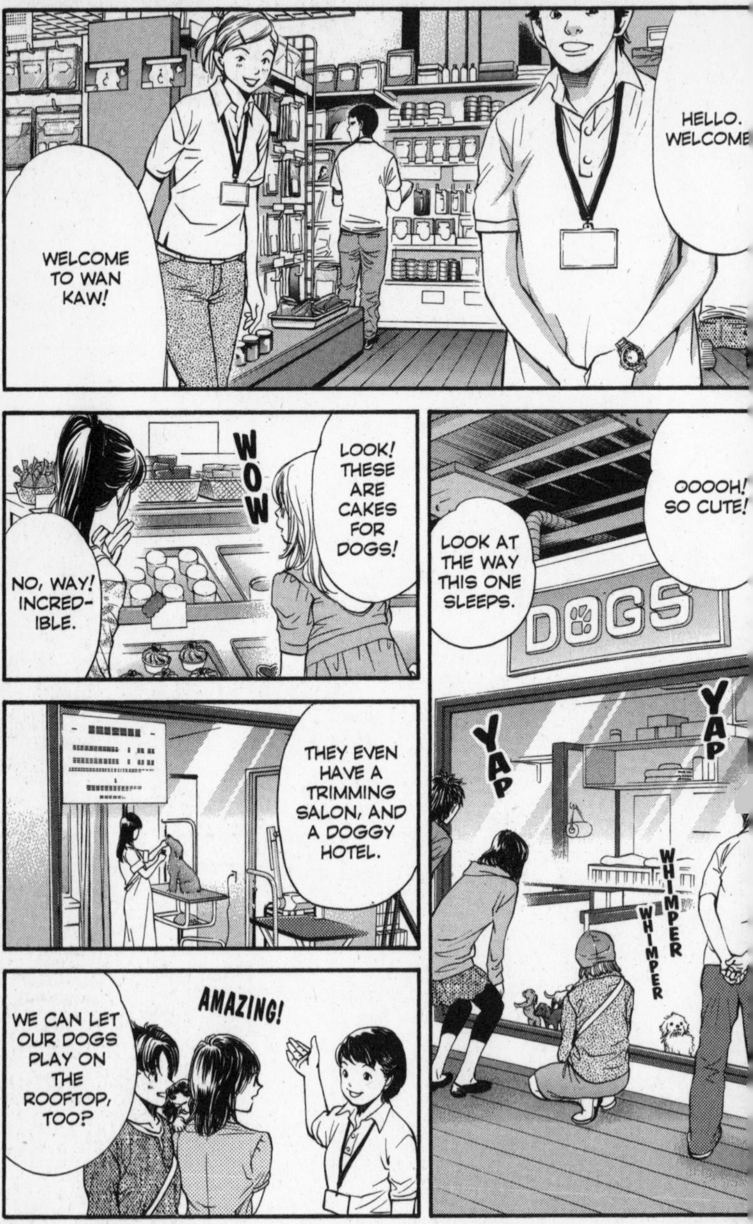
HELLO. WELCOME
WELCOME TO WAN KAW!
OOOOH! SO CUTE!
LOOK AT THE WAY THIS ONE SLEEPS.
DOGS
YAP
YAP
WHIMPER
WHIMPER
WOW
LOOK! THESE ARE CAKES FOR DOGS!
NO, WAY! INCREDIBLE.
THEY EVEN HAVE A TRIMMING SALON, AND A DOGGY HOTEL.
AMAZING!
WE CAN LET OUR DOGS PLAY ON THE ROOFTOP, TOO?

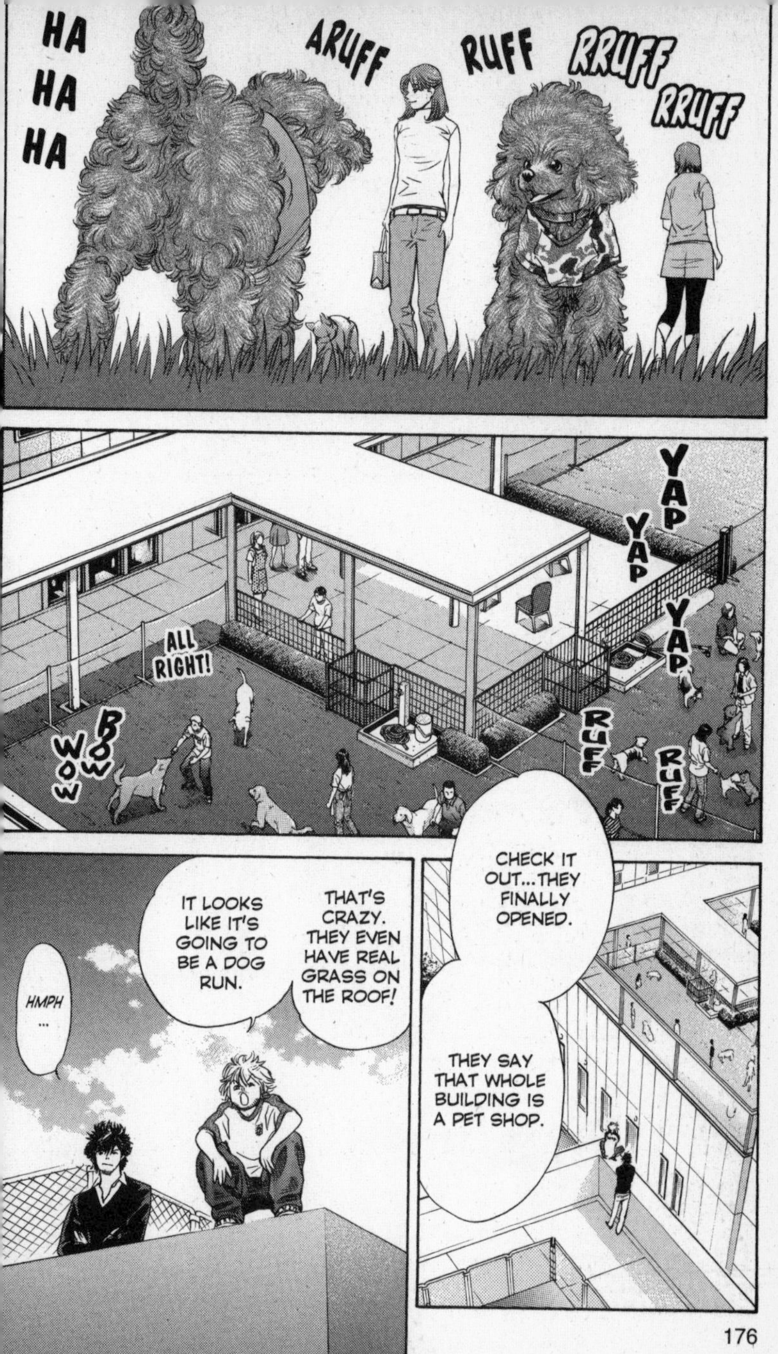
RRUFF RRUFF
RUFF
ARUFF
HA HA HA
YAP YAP
YAP YAP
RUFF
RUFF
ALL RIGHT!
BOW WOW WOW
CHECK IT OUT...THEY FINALLY OPENED.
THEY SAY THAT WHOLE BUILDING IS A PET SHOP.
THAT'S CRAZY. THEY EVEN HAVE REAL GRASS ON THE ROOF!
IT LOOKS LIKE IT'S GOING TO BE A DOG RUN.
HMPH ...

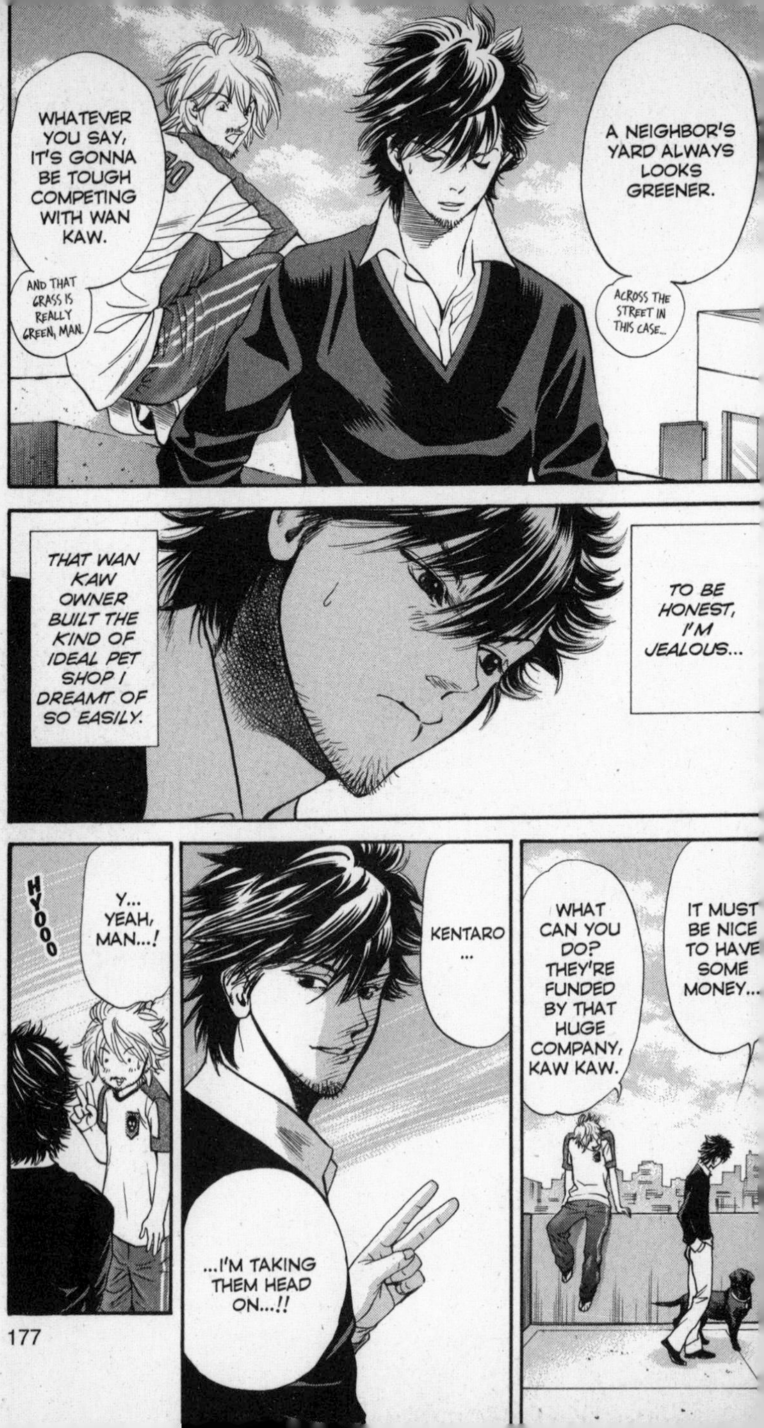
A NEIGHBOR'S YARD ALWAYS LOOKS GREENER.
ACROSS THE STREET IN THIS CASE...
WHATEVER YOU SAY, IT'S GONNA BE TOUGH COMPETING WITH WAN KAW.
AND THAT GRASS IS REALLY GREEN, MAN.
TO BE HONEST, I'M JEALOUS...
THAT WAN KAW OWNER BUILT THE KIND OF IDEAL PET SHOP I DREAMT OF SO EASILY.
IT MUST BE NICE TO HAVE SOME MONEY...
WHAT CAN YOU DO? THEY'RE FUNDED BY THAT HUGE COMPANY, KAW KAW.
KENTARO...
...I'M TAKING THEM HEAD ON...!!
HYOOO
Y... YEAH, MAN...!

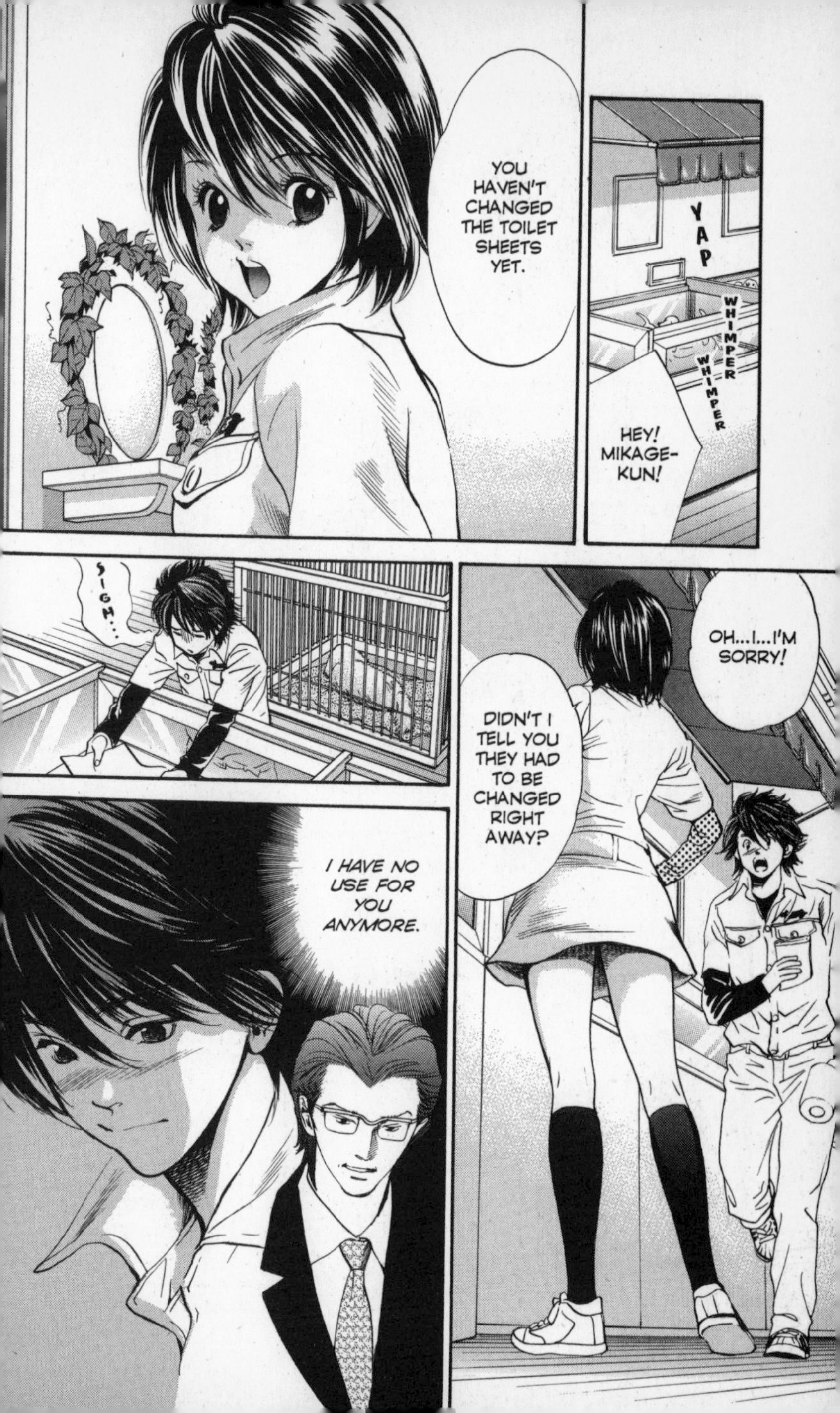

YAP
WHIMPER
WHIMPER
HEY! MIKAGE-KUN!
YOU HAVEN'T CHANGED THE TOILET SHEETS YET.
OH...I...I'M SORRY!
DIDN'T I TELL YOU THEY HAD TO BE CHANGED RIGHT AWAY?
SIGH...
I HAVE NO USE FOR YOU ANYMORE.

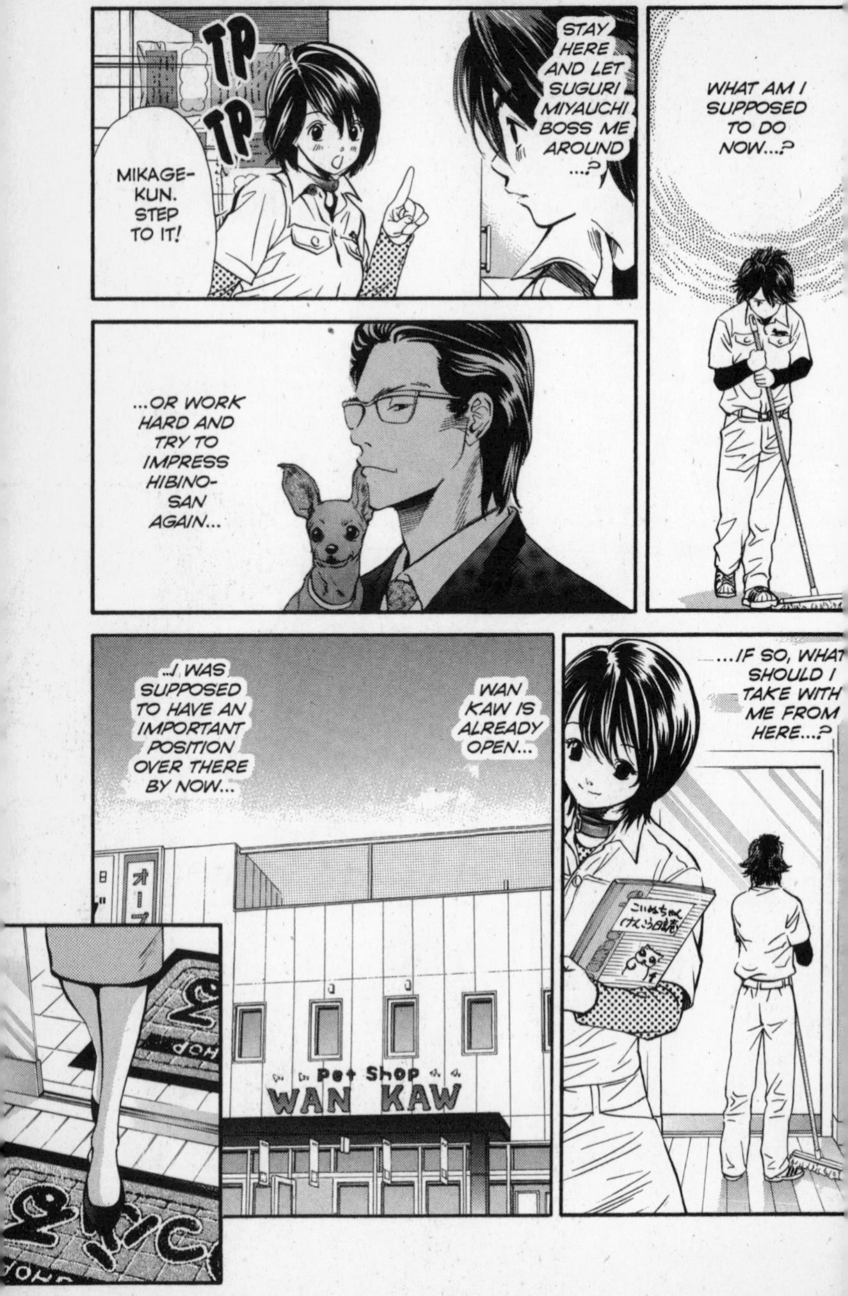
WHAT AM I SUPPOSED TO DO NOW...?
STAY HERE AND LET SUGURI MIYAUCHI BOSS ME AROUND ...?
TP TP
MIKAGE-KUN. STEP TO IT!
...OR WORK HARD AND TRY TO IMPRESS HIBINO-SAN AGAIN...
...IF SO, WHAT SHOULD I TAKE WITH ME FROM HERE...?
WAN KAW IS ALREADY OPEN...
...I WAS SUPPOSED TO HAVE AN IMPORTANT POSITION OVER THERE BY NOW...
Pet Shop
WAN KAW

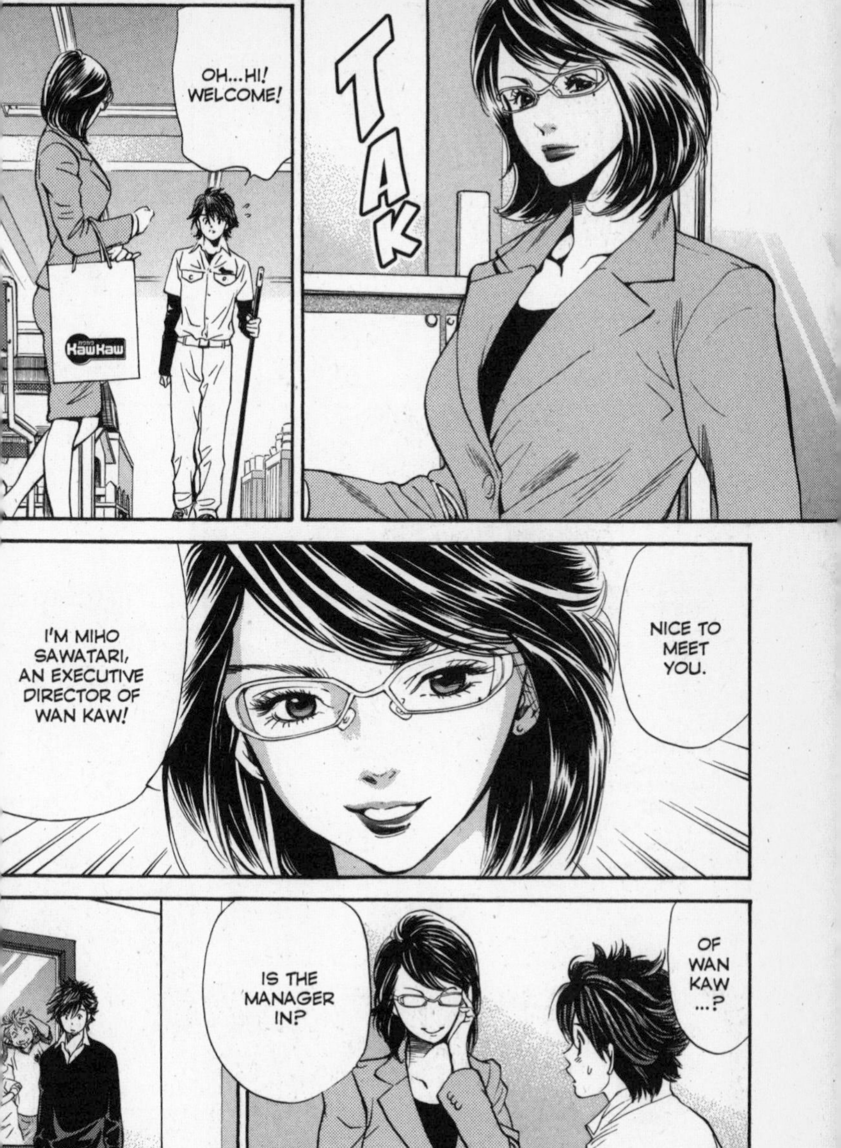
TAK
OH...HI! WELCOME!
NICE TO MEET YOU.
I'M MIHO SAWATARI, AN EXECUTIVE DIRECTOR OF WAN KAW!
OF WAN KAW ...?
IS THE MANAGER IN?

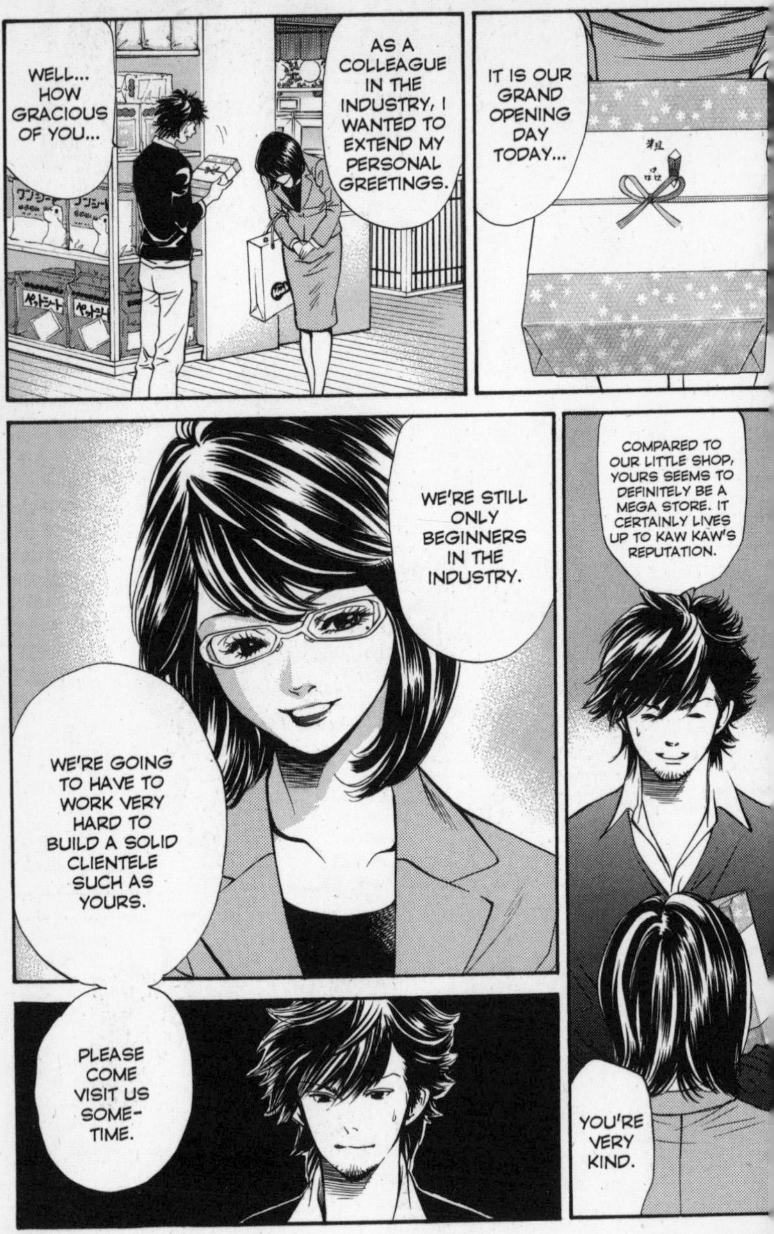
IT IS OUR GRAND OPENING DAY TODAY...
AS A COLLEAGUE IN THE INDUSTRY, I WANTED TO EXTEND MY PERSONAL GREETINGS.
WELL... HOW GRACIOUS OF YOU...
COMPARED TO OUR LITTLE SHOP, YOURS SEEMS TO DEFINITELY BE A MEGA STORE. IT CERTAINLY LIVES UP TO KAW KAW'S REPUTATION.
YOU'RE VERY KIND.
WE'RE STILL ONLY BEGINNERS IN THE INDUSTRY.
WE'RE GOING TO HAVE TO WORK VERY HARD TO BUILD A SOLID CLIENTELE SUCH AS YOURS.
PLEASE COME VISIT US SOME-TIME.

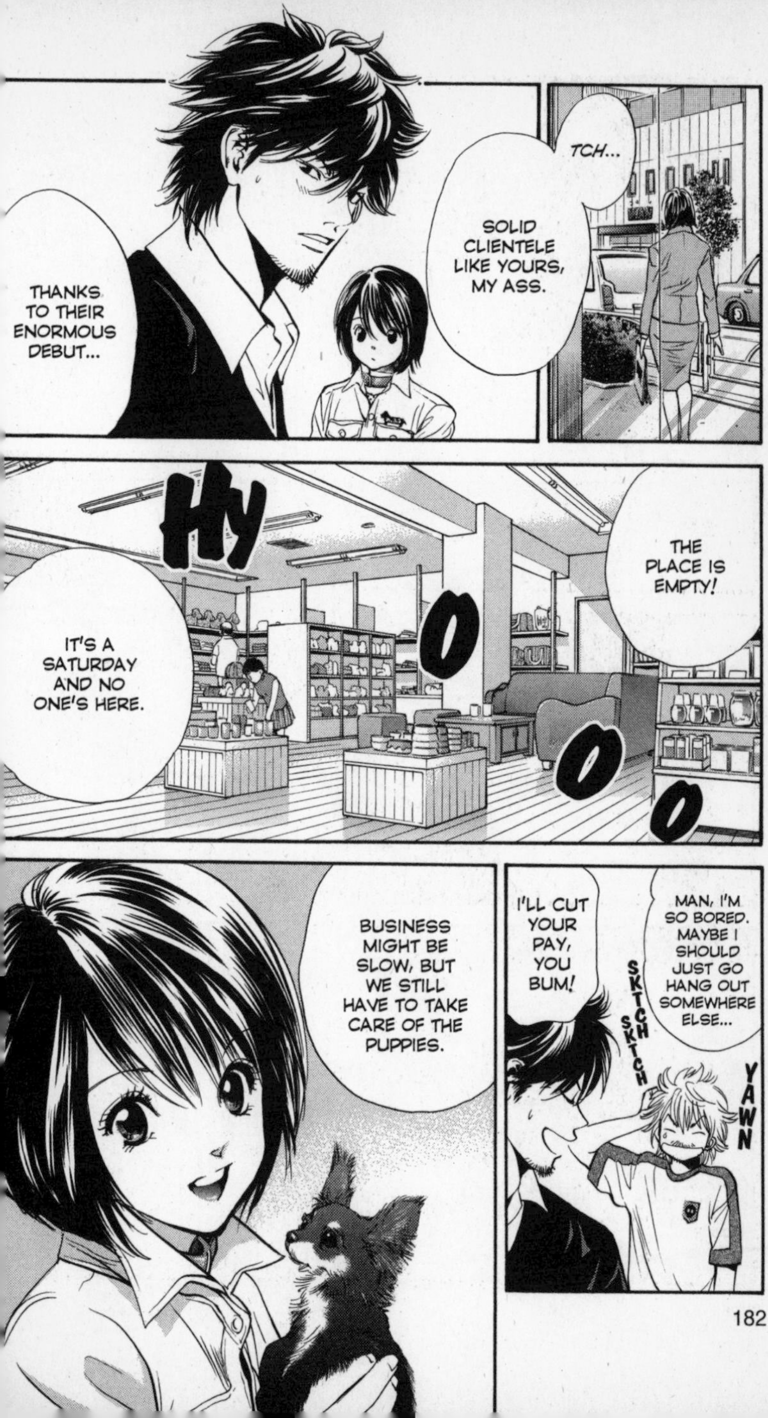
TCH...
SOLID CLIENTELE LIKE YOURS, MY ASS.
THANKS TO THEIR ENORMOUS DEBUT...
THE PLACE IS EMPTY!
HYOOO
IT'S A SATURDAY AND NO ONE'S HERE.
YAWN
MAN, I'M SO BORED. MAYBE I SHOULD JUST GO HANG OUT SOMEWHERE ELSE...
SKTCH SKTCH
I'LL CUT YOUR PAY, YOU BUM!
BUSINESS MIGHT BE SLOW, BUT WE STILL HAVE TO TAKE CARE OF THE PUPPIES.

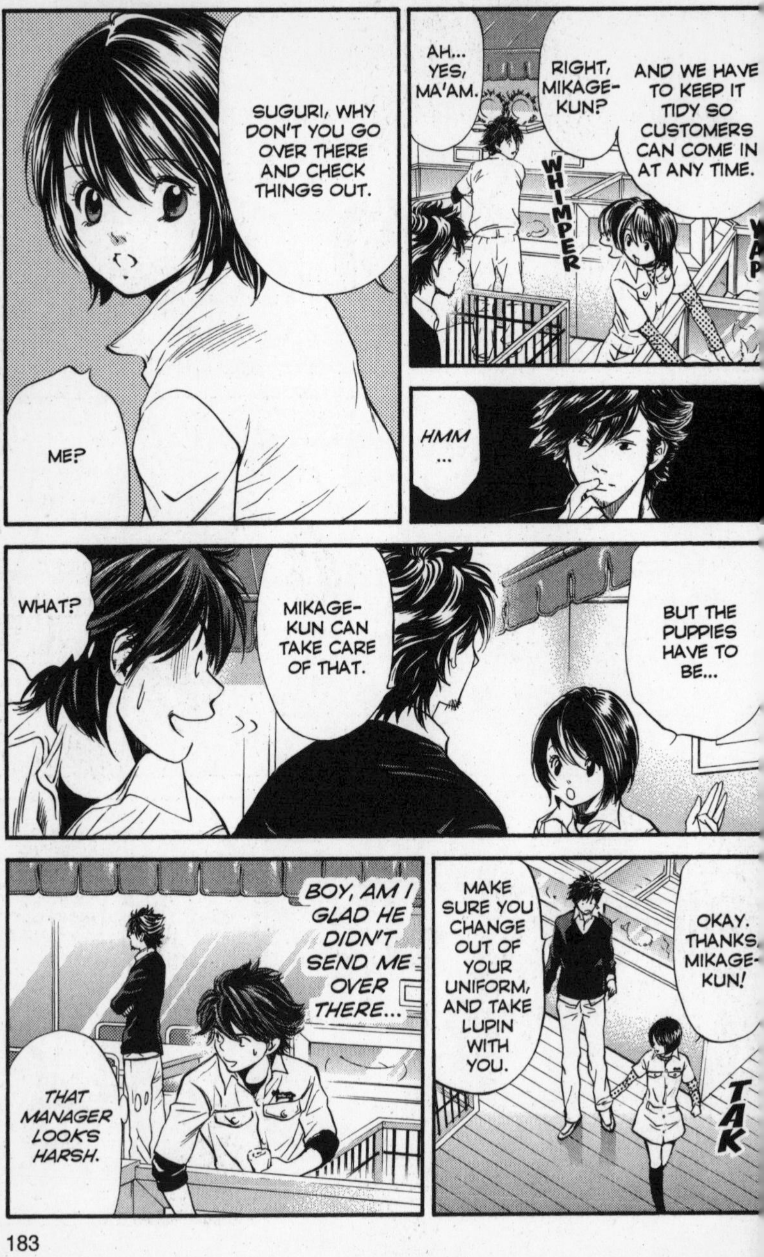
AND WE HAVE TO KEEP IT TIDY SO CUSTOMERS CAN COME IN AT ANY TIME.
RIGHT, MIKAGE-KUN?
AH... YES, MA'AM.
WHIMPER
HMM ...
SUGURI, WHY DON'T YOU GO OVER THERE AND CHECK THINGS OUT.
ME?
BUT THE PUPPIES HAVE TO BE...
MIKAGE-KUN CAN TAKE CARE OF THAT.
WHAT?
OKAY. THANKS, MIKAGE-KUN!
MAKE SURE YOU CHANGE OUT OF YOUR UNIFORM, AND TAKE LUPIN WITH YOU.
TAK
BOY, AM I GLAD HE DIDN'T SEND ME OVER THERE...
THAT MANAGER LOOKS HARSH.

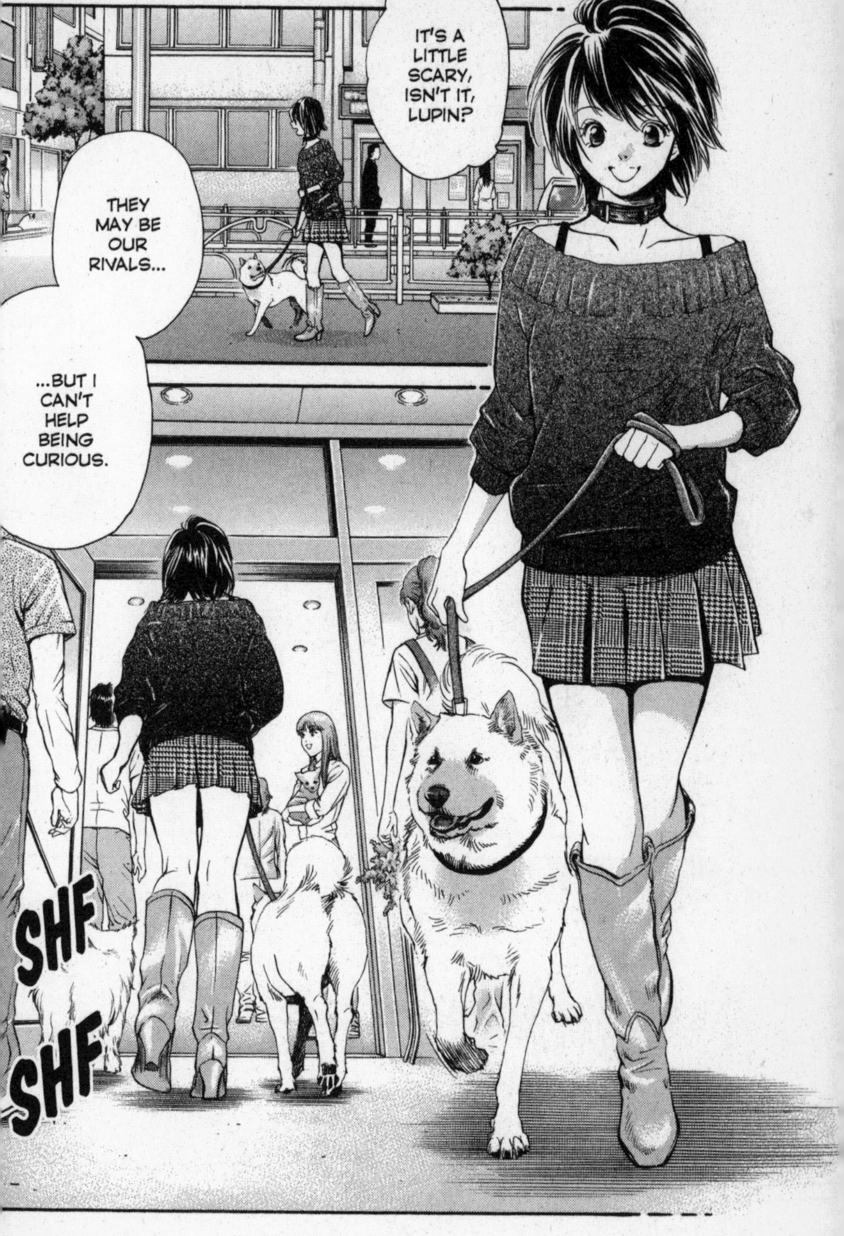

IT'S A LITTLE SCARY, ISN'T IT, LUPIN?
THEY MAY BE OUR RIVALS...
...BUT I CAN'T HELP BEING CURIOUS.
SHF
SHF

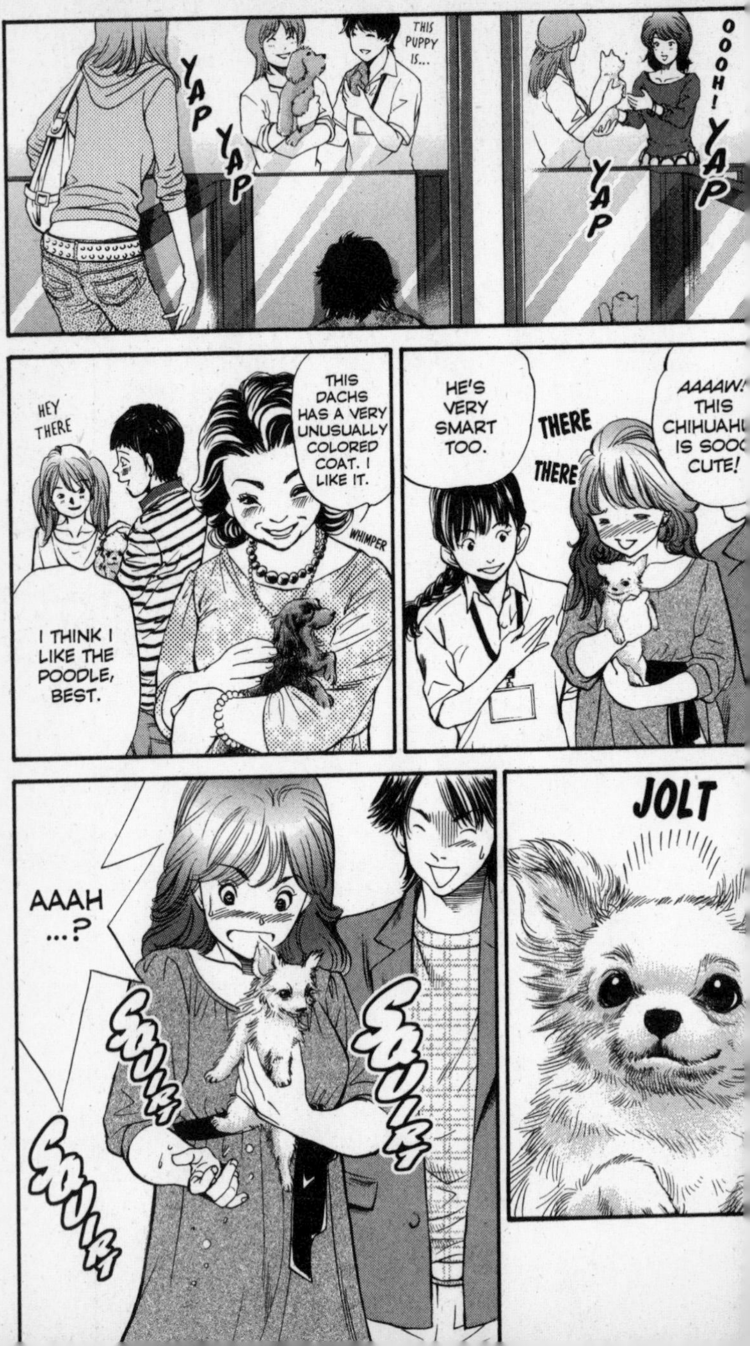
OOOOH!
YAP YAP
THIS PUPPY IS...
YAP YAP
AAAAW! THIS CHIHUAHU IS SOOO CUTE!
THERE THERE
HE'S VERY SMART TOO.
THIS DACHS HAS A VERY UNUSUALLY COLORED COAT. I LIKE IT.
WHIMPER
HEY THERE
I THINK I LIKE THE POODLE, BEST.
JOLT
SQUIRM SQUIRM
AAAH ...?
SQUIRM

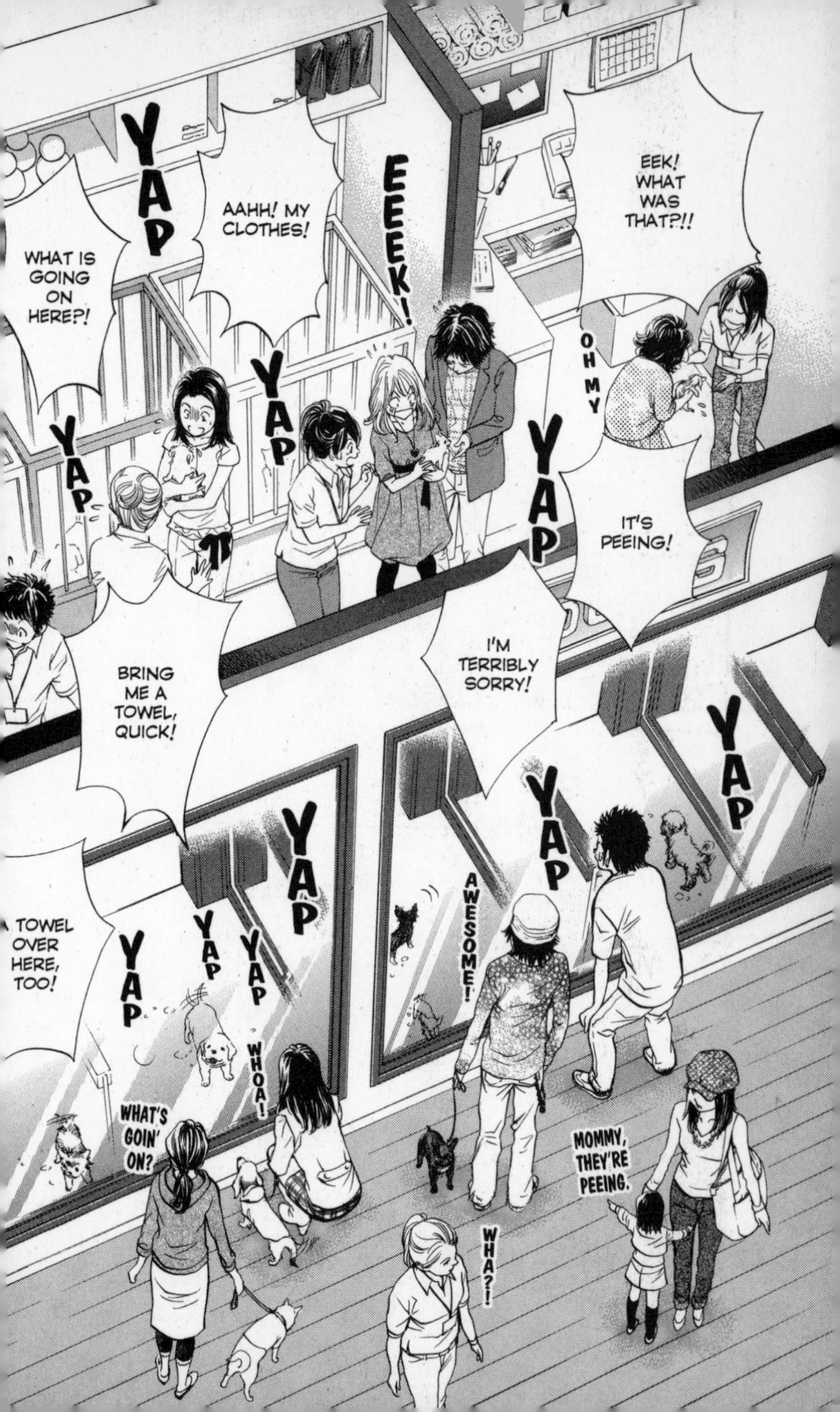

EEK! WHAT WAS THAT?!!
EEEEK!
AAHH! MY CLOTHES!
YAP
WHAT IS GOING ON HERE?!
OH MY
IT'S PEEING!
YAP
YAP
YAP
I'M TERRIBLY SORRY!
BRING ME A TOWEL, QUICK!
YAP
YAP
AWESOME!
YAP
YAP
YAP
YAP
TOWEL OVER HERE, TOO!
MOMMY, THEY'RE PEEING.
WHA?!
WHOA!
WHAT'S GOIN' ON?

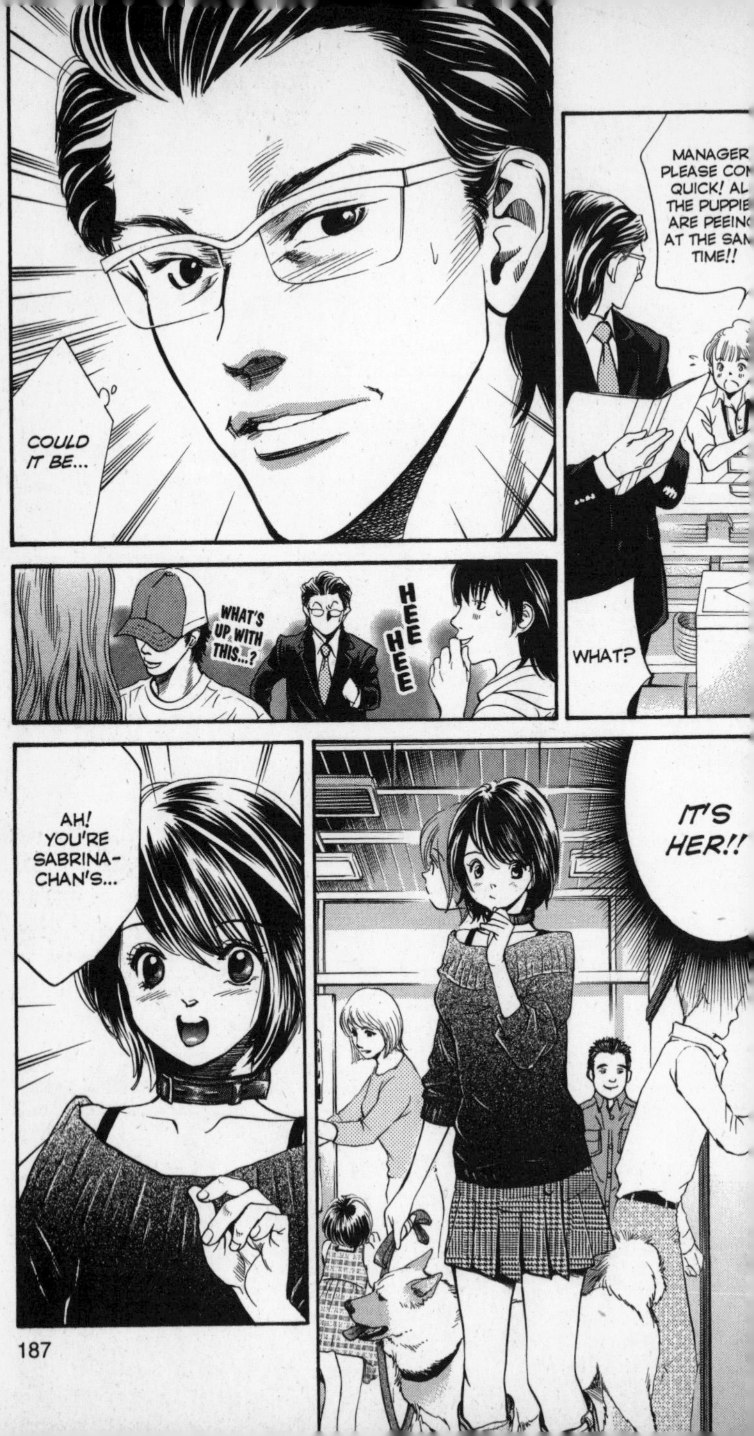
MANAGER PLEASE CO QUICK! AL THE PUPPIE ARE PEEIN AT THE SA TIME!!
WHAT?
COULD IT BE...
HEE HEE
WHAT'S UP WITH THIS...?
IT'S HER!!
AH! YOU'RE SABRINA-CHAN'S...

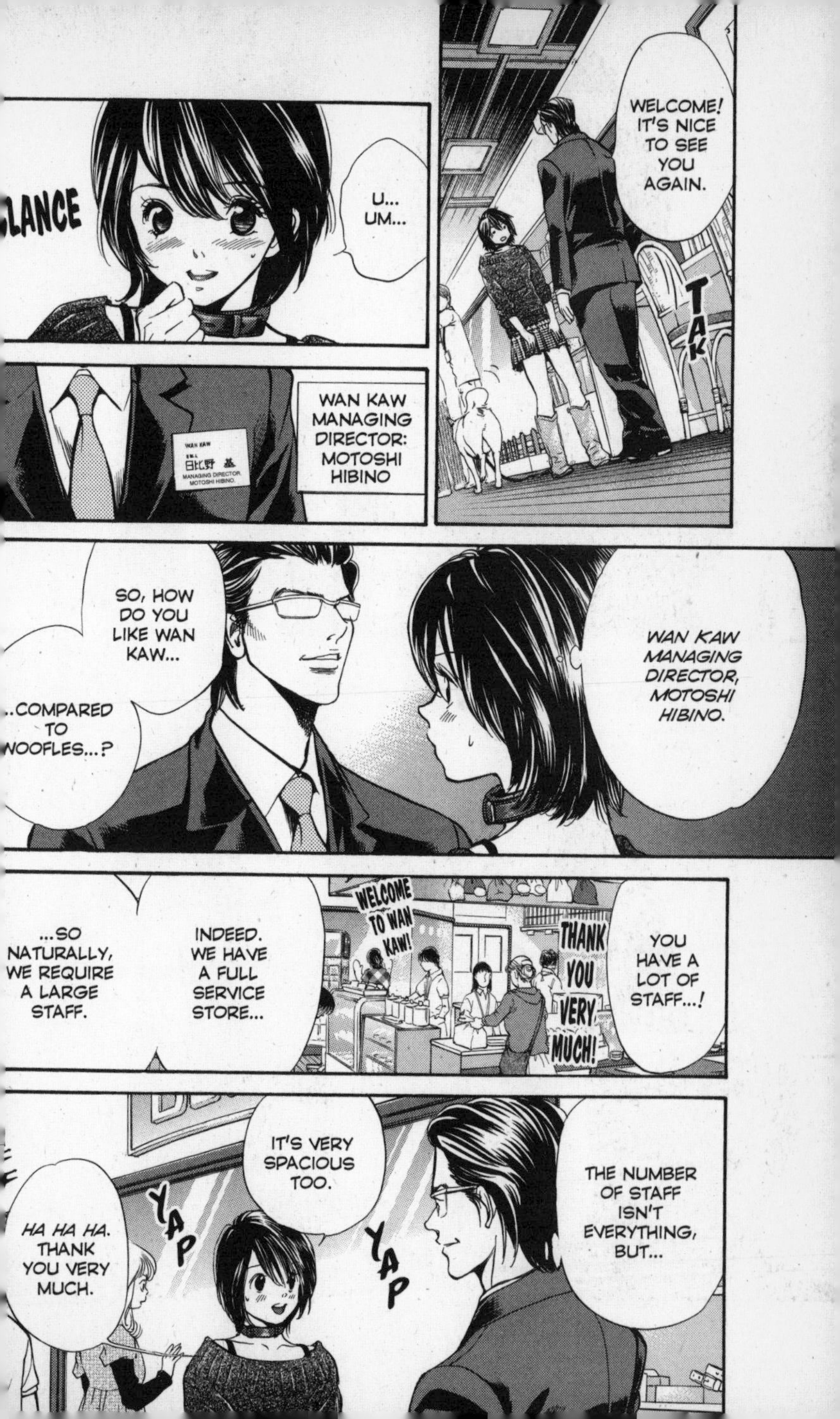
WELCOME! IT'S NICE TO SEE YOU AGAIN.
TAK
GLANCE
U... UM...
WAN KAW MANAGING DIRECTOR: MOTOSHI HIBINO
WAN KAW MANAGING DIRECTOR, MOTOSHI HIBINO.
SO, HOW DO YOU LIKE WAN KAW...
..COMPARED TO WOOFLES...?
YOU HAVE A LOT OF STAFF...!
THANK YOU VERY MUCH!
WELCOME TO WAN KAW!
INDEED. WE HAVE A FULL SERVICE STORE...
...SO NATURALLY, WE REQUIRE A LARGE STAFF.
THE NUMBER OF STAFF ISN'T EVERYTHING, BUT...
YAP
IT'S VERY SPACIOUS TOO.
YAP
HA HA HA. THANK YOU VERY MUCH.

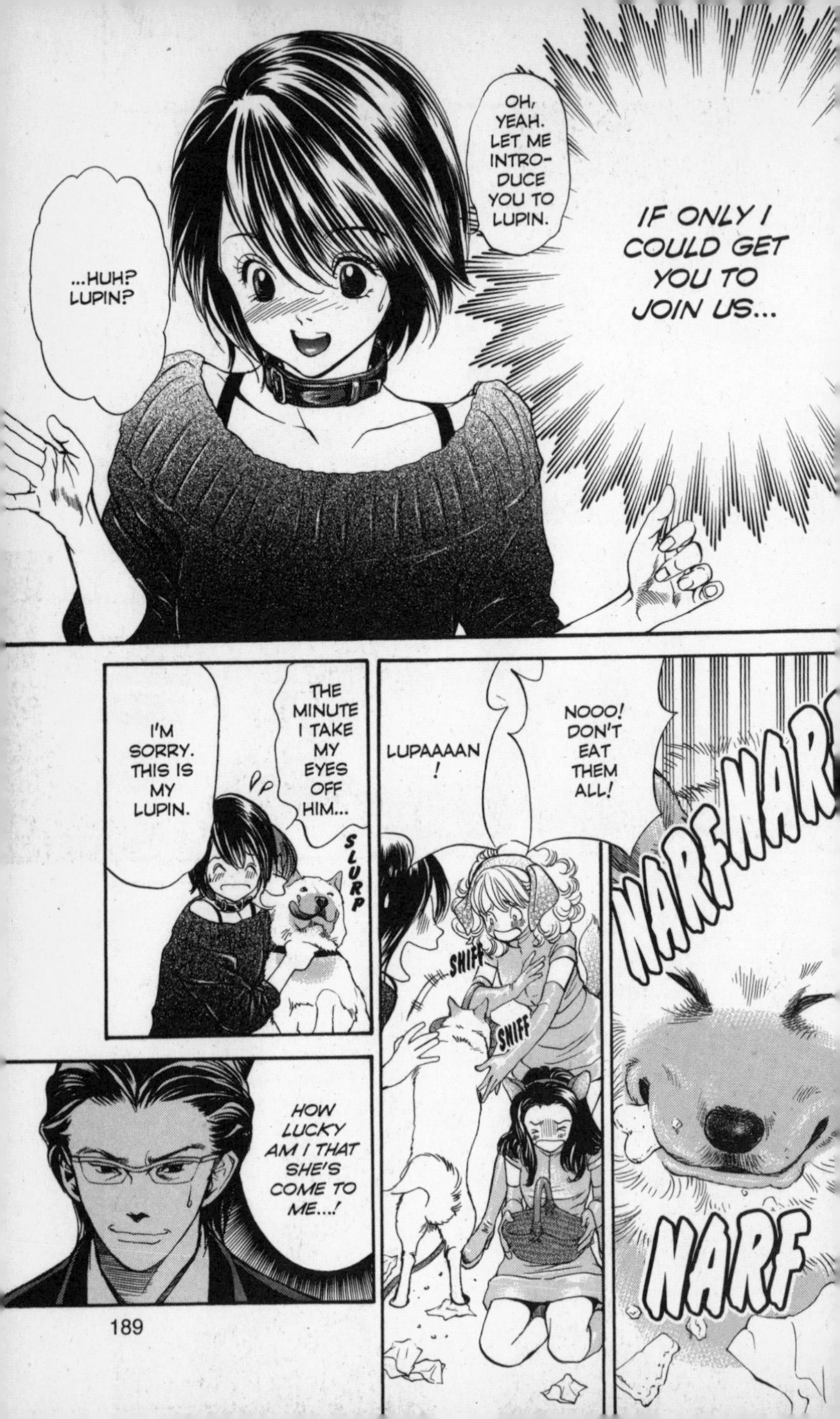
IF ONLY I COULD GET YOU TO JOIN US...
OH, YEAH. LET ME INTRO- DUCE YOU TO LUPIN.
...HUH? LUPIN?
NARFNARF
NARF
NOOO! DON'T EAT THEM ALL!
LUPAAAAN!
SNIFF
SNIFF
THE MINUTE I TAKE MY EYES OFF HIM...
I'M SORRY. THIS IS MY LUPIN.
SLURP
HOW LUCKY AM I THAT SHE'S COME TO ME...!

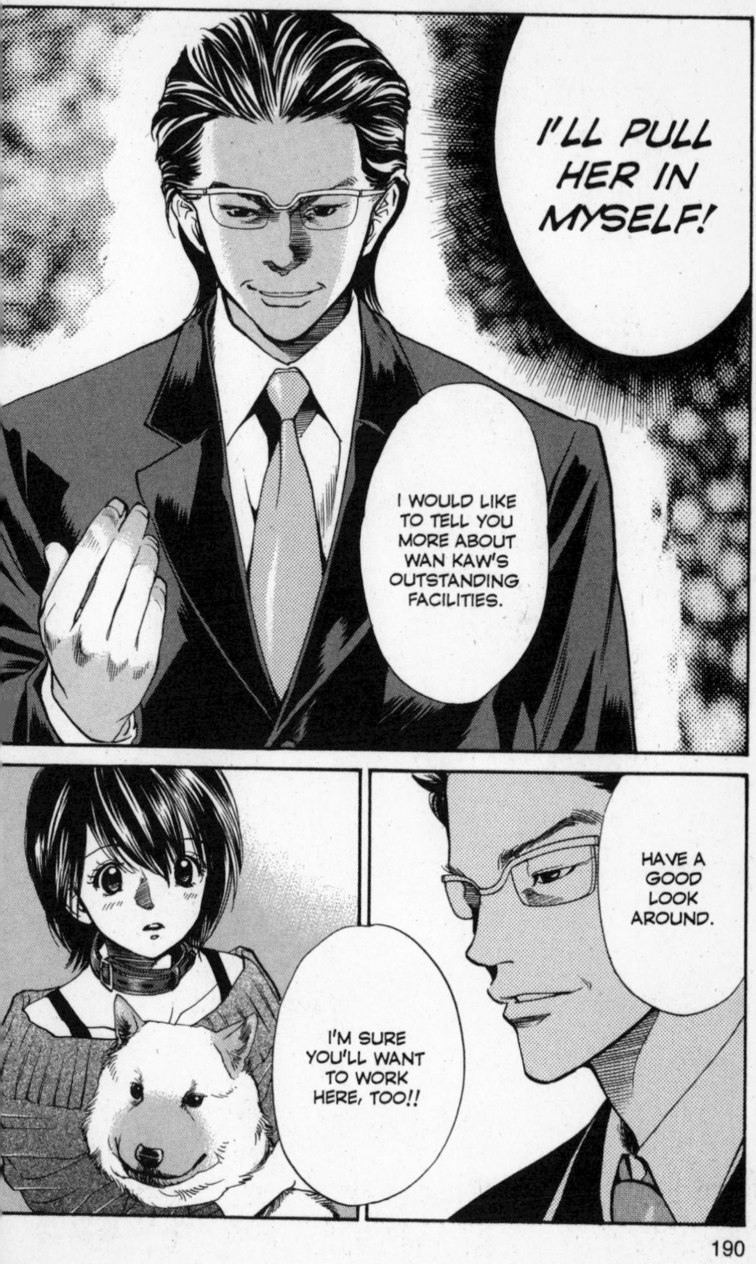
I'LL PULL HER IN MYSELF!
I WOULD LIKE TO TELL YOU MORE ABOUT WAN KAW'S OUTSTANDING FACILITIES.
HAVE A GOOD LOOK AROUND.
I'M SURE YOU'LL WANT TO WORK HERE, TOO!!

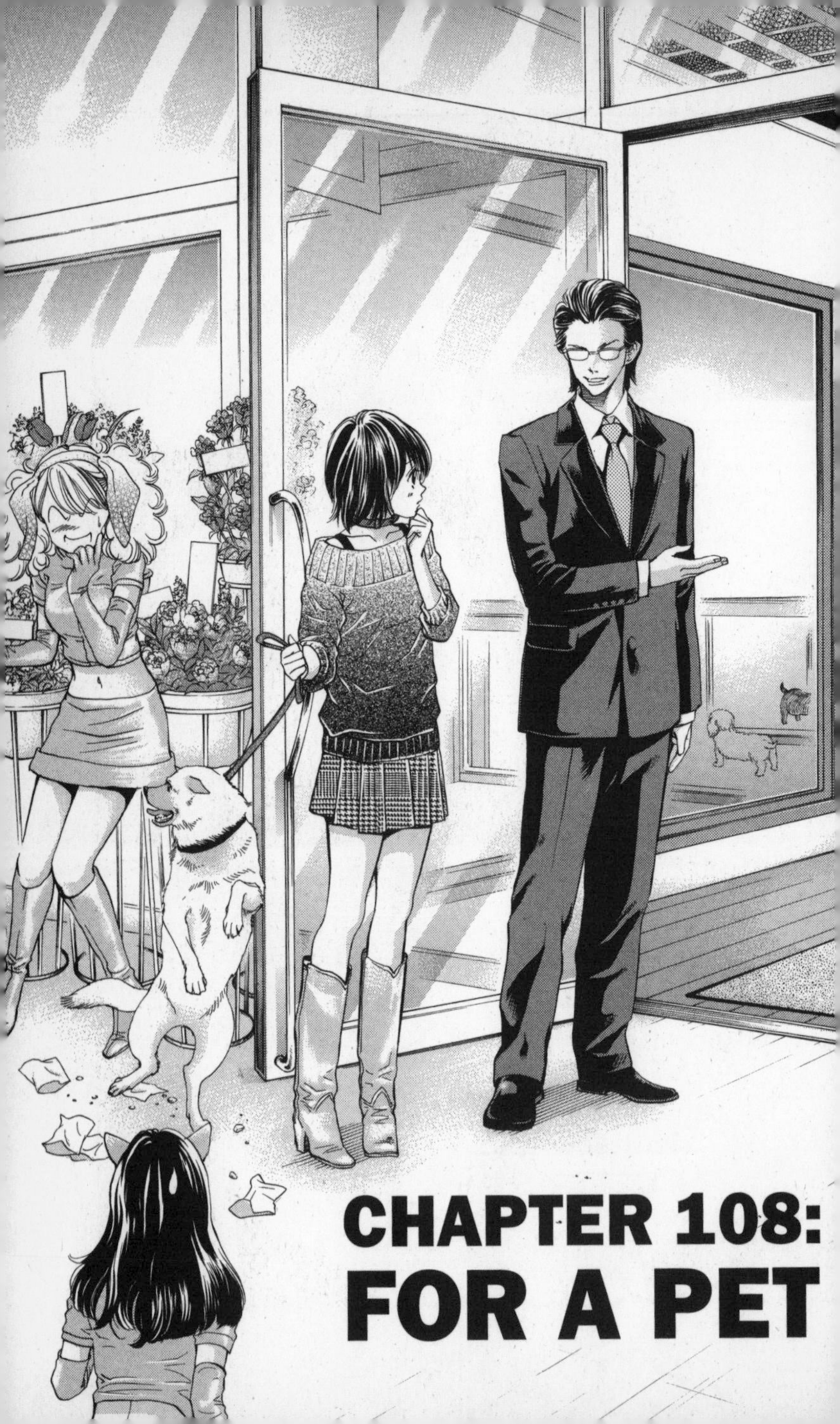

CHAPTER 108: FOR A PET

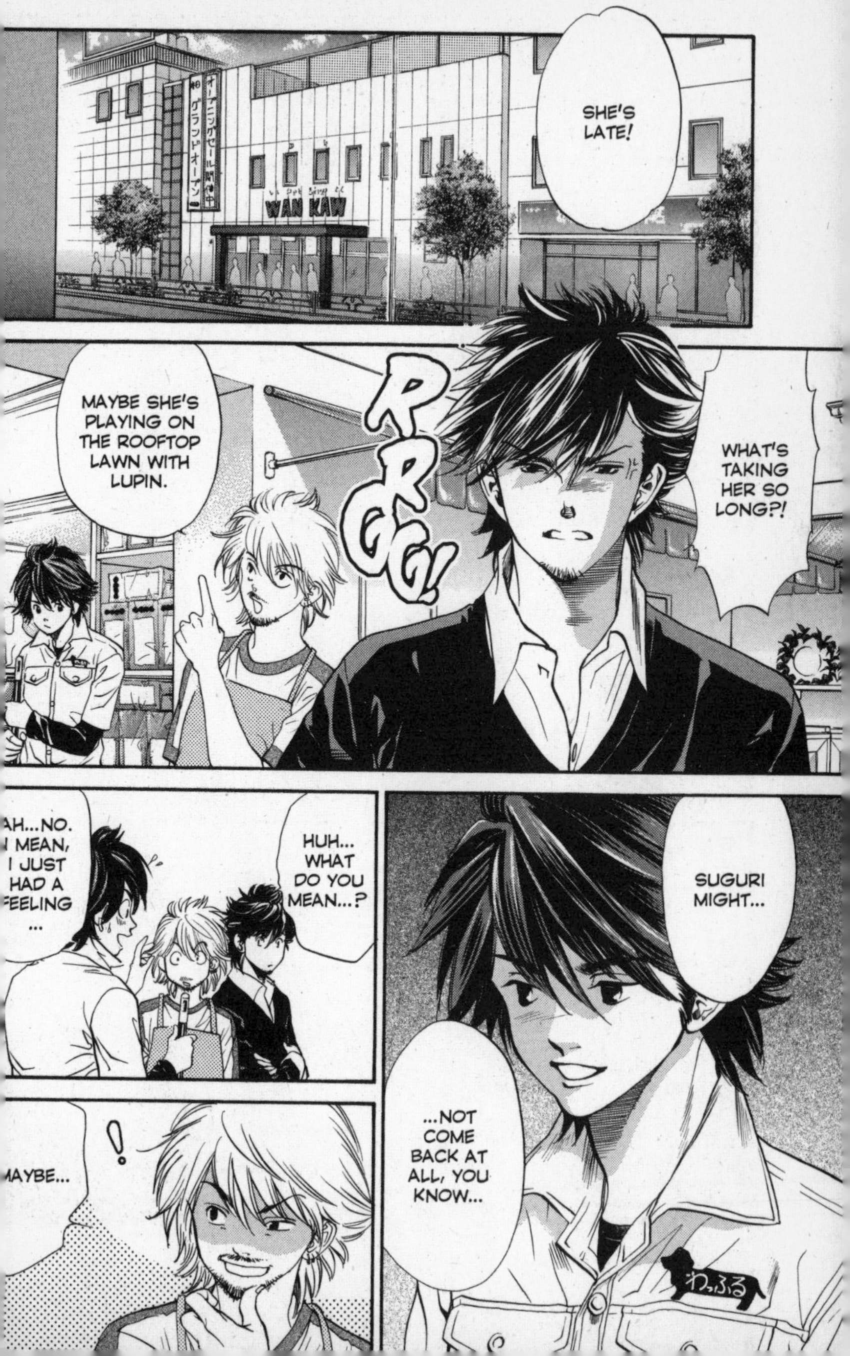

SHE'S LATE!
WAN KAW
WHAT'S TAKING HER SO LONG?!
RRGG!
MAYBE SHE'S PLAYING ON THE ROOFTOP LAWN WITH LUPIN.
SUGURI MIGHT...
...NOT COME BACK AT ALL, YOU KNOW...
わっふる
HUH... WHAT DO YOU MEAN...?
AH...NO. I MEAN, I JUST HAD A FEELING ...
!
MAYBE...

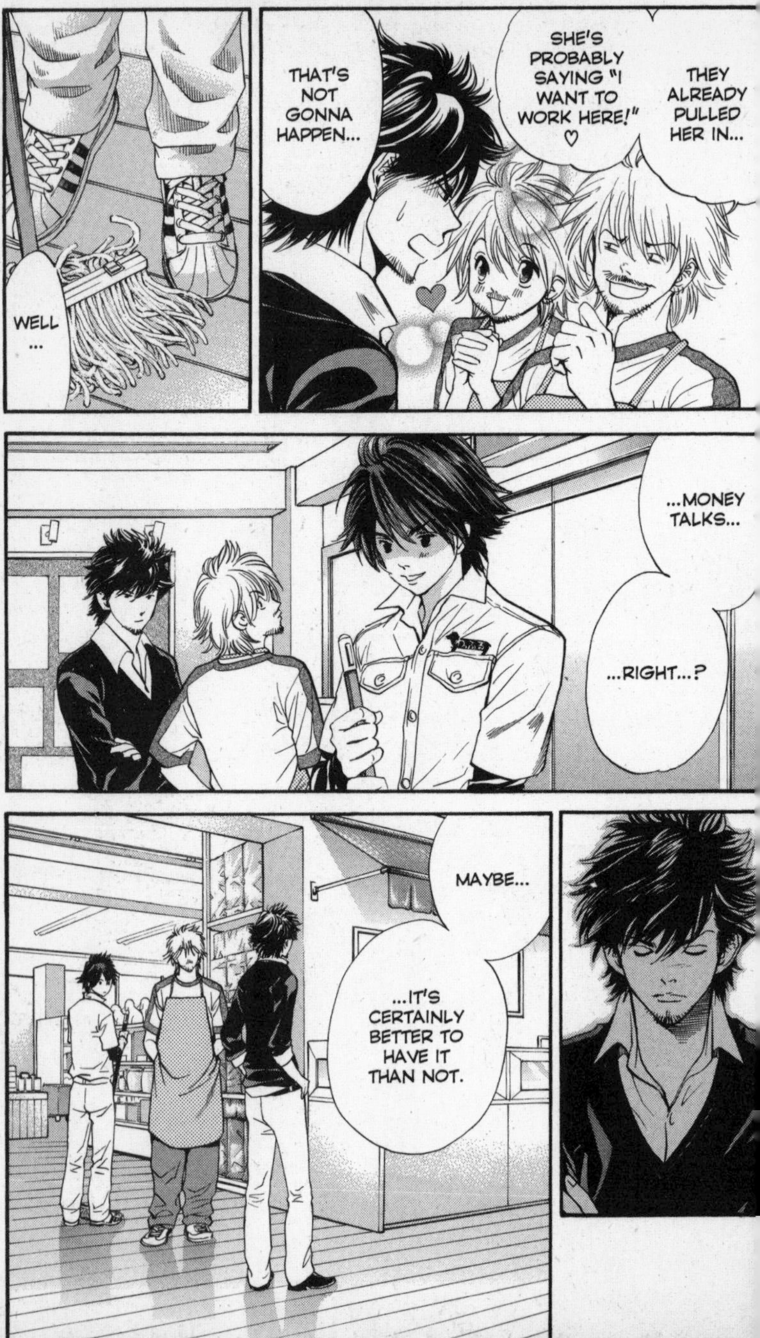
THEY ALREADY PULLED HER IN...
SHE'S PROBABLY SAYING "I WANT TO WORK HERE!" ♡
THAT'S NOT GONNA HAPPEN...
WELL ...
...MONEY TALKS...
...RIGHT...?
MAYBE...
...IT'S CERTAINLY BETTER TO HAVE IT THAN NOT.

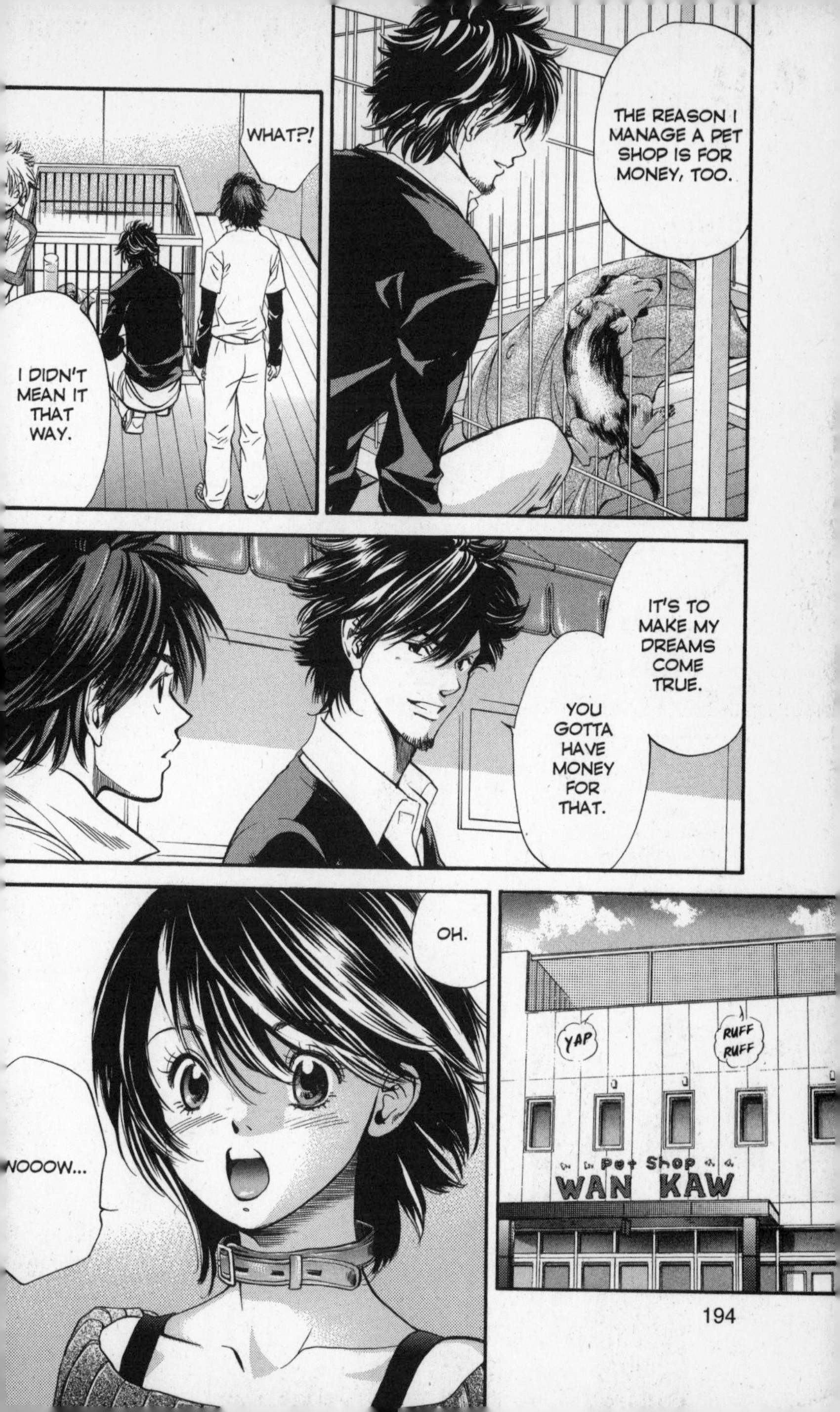
THE REASON I MANAGE A PET SHOP IS FOR MONEY, TOO.
WHAT?!
I DIDN'T MEAN IT THAT WAY.
IT'S TO MAKE MY DREAMS COME TRUE.
YOU GOTTA HAVE MONEY FOR THAT.
RUFF RUFF
YAP
Pet Shop
WAN KAW
OH.
NOOOW...

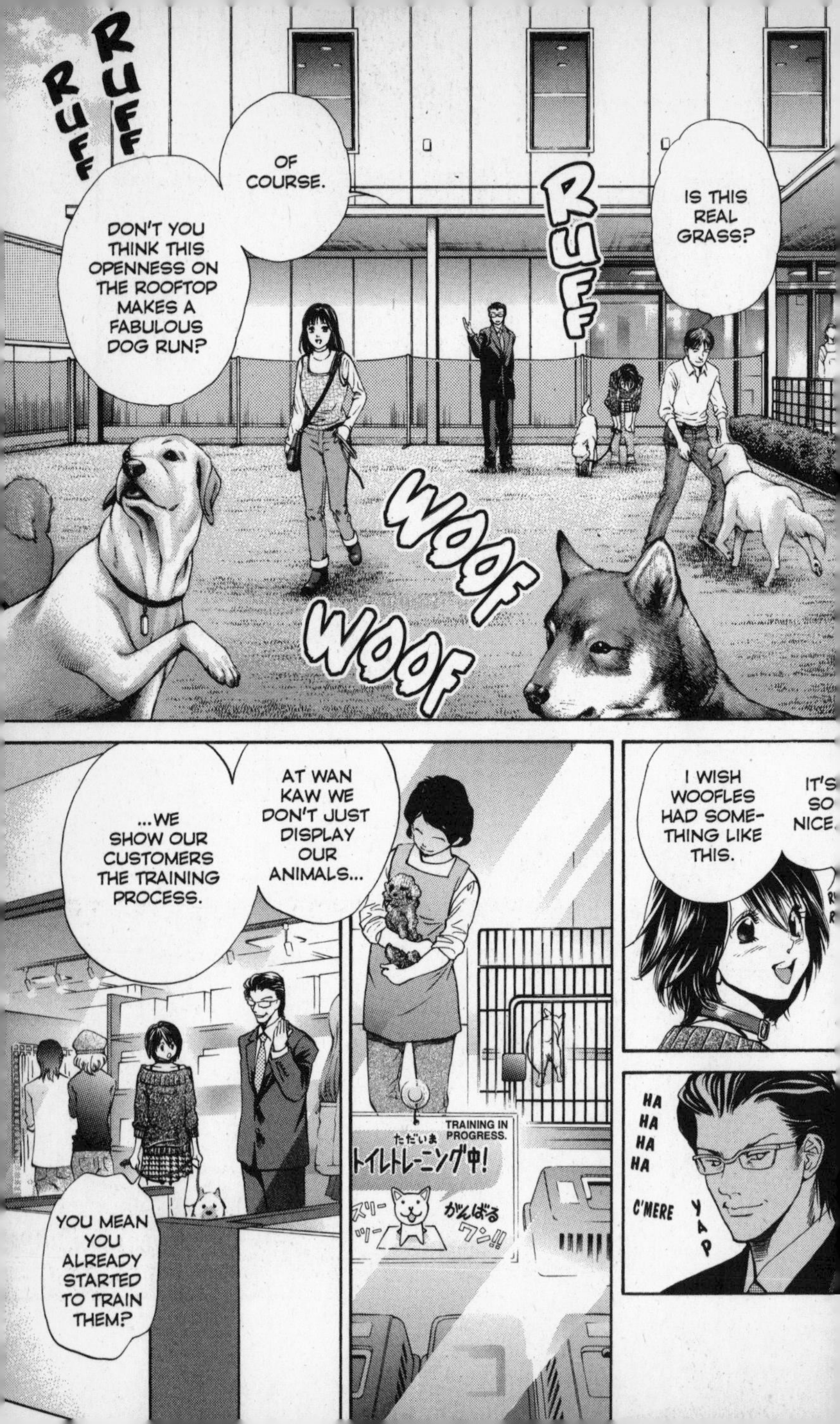
IS THIS REAL GRASS?
RUFF RUFF
OF COURSE.
DON'T YOU THINK THIS OPENNESS ON THE ROOFTOP MAKES A FABULOUS DOG RUN?
RUFF RUFF
WOOF WOOF
IT'S SO NICE.
I WISH WOOFLES HAD SOME-THING LIKE THIS.
HA HA HA HA
C'MERE
YAP
AT WAN KAW WE DON'T JUST DISPLAY OUR ANIMALS...
...WE SHOW OUR CUSTOMERS THE TRAINING PROCESS.
TRAINING IN PROGRESS.
ただいま
トイレトレーニング中!
スリー ツー
がんばる ワン!!
YOU MEAN YOU ALREADY STARTED TO TRAIN THEM?

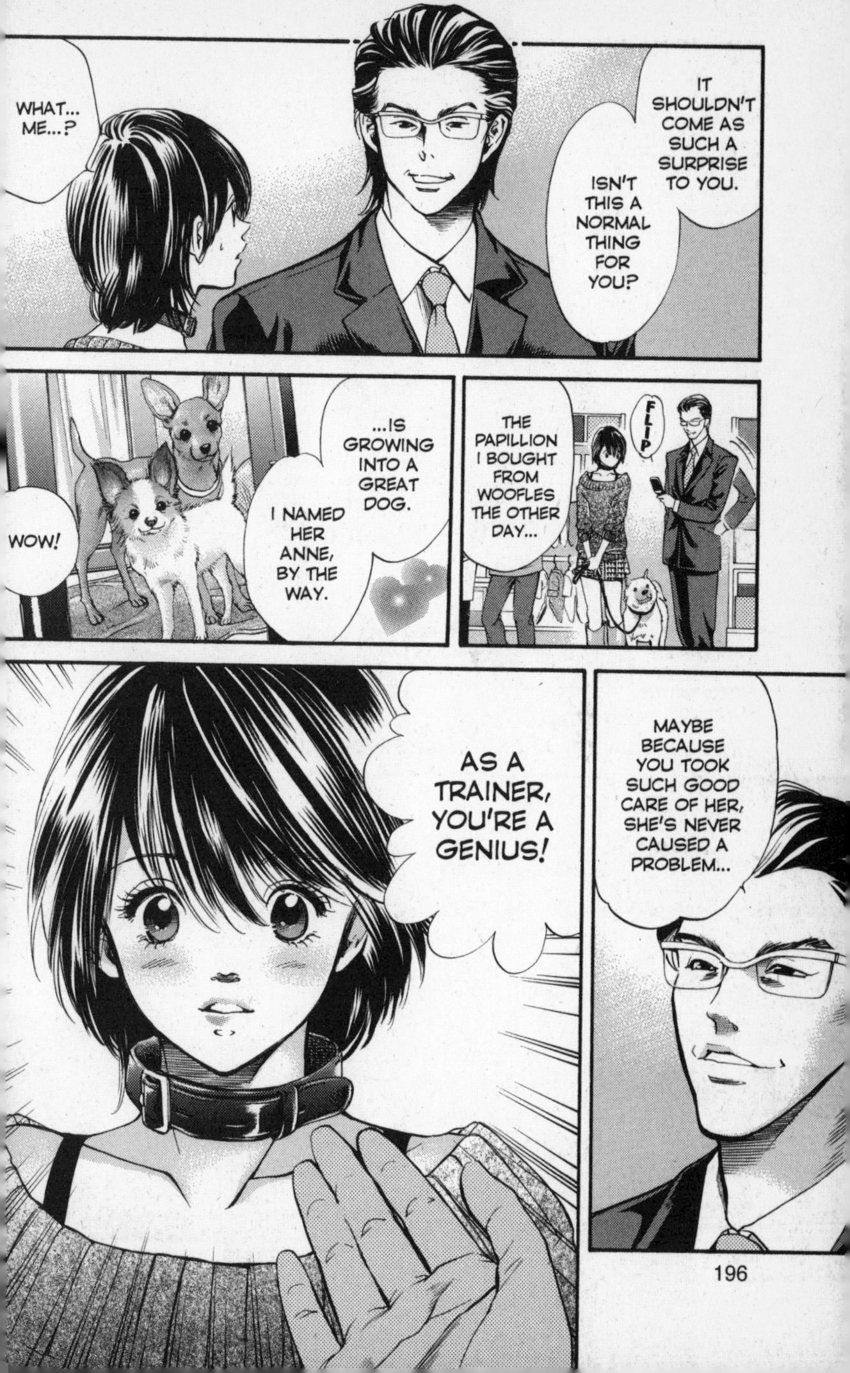
IT SHOULDN'T COME AS SUCH A SURPRISE TO YOU.
ISN'T THIS A NORMAL THING FOR YOU?
WHAT... ME...?
FLIP
THE PAPILLION I BOUGHT FROM WOOFLES THE OTHER DAY...
...IS GROWING INTO A GREAT DOG.
I NAMED HER ANNE, BY THE WAY.
WOW!
MAYBE BECAUSE YOU TOOK SUCH GOOD CARE OF HER, SHE'S NEVER CAUSED A PROBLEM...
AS A TRAINER, YOU'RE A GENIUS!

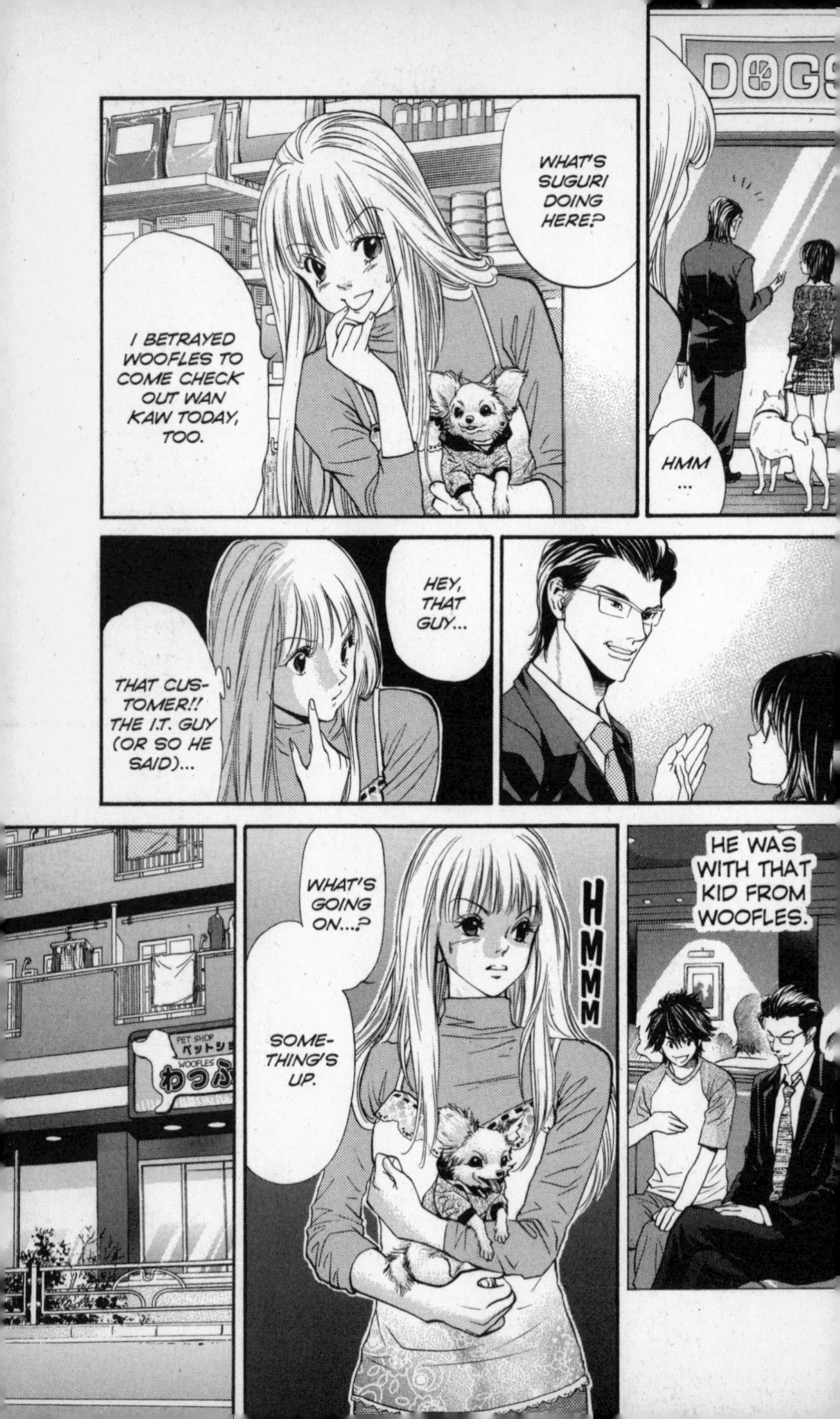
HMM ...
WHAT'S SUGURI DOING HERE?
I BETRAYED WOOFLES TO COME CHECK OUT WAN KAW TODAY, TOO.
HEY, THAT GUY...
THAT CUS-TOMER!! THE I.T. GUY (OR SO HE SAID)...
HE WAS WITH THAT KID FROM WOOFLES.
WHAT'S GOING ON...?
HMMM
SOME-THING'S UP.
PET SHOP
WOOFLES

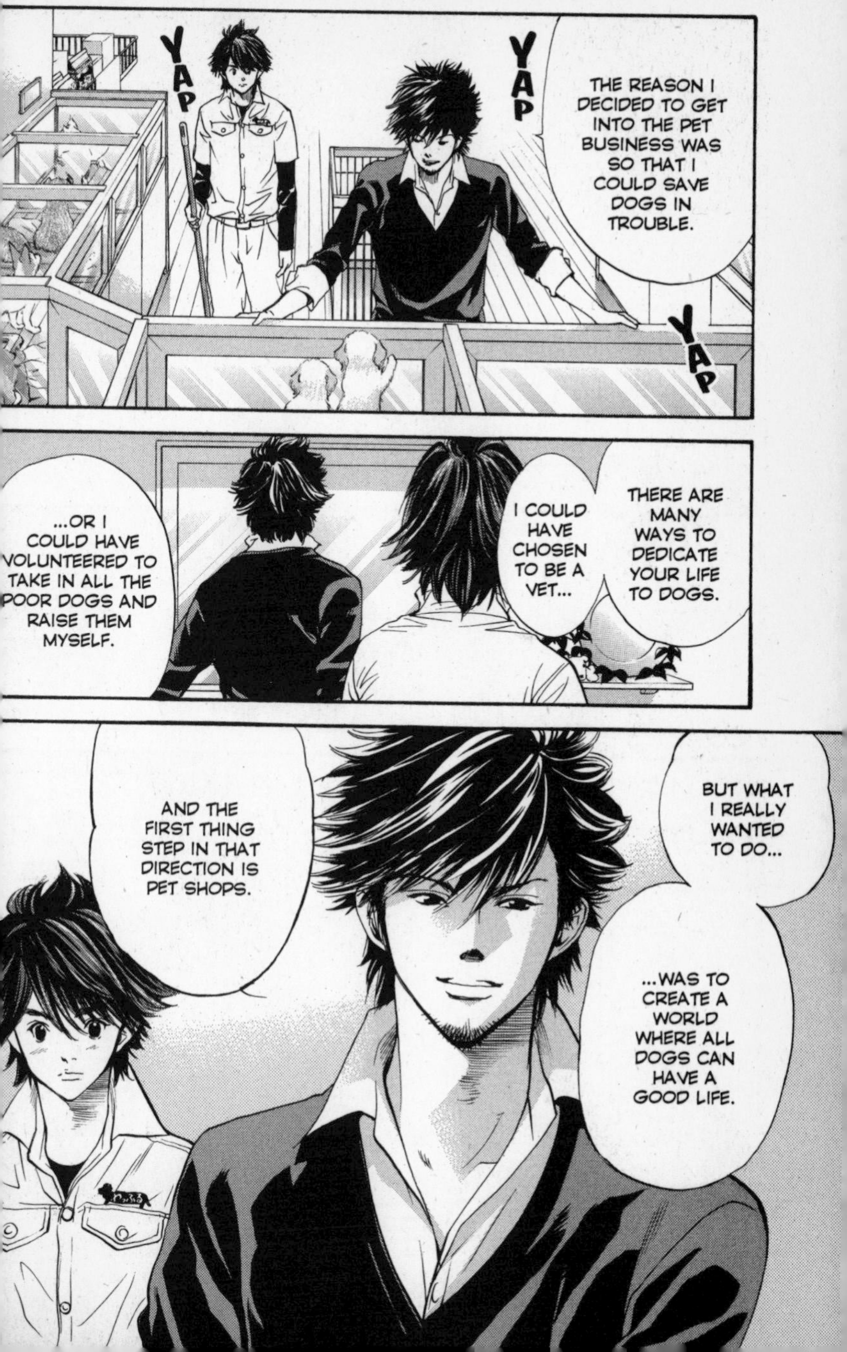
THE REASON I DECIDED TO GET INTO THE PET BUSINESS WAS SO THAT I COULD SAVE DOGS IN TROUBLE.
YAP
YAP
YAP
THERE ARE MANY WAYS TO DEDICATE YOUR LIFE TO DOGS.
I COULD HAVE CHOSEN TO BE A VET...
...OR I COULD HAVE VOLUNTEERED TO TAKE IN ALL THE POOR DOGS AND RAISE THEM MYSELF.
BUT WHAT I REALLY WANTED TO DO...
...WAS TO CREATE A WORLD WHERE ALL DOGS CAN HAVE A GOOD LIFE.
AND THE FIRST THING STEP IN THAT DIRECTION IS PET SHOPS.

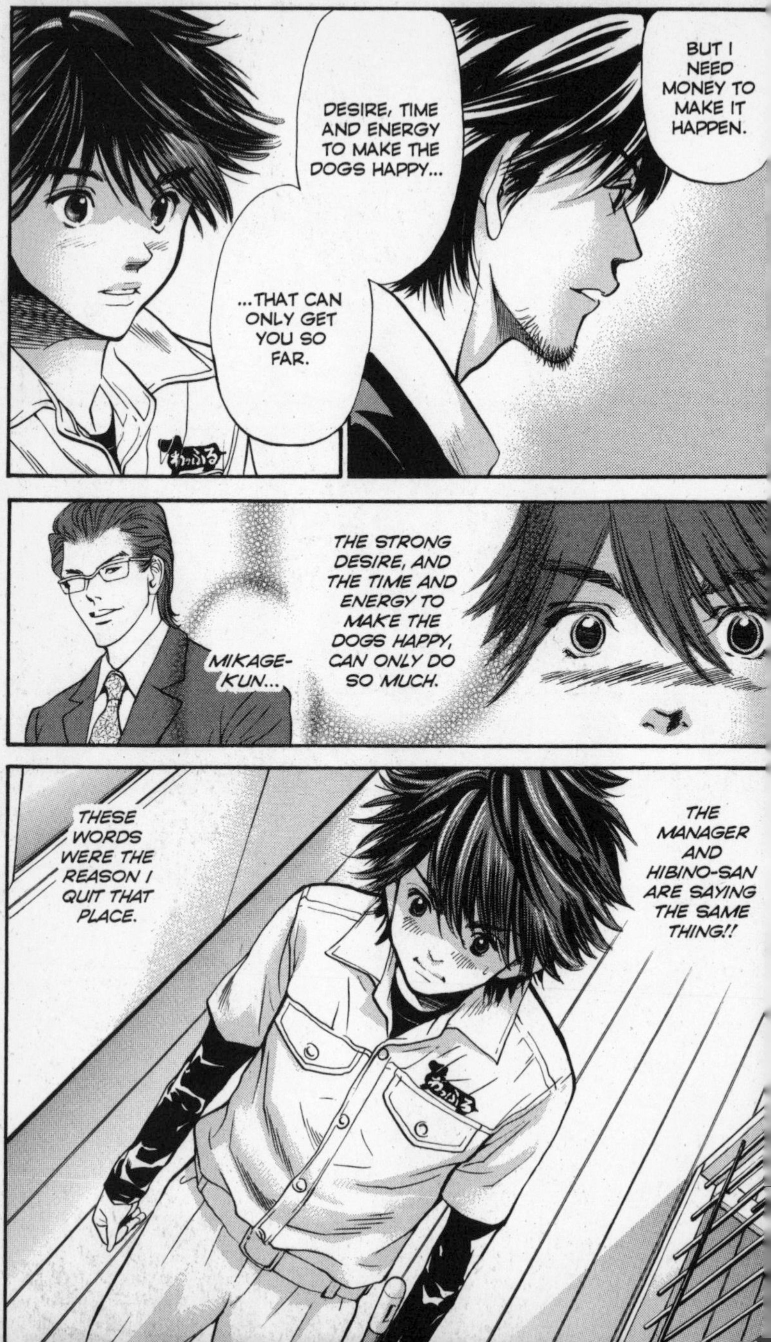
BUT I NEED MONEY TO MAKE IT HAPPEN.
DESIRE, TIME AND ENERGY TO MAKE THE DOGS HAPPY...
...THAT CAN ONLY GET YOU SO FAR.
THE STRONG DESIRE, AND THE TIME AND ENERGY TO MAKE THE DOGS HAPPY, CAN ONLY DO SO MUCH.
MIKAGE-KUN...
THE MANAGER AND HIBINO-SAN ARE SAYING THE SAME THING!!
THESE WORDS WERE THE REASON I QUIT THAT PLACE.

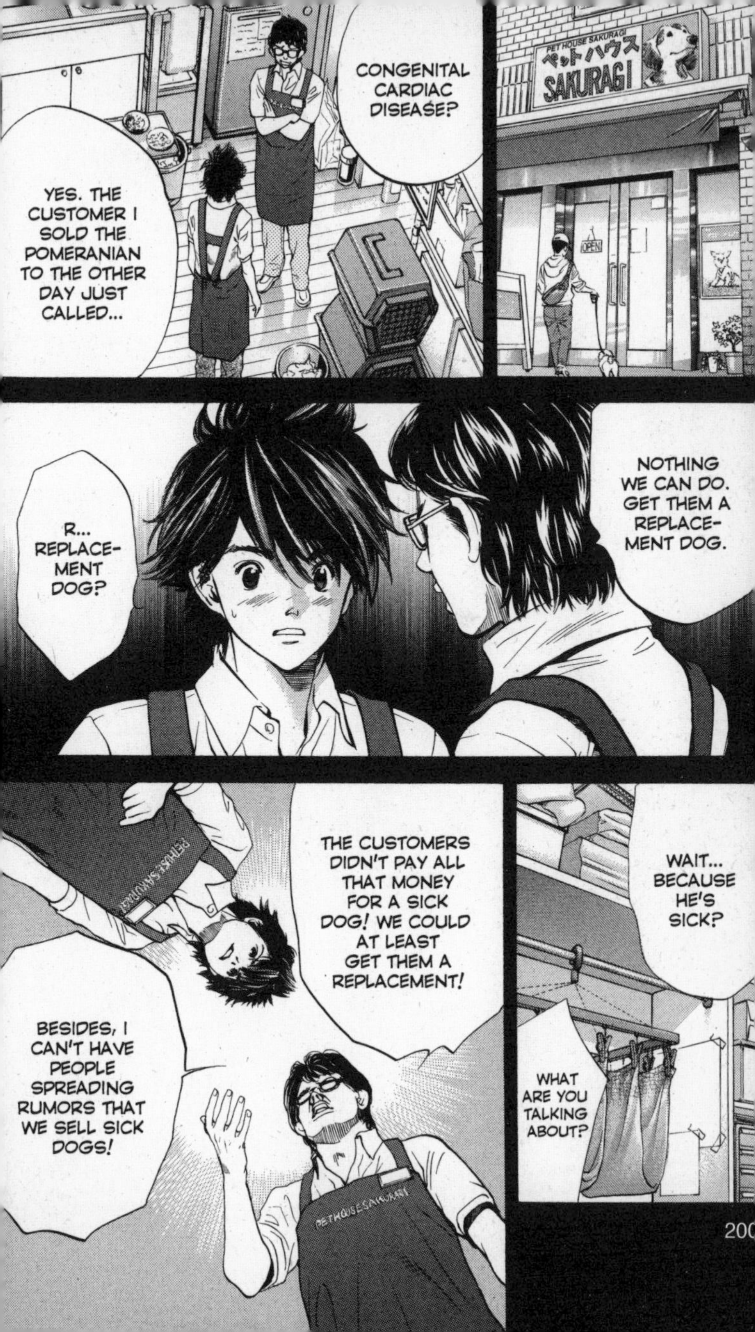
PET HOUSE SAKURAGI
ペットハウス
SAKURAGI
OPEN
CONGENITAL CARDIAC DISEASE?
YES. THE CUSTOMER I SOLD THE POMERANIAN TO THE OTHER DAY JUST CALLED...
NOTHING WE CAN DO. GET THEM A REPLACEMENT DOG.
R... REPLACEMENT DOG?
WAIT... BECAUSE HE'S SICK?
WHAT ARE YOU TALKING ABOUT?
THE CUSTOMERS DIDN'T PAY ALL THAT MONEY FOR A SICK DOG! WE COULD AT LEAST GET THEM A REPLACEMENT!
BESIDES, I CAN'T HAVE PEOPLE SPREADING RUMORS THAT WE SELL SICK DOGS!

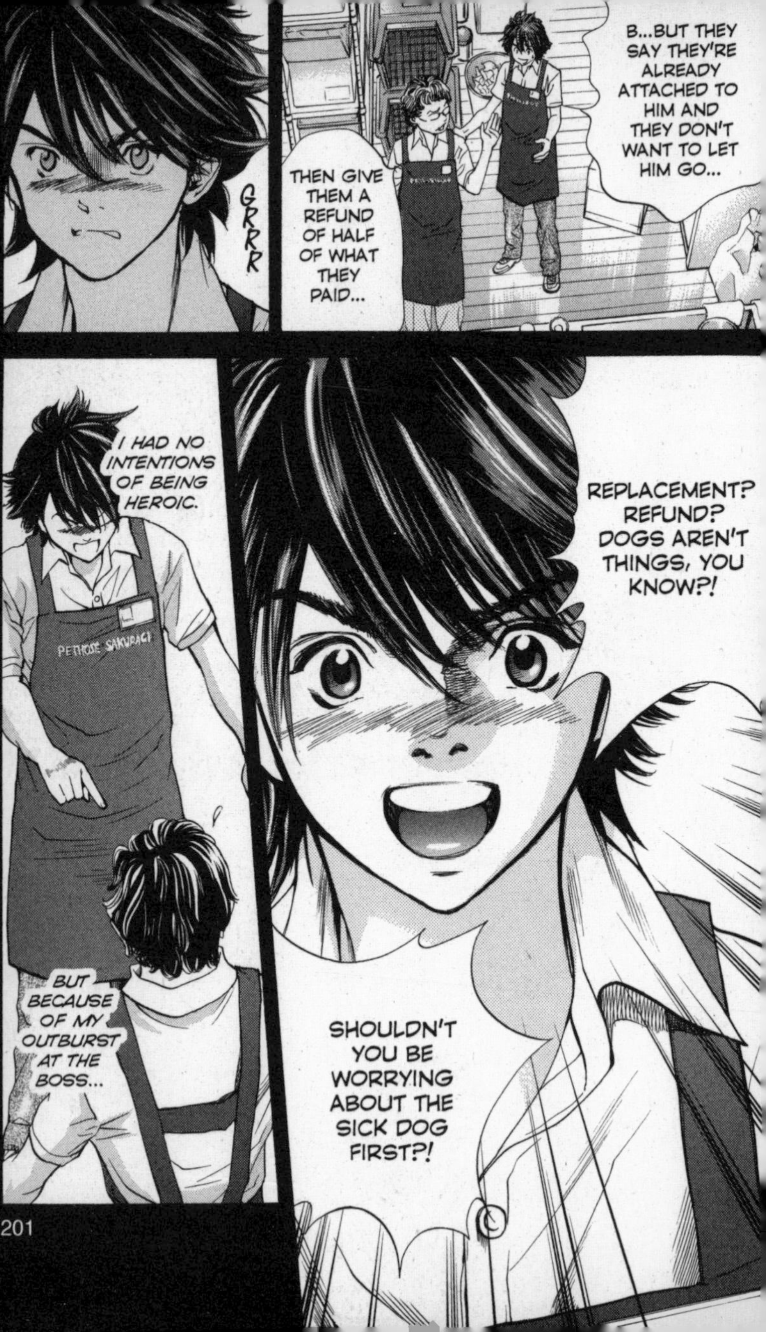
B...BUT THEY SAY THEY'RE ALREADY ATTACHED TO HIM AND THEY DON'T WANT TO LET HIM GO...
THEN GIVE THEM A REFUND OF HALF OF WHAT THEY PAID...
GRRR
REPLACEMENT? REFUND? DOGS AREN'T THINGS, YOU KNOW?!
SHOULDN'T YOU BE WORRYING ABOUT THE SICK DOG FIRST?!
I HAD NO INTENTIONS OF BEING HEROIC.
PETHOSE SAKURAGI
BUT BECAUSE OF MY OUTBURST AT THE BOSS...

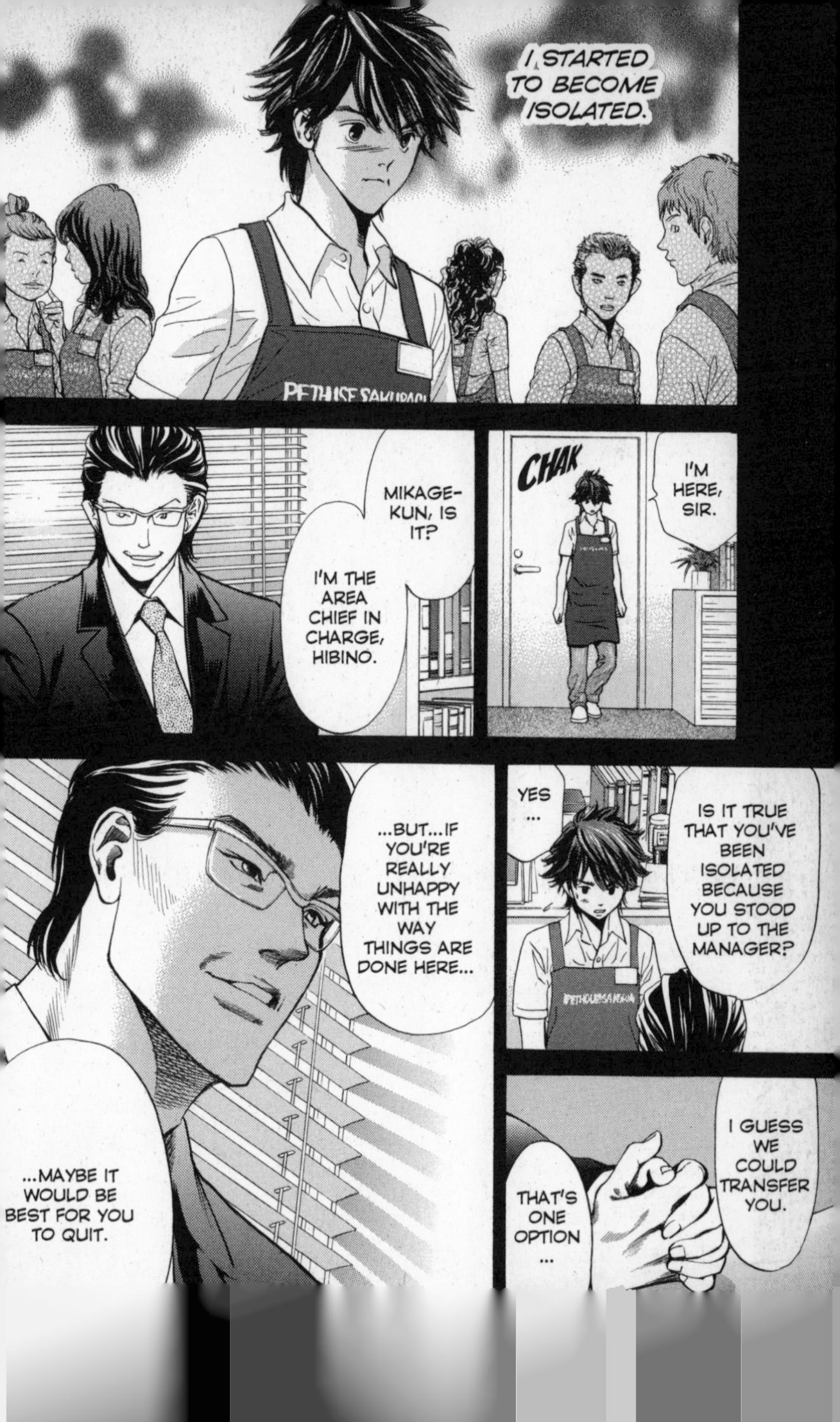
I STARTED TO BECOME ISOLATED.
CHAK
I'M HERE, SIR.
MIKAGE-KUN, IS IT?
I'M THE AREA CHIEF IN CHARGE, HIBINO.
IS IT TRUE THAT YOU'VE BEEN ISOLATED BECAUSE YOU STOOD UP TO THE MANAGER?
YES ...
I GUESS WE COULD TRANSFER YOU.
THAT'S ONE OPTION ...
...BUT...IF YOU'RE REALLY UNHAPPY WITH THE WAY THINGS ARE DONE HERE...
...MAYBE IT WOULD BE BEST FOR YOU TO QUIT.

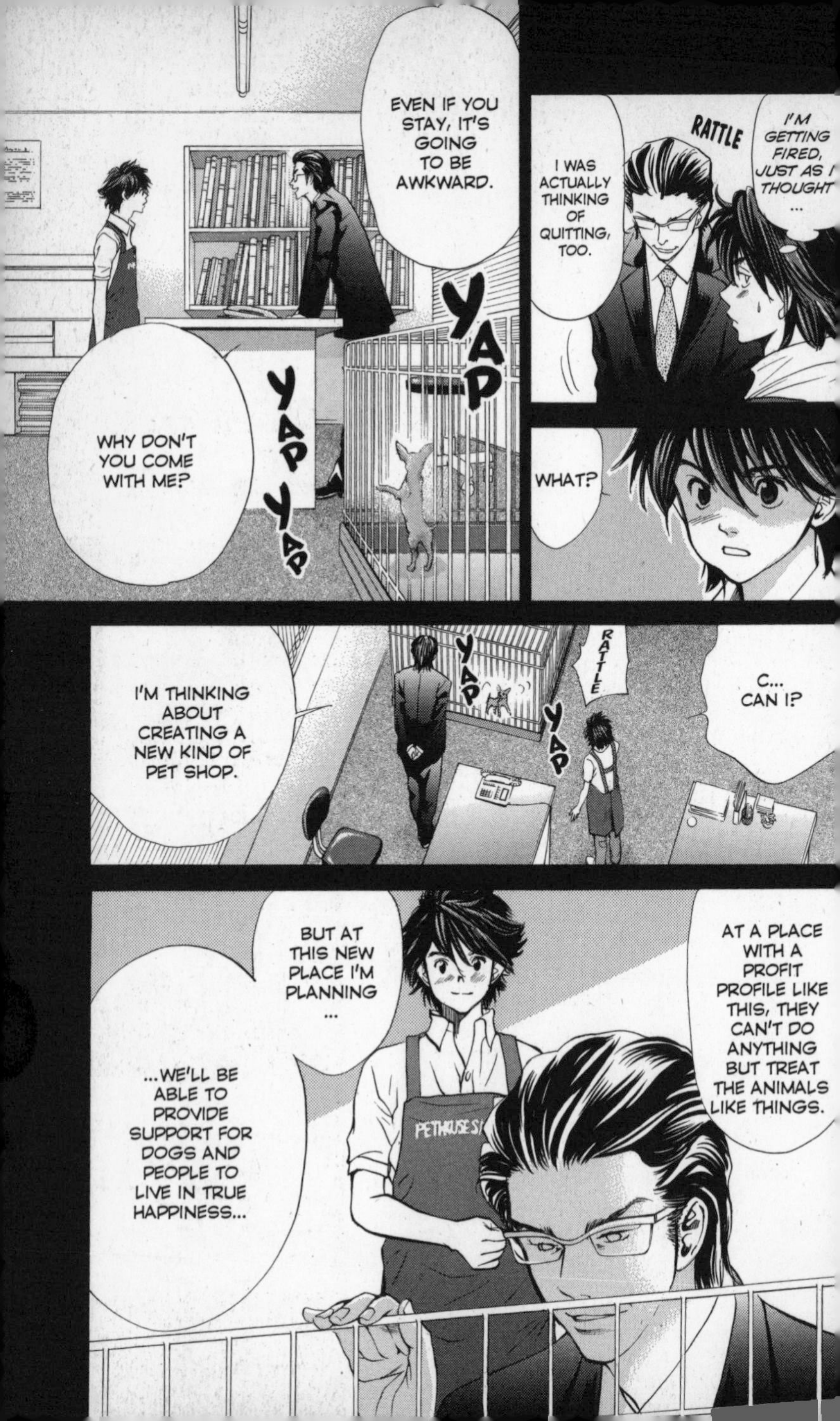

I'M GETTING FIRED, JUST AS I THOUGHT...
RATTLE
I WAS ACTUALLY THINKING OF QUITTING, TOO.
WHAT?
EVEN IF YOU STAY, IT'S GOING TO BE AWKWARD.
YAP YAP
YAP YAP
WHY DON'T YOU COME WITH ME?
C... CAN I?
RATTLE
YAP YAP
YAP YAP
I'M THINKING ABOUT CREATING A NEW KIND OF PET SHOP.
AT A PLACE WITH A PROFIT PROFILE LIKE THIS, THEY CAN'T DO ANYTHING BUT TREAT THE ANIMALS LIKE THINGS.
BUT AT THIS NEW PLACE I'M PLANNING...
...WE'LL BE ABLE TO PROVIDE SUPPORT FOR DOGS AND PEOPLE TO LIVE IN TRUE HAPPINESS...

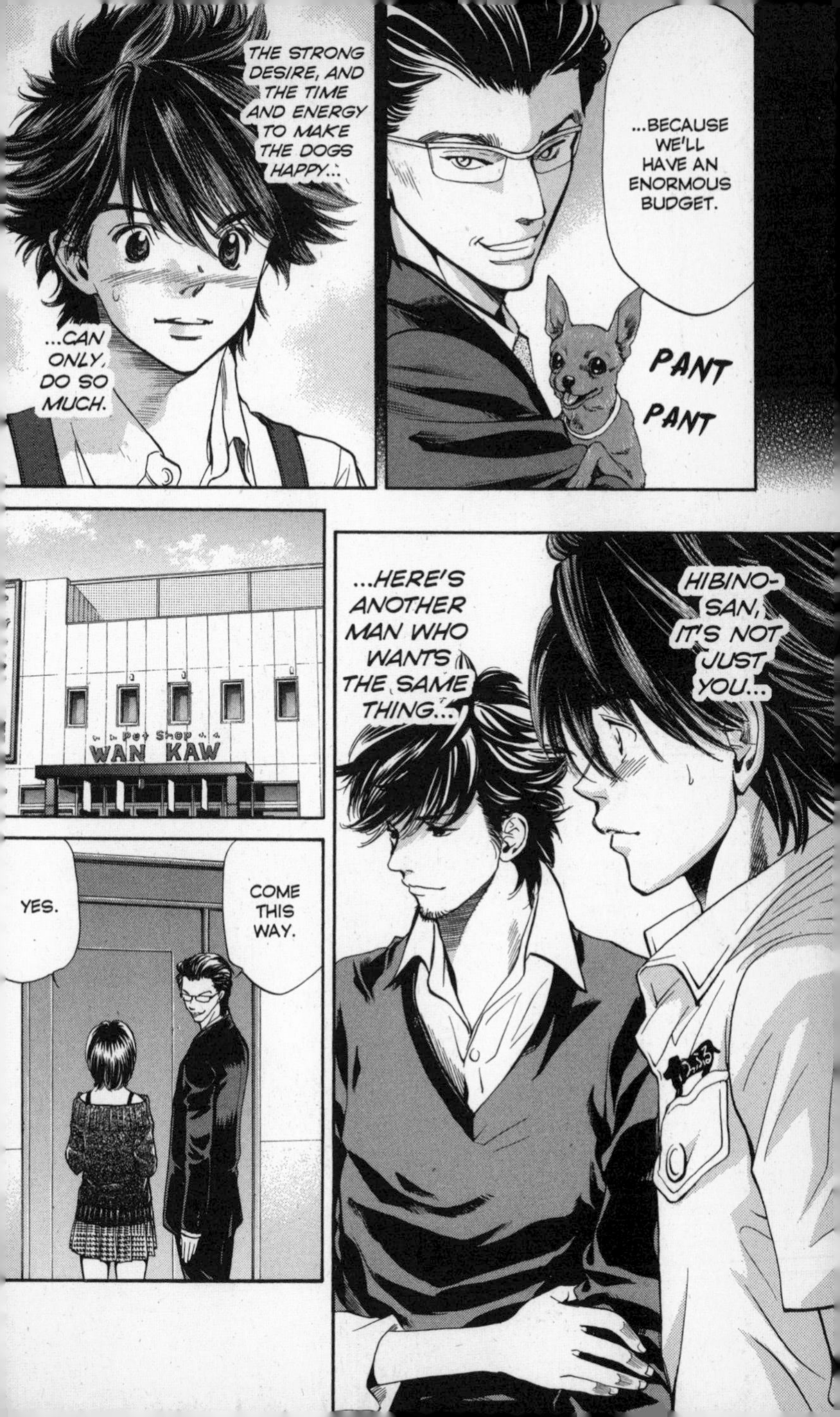
...BECAUSE WE'LL HAVE AN ENORMOUS BUDGET.
PANT
PANT
THE STRONG DESIRE, AND THE TIME AND ENERGY TO MAKE THE DOGS HAPPY...
...CAN ONLY DO SO MUCH.
HIBINO-SAN, IT'S NOT JUST YOU...
...HERE'S ANOTHER MAN WHO WANTS THE SAME THING...
Pet Shop
WAN KAW
COME THIS WAY.
YES.

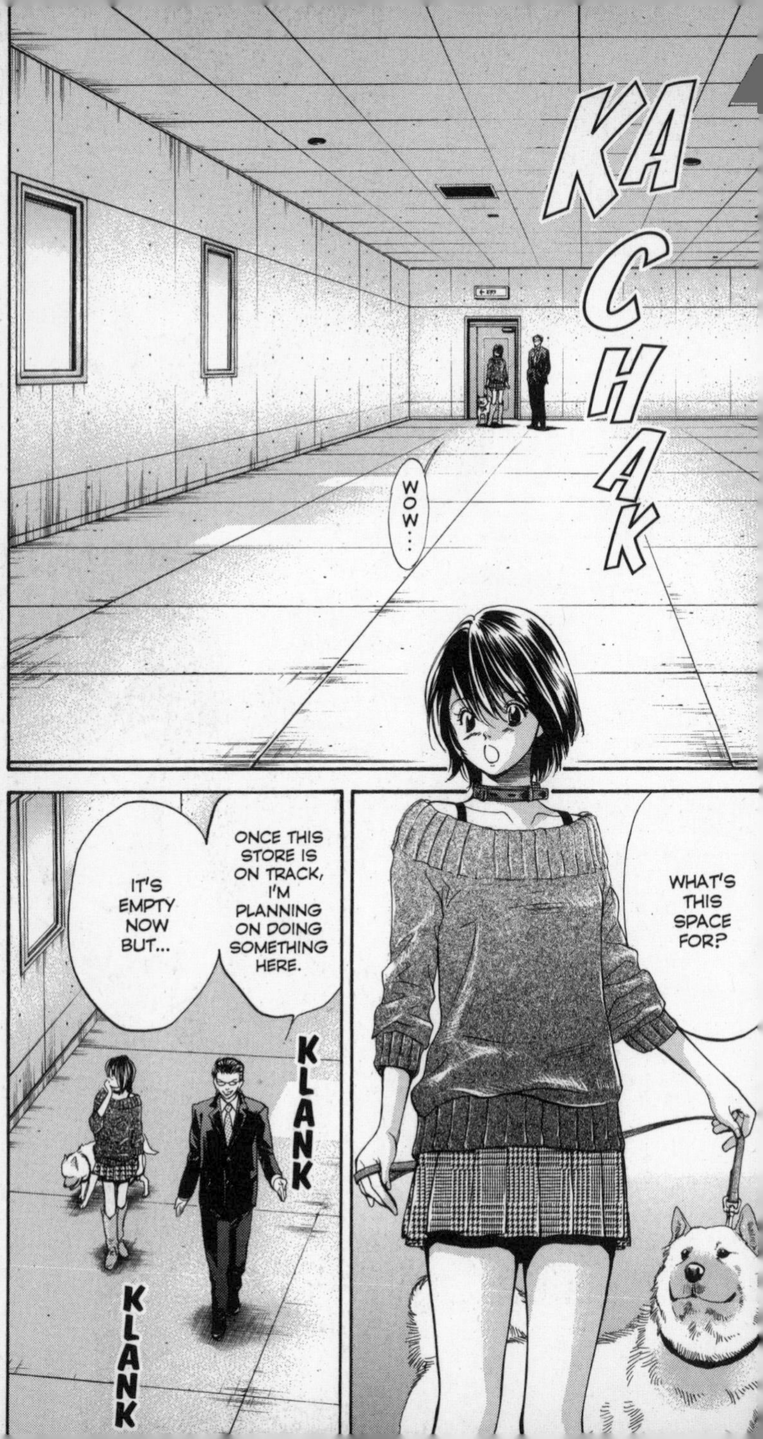
KA-CHAK
WOW...
WHAT'S THIS SPACE FOR?
ONCE THIS STORE IS ON TRACK, I'M PLANNING ON DOING SOMETHING HERE.
IT'S EMPTY NOW BUT...
KLANK
KLANK

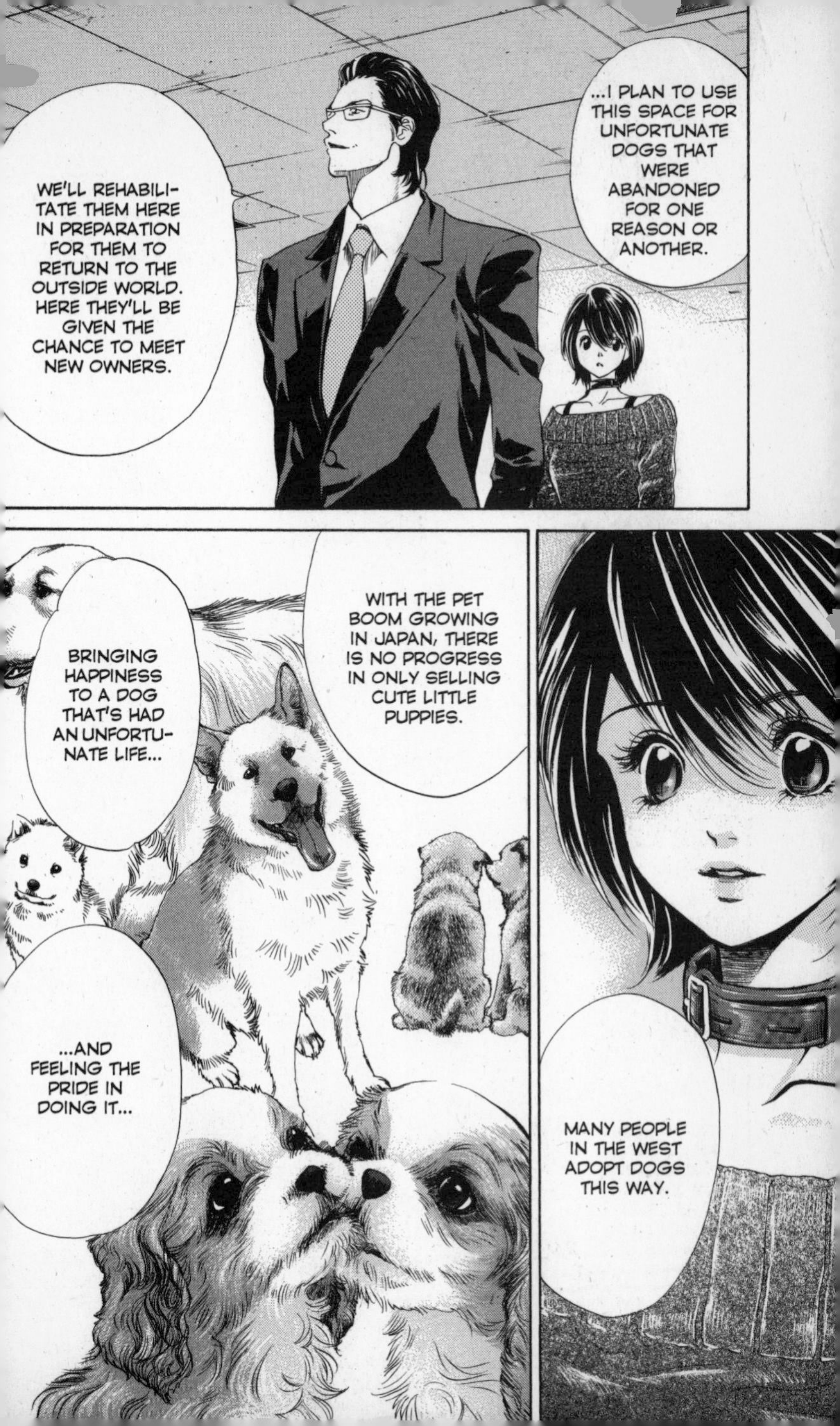
...I PLAN TO USE THIS SPACE FOR UNFORTUNATE DOGS THAT WERE ABANDONED FOR ONE REASON OR ANOTHER.
WE'LL REHABILITATE THEM HERE IN PREPARATION FOR THEM TO RETURN TO THE OUTSIDE WORLD. HERE THEY'LL BE GIVEN THE CHANCE TO MEET NEW OWNERS.
MANY PEOPLE IN THE WEST ADOPT DOGS THIS WAY.
WITH THE PET BOOM GROWING IN JAPAN, THERE IS NO PROGRESS IN ONLY SELLING CUTE LITTLE PUPPIES.
BRINGING HAPPINESS TO A DOG THAT'S HAD AN UNFORTUNATE LIFE...
...AND FEELING THE PRIDE IN DOING IT...

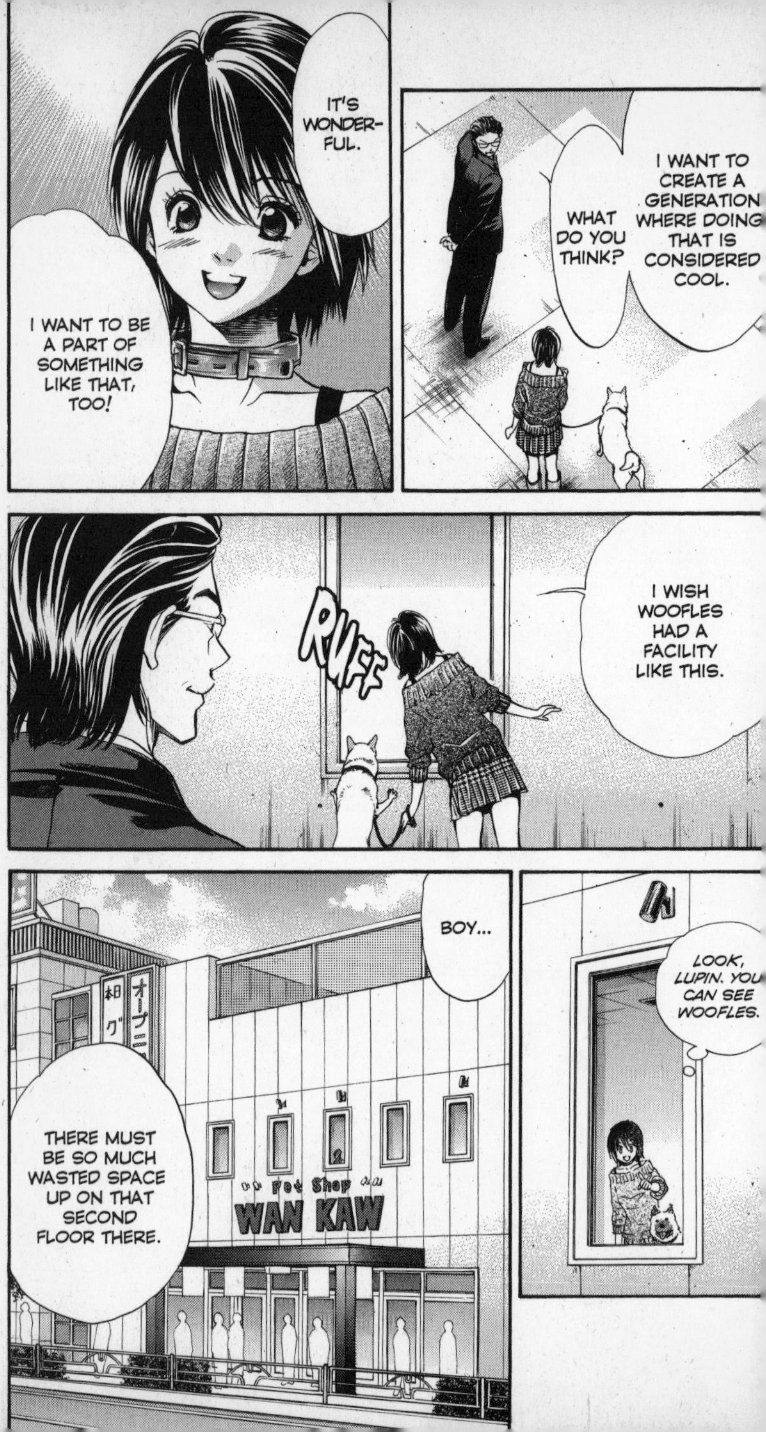
I WANT TO CREATE A GENERATION WHERE DOING THAT IS CONSIDERED COOL.
WHAT DO YOU THINK?
IT'S WONDER-FUL.
I WANT TO BE A PART OF SOMETHING LIKE THAT, TOO!
I WISH WOOFLES HAD A FACILITY LIKE THIS.
RUFF
LOOK, LUPIN. YOU CAN SEE WOOFLES.
BOY...
THERE MUST BE SO MUCH WASTED SPACE UP ON THAT SECOND FLOOR THERE.
Pet Shop
WAN KAW

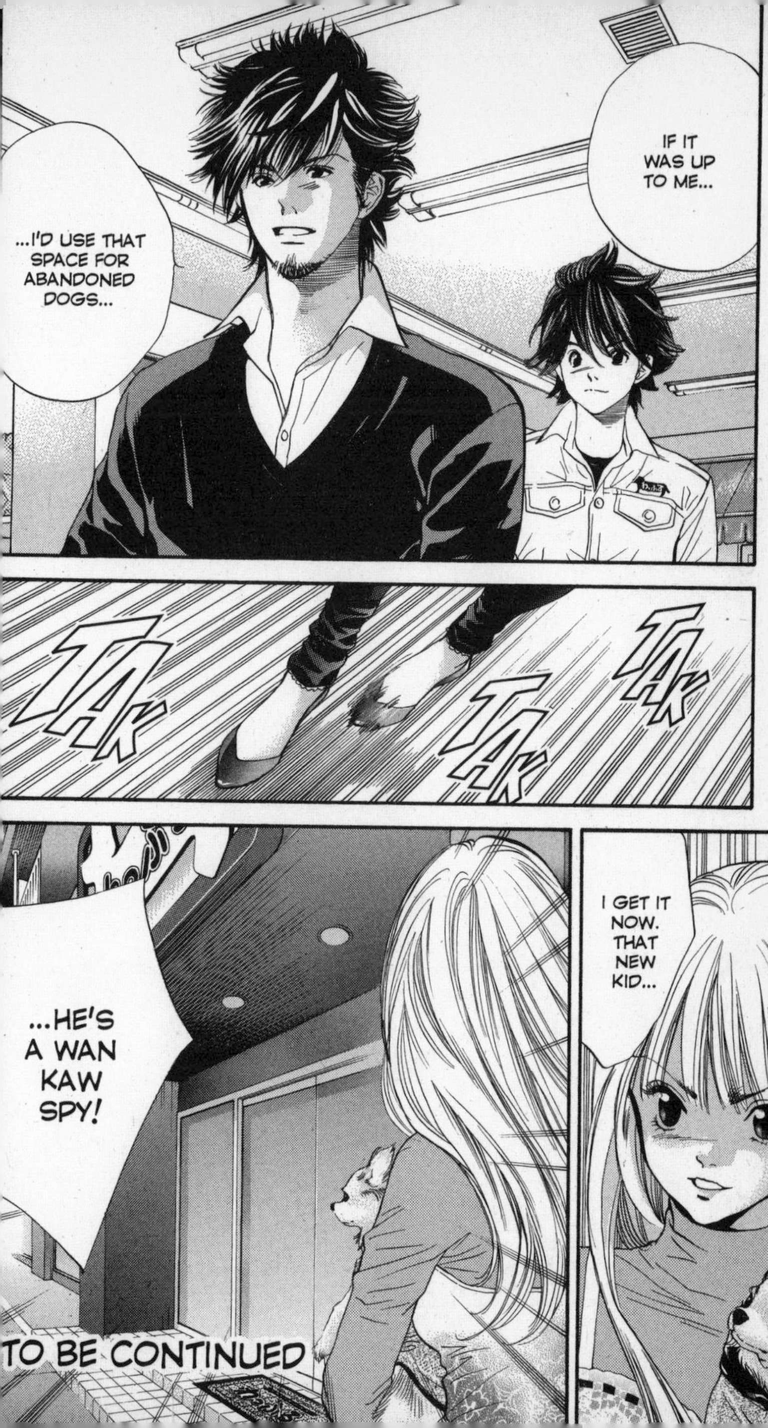
IF IT WAS UP TO ME...
...I'D USE THAT SPACE FOR ABANDONED DOGS...
TAK
TAK
TAK
I GET IT NOW. THAT NEW KID...
...HE'S A WAN KAW SPY!
TO BE CONTINUED

INUBA★KA

INUBAKA

Everybody's Crazy for Dogs!

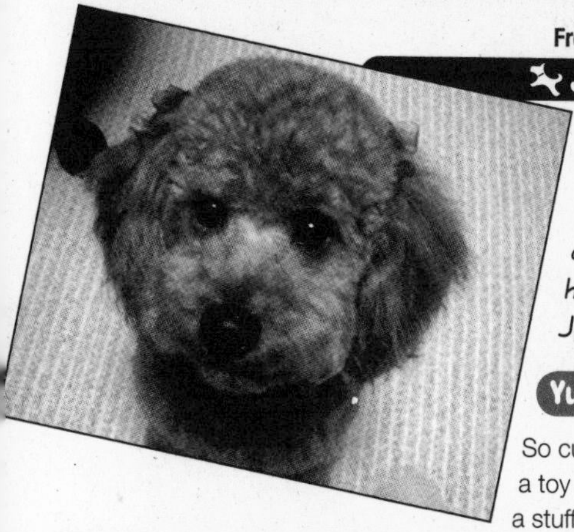

From Nakajima-san in Chiba Prefecture

Jenny-chan (toy poodle)

Jenny-chan, who loves to be on people's laps, is waiting for her owner's return. She can't wait to climb up on his lap and fall asleep, right Jenny-chan?

Yukiya Sakuragi

So cute! The teddy bear-style cut on a toy poodle makes them look just like a stuffed animal. I can almost hear her footsteps, "TAK TAK TAK." Well, maybe it's more than just a little "TAK TAK TAK" when she's on her way to greet her family. (lol)

Gomibuchi-san in Kanagawa Prefecture

Ku-kun (mutt)

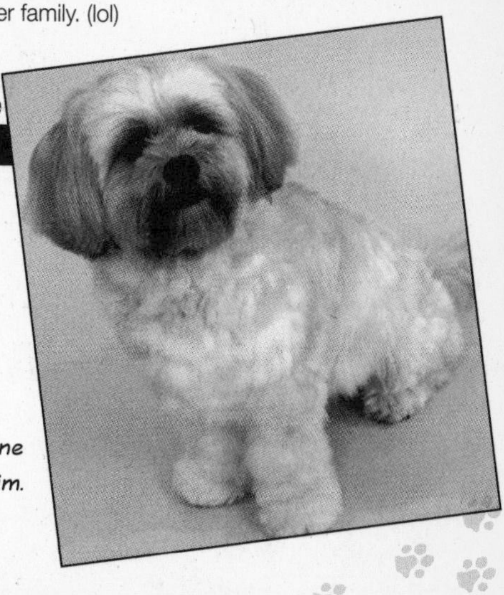

Ku-kun and his owner first met at an animal shelter. There were so many applicants who wanted to adopt the puppies there, the owner thought it might be impossible to get Ku-kun. But when it was Ku-kun's turn, the owner was the only one who raised his hand to adopt him. It was fate.

Yukiya Sakuragi

Yes! I'd say it was fate too! I assure you that Ku-kun will never betray the Gomibuchi family, who took him in from a shelter and gave him a loving home. Ku-kun knows he's a lucky doggy…

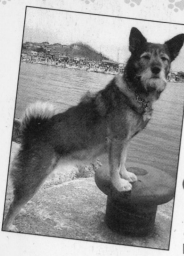

Specialty Ham-san in Okayama Prefecture
🐾 Ema-chan (mutt)

Ema-chan is good at begging. They say she begs with her paws, just like Lupin. This picture was taken during a walk. She's a girl, but she looks as cool as '70s' actor Yujiro Ishihara in this photo!

Yukiya Sakuragi

Pardon me! I thought she was a boy from this stunning pose! I hear people like to call her all sorts of things, like Mito Komon [Japanese historical character] and Santa Claus, but I can kind of see that (lol). She looks smarter than Lupin, though…

Kano-san in Tokyo
🐾 (Left) Mario-kun and (right) Komomo-chan (pugs)

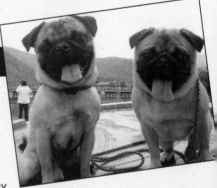

Both Mario-kun and Komomo-chan are very friendly and popular. They often get their picture taken by tourists on their walks. For some reason they tend to get barked at a lot by other dogs. But they are good dogs, because they never get into fights!

Yukiya Sakuragi

They look like close buddies! They seem to be smiling too. They must be quite mature to not get into fights (lol). We haven't had a pug as a main character in our stories yet, but I do want to draw one sometime soon! Hang in there just a little longer!

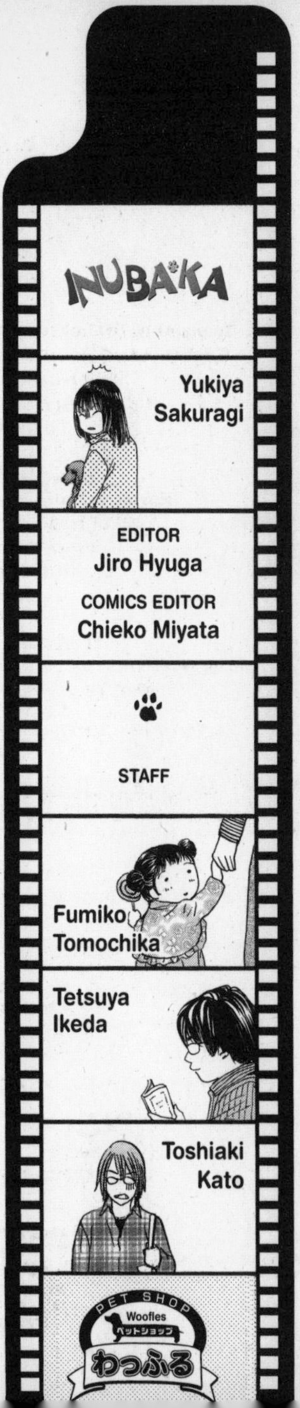
INUBAKA
Yukiya Sakuragi
EDITOR
Jiro Hyuga
COMICS EDITOR
Chieko Miyata
STAFF
Fumiko Tomochika
Tetsuya Ikeda
Toshiaki Kato
PET SHOP
Woofles
ペットショップ
わっふる

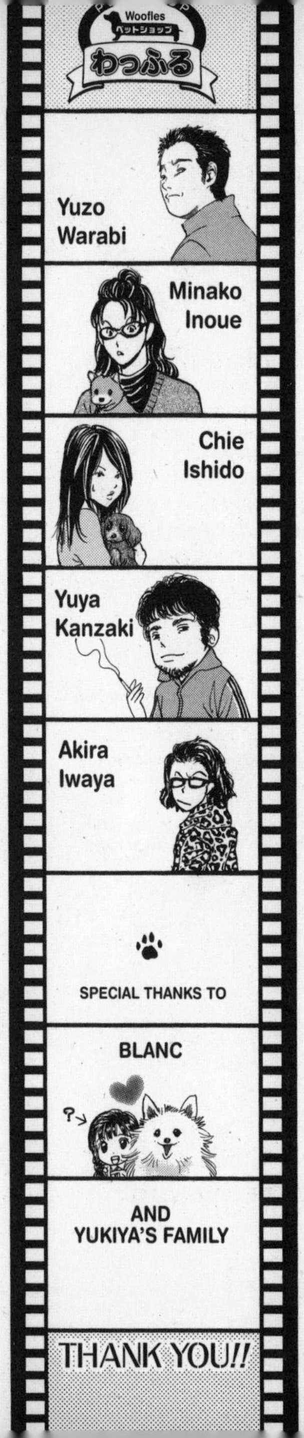
Woofles
ペットショップ
わっふる
Yuzo Warabi
Minako Inoue
Chie Ishido
Yuya Kanzaki
Akira Iwaya
SPECIAL THANKS TO
BLANC
?
AND
YUKIYA'S FAMILY
THANK YOU!!

Inubaka
Crazy for Dogs
Vol. #10
VIZ Media Edition

Story and Art by
Yukiya Sakuragi

Translation/Hidemi Hachitori, HC Language Solutions, Inc.
English Adaptation/Ian Reid, HC Language Solutions, Inc.
Touch-up Art & Lettering/Kelle Han
Cover and Interior Design/Hidemi Sahara
Editor/Ian Robertson

Editor in Chief, Books/Alvin Lu
Editor in Chief, Magazines/Marc Weidenbaum
VP of Publishing Licensing/Rika Inouye
VP of Sales/Gonzalo Ferreyra
Sr. VP of Marketing/Liza Coppola
Publisher/Hyoe Narita

INUBAKA © 2004 by Yukiya Sakuragi
All rights reserved. First published in Japan in 2004 by SHUEISHA Inc., Tokyo.
English translation rights arranged by SHUEISHA Inc.

Printed in the U.S.A.

Published by VIZ Media, LLC
P.O. Box 77010
San Francisco, CA 94107

10 9 8 7 6 5 4 3 2 1
First printing, August 2008

www.viz.com
store.viz.com

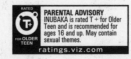

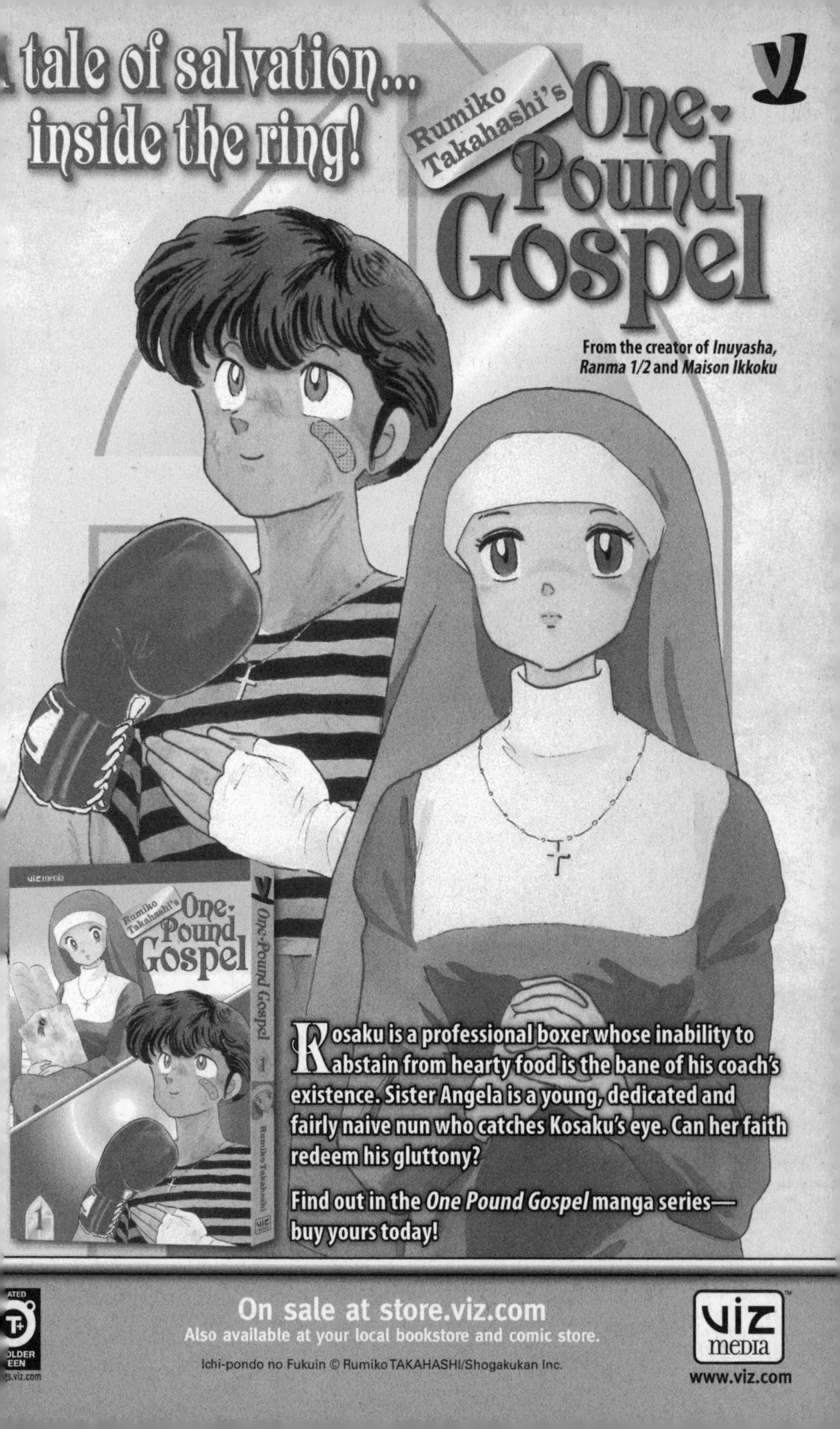
A tale of salvation...
inside the ring!
Rumiko Takahashi's
One-Pound Gospel
From the creator of *Inuyasha*, *Ranma 1/2* and *Maison Ikkoku*
viz media
Rumiko Takahashi's One-Pound Gospel
One-Pound Gospel 1 Rumiko Takahashi
Kosaku is a professional boxer whose inability to abstain from hearty food is the bane of his coach's existence. Sister Angela is a young, dedicated and fairly naive nun who catches Kosaku's eye. Can her faith redeem his gluttony?
Find out in the *One Pound Gospel* manga series—buy yours today!
On sale at store.viz.com
Also available at your local bookstore and comic store.
Ichi-pondo no Fukuin © Rumiko TAKAHASHI/Shogakukan Inc.
viz media
www.viz.com

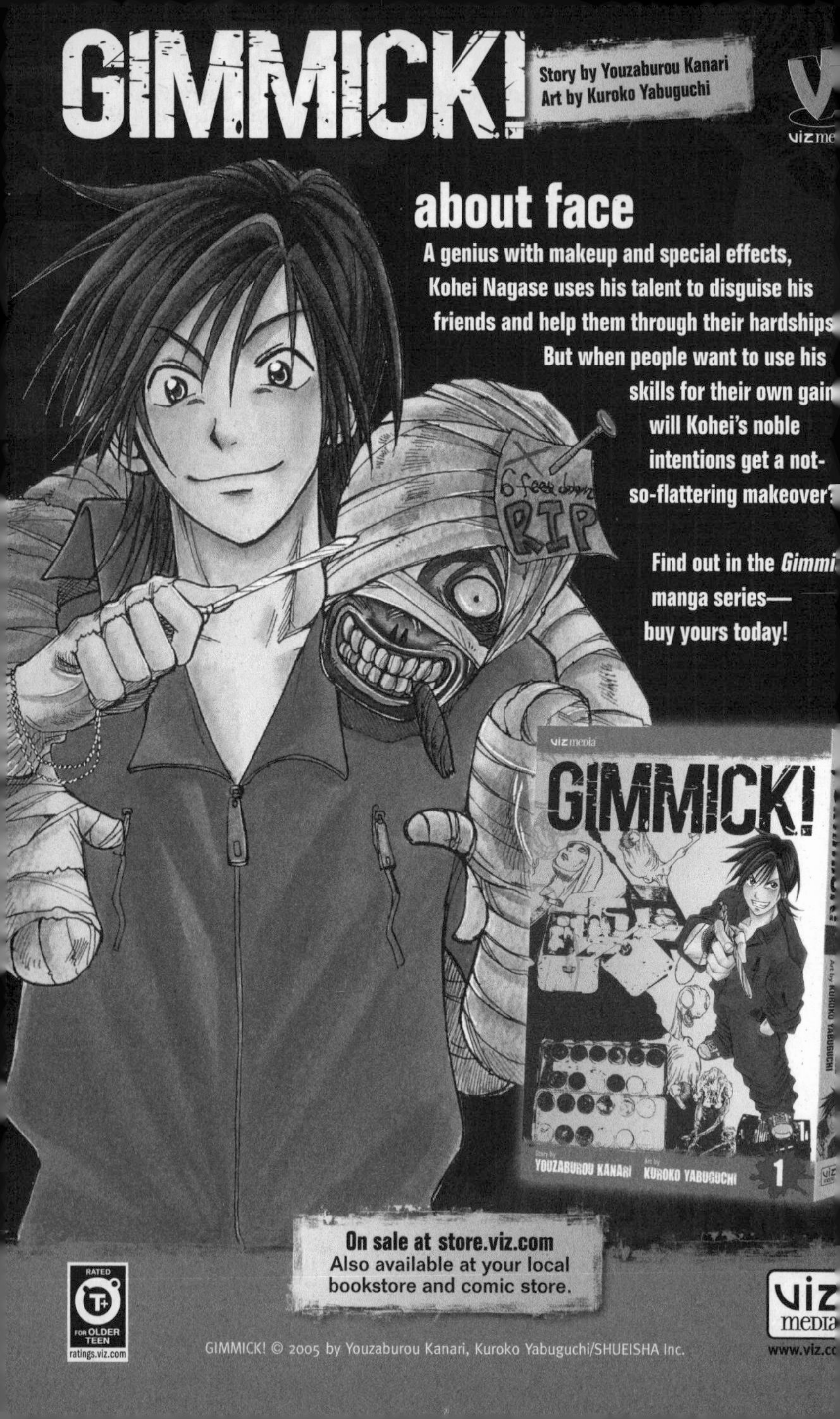
GIMMICK!
Story by Youzaburou Kanari
Art by Kuroko Yabuguchi
viz me
about face
A genius with makeup and special effects,
Kohei Nagase uses his talent to disguise his
friends and help them through their hardships
But when people want to use his
skills for their own gain
will Kohei's noble
intentions get a not-
so-flattering makeover
6 feet down
RIP
Find out in the Gimmi
manga series—
buy yours today!
viz media
GIMMICK!
Story by
YOUZABUROU KANARI
Art by
KUROKO YABUGUCHI
1
On sale at store.viz.com
Also available at your local
bookstore and comic store.
RATED
T+
FOR OLDER TEEN
ratings.viz.com
GIMMICK! © 2005 by Youzaburou Kanari, Kuroko Yabuguchi/SHUEISHA Inc.
viz media
www.viz.co

LOVE MAN…

LET US KNOW WHAT YOU THINK!

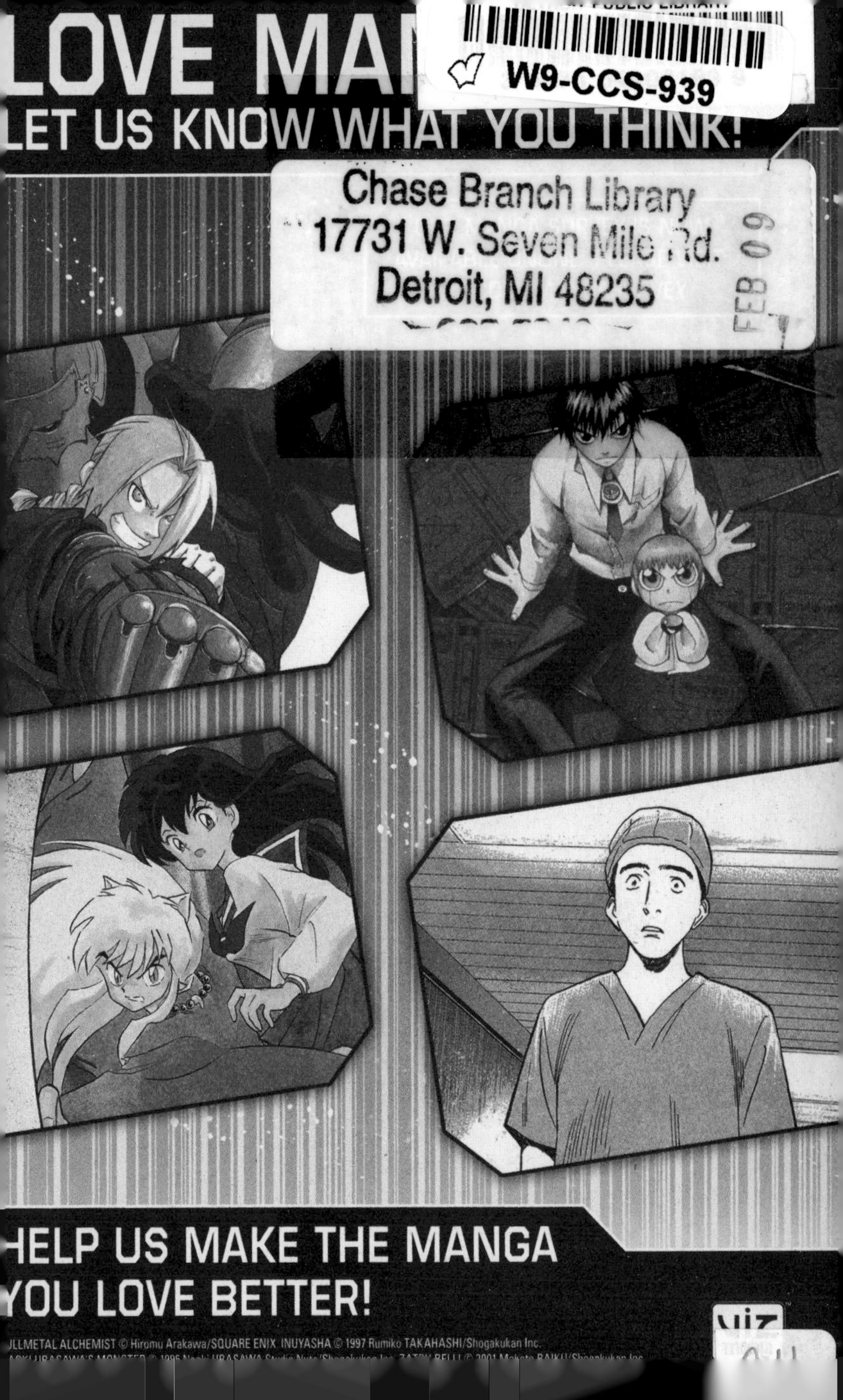

HELP US MAKE THE MANGA YOU LOVE BETTER!